SPECIAL FORCES FOREIGN WEAPONS HANDBOOK

SGM FRANK A. MOYER

Citadel Press
Secaucus, New Jersey

Copyright © 1983 by Paladin Press

All rights reserved. No part of this book
may be reproduced in any form, except by
a newspaper or magazine reviewer who wishes
to quote brief passages in connection
with a review.

Published by Citadel Press
A division of Lyle Stuart, Inc.
120 Enterprise Ave., Secaucus, N.J. 07094
In Canada: Musson Book Company
A division of General Publishing Co. Limited
Don Mills, Ontario

Queries regarding rights and permissions should be
addressed to: Lyle Stuart, 120 Enterprise Avenue,
Secaucus, N.J. 07094

Manufactured in the United States of America

ISBN 0-8065-1044-7

Neither the author nor the publisher assumes
any responsibility for the use or misuse of
information contained in this book.

TABLE OF CONTENTS

CONTENTS - III
INTRODUCTION - V
PISTOLS, SECTION 1 - 1
   Austria, 9mm Steyr, M12 - - - - - - - - - - - - - - - - - 2
   Belgium, 9mm, M35 (Browning H.P.) - - - - - - - - - - - - 6
   Great Britain, .455 Auto, Mark 1 (Webley) - - - - - - - - 10
   France, 7.65mm Long, M1935A - - - - - - - - - - - - - - - 14
   Germany, 7.63mm, MM1896 (Mauser "Broomhandle") - - - - - - 18
   Germany, 9 mm, P-38 - - - - - - - - - - - - - - - - - - - 23
   Germany, 9mm, P-08 ("Luger") - - - - - - - - - - - - - - - 27
   Italy, 9mm, M1910 (Glisenti) - - - - - - - - - - - - - - - 31
   Italy, 9mm, M1951 (Beretta) - - - - - - - - - - - - - - - 35
   Japan, 8 mm Jap, Type 14 (Nambu) - - - - - - - - - - - - - 39
   Japan, 8mm Jap, Type 94 ('Suicide Model") - - - - - - - - 43
   Russia, 7.63 mm, TT33 (Tokarev) - - - - - - - - - - - - - 47
   Russia, 9mm short, PM (Makarov) - - - - - - - - - - - - - 51
   Sweden, 9mm, M1940 (Lahti) - - - - - - - - - - - - - - - - 55

RIFLES AND CARBINES, SECTION II - - - - - - - - - - - - - - 59
   Belgium, 7.62mm NATO, FAL - - - - - - - - - - - - - - - - 60
   Belgium, 7.92mm, Type D (also Model 30 and Swedish model 21) - - - - 65
   Czechoslovakia, 7.62mm, Model 52 - - - - - - - - - - - - - 70
   Czechoslovakia, 7.62mm Short, Model 58 - - - - - - - - - - 74
   Denmark 7.62mm NATO, Madsen - - - - - - - - - - - - - - - 78
   Dominican Republic, .30 Carbine, Model 2 (Cristobal) - - - - - - - 82
   France, 7.5mm, Model 1949 - - - - - - - - - - - - - - - - 86
   Germany, 7.92mm, GEW-43 (Kar. 43) - - - - - - - - - - - - 90
   Germany, 7.62mm NATO, G3 - - - - - - - - - - - - - - - - - 94
   Germany, 7.92mm, FG-42 - - - - - - - - - - - - - - - - - 98
   Russia, 7.62mm, Model 40 (Tokarev) - - - - - - - - - - - - 103
   Russia, 7.62mm, M43, SKS - - - - - - - - - - - - - - - - 107
   Russia, 7.62mm M43, AK - - - - - - - - - - - - - - - - - 111
   Sweden, 6.5mm, AG42B (Ljungman) - - - - - - - - - - - - - 115

SUBMACHINE GUNS, SECTION III - - - - - - - - - - - - - - - 119
   Australia, 9mm, Mark 1-42 (Owen) - - - - - - - - - - - - - 120
   Great Britain, 9mm, Mark V Sten - - - - - - - - - - - - - 124
   Czechoslovakia, 7.62mm, Model 24 - - - - - - - - - - - - - 130
   Denmark, 9mm, Model 1950 (Madsen) - - - - - - - - - - - - 134
   Finland, 9mm, Model 1931 (Soumi) - - - - - - - - - - - - - 138
   France, 7.65mm Long, MAS-38 - - - - - - - - - - - - - - - 142
   France, 9mm, MAT-49 - - - - - - - - - - - - - - - - - - - 146
   France, 9mm, "Universal" (Hotchkiss) - - - - - - - - - - - 150

TABLE OF CONTENTS CONTINUED

    France, 9mm, M1948 Type C4 — 154
    Germany, 9mm, MP-40 (Schmeisser) — 158
    Germany, 9mm, MPK (Walther) — 162
    Germany, 7.92mm Short, MP-43 — 166
    Germany, 9mm, Steyr-Solothurn — 171
    Israel, 9mm, No 2 Mk A (Uzi) — 174
    Italy, 9mm, Model 38-42 (Beretta) — 179
    Italy, 9mm, LF-57 (Franchi) — 184
    Russia, 7.62mm, PPSH-41 — 188
    Russia, 7.62mm, PPS-43 — 193
    Sweden, 9mm, M45B (Carl Gustaf) — 197
    Switzerland, 9mm, F.V. Mk 4 (Rexim) — 201

MACHINEGUNS, SECTION IV. — 205
    Austria, 8mm, Model 07-12 (Schwarzlose) — 206
    Great Britain, .303 Lewis — 210
    Nationalist China, 7.92-mm, Mark 2 Bren. (also .30 Type 41) — 214
    Czechoslovakia, 7.92mm, ZB30 — 218
    Czechoslovakia, 7.62mm, Model 1952 — 221
    Denmark, 7.62mm NATO, Madsen-Saetter — 225
    Denmark, 8mm, Madsen — 229
    France, 7.5mm M29, Model 1924-29 — 233
    France, 7.5mm M29, Model 1931A — 236
    France, 8mm, Model 1914 — 241
    France, 7.5mm M29, Model 1952 — 245
    Germany, 7.92mm, MG-42 — 249
    Italy, 6.5mm Model 30 (Breda) — 254
    Japan, 6.5mm, Type 11 (Nambu) — 258
    Japan, 7.7mm, Type 99 — 262
    Japan, 7.62mm NATO, Model 1962 — 266
    Russia, 7.62mm, DP (Degtyarev) — 270
    Russia, 7.62mm, RP-46 — 274
    Russia, 7.62mm M-43 RPD — 278
    Russia, 7.62mm, SG-43 — 282
    Russia, 7.62mm, SPM (Maxim) — 286
    Russia, 7.62mm M43, RPK — 291

GLOSSARY OF SMALL ARMS TERMS, SECTION V — 295

REFERENCE DATA, SECTION VI — 317

INTRODUCTION

A requirement has long existed for a Foreign Weapons Guide directed to the needs of the average, non-professional individual interested in fire arms.

The publication desired was a very unique one because the purpose it was to serve was unique. The task began by investigating all publication sources existing that might fill the bill of a compact, concise, and yet informative publication. Among the sources investigated were Army Technical Manuals, Army Field Manuals, Department of the Army Pamphlets, Ordnance Manuals, other military publications, and a number of commercial publications. None of these in itself could provide the answer. The requirement became a matter of compiling certain data from many sources into this one handbook.

After thorough scrutinizing, 70 out of approximately 200 weapons were selected for coverage. Serious effort was made to avoid duplication of systems with the exception of certain submachine guns that differ in disassembly procedure. Some weapons which are considered obsolete by present-day standards were included because of the unusual system of operation they employed, giving the reader a better understanding of the multitude of designs that exist. Others were included because of their extreme simplicity and the fact that they could be produced by a number of "poor" countries. Mechanical difficulties such as stoppages and jams are omitted to keep the text simple.

It is emphasized that consideration was given to existing publications on the subject of small arms. Illustrations of the chosen weapons were not available in the disassembly format desired, so that each weapon covered had to be physically procured (from various sources) and photographed. In accordance with this, it is admitted that this publication will appear as a radical departure from the standard small arms textbook. Reminder is again interposed that this is a unique publication and with this in mind, technical data was obtained by set formula in the following manner:

Weight: All weapons were weighed with slings (when available), empty magazines, other necessary accouterments that normally accompany the weapon and bayonets if permanently attached. The weighing scales were calibrated every 30 days.

Overall Length: This demension was determined by laying the weapon on a one-inch grid background dimension sheet. A movable grid plate graduated in tenths of an inch was used to measure between major dimension lines at the muzzle and butt of the piece.

Practical Rate of Fire: This figure was derived by the use of a formula which considered the cyclic rate of fire and tactical use as variable factors, weight of weapon, type of mount normally used, and type and capacity of feed as fixed factors. In all cases, the rate of fire is stated as somewhat higher than the figures determined by formula based on two assumptions—that a 25 percent hit figure was a fair combat criteria and that the weapon was being operated by an expert. The writer's personal experience tipped the balance in favor of the shooter when an experience factor could be weighed.

Effective Range: No other data on a characteristic data chart is more controversial than the range figure. In this respect, Effective Range as stated in this book means accurate range. (That range at which 25 per cent of the shots will hit the normal tactical target for the weapon under question.) This figure was derived by a formula which considered the practical rate of fire, weight, type of mount used, and tactical application considered as fixed factors; the experience of the average operator with consideration given to the complexity of the specific weapon was treated as a variable factor.

Assembly, Disassembly, and Functioning: Assembly and disassembly instructions were researched in the following manner. All possible assembly and disassembly step-by-step procedures were applied by practical process with respect to each weapon. The most logical and the easiest was selected. The description of weapon functioning omitted lengthy discussion of obvious phases such as feeding, extraction and ejection, while elaborating on other phases which were deemed more important.

With emphasis of safety in mind, the loading and firing instructions generally include the procedure for placing the weapon on "SAFE" before loading and where applicable, setting the Fire Select Lever to type of fire desired before pulling the trigger. Mention of these simple steps, in each weapon coverage may seem unnecessary, but handling a strange weapon is dangerous enough without adding carelessness.

There is no question this publication could be larger, more detailed, include more weapons, teach more technical facts, and present more trouble shooting information. The purpose was to produce a simple, concise publication for use by individuals for whom such data is not readily available. It is felt that this has been done, but only you the user can verify this fact. In conclusion, you are assured that all factors were examined and exhausted to produce this special handbook.

Frank A. Moyer
Sergeant Major
US Army

PISTOLS

SECTION I

A pistol is defined as a short firearm intended to be held normally with one hand. Its chamber is formed by reaming and enlarging the breech end of the barrel so it will receive the cartridge. In this respect a pistol is differentiated from a revolver inasmuch as the cartridge, at the time of ignition, is fully seated and contained in the breech end of the barrel in a pistol, while in a revolver the cartridge is contained within a separate component (the cylinder) at the time of ignition. The term "pistol" originally referred to single shot weapons but under present day application refers to any hand gun in which the cartridge is placed in the chamber of the barrel, either manually or by mechanical means, before the primer is struck by the firing pin. The term "automatic pistol" is a misnomer when used in reference to mechanically fed hand guns. These weapons are properly classed as "auto-loaders" or "self-loading" arms. There is an extremely limited number of true "automatic pistols" in use today. The automatic pistol by proper definition is one in which the weapon mechanically feeds fresh ammunition into the chamber and fires it as long as the trigger is held to the rear. Hand guns of this type have seen little success; control of such a weapon during firing being almost impossible for any degree of accuracy, unless a shoulder stock is attached.

The pistols discussed in this handbook represent only a fraction of the auto-loading designs which may be encountered by Special Forces personnel. The weapons covered do represent a general cross-section of the most successful arms of this type; different locking systems are explained in detail to include of course the unlocked breech weapon, the straight blowback system. Many more hand guns should have been included, but the general purpose of the discussion was to present to the reader an idea of the various designs in use today. Understanding the function of a few will make it easier to understand the function of many more.

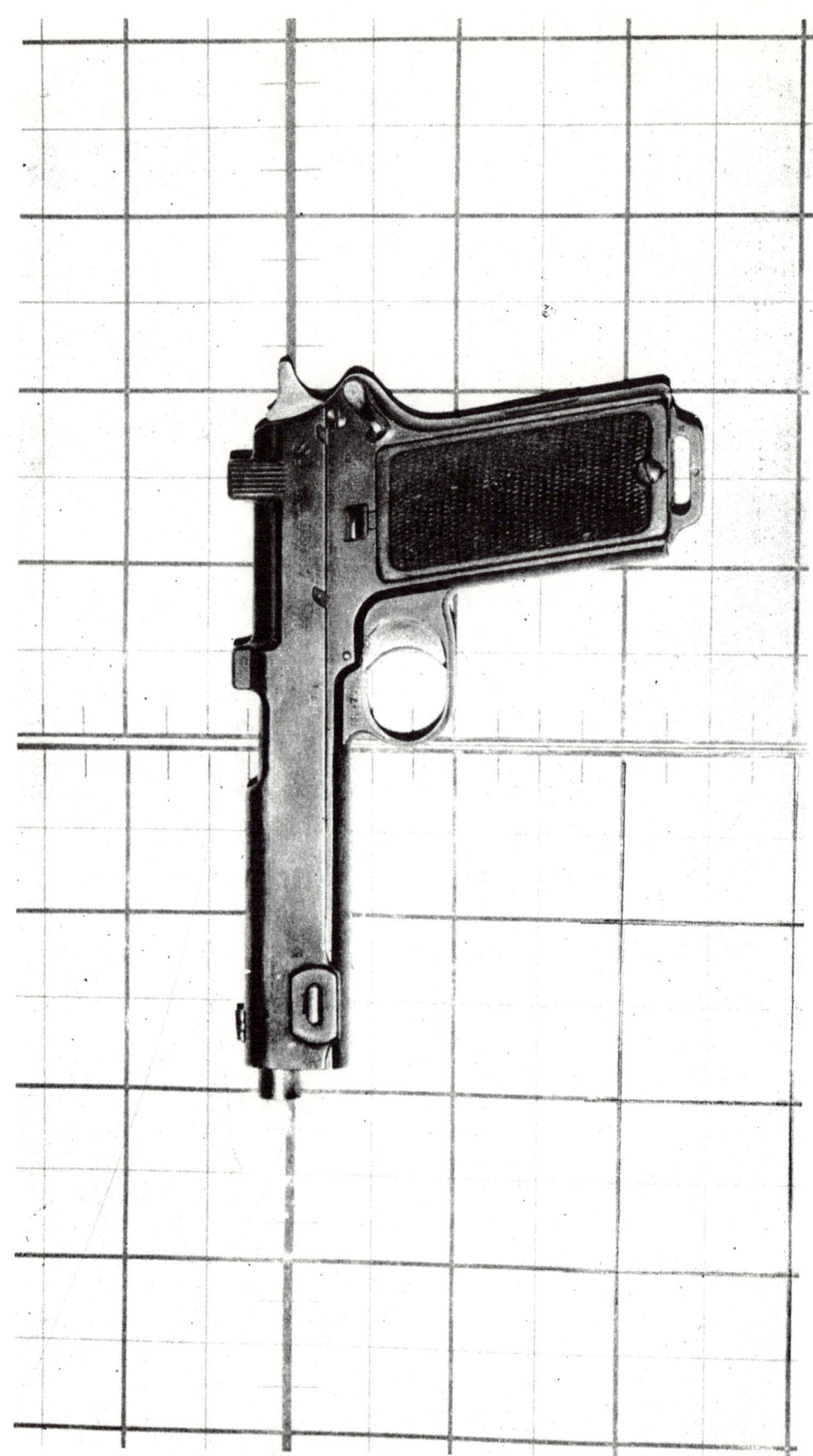

AUSTRIA   9-MM STEYR, M12

PISTOL   **AUSTRIA**

9-mm M12 (Steyr)

The 9-mm M12 Steyr-Hahn pistol is a recoil operated, locked breech pistol, which is chambered for a special 9-mm round. This 9-mm round is slightly longer than the standard 9-mm round used in the Luger pistol. Some of these weapons were rebarreled for the Luger cartridge during WWII and are marked "08" on the slide. This is an exceptionally well made pistol, though the shape of the grip and the heavy recoil make it an uncomfortable piece to fire. This weapon incorporates two unusual features; the breech is locked by a slight rotation of the barrel and remains in this locked position during the travel of the bullet down the barrel by the force the bullet exerts in following the rifling; the magazine is a permanent component of the pistol grip and is loaded through the top of the receiver from a strip clip. Because of this unique loading feature, the fact that there is no magazine to remove if it becomes necessary to unload the pistol, the cartridges in the magazine are removed by opening the slide and locking it open by the safety catch and pressing on the latch on the left side of the receiver above the stock. This allows the magazine spring and follower to force the cartridges up and out through the top of the receiver.

FUNCTIONING

This is a locked breech pistol which is locked by the rotation of the barrel in which cam surfaces on the barrel engage locking slots in the slide. An automatic disconnector is incorporated in the design which prevents the pistol from being fired until the slide is fully forward and the trigger has been released. Eight rounds are stripped into the magazine contained in the pistol grip from a strip clip. The safety is pushed down, the slide is released. As the slide strikes the rear of the barrel it forces it forward. A camming rib on the barrel riding in a mating slot in the receiver forces the barrel to turn clockwise so that the locking lugs on the barrel engage locking slots in the slide. A round has been chambered, the hammer has been forced back and engaged by the sear and the disconnector has moved up to connect the sear and the trigger. When the trigger is pulled and the cartridge is fired the barrel and slide start to move rearward. The barrel is rifled with a right hand twist. The bullet in the barrel following the rifling tends to twist the barrel to the right. The barrel must turn to the left to disengage from the slide, and as long as the bullet is in the barrel the barrel and slide remain locked together until the bullet leaves the muzzle. When the barrel unlocks from the slide, the slide continues to the rear, compressing the recoil spring and then moves forward under the force of the compressed recoil spring and chambers a new round. Extraction and ejection of the empty case is accomplished as in other pistols.

CHARACTERISTIC DATA

Caliber	9-mm Steyr
Operation	Recoil
Type of Feed	Fixed box—8 rd cap
Weight, empty	34 oz.
Overall length	8.5 inches
Effective Range	75 meters
Muzzle velocity	1,200 fps

FIELD STRIP PROCEDURE

STEP   ACTION

1. Press the locking points of the Slide Retaining Pin together.
2. Remove Slide Retaining Pin.
   (Recoil Spring and Guide may be removed at this point.)
3. Pull Slide back slightly and raise up.
4. Continue to pull Slide to the rear and lift it off the Receiver.
5. Lift Barrel Out of the Slide.

ASSEMBLY PROCEDURE

Proceed in the reverse order. Assemble Barrel to Slide. Engage Slide with Receiver, slide forward and down into locked position. If the Recoil Spring and Guide were removed, assemble into Receiver from the front. Put Slide Retaining Pin in place.

LOADING AND FIRING

To load: Pull the Slide to the rear and push the Safety Lever up to lock the slide open. Place an 8-round Strip Clip into the feed guides in the top of the Receiver. Push the cartridges down into the pistol grip. Remove the empty Strip Clip. Push down on the Safety Lever and the Slide will move forward and chamber the first round.

To fire: Press the trigger the weapon will fire. The trigger must be pulled for each round fired. When the last shot has been fired the slide will remain to the rear.

SLIDE
BARREL
(note rotary locking
lugs)
RECEIVER
GROUP
SLIDE LOCK PIN

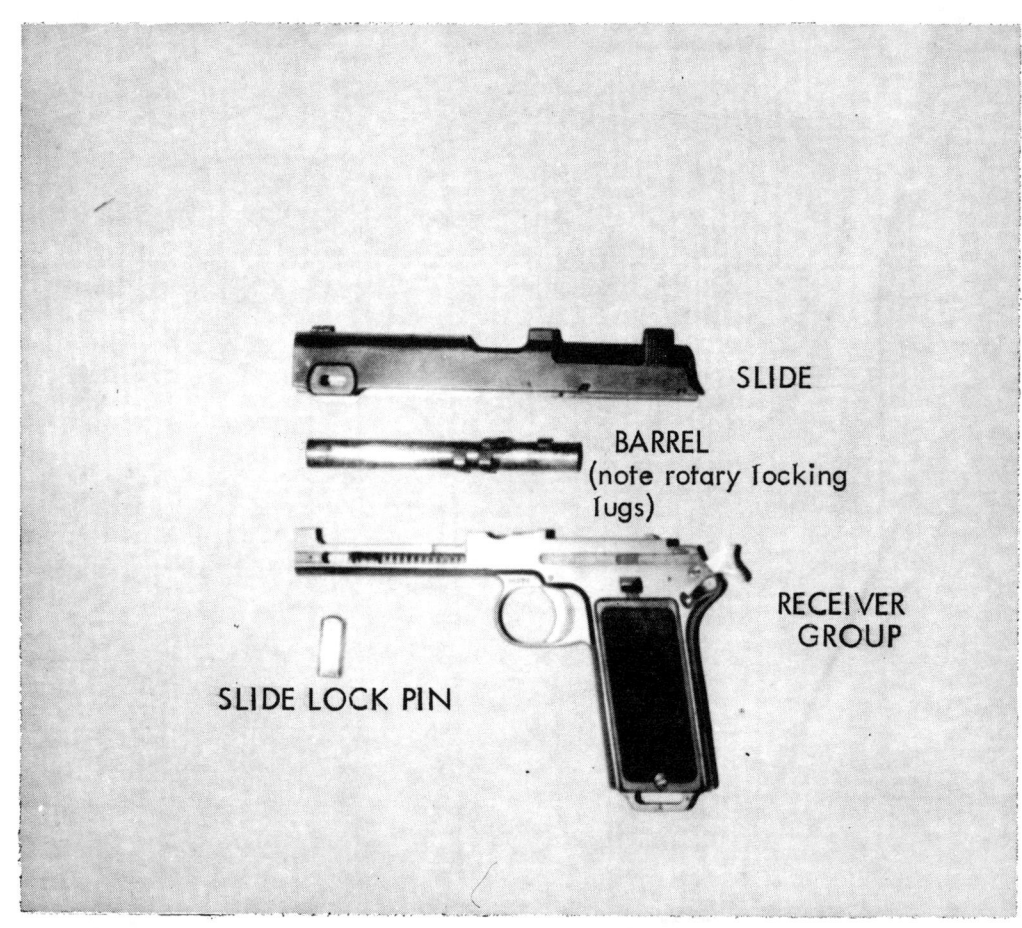

9-mm M12

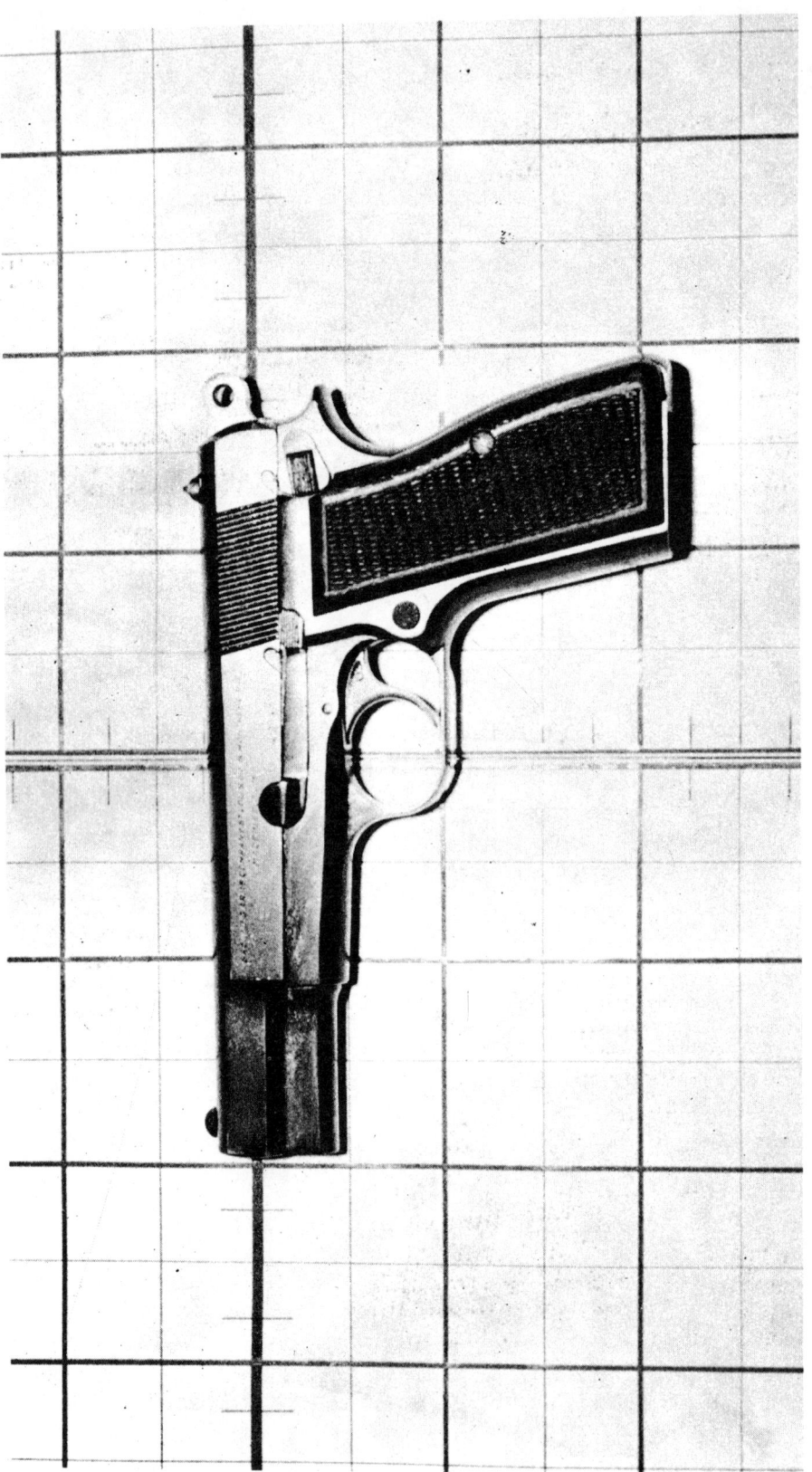

BELGIUM 9-MM, M35

PISTOL BELGIUM

9-mm M35 BROWNING (HI POWER)

This pistol, manufactured by Fabrique Nationale d'Armes de Guerre, Herstal-Liege, Belgium, was first placed on the market in two models in 1935. One model (illustrated), has fixed front and rear sights. The other model has an adjustable rear sight, provision for attachment of a shoulder stock and a special combination holster and shoulder stock. Under German occupation and supervision during WW II, an automatic variant is reported to have been produced. A light weight type, with light metal alloy frames has been manufactured as a post WW II production. This weapon was manufactured in Canada as the No. 1, Mk. 1, No. 2, Mk. 1, No. 2 Mk 1*, S.L. No. 2 Mk 1 and S.L. No. 2 Mk 1*. With variant markings the pistol was supplied to the Chinese Nationalist Army. It was manufactured by German occupation forces during WW II. Commercial and military contract sales to: Belgian, French, Rumanian and Latvian armies.

FUNCTIONING

Designed by John Browning in 1926, this piece is similar in design and function to the U.S. M1911A1 pistol. Recoil operated, with a locked slide, the barrel is locked to the slide by a camming wedge on the underside of the barrel. The disconnector and sear differ from the standard Browning practice in that the sear is mounted in the slide. The pivoting trigger pivots the sear. Forward motion of the slide cams the trigger lever out of engagement with the sear until it is released and repulled.

NOTES TO REMEMBER

1. Hold the slide firmly when removing it from the receiver. The recoil spring is fully compressed at this point in disassembly. If the slide slips from the person's hand, it will be forced violently from the receiver. It may injure the disassembler or cause damage to the slide or receiver.

2. Post WW II production pieces have a magazine safety incorporated into the design. When the magazine is removed, the trigger cannot be pulled. In order to pull the trigger and drop the hammer, a magazine must be inserted in the handle. An empty magazine should be used.

CHARACTERISTIC DATA

Caliber. 9-mm
Operation . . . . .Recoil
Type of Feed . . . . .Box-13 rd cap
Weight w/empty magazine . . . . 32 oz
Overall length . . . . .7.8 in
Effective range . . . . .70 meters

FIELD STRIP PROCEDURE

STEP   ACTION
1. Pull Slide to the rear.
2. Push Thumb Safety up into 2nd Notch in Slide.
3. Pressing in on Magazine Catch, remove magazine.
4. Push out Slide Stop by pressing on Slide Stop pin on right side of Receiver. Hold Slide firmly, release Thumb Safety and allow Slide to move forward. Lift off of Receiver.
5. Holding the Slide Assembly upside down, move the Recoil Spring Guide toward the muzzle slightly.
6. Disengage the Recoil Spring Guide head from the Barrel Nose. Remove Recoil Spring and Guide and Barrel from the Slide.

ASSEMBLY PROCEDURE

Proceed in reverse order. Hold Slide upside down, put Barrel into place. Assemble Recoil Spring and Guide and assemble to Slide, make sure Recoil Spring Guide head is firmly in place against Barrel Nose. Assemble Slide Assembly to Receiver, push Slide all the way to the rear and engage Thumb Safety in 2nd Notch in Slide. Put Slide Stop Pin in the hole in the Receiver and press in firmly.

LOADING AND FIRING

To load: Pull the Slide to the rear, lock open with the Slide Stop, insert a loaded Magazine into the Handle. Push down on the Slide Stop and allow the Slide to go forward and chamber a round. Push the Thumb Safety up into the rear (1st) Notch in the Slide.
To fire: Push Thumb Safety down. Pull the Trigger, the weapon will fire one shot for each pull of the Trigger.
NOTE: Some models have a Magazine Safety which locks the Sear when the Magazine is removed. If the Hammer will not fall when the Trigger is pulled, slide a Magazine in place, pull Trigger. This pistol can be carried with a round in the chamber and the Hammer down; hold the Hammer with the thumb of one hand and pull the Trigger, let the Hammer down gently on the Firing Pin Stop. Pull Hammer back to fire.

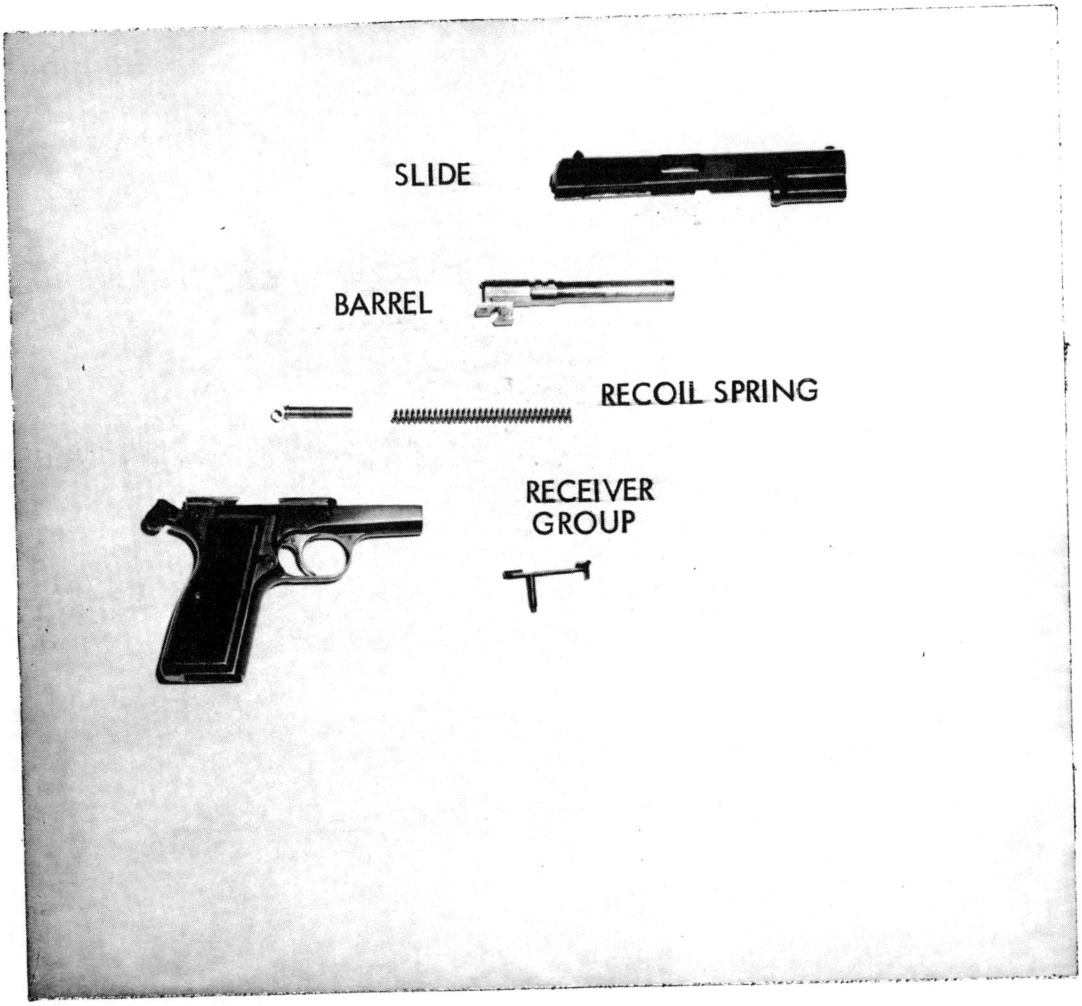
SLIDE
BARREL
RECOIL SPRING
RECEIVER
GROUP

9-mm M35 Browning

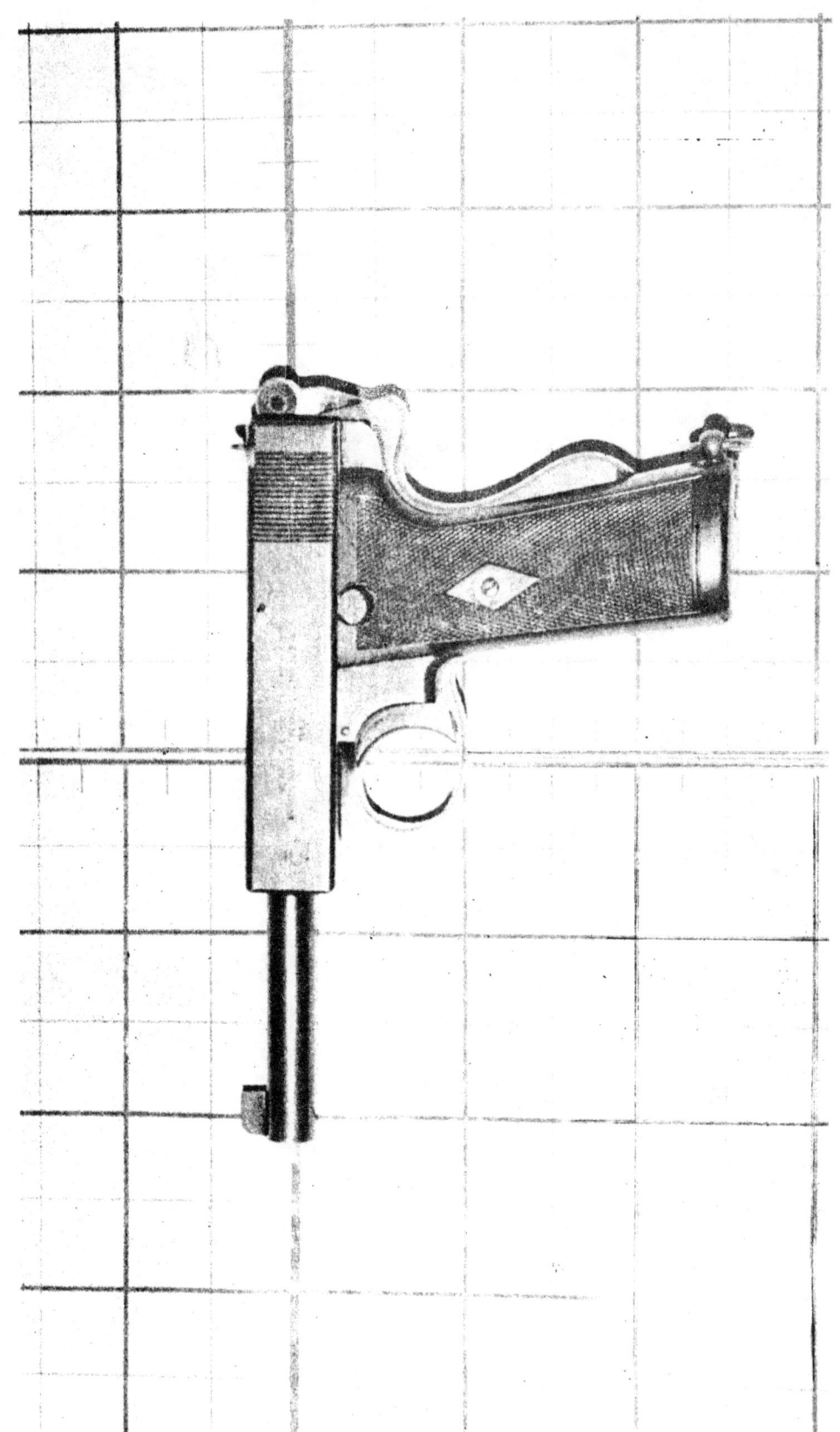

GREAT BRITAIN .455 AUTO, MARK 1

PISTOL   **GREAT BRITAIN**

.455 SELF LOADING PISTOL MARK 1

The British .455 Mark 1 Pistol is a recoil operated, locked breech weapon chambered for a round which is very similar to the U.S. .45 caliber round used in the M1911A1 Pistol. The round is semi-rimmed instead of rimless and the bullet is blunter than the .45 caliber round. The .455 round will not chamber in the U.S. Pistol. The .455 Mark 1 Pistol manufactured by Webley and Scott was adopted by the Royal British Navy in 1913. An earlier model produced in 1904 and a .38 caliber model produced in 1910 were never successful, but are not to be confused with the Mark 1. Straight blowback model pistols made by Webley and Scott were chambered for .25, .32, .380 and 9-mm ammunition and resemble the .455 caliber recoil operated pistol. Harrington and Richardson of the United States manufactured a modification of the Webley pistol in .32 ACP caliber. The Mark 1 Pistol was a difficult pistol to hold and fire because of the shape and angle of the grip. One design item of note is the two-position magazine system. The magazine could be inserted until the first engagement notch of the magazine engaged the magazine catch, and the piece would not load from the magazine but could be loaded single shot manually. The loaded magazine was thus kept in reserve. Pushing the magazine up to engage the second notch of the magazine brought the magazine into use.

FUNCTIONING

With a loaded magazine fully inserted the slide is drawn to the rear and released. The slide moves forward strips a round from the magazine and chambers it. The hammer remains held to the rear by the sear. The locking system involves the movement of the barrel up and down along inclined grooves in the receiver. Angled grooves on either side of the receiver are engaged by lugs on each side of the barrel. When the forward moving slide strikes the rear of the barrel, the barrel is forced forward and up so that a shoulder on the top of the barrel is abutted against a mating recess in the top of the slide. When the round is fired, the barrel and slide move to the rear. The lugs on the barrel riding in the grooves in the receiver direct the rear of the barrel downward pulling the locking shoulder on the top of the barrel out of the recess in the top of the slide. The rearward movement of the barrel stops at this point and the slide continues to the rear to extract and eject the empty case. The slide then moves forward under impulse of the compressed recoil spring which is a "V" shaped leaf spring contained under the right stock. The hammer remains to the rear. Pulling the trigger will repeat the firing cycle.

CHARACTERISTIC DATA

Caliber . . . . .455 Webley SL
Operation . . . . .Recoil
Type of Feed . . . . .Box—7 rd cap
Weight, empty . . . . 38 oz
Overall length . . . . 8.5 in
Effective range . . . . .70 meters

FIELD STRIP PROCEDURE

STEP   ACTION

1. Draw the Slide slightly to the rear and press in on the Recoil Lever Stop. This locks the Recoil Spring out of action.
2. Push the Slide forward.
3. Pull the Slide Stop out as far as it will go.
4. Pull the Slide to the rear as far as it will go.
5. Lift the Barrel out of the Receiver.
6. Push the Slide forward off the Receiver.

ASSEMBLY PROCEDURE

Assemble in the reverse order. Slide the Slide on to the front of the Receiver and push all the way to the rear. Assemble the Barrel to the Receiver. Push the Slide forward slightly, pushing in on the Slide Stop at the same time. Move the Slide slightly to the rear until the Recoil Lever Stop disengages from the Recoil Spring and the Recoil Spring again becomes operational.

LOADING AND FIRING

To load: Insert a loaded magazine fully into the grip. There is no Safety Lever on this weapon. The only Safety is a Grip Safety and this Grip Safety located in the rear of the Grip must be pushed in fully to fire the pistol. Draw the Slide to the rear and release it. The Slide will move forward and chamber a round. The Hammer will be held to the rear by the Sear.

To fire: Grip the Pistol Grip firmly so the Grip Safety is pushed in. Pull the Trigger. The weapon will fire for each pull of the Trigger until the Magazine is empty. The slide will remain to the rear after the Magazine is empty. When the Magazine is removed, the Slide Stop will hold the Slide open.

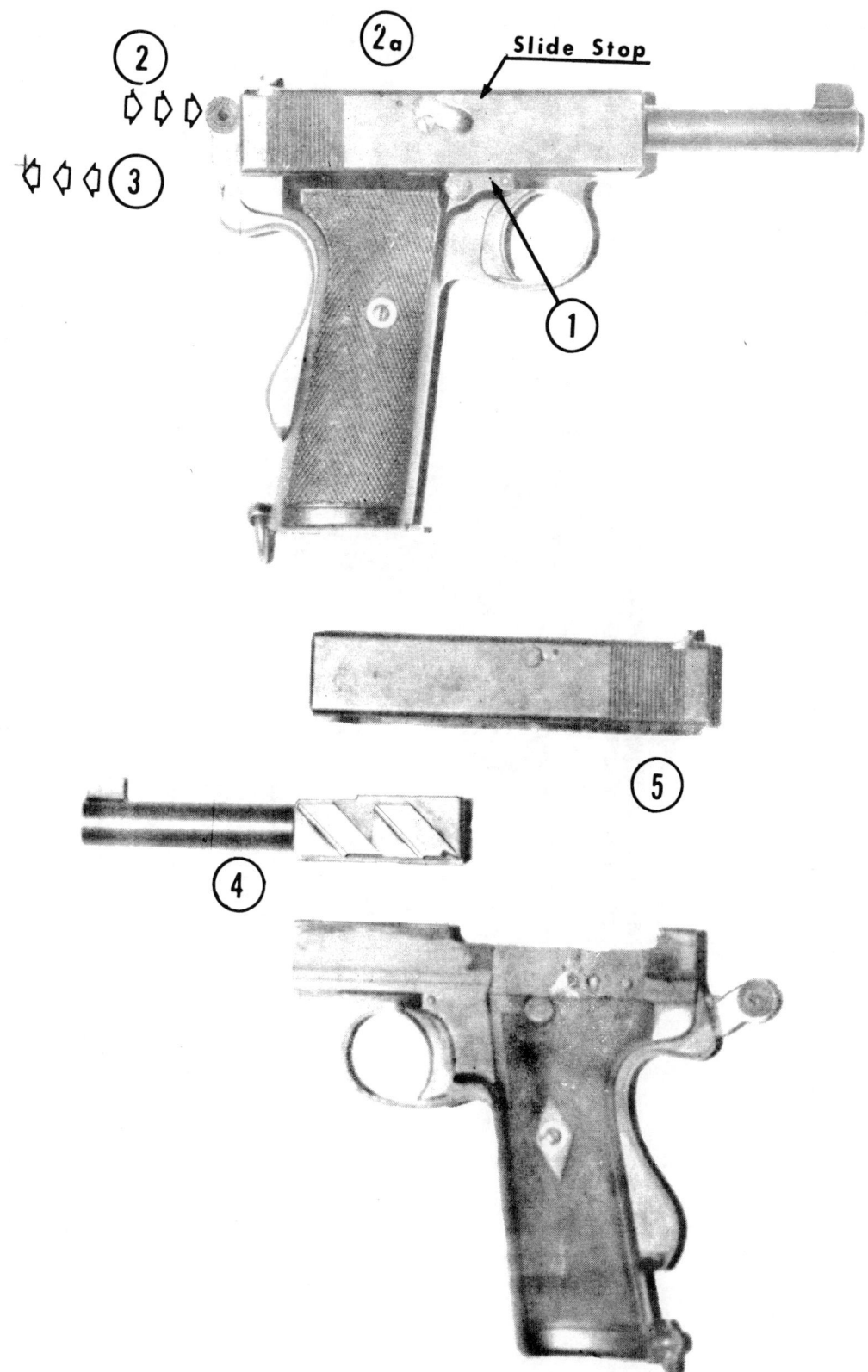

.44·5 Self Loading Pistol Mark I

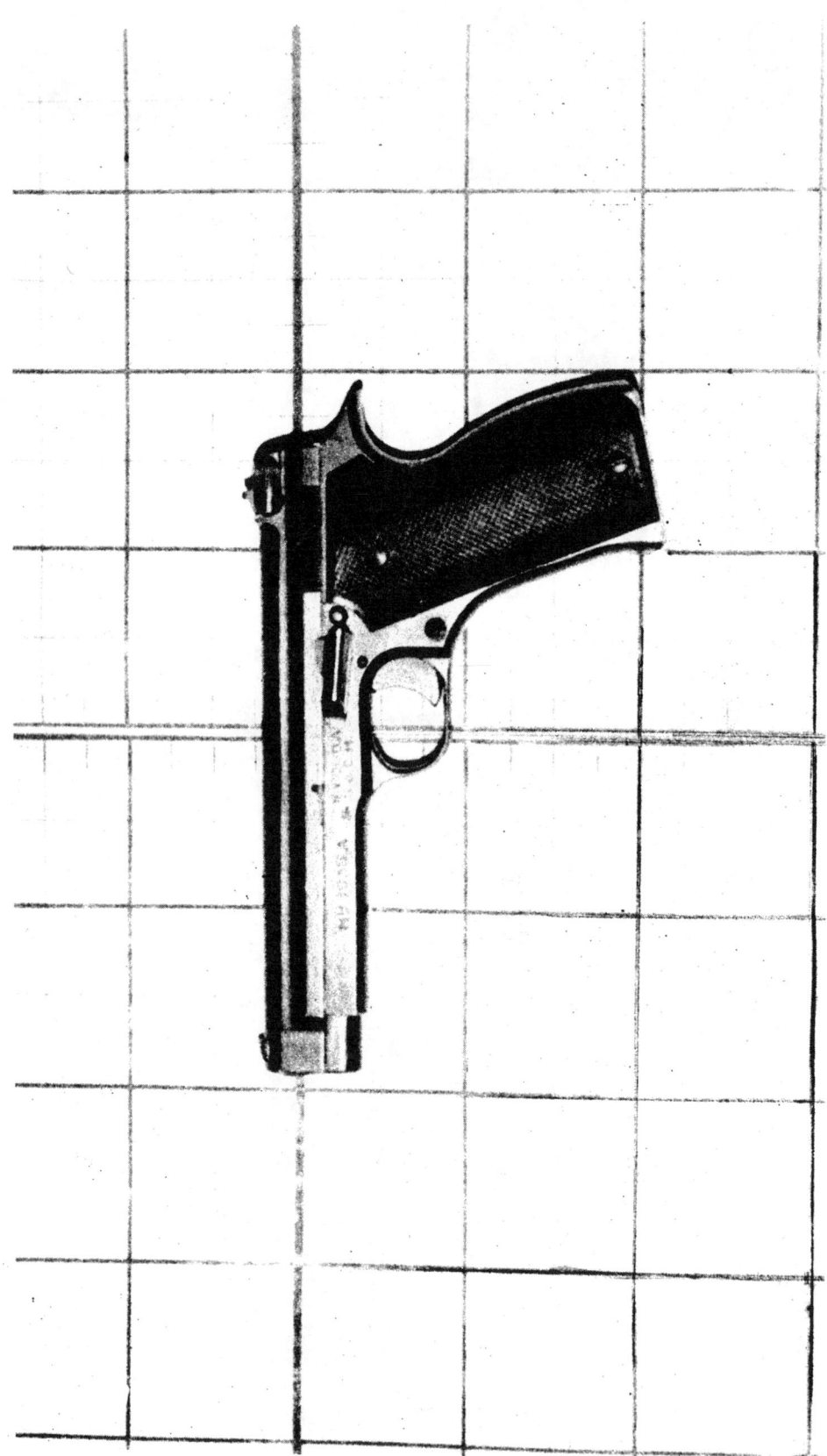

FRANCE 7.65-MM LONG, M1935A

PISTOL   **FRANCE**

7.65-mm M1935A (MAS)

The French M1935A MAS Pistol is chambered for a special 7.65-mm cartridge, which has a longer case than either the Luger 7.65-mm or the Colt 7.65-mm rounds. The French MAS-38 submachinegun is also chambered for this round, and though the round is considered weak for a submachinegun round, it is more than adequate for a pistol. The M1935A pistol is patterned after the U.S. model 1911A1 pistol and resembles it in many respects with the exception of being slightly smaller than the U.S. piece. The French pistol does not however have a grip safety, the only safety being a lever mounted on the top left rear of the slide. The exposed hammer does not have a "spur" but is instead a "burr" type and is almost completely protected by the slide when in the forward position. The finish of the piece is generally poor, being a black enamel. The M1935A has been replaced by the 9-mm M1950 Pistol in the French Army. The M1935A may still be encountered in the hands of police units.

FUNCTIONING

The M1935A Pistol is a locked breech pistol. The locking of the barrel to the slide is accomplished by a link, one end of which is attached to the breech end of the barrel, the other end firmly affixed to the receiver. With a loaded magazine in place, the slide is drawn to the rear and released. As the slide moves forward under impulse of the compressed recoil spring a round is stripped from the magazine and chambered. When the breech block strikes the rear of the barrel, it forces the barrel forward, and the rear of the barrel pivots about the fixed link moving up so the locking lugs on the top of the barrel engage mating locking grooves in the top of the slide. Upon firing, the slide and barrel move to the rear a short distance locked together. The link being firmly attached to the receiver then pulls the barrel down out of engagement with the slide and the slide continues to the rear. Extraction and ejection of the empty case is accomplished at this time. The slide moves forward and chambers the next round and the hammer is held to the rear by the sear. Pulling the trigger repeats the cycle.

CHARACTERISTIC DATA

Caliber	7.65-mm Long
Operation	Recoil
Type of Feed	Box—8 rd cap
Weight, empty	25.3 oz
Overall length	7.8 in
Effective Range	65 meters

FIELD STRIP PROCEDURE

STEP ACTION

1. Press the Slide Stop Pin out of the Receiver from the right side.
1a. Remove the Slide Stop.
2. Slide the Slide with Barrel, Recoil Spring and Guide off the front of the Receiver.
3. Lift the assembled Recoil Spring and Guide from the Slide.
4. Remove the Barrel from the Slide.

ASSEMBLY PROCEDURE

Assemble in the reverse order. Slide the Barrel into the Slide. Assemble the Recoil Spring and Guide into the Slide making sure that the rear of the Recoil Spring Guide engages the Barrel Link. Assemble the Slide to the Receiver. Line up the Barrel Link with the hole in the Receiver and push the Slide Stop Pin through the Receiver.

LOADING AND FIRING

To load: Insert a loaded Magazine. Push the Safety Lever up to "SAFE". Draw the Slide to the rear and release it. The Slide will move forward, strip a round from the Magazine, and chamber it.

To fire: Push the Safety Lever down. Pull the Trigger. The weapon will fire for each pull of the Trigger until the Magazine is empty. The Slide will remain to the rear after the Magazine is empty. When the Magazine is removed the Slide Stop will hold the Slide open. NOTE: This weapon has a Magazine Safety. When the Magazine is removed the weapon cannot be fired.

1
Slide Stop
2
4
3
1a

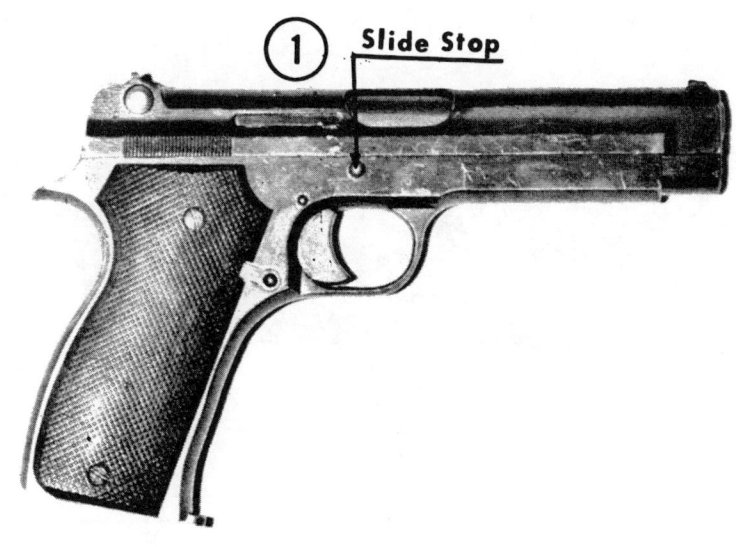

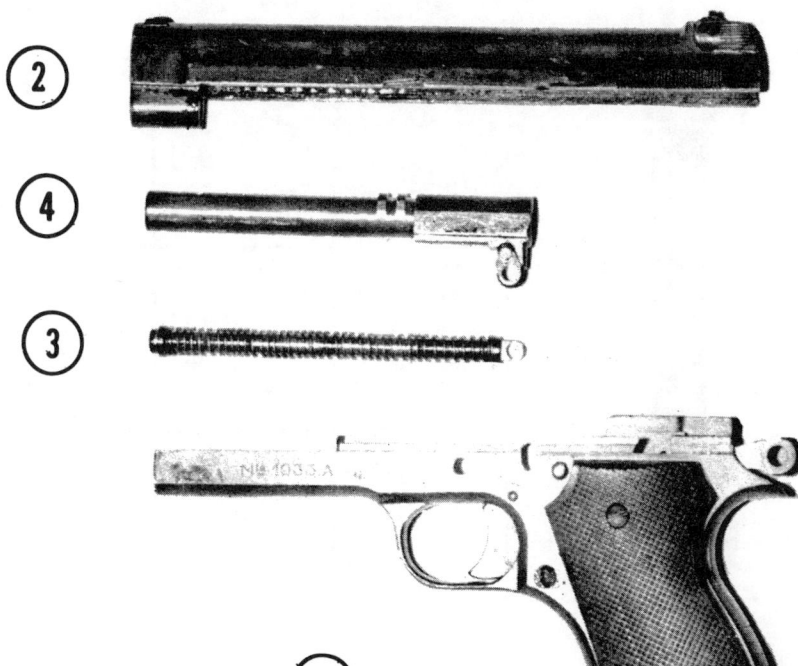

7.65-mm M1935A

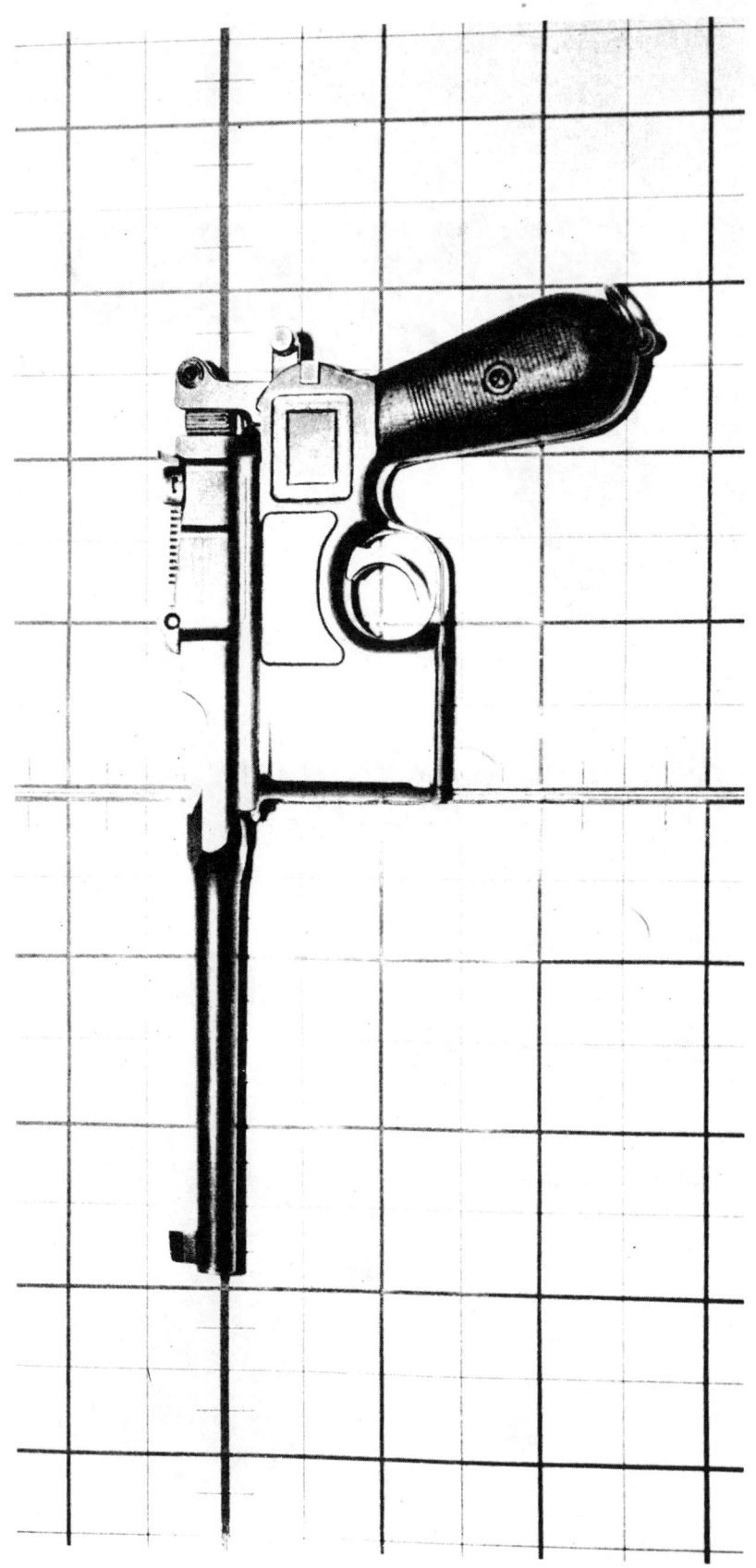

GERMANY 7.63-MM, MM1896

PISTOL   GERMANY

7.63-mm 1896 MILITARY MODEL

The 7.63-mm Mauser pistol is a recoil operated, fixed magazine-fed pistol. This pistol, designed by Paul Mauser of Oberndorf, Germany in 1896, was the first of the true military pistols. It is one of the few pistols in the world today which does not utilize a detachable magazine, the ammunition being loaded from a strip clip into the fixed-magazine, built into the frame forward of the trigger guard. The design of this weapon has changed very little since the original system was produced in 1896. The lock-frame and hammer mechanism is extremely complicated for a pistol, but because of the large magazine capacity (10 rounds), shoulder stock attachment, relatively long barrel and adjustable, accurate sights, it is well liked by both military and civilian shooters. The black-jack shaped grip, and forward heavy balance of the piece makes it an awkward weapon to shoot until one has mastered the feel and balance. The pistol has been chambered for 9-mm and can usually be identified in this caliber by a large number "9" carved in the stock. Models exist with a change lever incorporated into the design which permits full-automatic fire, and in this pistol the detachable shoulder stock must be used. Other models exist in which a detachable 20-round magazine is used in conjunction with a long carbinetype barrel, removable shoulder stock and incorporating a change lever. As such, it becomes a true machine-pistol.

FUNCTIONING

This is a locked breech pistol and because of the special ballistics of the round it fires, it is somewhat more accurate than a conventional pistol. With the bolt locked to the rear, the bolt remains open if the magazine is empty, a strip-clip holding 10 rounds is placed in the feed guide at the top of the magazine housing. The ammunition is pushed down into the magazine compressing the magazine spring. Removing the empty clip releases the bolt and the bolt will move forward to chamber the first round. The hammer remains to the rear in the cocked position held by the sear. The bolt lock is forced up into the recesses in the bottom of the bolt, firmly locking the bolt against the breech. Pulling the trigger pivots the sear out of engagement with the hammer allowing the hammer to swing forward against the striker. The barrel, barrel extension, lock and lock frame move to the rear a short distance locked together (approximately 3/16"). The rear bottom toe of the lock drops into a recess in the lock frame, disengaging from the bolt and the bolt moves to the rear extracting and ejecting the fired case. The bolt then moves forward and chambers a new round. The hammer is held back by the sear and the pistol is ready to fire again.

CHARACTERISTIC DATA

Caliber 7.63-mm
Operation ....Recoil
Type of feed..Fixed Box—10 rd cap
Weight, Empty ....45 oz
Overall length ....12.2 in w/out stock
Barrel length..5.25 in
Effective range ....80 meters
Muzzle velocity ....1426 fps

FIELD STRIP PROCEDURE

STEP   ACTION

1. Press in on the Locking Stud located at the rear of the Magazine Floor Plate. Slide Floor Plate forward and off. Remove Magazine Spring and Follower.
2. Draw the Hammer back. Press up on the Receiver Lock located beneath the base of the Hammer.
3. Slide the Barrel and Barrel Extension with the attached Lock Frame to the rear of the Receiver.
4. Pivot the Lock Frame Assembly down and remove from engagement with the Barrel Extension. Lift the Bolt Lock off of the Lock Frame Assembly.

ASSEMBLY PROCEDURE

Proceed in the reverse order. Assemble the Bolt Lock to the underside of the Barrel Extension, engaging the locking recesses in the Bolt. Attach the Lock Frame Assembly onto the Bolt Lock by inserting the rear toe of the Lock into its recess in the top of the Lock Frame Assembly. Holding the two firmly together, slide into the guides in the Receiver and push forward until the Receiver Lock is engaged. Assemble Magazine Spring and Follower into the Magazine Housing and slide Floor Plate into place.

LOADING AND FIRING

To load: Draw Slide to the rear. Insert loaded strip clip into feed guides and press ammunition down into the Magazine. Remove strip clip and Bolt will ride forward and chamber the first round. If the Safety, located on the left side of the Hammer is up, the weapon is on Safe. Push the Safety down and the pistol is ready to fire.

To fire: Pull the Trigger and the weapon will fire. This is a semi-automatic pistol and the Trigger must be pulled for each round fired.

BARREL & SLIDE ASS'Y
FIRING MECHANISM
RECEIVER GROUP
MAGAZINE FOLLOWER, SPRING AND BOTTOM PLATE

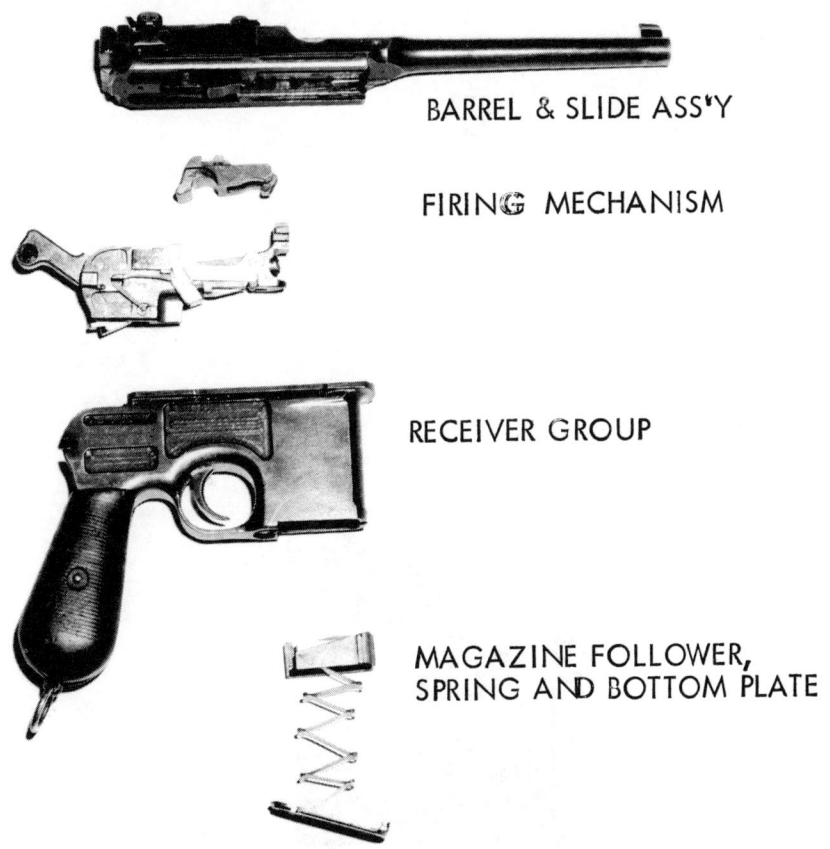

7.63-mm 1896 Military Model

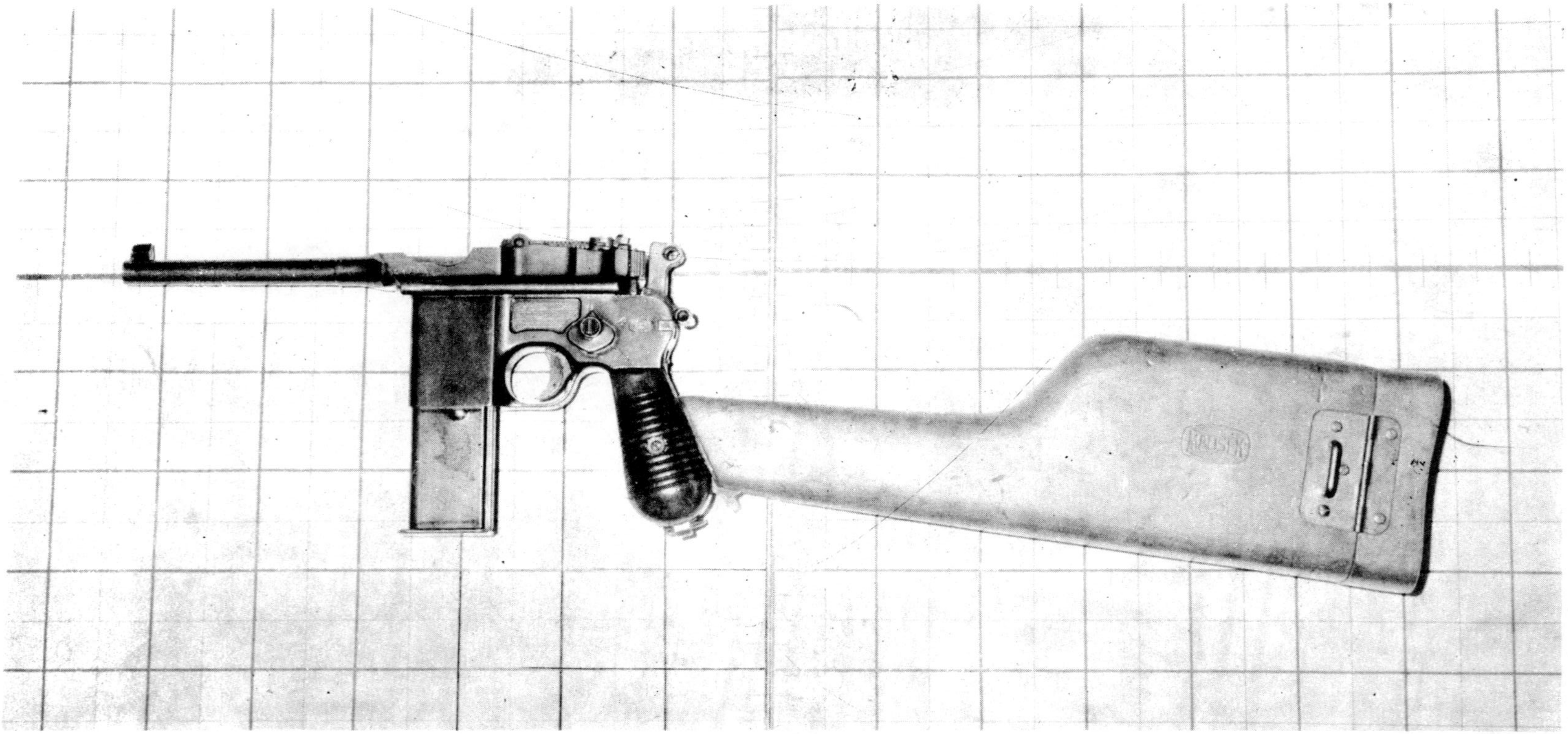

GERMANY 7.63-MM, MP1932

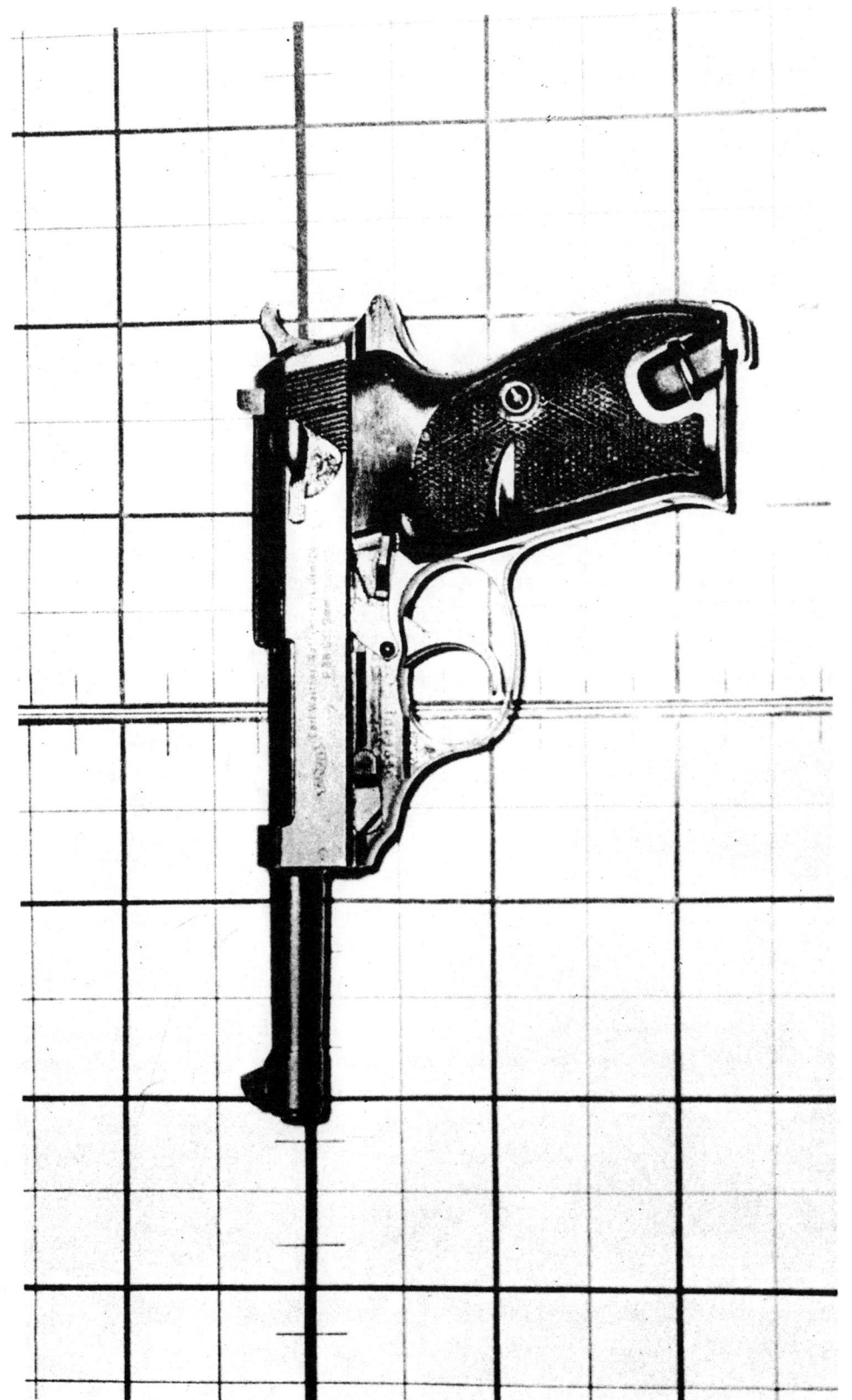

GERMANY 9-MM, P-38

PISTOL   **GERMANY**

9-mm PISTOLE 38 (P-38)

The 9-mm Walther Military Model (Heeres Pistole), P-38, originally manufactured at Walther, Zell Mehlis, was intended to replace the German Pistole 08 (P-08) as the standard handgun of the German Army. War requirements, however, kept the P-08 in production. The Swedish version of this pistol is listed as the Pistol m/39, the Norwegian service (post WWII) arm as the 9-mm Pistol m/38. It was also used extensively by the Czech police (post WWII). Commercial versions of this arm were in production prior to 1939 and were sold in the United States through arms import houses. It can be found in .22 caliber rimfire, .38 ACP and .45 ACP. Many experimental variations exist as well as many standardized design models. Differences in barrel lengths, material, and firing pin safeties exist in the standardized models. The weapon is very unusual in that it incorporates a double-action hammer, seldom successful or considered, in the design of an auto-loading pistol. The Austrian Roth-Steyr, M1907 utilized a striker, cocked and released by the trigger. In the case of the P-38, the double-action feature has considerable merit (as a military side-arm) over conventional pistols. With the weapon loaded, the hammer can be dropped by applying the safety. To fire it is only necessary to pull the trigger, the hammer functions in the manner of a double-action revolver. In the event of a misfire the trigger can be repeatedly pulled until the cartridge discharges. A loaded chamber indicator, a floating pin which protrudes from the rear of the slide above the hammer, indicates by sight, or feel, whether a round is in the chamber. This weapon has all the good-holding points of the P-08, a positive swinging-block locking system similar to the Mauser pistol, the sturdiness of the U.S. M1911A and an extremely simple takedown procedure.

FUNCTIONING

This is a recoil operated pistol with a positively locked slide. If the double-action feature is used to fire the first round, the hammer will be cocked by the rearward movement of the slide after the round is fired, and the cocking action thereafter is similar to standard auto-loading pistol principles. The barrel is locked to the slide for a short recoiling distance by lugs on a pivoting lock attached to the barrel assembly. At the end of 5/16" rearward travel of the locked parts, the lock is cammed down by a locking plunger which butts against the receiver at this point in travel. The slide continues to the rear compressing two small recoil springs. Moving forward after completing its rearward movement, the slide strips a round from the magazine and chambers it. The lock is forced up into engagement with the slide by a camming surface on the bottom of the lock. Extraction and ejection is the same as for similar auto-loaders.

CHARACTERISTIC DATA

Caliber	9-mm
Operation	Recoil
Weight with empty magazine	34 oz
Overall length	8.6 in
Barrel length	4.9 in
Magazine capacity	8 rds
Effective range	70 meters

FIELD STRIP PROCEDURE

STEP   ACTION

1. With Magazine removed and Chamber empty, push thumb Safety Lever down to "SAFE."
2. Draw the Slide to the rear and lock open with the Slide Stop.
3. Turn the lever-type Locking Pin down and around as far as it will go. Holding the Slide firmly, push down on the Slide Stop and allow the Slide and Barrel Assembly to slide forward. The trigger must be pulled to release the Slide and Barrel Assembly.
4. Hold the Barrel and Slide upside down and press in on the Lock Plunger. This will cam the Locking Lugs on the Lock out of engagement with the Slide.
5. Slide the Barrel and Lock forward out of the Slide. The Lock may be lifted from the Barrel Assembly. No further disassembly is necessary for general cleaning.

ASSEMBLY PROCEDURE

Proceed in the reverse order. Replace the lock in the Barrel Assembly by pressing down firmly. With the Receiver held upside down, slide the Barrel Assembly and Lock into the Receiver. Holding the Lock in the "locked" position (pushed in against the Barrel), slide the Slide and Barrel Assembly onto the Receiver. Push all the way to the rear and raise the Slide Stop to hold the Slide open. Pivot the Locking Pin back and up. Release the Slide Stop and allow the Slide to move forward.

LOADING AND FIRING

To load: Draw the Slide to the rear and lock open with the slide Stop. Insert a loaded Magazine. Push down on the Slide Stop. The Slide will move forward and chamber a round. If the Safety was on "FIRE", the Hammer will remain cocked back and the weapon is ready to fire. If the Safety was on "SAFE", the Hammer will follow the Slide forward, resting against the blocked Firing Pin. To Fire: With the Safety in the "SAFE" position, push the Safety up. The Hammer can now be thumb-cocked for the first round or a pull of the Trigger will draw the Hammer back and release it.

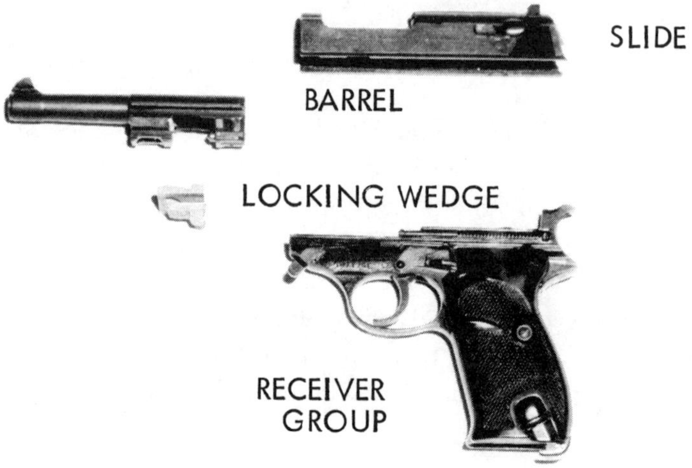
SLIDE
BARREL
LOCKING WEDGE
RECEIVER
GROUP

9-mm Pistole 38

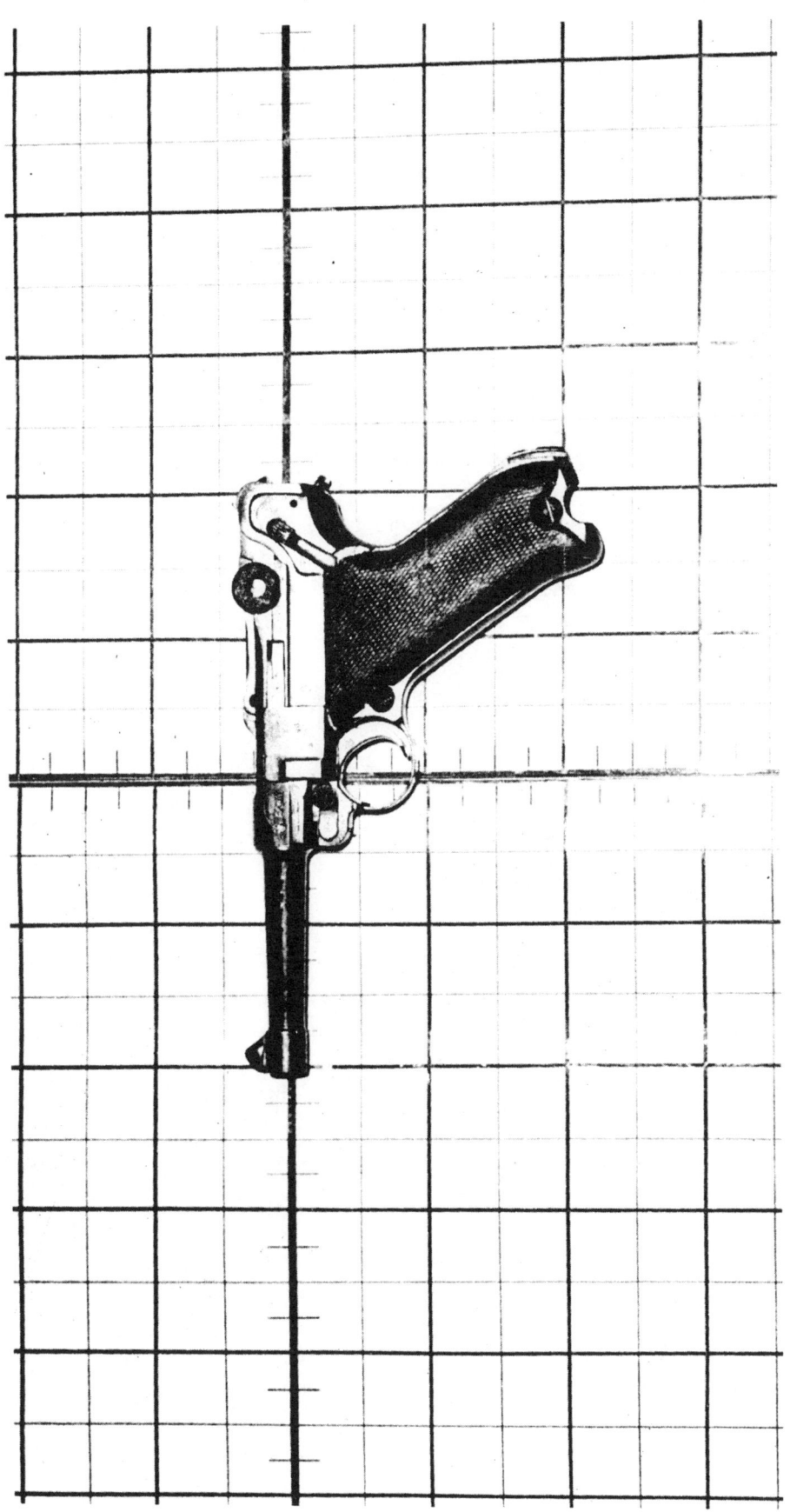

GERMANY 9-MM, P-08

PISTOL   **GERMANY**

9-mm PISTOLE 08 (LUGER)

The 9-mm Pistole 08 (P-08), commonly known as the Luger Pistol, is probably one of the most popular, best known handguns in the world. It has been produced in 7.65-mm and 9-mm caliber and units to convert to .22 caliber are available. A few were made in caliber .45 ACP for tests by the United States in the early 1900's. Very few changes have been made in the Luger design since 1900. These have included changes in the movement of the safety lever and the inclusion, in very limited quantities, of a magazine safety. The Luger may be encountered with various barrel lengths, addition of a grip safety, different rear sight locations and types, and may be found with or without the stock attachment lug on the grip. It is probably one of the best "pointing" pistols in existence and its main mechanical fault is the total exposure to the elements of the major moving parts, the breechblock, toggle and toggle joint assembly. This, plus the excessive breakage of the recoil spring (later improved) and the failure of the magazine catch to hold the magazine in proper feeding position were some of the reasons for the failure of acceptance of the pistol as the standard military sidearm for U.S. armed forces. A wooden shoulder stock, forearm, and 32-round drum magazine are available for this weapon. Some models are reported to have been modified for full-automatic fire also.

FUNCTIONING

This is a recoil operated, locked-breech action pistol. With a loaded magazine inserted in the grip, the large knobs on either side of the toggle joint are pulled up and to the rear to draw open the breechblock. Releasing the knobs allows the assembled toggle joint assembly and breechblock to move down and forward into an in-line position under the impulse of the recoil spring contained in the rear of the grip. Pulling the trigger causes the trigger bar ("L" shaped) to press against the sear which is holding the firing pin to the rear. The firing pin is released and moves forward under the impulse of the compressed firing pin spring and strikes the primer. The breechblock is locked against the face of the chamber by the "straight-line" structure of the fore and rear toggle pieces and toggle joint assembly. After a short rearward travel of the locked barrel and receiver assembly, the toggle joint knobs are forced up and in so doing, the "straight-line" is broken and the breechblock moves away from the face of the chamber, extracting and ejecting the empty cartridge case. At the completion of this rearward movement of the breechblock, the recoil spring forces the opened toggle system to move forward again, forcing the breechblock against the face of the chamber during which time it has stripped the top round from the magazine and chambered it. Another pull of the trigger will repeat this cycle.

CHARACTERISTIC DATA

Caliber 9-mm
Operation . . . . .Recoil
Type of Feed . . . . .Box 8 rd cap
Weight, empty . . . . 30 oz
Overall length . . . . 8.7 in
Effective range . . . . 70 meters

FIELD STRIP PROCEDURE

STEP   ACTION

1. With the Chamber empty and the Magazine removed, push back slightly on the Barrel and pivot the Side Plate Retaining Pin down and remove.
2. Lift off the Side Plate.
3. Slide the Barrel and Receiver Assembly with Breechblock and Toggle Assembly forward off the frame.
4. Buckle the Toggle up slightly by pressing on the underside of the Toggle Joint and push the Toggle Assembly Retaining Pin out. Slide the Breechblock and Toggle Assembly out of the Receiver Assembly guides.

ASSEMBLY PROCEDURE

Proceed in the reverse order. Slide the Toggle and Breechblock Assembly into the Receiver Assembly guides. Buckle the Toggle up slightly and press the Toggle Retaining Pin into place. Mate the Receiver Assembly with the Frame and slide into place. NOTE 1: Make sure the HOOK attached to the rear of the Toggle Assembly drops into place in front of the Recoil Spring Claw, visible just forward of and below the inclined ramp at the rear of the Frame. Push the Barrel to the rear slightly and assemble the Side Plate Retaining Pin. Place the Side Plate into position. NOTE 2: The TONGUE at the rear of the Side Plate must slip beneath the recess in the Frame and the Projecting arm of the Trigger Bar must fall into the proper slot above the Trigger. Pivot the Side Plate Retaining Pin up to lock the Barrel Assembly and Frame together.

LOADING AND FIRING

To load: Push the Safety Lever up to "SAFE." Insert a loaded Magazine into the pistol grip. Grasp the serrated Toggle Knobs and pull up and back to pull the Breechblock to the rear. Release the Knobs and the Breechblock will move forward and chamber a round.

To fire: Push the Safety to "Off." Pull the Trigger. The weapon will fire one shot for each pull of the Trigger until empty. When the last round has been fired, the Breechblock will remain to the rear with the Toggle Joint in the "up" position.

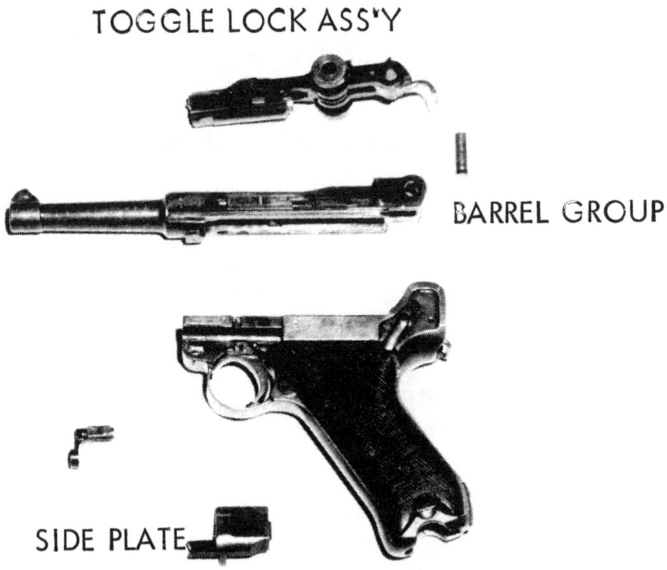
TOGGLE LOCK ASS'Y
BARREL GROUP
SIDE PLATE

9-mm Pistole 08

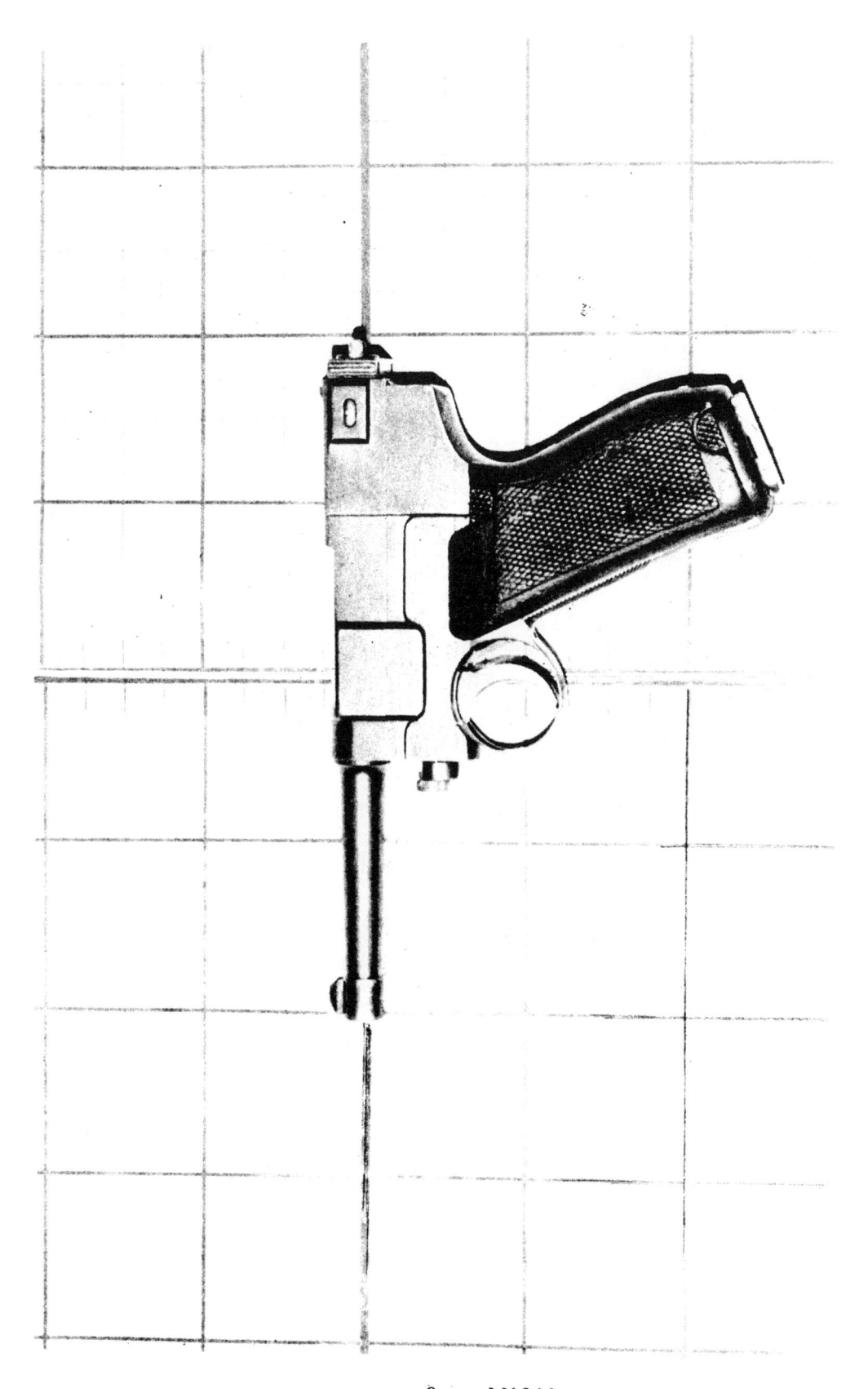

ITALY   9-MM, M1910

9-mm M1910

PISTOL   ITALY

9-mm M1910 GLISENTI

The Italian 9-mm Glisenti Pistol is a recoil operated, locked breech weapon, which incorporates a number of unusual design features in its construction. It was patented in 1906 and presented for tests in the United States in 1907. Officially adopted as the Italian service pistol in 1910, it saw service in both WWI and WWII. It has been replaced by the Italian 9-mm Beretta M1951. As a military arm, it was overly complicated and bulky. A relatively weak prop-up lock is capable of handling the ammunition designed for this weapon, but the standard German 9-mm ammunition should not be fired in it. A double sear system, one sear holding the firing pin in the cocked position and the other sear mounted on the trigger and a separate barrel return spring, are two of the unusual design components.

FUNCTIONING

With a loaded magazine inserted, the slide is drawn to the rear and released. As the slide moves forward under impulse of the compressed recoil spring, it strips a round from the magazine and chambers it. The prop-up lock located in the upper rear portion of the receiver is swung upward under the impulse of a leaf spring located in the grip. The nose of the lock which passes through an opening in the bottom of the barrel extension now engages a locking notch cut in the bottom of the bolt. The barrel has also been pushed forward under impulse of the barrel return spring. The firing pin sear has engaged the firing pin and holds it in the cocked position and the trigger sear contacts the firing pin sear. A grip safety is located on the front of the grip and must be pressed in before the trigger can be pulled. When the trigger is pulled, the trigger sear lifts the tail of the firing pin sear and releases the firing pin. The barrel and barrel extension, with the bolt locked against the barrel by the prop-up lock starts to the rear when the round is fired. After five-sixteenths of an inch of travel the barrel extension butts against a shoulder in the rear of the receiver. At this point the prop-up lock has pivoted rearward and downward to the point where the nose no longer engages the bolt and the bolt continues to the rear. The recoil spring, which is housed around the firing pin in the bolt, is compressed at this time. As the bolt starts forward it strips a round from the magazine, the prop-up lock swings up into position, the round is chambered, and the barrel return spring forces the barrel with attached extension and locked bolt forward the last ¼ inch. In this respect the round is actually chambered before the action is fully forward. Pressing in on the grip safety and pulling the trigger will repeat the firing cycle.

CHARACTERISTIC DATA

Caliber . . . . 9-mm Glisenti
Operation . . . . Recoil
Type of Feed . . . . Box 7 rd cap
Weight empty . . . . 34 ozs
Overall length . . . . 8.3 in
Effective range . . . . 60 meters

FIELD STRIP PROCEDURE

STEP   ACTION

1. Push in on Dismounting Plunger Retaining Pin.
2. Holding this pin in pull out on the Dismounting Plunger and turn it to lock open.
3. Lift the Side Plate off.
4. Press in on the Stock Release Plunger and remove left Stock.
5. Pull the Bolt to the rear. No further disassembly is necessary for normal cleaning.

ASSEMBLY PROCEDURE

Assemble in the reverse order. Pull the Bolt back slightly and allow it to move forward. Replace the left Stock. Replace the Left Side Plate. Turn the Dismounting Plunger to unlock and allow it to snap into position.

LOADING AND FIRING

To load: Place a loaded magazine in the magazine well. Draw the Bolt to the rear and release it, the Bolt will move forward and chamber a round. A Safety Lever located on the rear face of the Bolt can now be turned to "SAFE". This Safety Lever can only be turned when the weapon is cocked.

To fire: Turn the Safety Lever off. Press the grip firmly to function the Grip Safety. Pull the trigger. The weapon will fire each time the Trigger is pulled until the Magazine is empty. The Bolt will stay to the rear when the Magazine is empty.

SIDE PLATE

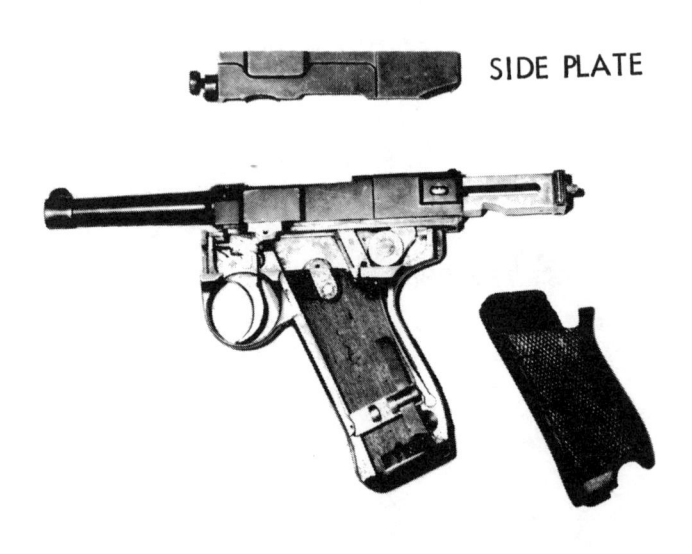

9-mm M1910

ITALY   9-MM, M1951

PISTOL

ITALY

9-mm M1951 (BERETTA)

The Model 1951 Beretta pistol is a recoil operated pistol with the typical Beretta open-top slide. Chambered for the 9-mm Luger cartridge, it is a well balanced, compact weapon which utilizes the Walther locking wedge system to lock the barrel to the slide during firing. Adopted by the Italian Army and Navy in 1951, it is also the official side arm for Israeli and Egyptian armed forces. It is very similar in appearance to the Model 1934, 9-mm Corto Beretta pistol, though slightly larger. Although the locking system is similar to the Walther P-38 pistol, it is not a double action firing pistol. With a cartridge in the chamber and the hammer down the hammer must be manually cocked to prepare the weapon for firing. A disconnector makes the weapon inoperative until the slide is fully forward. The safety is a push-through button located in the upper rear portion of the pistol grips. This weapon is also known as the M951.

FUNCTIONING

This is a recoil operated, locked breech pistol, in which the barrel is locked to the slide by a wedge being cammed up into grooves in the slide when the action is closed. With a loaded magazine inserted, the slide is drawn to the rear and released. When the slide reaches its forward position a locking wedge attached to the underside of the barrel is cammed upward to engage grooves in the inside of the slide. When the trigger is pulled the sear releases the hammer, the hammer strikes the rebounding type firing pin and the primer is struck. The slide and barrel move to the rear locked together for a short distance (7/16 in), an unlocking plunger which abuts the rear of the locking wedge, strikes a ledge in the receiver and forces the locking wedge down out of engagement with the slide. The slide continues to the rear compressing the recoil spring, which is located beneath the barrel. Extraction and ejection take place at this time. As the slide moves forward it strips a round from the magazine and chambers it. The hammer is held back by the sear and the weapon is ready to fire again.

CHARACTERISTIC DATA

Caliber 9-mm
Operation .... Recoil
Type of Feed .... Box - 8 rd cap
Weight, empty .... 25.2 ozs
Overall length .... 8 in
Effective range .... 70 meters

FIELD STRIP PROCEDURE

STEP   ACTION

1. Draw Slide to the rear and swing Dismounting Lever, located on right side of Receiver, forward and up to engage dismounting notch in Slide.
2. Pull Slide Assembly and Barrel forward off of Receiver.
3. Remove Recoil Spring and Guide from Slide. (Barrel may also be removed from Slide.)

ASSEMBLY PROCEDURE

Assemble in the reverse order. Assemble Recoil Spring and Guide to Slide. Slide Slide Assembly and Barrel onto Receiver. Push to the rear until Dismounting Lever aligns with dismounting notch and swing dismounting Lever down to the rear.

LOADING AND FIRING

To load: Insert a loaded Magazine into the Pistol Grip. Push Safety Button from right to left to "SAFE." Draw the Slide to the rear and release. The Slide will move forward and chamber a round and the Hammer will be held back by the Sear.

To fire: Push the Safety Button from left to right to "FIRE". Pull the Trigger. The weapon will fire. The Trigger must be pulled for each shot fired. When the Magazine is empty the Slide Stop will hold the Slide open.

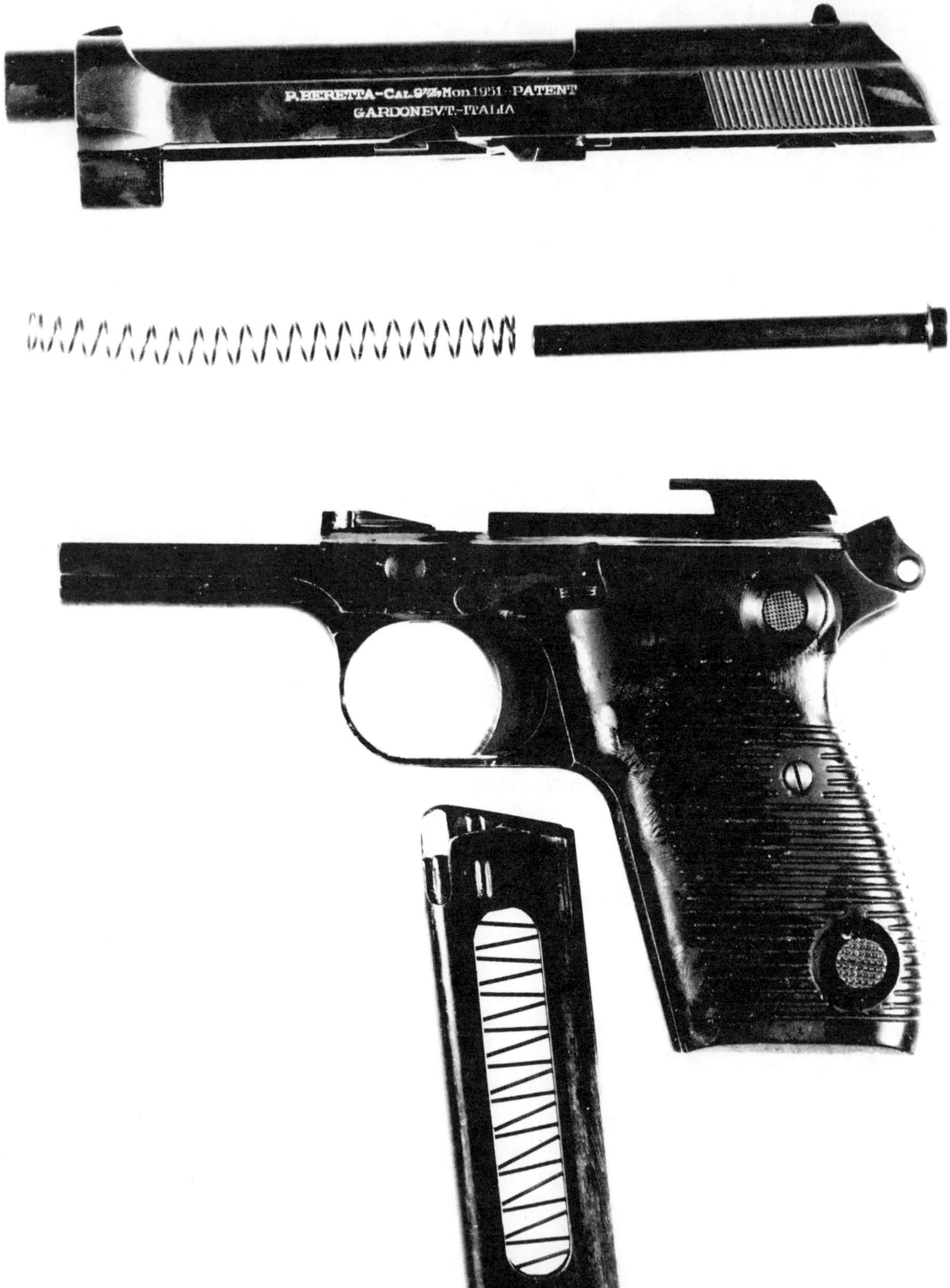
P. BERETTA-CAL.9m/m Mod.1951-PATENT
GARDONE V.T.-ITALIA

9-mm M1951

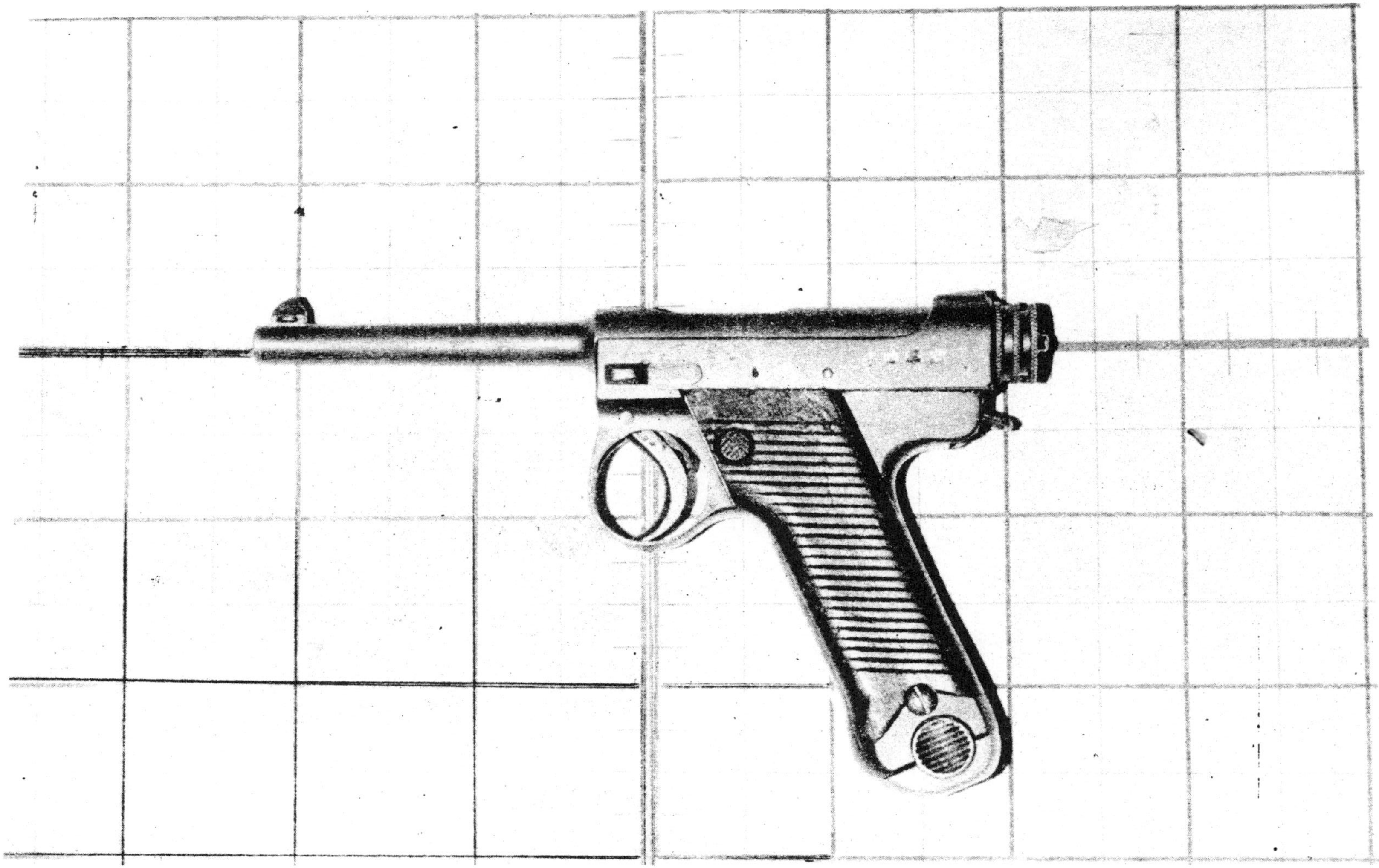

JAPAN 8-MM JAPANESE, TYPE 14

PISTOL   **JAPAN**

8-mm TYPE 14 (M1925)

The Japanese Type 14 Pistol is a recoil operated, locked breech weapon which is chambered for a relatively weak, bottle-neck cartridge. It is a modification of the 1914 Model Nambu pistol and though called the Type 14, which signifies manufacture in 1925, it is not to be confused with the original Nambu which was a much better arm. The modifications involved were those required for mass production demands. The Type 14 differs from the 1914 model in that it has no grip safety, a pivoting safety lever is mounted on the left of the receiver above the trigger guard, and two recoil springs are used, mounted on either side of the model. The type 14 has certain desirable features as a military arm, the angle of the grip and the long barrel being two of them. The underpowered, bottle-necked cartridge more than offsets any advantage gained by the long barrel and good holding characteristics of the weapon.

FUNCTIONING

With a loaded magazine inserted in the grip, the bolt is drawn to the rear and released. The bolt rides forward under impulse of the compressed recoil springs and chambers a round. The striker is held to the rear by the sear. The bolt lock is a "T" shaped piece, lying down. Its long stem is pivoted from a lug attached to the barrel extension. When locked, one end of the cross of the "T" is riding on a flat surface in the receiver which forces the other end of the cross up through a hole in the barrel extension into a notch in the bottom of the bolt. In this position the bolt and barrel extension are locked firmly together. Pulling the trigger draws the trigger bar forward and pulls the sear out of engagement with the firing pin. The barrel and attached barrel extension with the bolt locked to the extension move to the rear in recoil. After a fractional movement of recoil, the cross of the "T" which is riding on the flat surface in the receiver reaches an opening at the rear of the flat surface and drops into this opening. This motion pulls the other end of the cross of engagement with the bolt, the barrel extension stops its rearward travel, and the bolt continues to the rear to extract and eject the empty case. The bolt upon reaching its rearmost movement, starts forward again chambering a round; the firing pin is held back by the sear and the cycle is ready to be repeated when the trigger is pulled. During this forward movement, the bolt lock has been cammed up out of the cut in the receiver to rest on the flat surface with the opposite cross of the "T" engaging the bolt.

CHARACTERISTIC DATA

Caliber . . . . 8-mm Nambu
Operation . . . . .Recoil
Type of Feed . . . . .Box - 8 rd cap
Weight, empty . . . . 29.2 ozs
Overall length . . . . 9.2 in
Effective range . . . . 60 meters

FIELD STRIP PROCEDURE

STEP   ACTION

1. Press in on the Firing Pin Extension and unscrew the Bolt Nut.
2. As the Nut is removed the Firing Pin Spring will force the Firing Pin Extension out of the Bolt.
3. Remove Magazine, press muzzle against an object and push the Barrel to the rear.
4. With the Barrel pushed to the rear, press in on the Magazine Release Button.
5. Grasp the Trigger Guard and pull it straight down the front strap of the Pistol Grip. It may be necessary to remove the Left Stock.
6. Slide Barrel, Barrel Extension and Assembled Bolt forward off the Receiver.
7. Remove the Bolt Lock from its pivot attachment on the bottom of the Barrel Extension.
8. Remove the Bolt and the two Recoil Springs from the Barrel Extension.

ASSEMBLY PROCEDURE

Assemble in the reverse order. Assemble the two Recoil Springs to the Bolt and slide the Bolt into the Barrel Extension. Assemble the Bolt Lock to the pivot block on the bottom of the Barrel Extension. CAUTION NOTE: This weapon can be assembled without this Bolt Lock. *If fired without the Bolt Lock in place it will function as a straight blowback weapon and the weapon or firer may be injured.* Slide the Barrel, Barrel Extension and assembled Bolt onto the Receiver. Push the Barrel to the rear and holding it in this position, slide the trigger guard into position. The Magazine Release Button must be depressed during this assembly. Assemble the Firing Pin Extension to the Bolt and screw the Bolt Nut onto the Bolt.

LOADING AND FIRING

To load: Place a loaded Magazine in the Magazine well and push up firmly. Draw the Bolt to the rear and release. Push the Safety Lever up to "SAFE."

To fire: Push the Safety Lever down. Pull the Trigger. The weapon will fire for each pull of the Trigger until the Magazine is empty. When the Magazine is removed, the Slide Assembly will move forward. There is no hold-open device in this weapon.

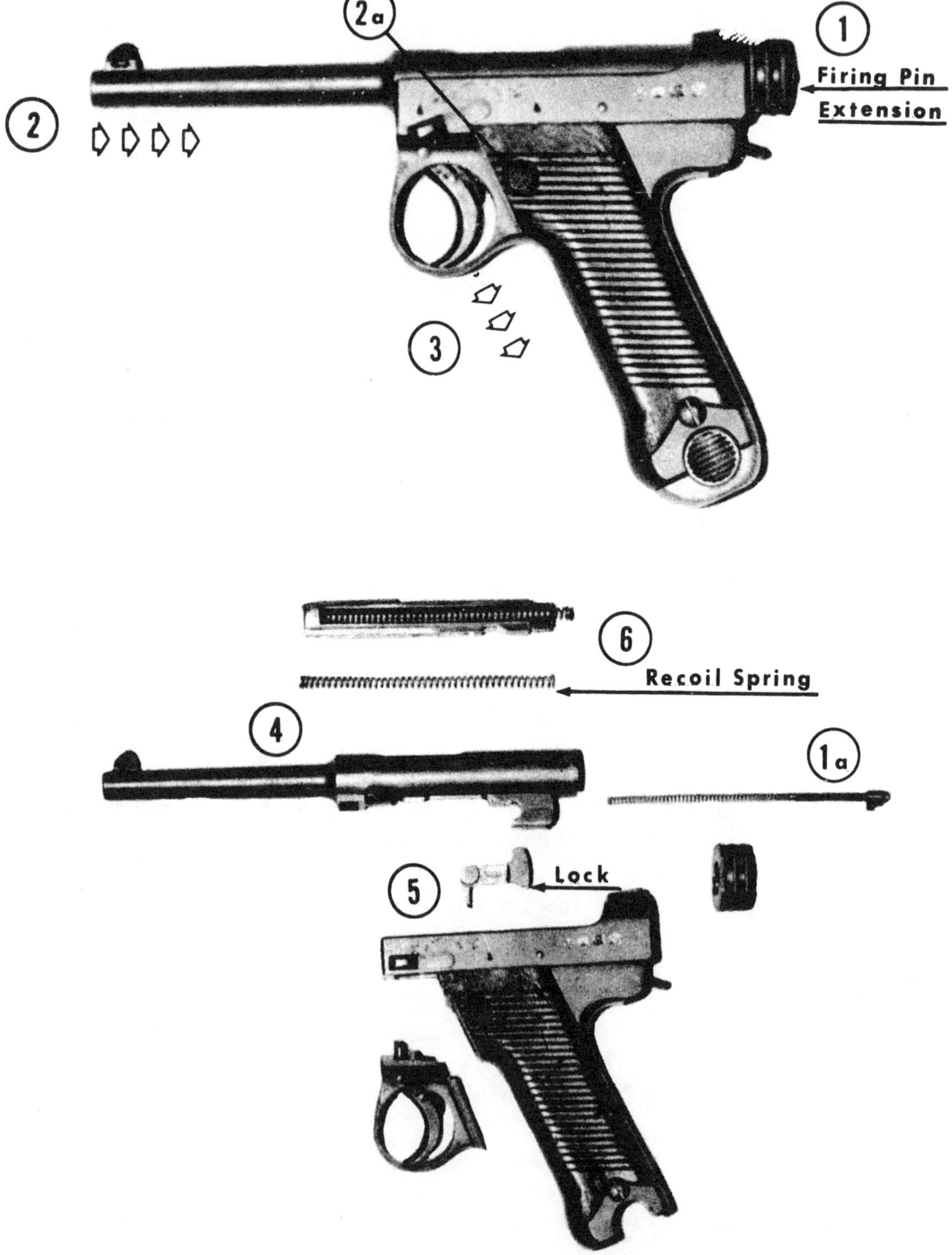
2a
1
Firing Pin Extension
2
3
6
Recoil Spring
4
1a
5
Lock

8-mm TYPE 14 (M1925)

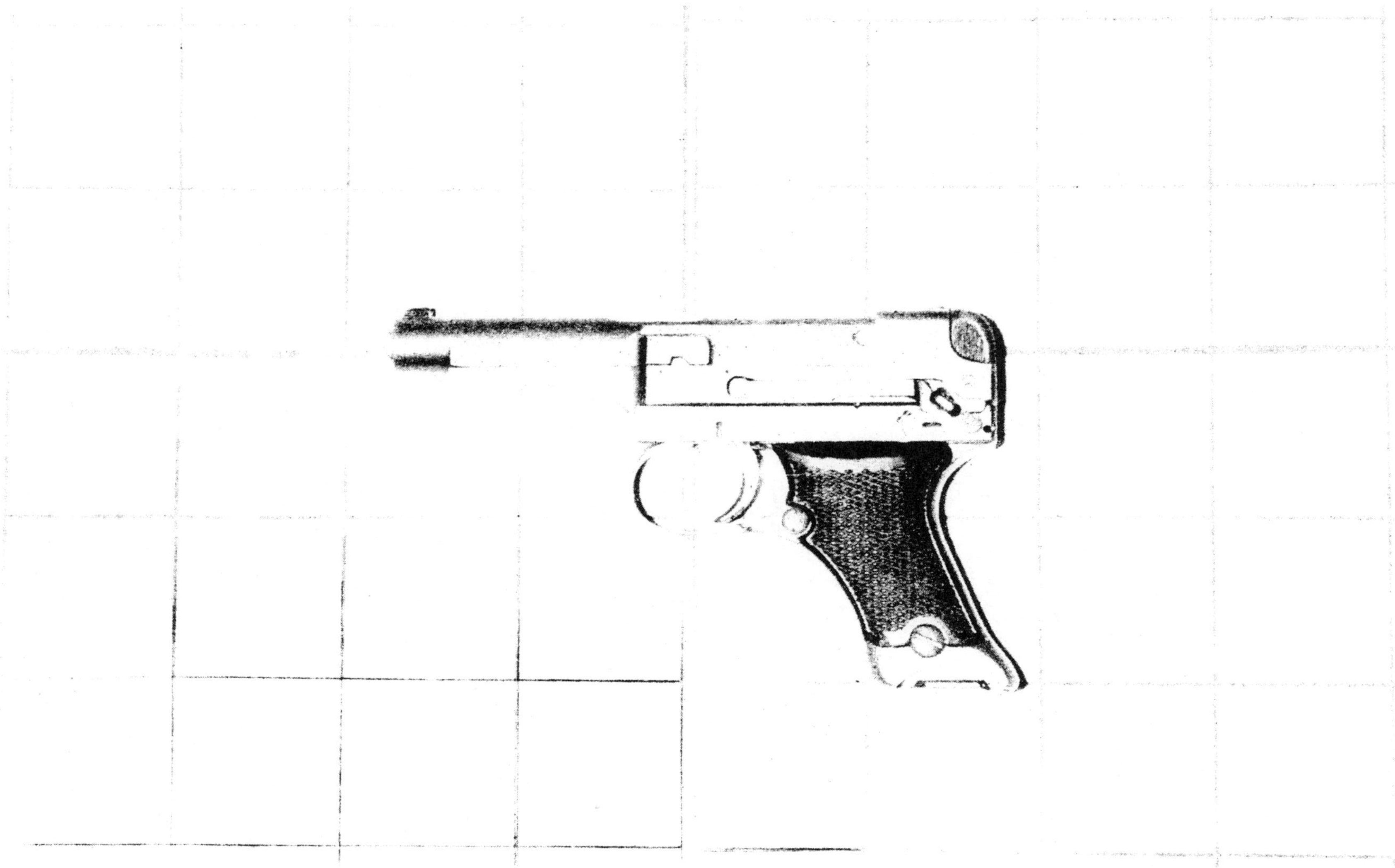

8-MM JAPANESE, TYPE 94

PISTOL   **JAPAN**

8-mm TYPE 94 (1934)

The Japanese Type 94 Pistol is a recoil operated locked breech weapon which is chambered for the bottle-necked Japanese 8-mm cartridge. It is a poorly designed, awkward handling pistol, with a number of inherently dangerous features. It was manufactured primarily for export, but during WWII was issued in some numbers to Officers of the Japanese Air Force. The bolt lock is an "H" shaped wedge, which is forced up to engage the locking grooves in the slide, while the lower portion of the block rides in a horse-shoe shaped lug on the bottom of the barrel. A thumb safety is located on the left side of the receiver, well to the rear, and is difficult to operate. The sear, connecting the trigger and the firing pin, is located on the left side of the receiver, recessed in a shallow cut-out. When the piece is cocked, (the firing pin held to the rear) the rear end of the sear protrudes from the shallow recess slightly. Pressing the sear with the thumb will release the firing pin. During WWII many people believed this weapon was designed this way on purpose. A Japanese Officer surrendering, could present his pistol butt first - press the exposed sear when doing so - and commit suicide. Hence the name "Suicide Gun" given to this piece.

FUNCTIONING

A loaded magazine is inserted in the grip, the knurled projections at the rear of the slide assembly are grasped, and the slide is pulled forward by the recoil spring which encircles the barrel. Moving forward, the breechblock which is carried in the rear of the slide, strips a round from the magazine and chambers it. Seven-thirty-seconds of an inch from being completely forward, the breechblock strikes the breech end of the barrel and drives it forward. The lock carried in a horse-shoe shaped lug on the bottom of the barrel is in its lowermost position resting in a cut-out in the receiver. The forward movement of the barrel forces the lock to move upward, the outside edges of the lock are engaged in 45 degree-angle inclined grooves in the slide, until the bottom surface of the lock is resting on a flat surface above and forward of the unlocking cut-out. The slide assembly and barrel are now locked together. Upon firing, the slide assembly and barrel move to the rear, the lock reaches the drop-off point and is cammed down out of engagement with the slide and the barrel stops against a shoulder in the receiver. The slide continues to the rear extracting and ejecting the empty case. The slide moves forward under impulse of the recoil spring chambering a round and the firing pin is held back by the sear. Pulling the trigger will repeat the firing cycle.

CHARACTERISTIC DATA

Caliber . . . . 8-mm Nambu
Operation . . . . Recoil
Type of Feed . . . . Box - 6 rd cap
Weight, empty . . . . .27 ozs
Overall length . . . . 7.1 in
Effective range . . . . 50 meters

FIELD STRIP PROCEDURE

STEP   ACTION

1. Draw the Slide Assembly all the way to the rear, grasp the Slide Assembly and Receiver at the forward end and hold firmly. Push in on the Firing Pin (through the opening under the Cocking Knobs).
2. Push the Breechblock Retainer through the Slide Assembly from right to left.
3. Release the Slide Assembly slightly and allow it to move forward under impulse of the compressed Recoil Spring.
4. Grasp the Cocking Knobs and pull the Breechblock from the rear of the Slide. Allow the Slide, Barrel, and Recoil Spring to come off the Receiver forward.
5. Lift the Barrel out of the Receiver. Lift out the Lock.
6. Remove the Recoil Spring from around the Barrel.

ASSEMBLY PROCEDURE

Assemble in the reverse order. Slide the Recoil Spring around the Barrel, Assemble the Lock and Barrel to the Receiver. Assemble the Slide to the Receiver and push all the way to the rear. Hold the Slide and Receiver firmly in this position. Slide the Breechblock into the rear of the Slide. Start the Breechblock Retainer into the hole in the Slide. Push in slightly on the Firing Pin and push the Breechblock Retainer fully through the Slide Assembly. Release the Slide Assembly and let it move forward.

LOADING AND FIRING

To load: Insert a loaded Magazine in the Butt. Grasp the Cocking Knobs and draw the Slide Assembly to the rear and release. Push the Safety Lever up to "SAFE".

To fire: Push the Safety Lever down. Pull the Trigger. The weapon will fire for each pull of the Trigger until the Magazine is empty. The Slide Assembly will remain to the rear when the Magazine is empty. When the Magazine is removed the Slide Assembly will move forward. There is no hold-open device in this weapon.

BOLT
BARREL
SLIDE
RECEIVER GRP

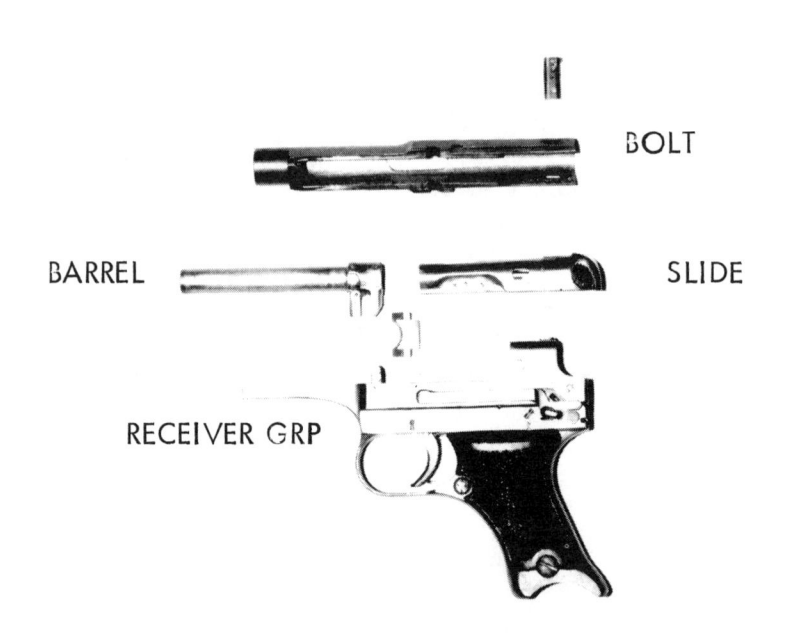

8-mm Type 94

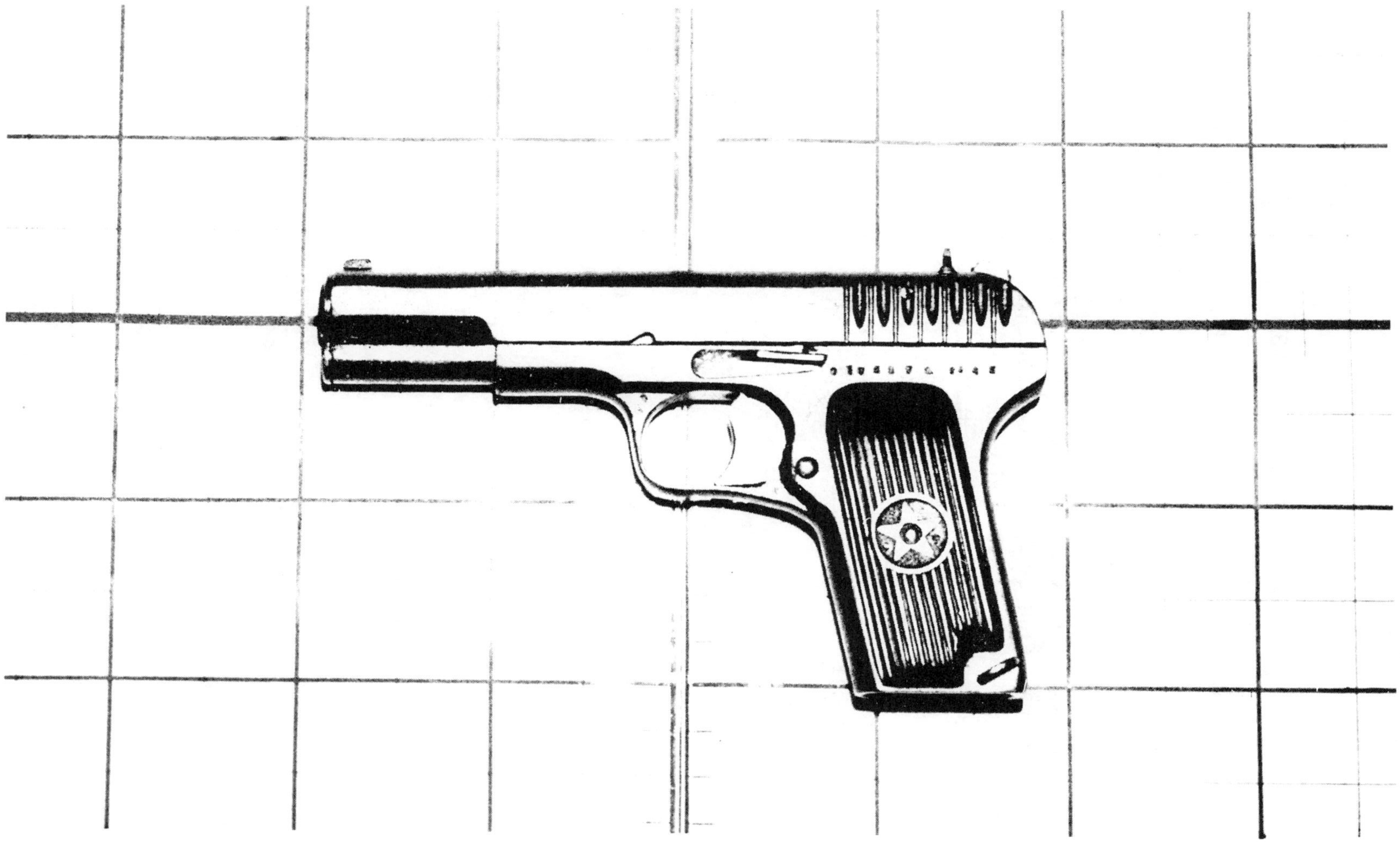

RUSSIA   7.63-MM TT33

PISTOL   U.S.S.R.

7.62-mm TOKAREV (TT-33)

The TT-33 pistol is a locked breech pistol designed from the Colt-Browning system. While the general design and the locking system were copied directly from the U.S. M1911A1 pistol, it has been simplified in both the manufacture and operation so that it represents a completely modernized version of this world-accepted sidearm. The pistol was designed by F. V. Tokarev at the Tula arsenal in 1933, hence the designation, TT-33. It has been furnished by the Soviets to all the satellite and bloc countries since the end of WWII, having been replaced in the Soviet Army by the Makarov and Stechkin pistols. It is manufactured by Poland, Hungary (as the Model 48) and Communist China (Type 51). Two notable improvements in the design of this weapon over the U.S. M1911A1, are the stronger barrel bushing and the hammer mechanism sub-assembly. The barrel locking system has been improved though it functions in the same manner as other weapons utilizing the Browning system. The locking ribs on the Tokarev barrel run entirely around the barrel circumference, which while not improving the locking facility, do contribute to barrel strength as well as ease of manufacture.

FUNCTIONING

This is a locked breech pistol in which the barrel is forced by a linkage system up into engagement with locking ribs in the top of the slide when the slide is forward. A round is loaded into the barrel in the conventional manner and the hammer stays in the cocked postion held by the sear. When the trigger is pulled, the hammer pivots forward to impinge on the firing pin, which is a rebounding type striker, and the primer is struck. The barrel and slide are locked together during the time of bullet travel down the barrel by locking ribs on the top of the barrel being held in engagement with corresponding ribs in the top inside surface of the slide. After a short locked movement, a link attached to the rear bottom of the barrel pulls the barrel down out of engagement with the slide and the slide continues to the rear alone. This movement of the slide cocks the hammer back to be engaged by the sear. A disconnector prevents the sear from engagement with the trigger until the slide has returned to its forward locked position. Pulling the trigger will again fire the pistol.

CHARACTERISTIC DATA

Caliber	7.62-mm Type "P"
Operation	Recoil
Type of Feed	Box - 8 rds
Weight, empty	32 ozs
Overall length	7.7 in
Effective range	50 meters

FIELD STRIP PROCEDURE

STEP   ACTION

1. Press in on the Recoil Spring Plug.
2. Swing the Barrel Bushing to the right until the locking lugs in the bushing disengage from the slide and remove. The Recoil Spring will now protrude from the front of the slide.
3. Push the Slide Stop Clip which holds the Slide Stop in place, to the rear. Withdraw the Slide Stop from the Receiver.
4. Push the Slide and Barrel assembly forward off the Receiver. Raise up on the Recoil Spring Guide and remove the Recoil Spring and Guide from the Slide. Remove the Barrel from the Slide.
5. Lift the Receiver sub-assembly (which contains the Hammer, Sear and Disconnector) from the top rear of the Receiver.

ASSEMBLY PROCEDURE

Assemble in the reverse order. Slide the Receiver sub-assembly into the rear of the Receiver. Slide the Barrel into the Slide. Assemble the Recoil Spring Guide to the Recoil Spring and assemble the Spring to the Slide. Slide the assembled Slide and Barrel onto the Receiver. Place the Slide Stop in its hole in the Receiver making sure the Slide Stop Pin has engaged the Barrel Link. Assemble the Barrel Bushing to the Slide, push in on the Recoil Spring Plug and swing the Bushing down so that the Bushing lug engages the mating groove in the Slide. Push the Slide Stop Clip forward.

LOADING AND FIRING

To load: Place a loaded Magazine in the Grip. This pistol has no manual Safety Lever, half cock of the Hammer is the only safety feature. Draw the Slide to the rear and release it. The Slide moving forward will strip a round from the Magazine and chamber it. The Hammer will remain cocked to the rear.

To fire: Pull the Trigger the weapon will fire. This is a semi-automatic weapon and will fire one shot for each pull of the trigger.

SLIDE
BARREL
HAMMER ASS'Y
RECOIL SPRING & GUIDE
RECEIVER ASS'Y

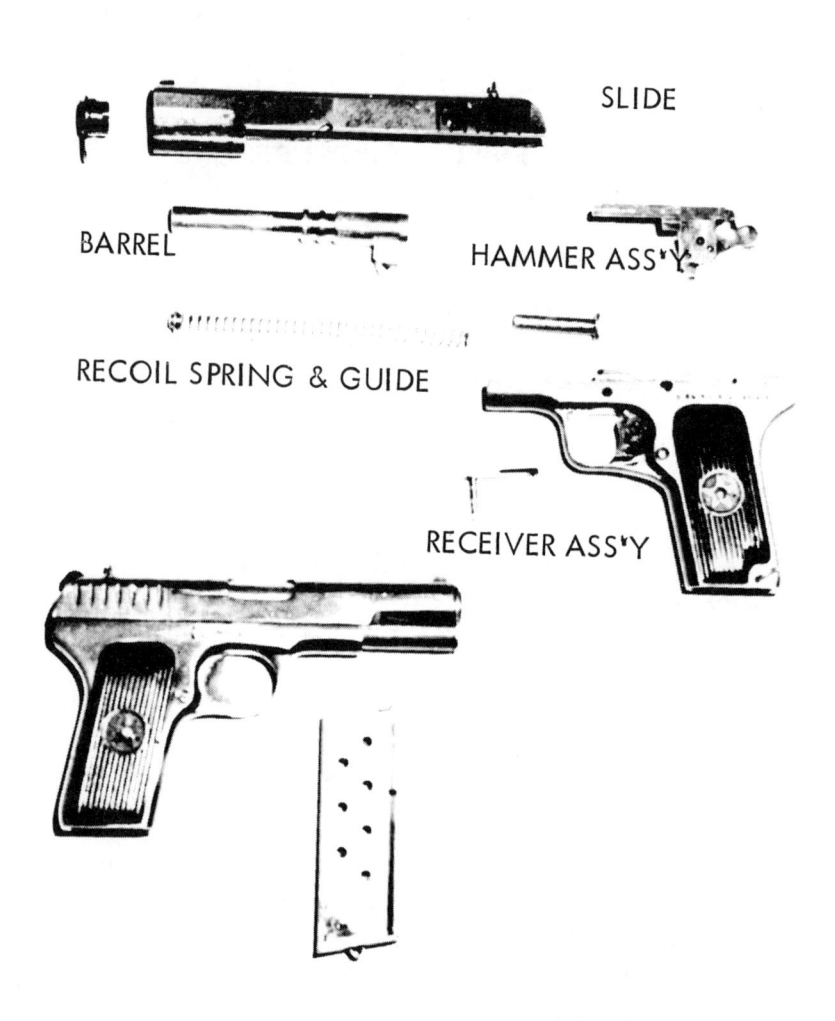

7.62-mm Tokarev

RUSSIA   9-MM, PM

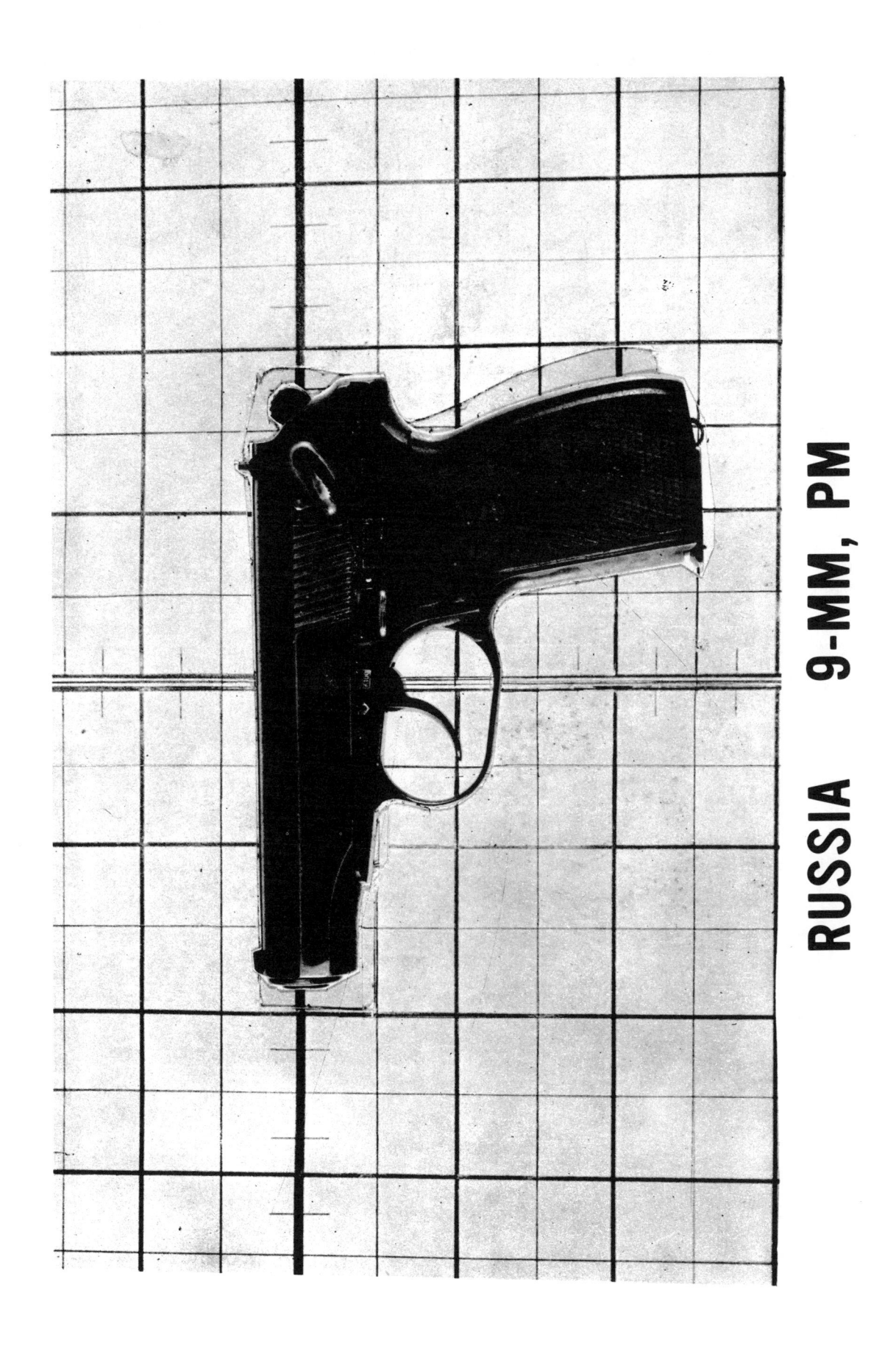

PISTOL   U.S.S.R.

9-mm PM (MAKAROV)

The Soviet 9-mm PM (Pistolet Makarov) Pistol is chambered for a special 9-mm round developed by the U.S.S.R. which is also fired in the new Soviet Stechkin (APS) Pistol. This round is less powerful than the 7.62-mm round fired in the Soviet TT33 Pistol which the PM (and the APS) is replacing. The cartridge is slightly longer than the 9-mm Corto (.380 ACP) round and slightly shorter than the 9-mm Luger round. The PM Pistol is a Soviet scaled-up version of the German Walther PP (Polizei Pistole) developed by the Walther firm in 1929. It is a blowback operated pistol with the recoil spring surrounding a fixed barrel. It is a well made, compact weapon, though its barrel length of only 3-7/8 inches makes it a relatively inaccurate pistol.

FUNCTIONING

The 9-mm PM Pistol is a straight blowback pistol copied from the German M1929 Walther PP pistol. A thumb safety lever is located on the left rear side of the slide, which blocks the firing pin and locks the sear when hammer is down. With a loaded magazine inserted in the pistol grip, the slide is drawn to the rear and released. The slide moves forward under impulse of the compressed recoil spring which surrounds the barrel, strips a round from the magazine and chambers it. The hammer is held to the rear by the sear. If the safety lever is pushed to "SAFE" a steel bar will rise to interfere with the hammer striking the firing pin and the hammer will be released to fall onto the bar. If the safety lever is pushed to "SAFE" with the hammer in the forward position, the steel bar will block the hammer from the firing pin and also lock the sear so the trigger will now draw the hammer back to fire. When the safety lever is turned to "FIRE," with the hammer held back, the trigger is pulled, the hammer is released and the weapon will fire. If the safety lever is pushed to "FIRE" when the hammer is forward, the trigger is pulled, the hammer is drawn to the rear in a double-action movement, released and the weapon will fire.

CHARACTERISTIC DATA

Caliber	9-mm Soviet
Operation	Blowback
Type of Feed	Box - 8 rd
Weight, empty	.25 ozs
Overall length	6.3 in
Effective range	50 meters

FIELD STRIP PROCEDURE

STEP ACTION

1. Pull down on the Trigger Guard.
2. Draw the Slide to the rear, raise the rear up and then slide forward.
3. Remove Slide from Receiver.
4. Recoil Spring may be removed.

ASSEMBLY PROCEDURE

Assemble in the reverse order. If the Recoil Spring has been removed replace it around the Barrel. Slide the Slide over the Barrel, draw fully to the rear, drop down and push forward. Swing the Trigger Guard up and lock.

LOADING AND FIRING

To load: Insert a loaded Magazine in the Pistol Grip. Push the Thumb Safety Lever to "SAFE." Draw the Slide to the rear and release. The Slide will move forward and chamber a round. The Hammer will drop onto the Firing Pin Safety Bar. If the Safety Lever is pushed to "SAFE" after a round has been chambered, the Hammer will drop.

To fire: Push the Thumb Safety Lever to "FIRE." Pull the Trigger. The Hammer will be drawn back in a double-action movement and then released. The weapon will fire. The Slide will remain open after the last round has been fired.

2
1
2a
3

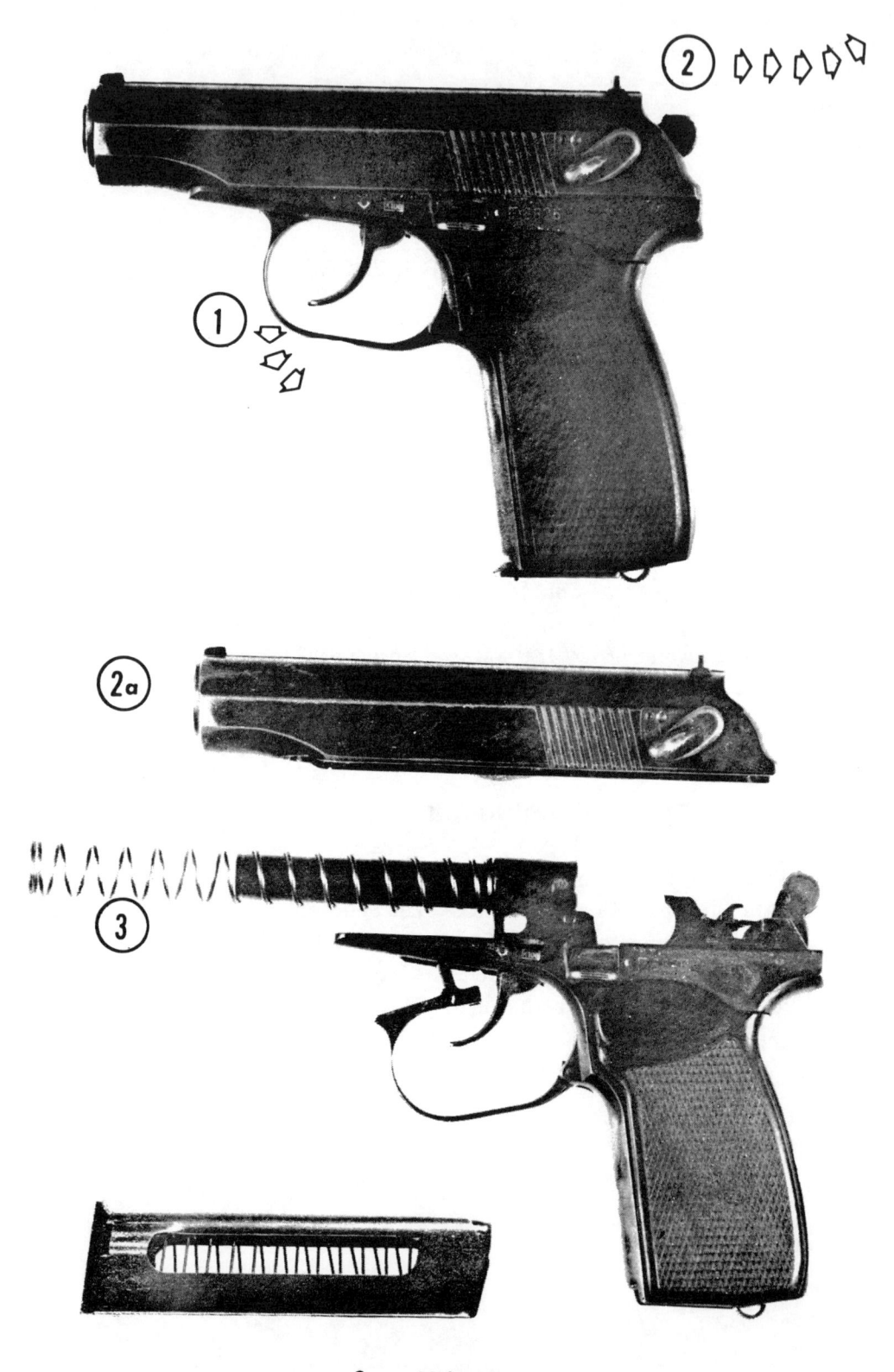

9-mm Makarov

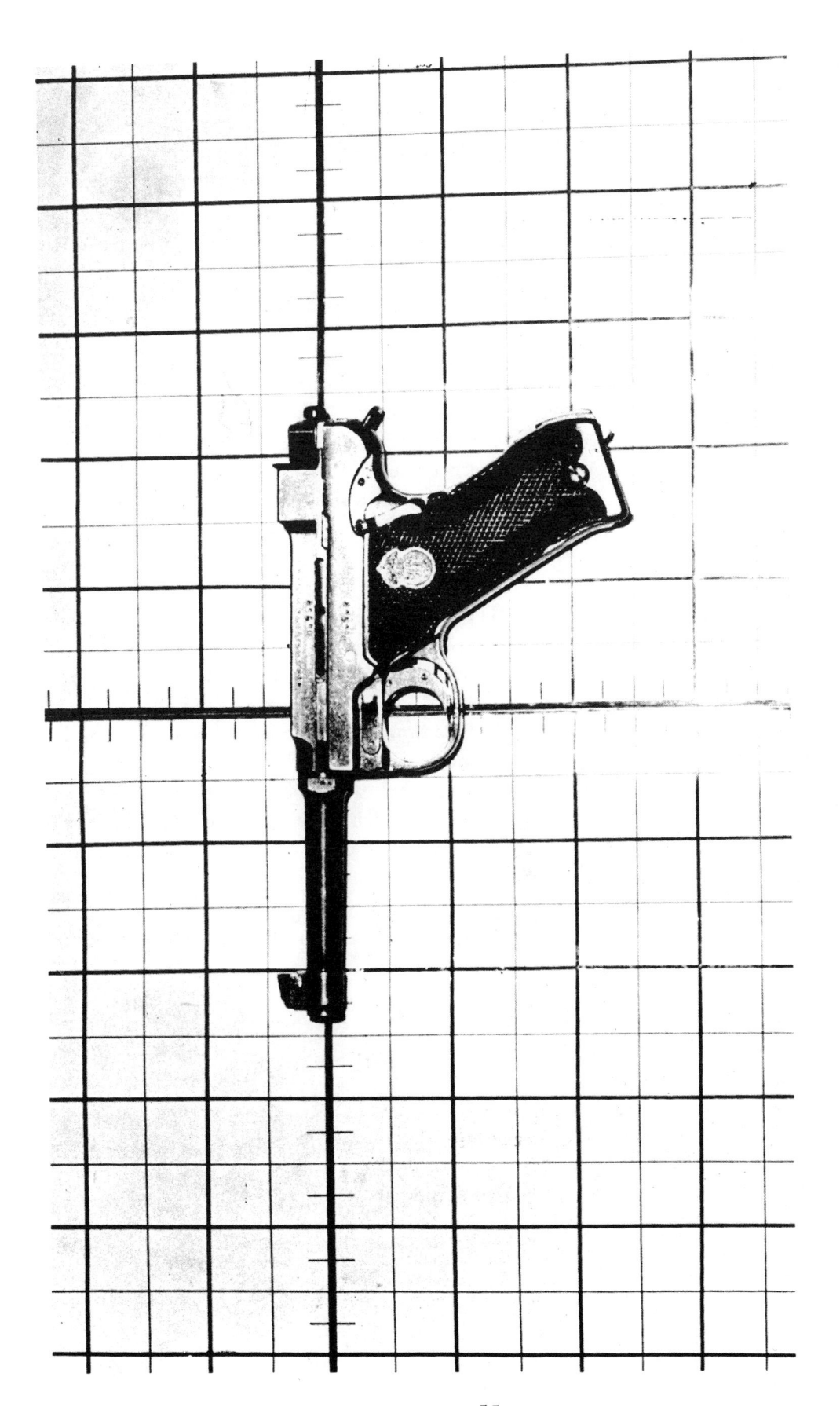

SWEDEN   9-MM, M1940

PISTOL SWEDEN

9-mm M1940 (Lahti)

The Swedish M1940, 9-mm Pistol is a locked breech pistol which has excellent holding characteristics, an extremely strong action, and incorporates in its rather unusual design an accelerator similar in function to that found in the U.S. Browning machineguns. This same weapon is used in Finland where it is known as the Model L-35 (Lahti). It resembles the Luger Pistol in grip shape and exposed barrel, but has a more square shaped receiver with a reciprocating bolt. The accelerator, which is contained in the forward portion of the receiver, functions against the bolt during recoil. The barrel strikes the accelerator at the time the barrel stops its rearward movement and the breech lock has disengaged, imparting a strong blow to the unlocked bolt assisting it in its rearward travel. Of questionable value for an arm of this size, the accelerator does have certain advantages in extremely cold climate. It is understandable, considering the climate of the two countries using this weapon, why such a feature was incorporated into the piece.

FUNCTIONING

The lock in this weapon is a "U" shaped block, positioned upsidedown in a bulge located near the rear of the barrel extension. With a magazine inserted, the knurled wings at the rear of the bolt are grasped and the bolt is drawn to the rear and released. The bolt moves forward under impulse of the compressed recoil spring which is contained in the bolt (the rear of the recoil spring guide protrudes from the rear of the bolt). A round is stripped from the magazine and chambered. The bolt lock which rides up and down to engage or disengage the locking recess in the bolt is now cammed down so that the lock cross piece lies in the recess in the top of the bolt. The side arms of the lock are mated with the vertical cuts in the barrel extension. When the trigger is pulled, the trigger bar disengages the sear from the hammer and the hammer pivots forward to strike the firing pin. The barrel and barrel extension with the bolt locked to the barrel extension moves to the rear under the forces of recoil. After a short initial movement, cam surfaces on each side of the lock, cam the lock up out of engagement with the locking recess in the top of the bolt and the bolt continues to the rear extracting and ejecting the empty case. At the moment the barrel and barrel extension come to a stop, the accelerator located behind the barrel with the accelerator claws abutting the bolt, transmits the barrel movement energy to the bolt assisting it in its rearward movement. The bolt reaches its rearmost point of travel and starts forward, strips a round from the magazine and chambers it. The hammer is held in the cocked position by the sear. Pulling the trigger again will repeat the firing cycle.

CHARACTERISTIC DATA

Caliber 9-mm
Operation . . . . .Recoil
Type of Feed . . . . .Box 8 rd cap
Weight, empty . . . . .37.5 oz
Overall length . . . . .10.7 in
Effective range . . . . 70 meters

FIELD STRIP PROCEDURE

STEp   ACTION

1. Insert an empty Magazine. Pull the Bolt to the rear. Remove the Magazine. Push the Barrel to the rear slightly and pivot the Receiver Lock down.
2. Pull the Bolt to the rear slightly, to free it from the hold open device, then ease the barrel and Extension with Bolt, forward off the Receiver.
3. Push the Breech Lock up out of engagement with the Bolt and remove the Bolt from the Barrel Extension.

ASSEMBLY PROCEDURE

Assemble in the reverse order. Slide Bolt into the Barrel Extension. Slide Barrel and Extension with assembled Bolt onto the Receiver. Pull the Bolt to the rear. Push Barrel to the rear slightly and pivot Receiver Lock up to locking position. Pull back on Bolt slightly and release it.

LOADING AND FIRING

To load: Swing the Safety Lever located to the rear of the Left Stock back to "SAFE". Insert a loaded Magazine. Grasp the knurled wings on the Bolt and pull to the rear. Release the Bolt. The Bolt will run forward and chamber a round.

To fire: Push the Safety Lever foward. Pull the Trigger. The weapon will fire for each pull of the Trigger until the Magazine is empty. The Bolt will remain to the rear when the Magazine is empty. To close the piece, remove the Magazine and pull the Bolt to the rear slightly and release it.

BARREL ASSEMBLY

BOLT

9-mm M1940

RIFLES AND CARBINES

SECTION II

A rifle, by general definition, is a shoulder fired, air-cooled firearm, which fires a spin stabilized projectile. Rotation is imparted to the projectile by lands and grooves, commonly referred to as "rifling," engraved in the inner walls of the barrel. In the field of military rifles, the cartridge is fed from a container, the magazine, into the chamber by either manual or mechanical means. The ammunition generally consists of a metal, center primed, cartridge case, a metal jacketed bullet and a propelling charge. There is no hard and fast rule as to what constitutes a "rifle caliber cartridge," a generic term, except the fact that a rifle, because of its tactical role, fires a cartridge larger than that chambered by the hand held pistol or revolver. Rifle ammunition recently introduced into various army inventories has maintained the "rifle caliber" (bullet dimension), but due to improvements in propellent composition, utilize a shorter case. At this writing they are referred to as "intermediate size cartridges." Such cartridges lack the velocity, range and penetration capabilities of full size cartridges and thus should not be compared with the 7.62-mm NATO round, which while "intermediate" in size still retains velocity, range and penetration capability comparable to a full size military cartridge.

Considerable confusion exists when the question of defining a carbine arises. By original definition a carbine was a short barreled rifle, generally somewhat lighter and easier to handle than a full-length rifle, but chambered for a conventional rifle size round. In the early 1940's, with the introduction of the U.S. .30 caliber Carbine, the definition also included a differentiation in cartridge size. Thus while the Soviet SKS Carbine meets the criteria in definition, in regard to barrel length and weight, it is chambered for the standard Soviet short round which is also utilized by Soviet machine guns and rifles. This places the SKS in the class of being a short barreled military rifle, a true carbine.

Problems in definition also arise when one tries to draw the line between an Automatic Rifle (AR), a light Machinegun (LMG) and an Assault Rifle (ASR). The AR is designed to be fired from the shoulder or hip, is usually fed from a box magazine, may utilize a bipod on occasion and seldom weighs more than 20 pounds. The LMG is usually fired from a bipod or tripod, is box magazine or belt fed, may on occasion be fired from the shoulder and seldom weighs more than 25 pounds. The ASR is usually fired from the shoulder though some models have bipods attached, is normally fed from a box magazine, is capable of selective fire and seldom weighs more than 11 pounds. Different armies have different definitions so it depends on which side you're on as to what weapon you may be handling.

Regardless of definition problems, the rifles and carbines covered in this handbook represent a fraction of the various rifles and carbines which may be encountered. The weapons covered do represent a general cross-section of various auto-loading systems in use today. Different locking systems discussed in detail include the unlocked breech weapons (delayed blowback).

BELGIUM   7.62-MM NATO, FAL

RIFLE   BELGIUM

7.62-mm (NATO) FN RIFLE (FAL)

The FN Light Automatic Rifle is a gas-operated, magazine-fed rifle which is produced in a number of variations, and is used by more than twenty countries. This weapon, the Model 1958 (FAL) evolved from the Belgian Semi-automatic rifle introduced in 1940. This later model is a selective fire weapon, most earlier models were capable of semi-automatic fire only. The design of the weapon embodies many favorable features of the Russian Tokarev gas system. The hammer mechanism is an adaptation of the Browning hammer hook system, used in the U.S. M1 Rifle.

FUNCTIONING

This is a gas-operated weapon in which a gas piston mounted above the barrel, operating on a tappet principle similar to the U.S. Carbine and Russian Tokarev systems, strikes the front surface of a bolt carrier to initiate unlocking action. The weapon fires from a closed bolt. With a loaded magazine in place, the operating handle is drawn to the rear and released. The carrier and bolt under impulse of the compressed recoil spring located in the stock, move forward, strips a round from the magazine and chambers it. As the bolt comes to a stop against the breech, the carrier continues to move a slight additional distance during which time, cams in the carrier and a ramp in the receiver, force the rear of the bolt down over a locking shoulder in the bottom of the receiver. When the trigger is pulled, the hammer pivots forward, impinges against the striker and fires the round. Gas is tapped from the barrel into the gas cylinder and strikes the gas piston. The piston is driven to the rear striking the forward face of the carrier. The carrier moves to the rear slightly before cams in the carrier engage mating lugs on the upper rear section of the bolt. As the carrier continues to move to the rear, the engaged camming surfaces lift the rear of the bolt into an unlocked position and carries it to the rear. The gas piston, under impulse of the gas piston spring, moves forward, the bolt and carrier continue to the rear compressing the recoil spring contained in the stock. The bolt and carrier then move forward and chamber a round and the hammer, if the select lever is set for semi-automatic, remains held in the cocked position by the sear. Pulling the trigger will release the hammer, which will pivot forward to strike the firing pin. The hammer will automatically be released if the select lever is set for full-automatic, and the weapon will continue to fire as long as the trigger is held to the rear. This weapon has a bolt hold-open device which functions when the magazine is empty, or which may be applied manually when there is no magazine in place.

FIELD STRIP PROCEDURE

STEP   ACTION

1. With the Bolt forward, press down or back, on Stock Release lever and pivot Stock down.
2. Slide Receiver Cover off to the rear.
3. Grasp the Recoil Spring Guide Rod attached to the rear of the Carrier and pull Carrier and attached Bolt out of the Receiver.
4. Disengage the Bolt from the Carrier by sliding the bolt to the rear, pushing in on the firing pin and lifting the front of the bolt up and out of the carrier.
5. Press the Gas Plug plunger in and turn Plug to the left. Remove the Gas Plug and Gas Piston with attached Spring from the Gas Cylinder.

ASSEMBLY PROCEDURE

Assemble in the reverse order. Slide the Gas Piston and Spring into the Gas Cylinder and lock the Gas Plug into place. Attach the bolt to the Carrier and slide into the Receiver guides. Slide the Receiver Cover onto the Receiver. Pivot the Stock up. The Stock Release Lever will engage automatically.

LOADING AND FIRING

To load: Move the safety/select lever up, to place weapon on Safe. Place a loaded Magazine into the Magazine Well and latch. Draw the Operating handle to the rear, and release. Bolt and Carrier will move forward and chamber a round. Place the Select Lever on type of fire desired. Down for semi-automatic, forward for full-automatic.

To fire: Pull the Trigger, the weapon will fire full or semiautomatic depending on the position of the Select Lever. When the Magazine is empty the Bolt will remain to the rear.

BOLT COVER

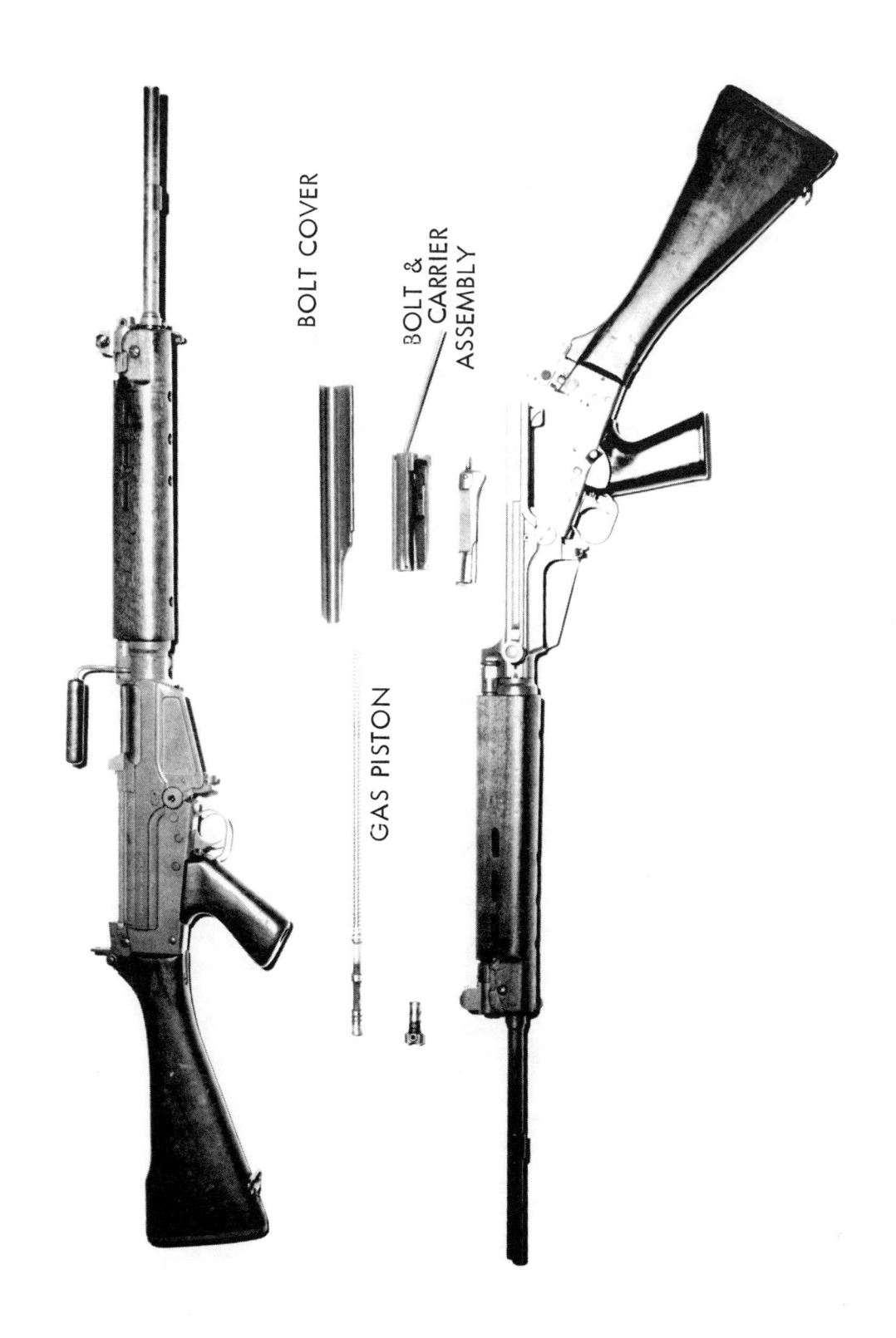

BOLT & CARRIER ASSEMBLY

GAS PISTON

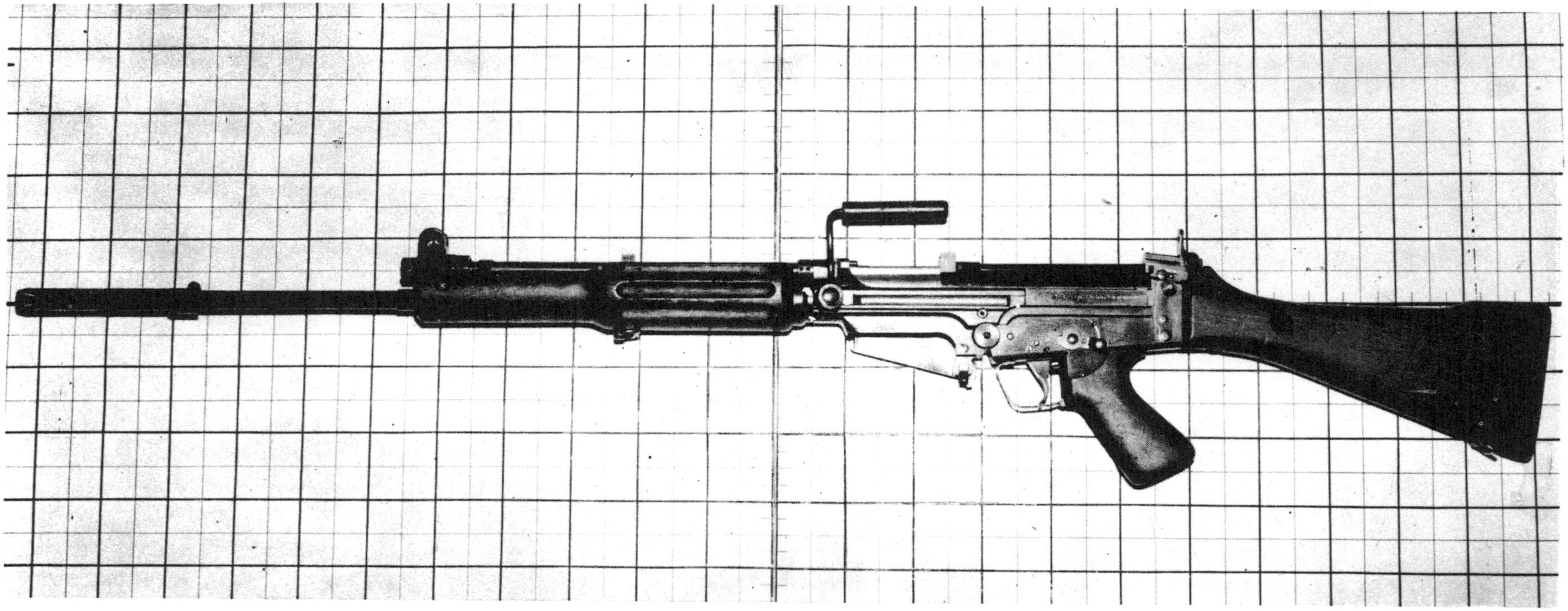

BELGIUM 7.62-MM NATO, FN

BELGIUM 7.92-MM, TYPE D

RIFLE   BELGIUM

7.92-mm TYPE D (BROWNING)

The Belgian Type D Automatic Rifle is an FN manufactured, improved version of the U.S. Browning Automatic Rifle. While basic design features of the U.S. Browning were retained, a number of improvements were built into this weapon which include a quick-change barrel, simplified disassembly procedure, improved gas regulation system, and a rate-of-fire device. This allows a slow automatic rate of fire to be employed which can be regulated by trigger manipulation to single-shot fire when desired. This weapon is manufactured in a number of calibers and may be tactically employed as an automatic rifle or as a light machinegun. Dust covers are provided to protect both the ejection port opening and the magazine port opening.

FUNCTIONING

This is a gas-operated weapon which fires from an open bolt, full-automatic only. A rate-of-fire device is incorporated in the trigger group mechanism, which functioning through a double sear system, allows the piece to be fired at a cyclic rate of fire of 600 rpm (fast) or 350 rpm (slow). At the slow rate of fire, proper trigger manipulation (tapping of the trigger) will produce semi-automatic or single shot fire. An exhaust type gas regulator permits adjustments for the amount of gas utilized for proper functioning of the mechanism. With a loaded magazine in place, the bolt handle, located on the left side of the receiver, is drawn to the rear and then pushed forward. The ejection port cover opens automatically when the action is cocked, or if the cover has been closed after the action has been cocked, it will open automatically when the bolt moves forward to fire. The sear bent in the bottom of the slide is now engaged by the right sear. When the trigger is pulled, the sear will release the slide. The bolt carried in grooves in the receiver is attached to the rear upper portion of the slide by a link. As the slide and attached bolt move forward under impulse of the compressed recoil spring, the bolt strips a round from the magazine and chambers it. As the bolt comes to a halt against the rear face of the barrel, the slide continues to move forward and in so doing, the link connecting the slide and bolt forces the locking arm at the rear of the bolt up into a recess in the top of the receiver. At this point, the hammer carried in the rear of the slide strikes the firing pin carried in the bolt driving it against the primer. Gas is tapped from the barrel into the gas cylinder to impinge against the gas piston which is a forward extension of the slide. The slide moves a short distance to the rear, through the linkage between the bolt and the slide; the locking arm is pulled down out of the locking recess in the top of the receiver and the bolt moves to the rear extracting and ejecting the empty case. If set for fast fire this cycle will be repeated until the trigger is released. If set for slow fire, the left sear will engage the slide momentarily after the right sear has released it, thus causing a hesitation in the forward movement of the slide and attached bolt, which results in the slower rate of fire.

1. Trigger Guard Pin
2. Retaining Pin

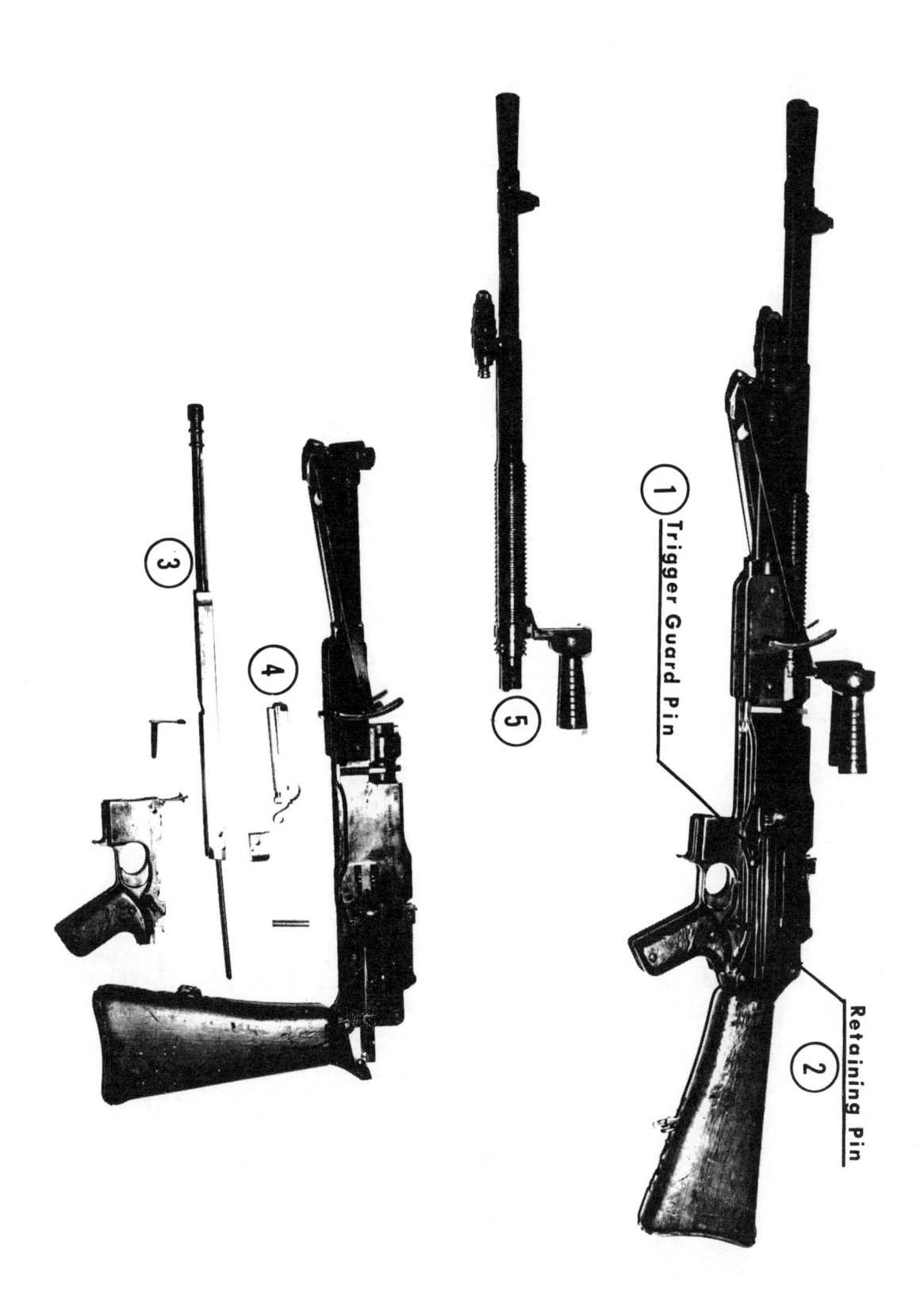

7.92-mm Type D

CHARACTERISTIC DATA

Caliber	7.92-mm
Operation	Gas
Type of Fire	Full-auto only
Rate of Fire	600 rpm (fast)
	350 rmp (slow) (Practical 250)
Type of Feed	Box - 20 rd cap
Weight, empty	21.2 lbs
Overall length	45.2 in
Effective range	1,480 meters

FIELD STRIP PROCEDURE

STEP   ACTION

1. Withdraw Trigger Guard Pin and remove Trigger Guard Assembly.
2. Pull Retaining Pin out to the left and pivot Stock down.
3. Grasp Recoil Spring Guide and pull Slide with attached Hammer, Bolt and Bolt Link out of the rear of the Receiver.
4. Push out the Link Pin which holds the Hammer and Link to the Slide and remove the Bolt with Link and the Hammer from the Slide.
5. Grasp the Carrying Handle and swing it down to the right, engage the dismounting stud with the dismounting notch in the Barrel Locking Nut, press in on the Dismounting Lever, swing the Carrying Handle upward and pull forward to remove Barrel from Receiver.

ASSEMBLY PROCEDURE

Assemble in the reverse order except that the Barrel may be assembled last. Assemble the Hammer to the Slide, insert Link into position in the Slide and push Link Pin through Slide. Slide assembled Slide, Bolt, Hammer and Link into Receiver, making sure that the Bolt engages the grooves in the Receiver. Pivot Stock up into position and push Retaining Pin through. Place Trigger Guard Assembly into position and replace Trigger Guard Pin.

LOADING AND FIRING

To load: Place Safety Lever on "SAFE." Insert Magazine into Receiver. Draw Bolt Handle to the rear and then push forward. Close Ejection Port Cover.

To fire: Set Select Lever to type fire desired. Pull Trigger. Weapon will fire. If Select Lever is set at "M," fast automatic fire, the weapon will fire at a cyclic rate of 600 rpm until the Trigger is released or the Magazine is empty. If Select Lever is set at "R." slow automatic fire, the weapon will fire at a cyclic rate of 350 rpm until the Trigger is released or the Magazine is empty. Semi-automatic fire may be obtained by tapping the Trigger when Select Lever is set at "R."

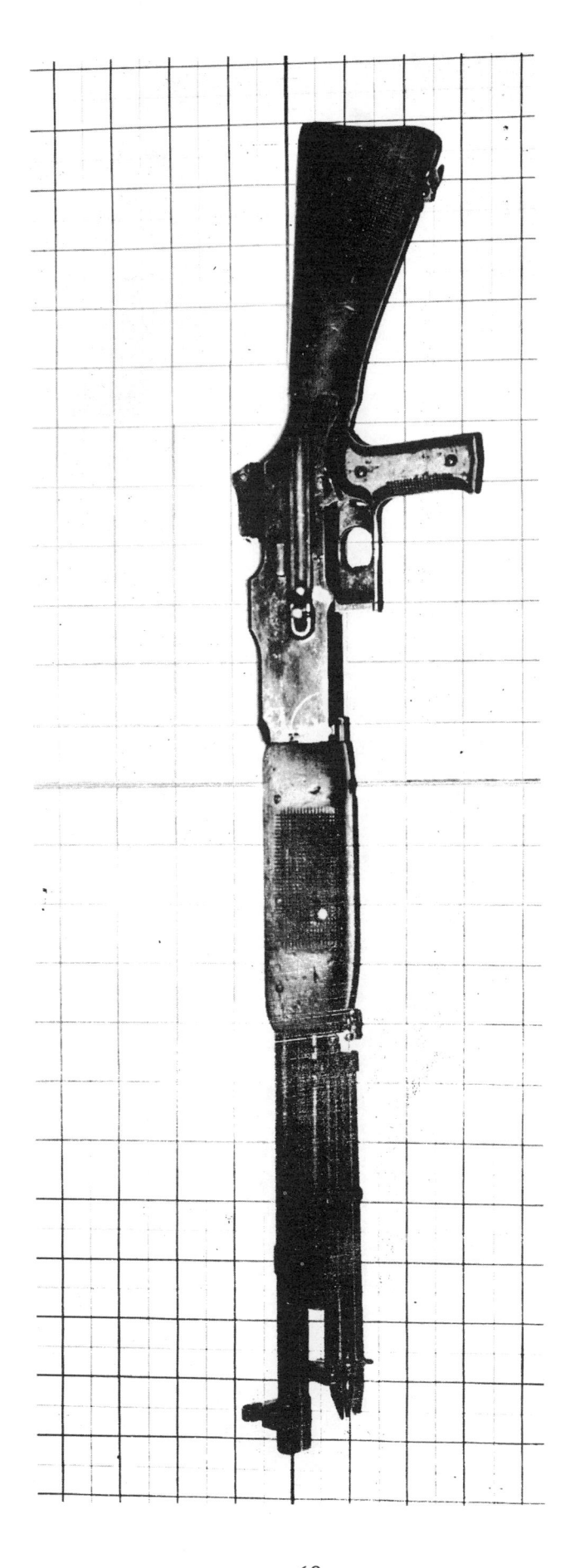

SWEDEN 6.5-MM, MODEL 21

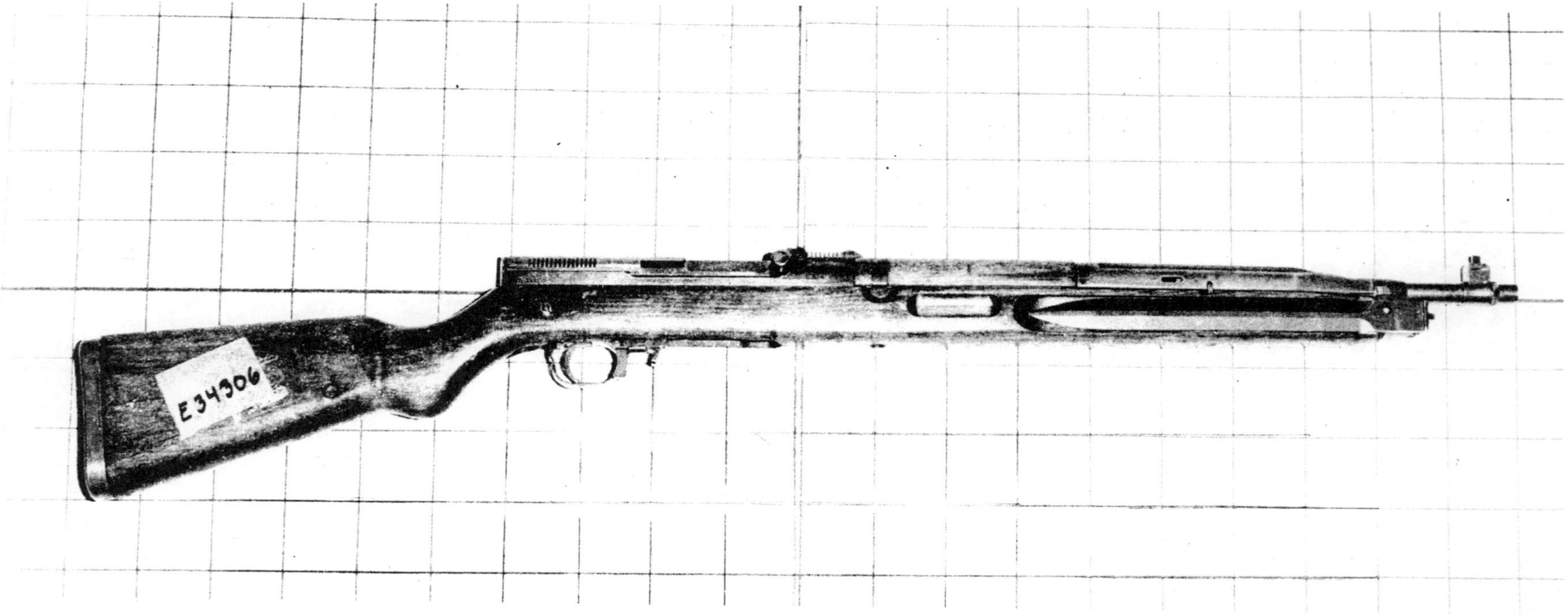

CZECHOSLOVAKIA   7.62-MM, MODEL 52

RIFLE — CZECHOSLOVAKIA

7.62-mm MODEL 52

The Czechoslovakian Model 52 Semi-automatic Rifle is chambered for a special short round similar to the Soviet M1943 round. A later version of this weapon, the Model 52/57 has been produced, chambered for the Soviet M1943 round. This later model is gradually being replaced by an assault rifle designated the Model 58 which is also chambered for the Soviet M1943 cartridge. The trigger mechanism of the Model 52 is similar to the U.S. M1 rifle system, employing a double sear; bolt locking is achieved by the front of the bolt tipping down into the recesses in the receiver; unlocking is accomplished by a sleeve above the barrel forcing the bolt carrier rearward under impulse of gas from the barrel. A permanently attached bayonet pivots flat against the right side of the forearm when not in use.

FUNCTIONING

The 7.62-mm Model 52 Semi-automatic Rifle is a gas-operated rifle which utilizes a tilting-bolt locking system. The gas operation system is unusual in that it does not employ a gas piston of conventional design but rather a sleeve shaped component which is forced rearward by gas being trapped in a sliding collar which surrounds the barrel at the gas tap-off point. With a loaded magazine in place, the bolt handle is drawn to the rear, drawing with it the bolt carrier and bolt and compressing the recoil spring. When the bolt handle is released the bolt carrier and bolt are forced forward by the recoil spring, a round is stripped from the magazine by the face of the bolt and chambered. When the bolt stops against the rear face of the barrel, the carrier continues forward for 0.3 of an inch more, at which time, the front of the bolt is tilted (or cammed) down so that locking lugs on the bolt engage locking recesses in the receiver. The hammer is now held to the rear by the trigger. When the trigger is pulled the trigger releases the hammer which pivots forward to strike the firing pin and the cartridge is fired. Gas is tapped from the barrel into a sliding-collar type gas chamber around the barrel. This collar moves rearward sharply, forcing the operating sleeve which partially surrounds the upper portion of the barrel, to move rearward. The rear of this operating sleeve is abutting the front face of the bolt carrier, and this rearward movement imparts a thrust to the bolt carrier, which moves it to the rear. In this movement, the bolt carrier lifts the front of the bolt up to disengage the bolt locking lugs from the locking recesses in the receiver. The bolt carrier and bolt continue to the rear, extracting and ejecting the empty case, compressing the recoil spring and then moves forward again to chamber a round, and the firing cycle is ready to be repeated when the trigger is pulled.

CHARACTERISTIC DATA

```
Caliber ........................................................7.62-mm Short
Operation ..............................................................Gas
Type of Fire .................................................Semi-auto only
Rate of Fire .........................................................30 rpm
Type of Feed ...............................................Box - 10 rd cap
Weight, empty .......................................................8.7 lbs
Overall length ......................................................39.4 in
Effective range ..................................................470 meters
```

FIELD STRIP PROCEDURE

STEP   ACTION

1. Push forward on the Receiver Cover until it disengages from the Receiver and carefully slide rearward and remove. (The Recoil Spring is compressed during the movement of the Receiver Cover.)
2. Push forward on the Recoil Spring and remove the Recoil Spring and Recoil Spring Guide from the Receiver.
3. Slide the Bolt Carrier and Bolt to the rear until the Bolt Carrier reaches the dismounting notches in the Receiver, lift the Bolt Carrier and Bolt up out of the Receiver. Remove the Bolt from the Bolt Carrier.
4. Press in on the Upper Hand Guard Retaining Clips at the rear of the Upper Hand Guard and remove the Upper Hand Guard from the Barrel.
5. Remove the Operating Sleeve from the top of the Barrel.

ASSEMBLY PROCEDURE

Assemble in the reverse order. Place the Operating Sleeve into position on top of the Barrel. Assemble the Upper Hand Guard to the top of the Barrel and engage the Retaining Clips. Assemble the Bolt to the Bolt Carrier and slide onto the Receiver until the dismounting notches in the Receiver line up with the Bolt Carrier, then slide down and forward to engage. Assemble the Recoil Spring and Recoil Spring Guide into the Receiver, engaging the Recoil Spring Guide inside of the cover, and slide Receiver Cover onto Receiver from rear to front until it engages.

LOADING AND FIRING

To load: Draw the Bolt Handle to the rear. The Bolt will remain held to the rear by the Bolt hold-open device. Insert a five-round clip into the charger guide grooves in front of the Receiver Cover. Push the cartridges down into the Magazine. Repeat until ten rounds have been loaded into the Magazine. Pull the Safety Lever, located at the right of the Trigger Guard, to the rear to the "SAFE" position. Draw the Bolt handle slightly to the rear to disengage the Bolt from the hold-open device and release. The Bolt will move forward and chamber a round.

To fire: Push the Safety Lever forward. Pull the Trigger. The weapon will fire. This weapon fires semi-automatic only and the Trigger must be pulled for each shot.

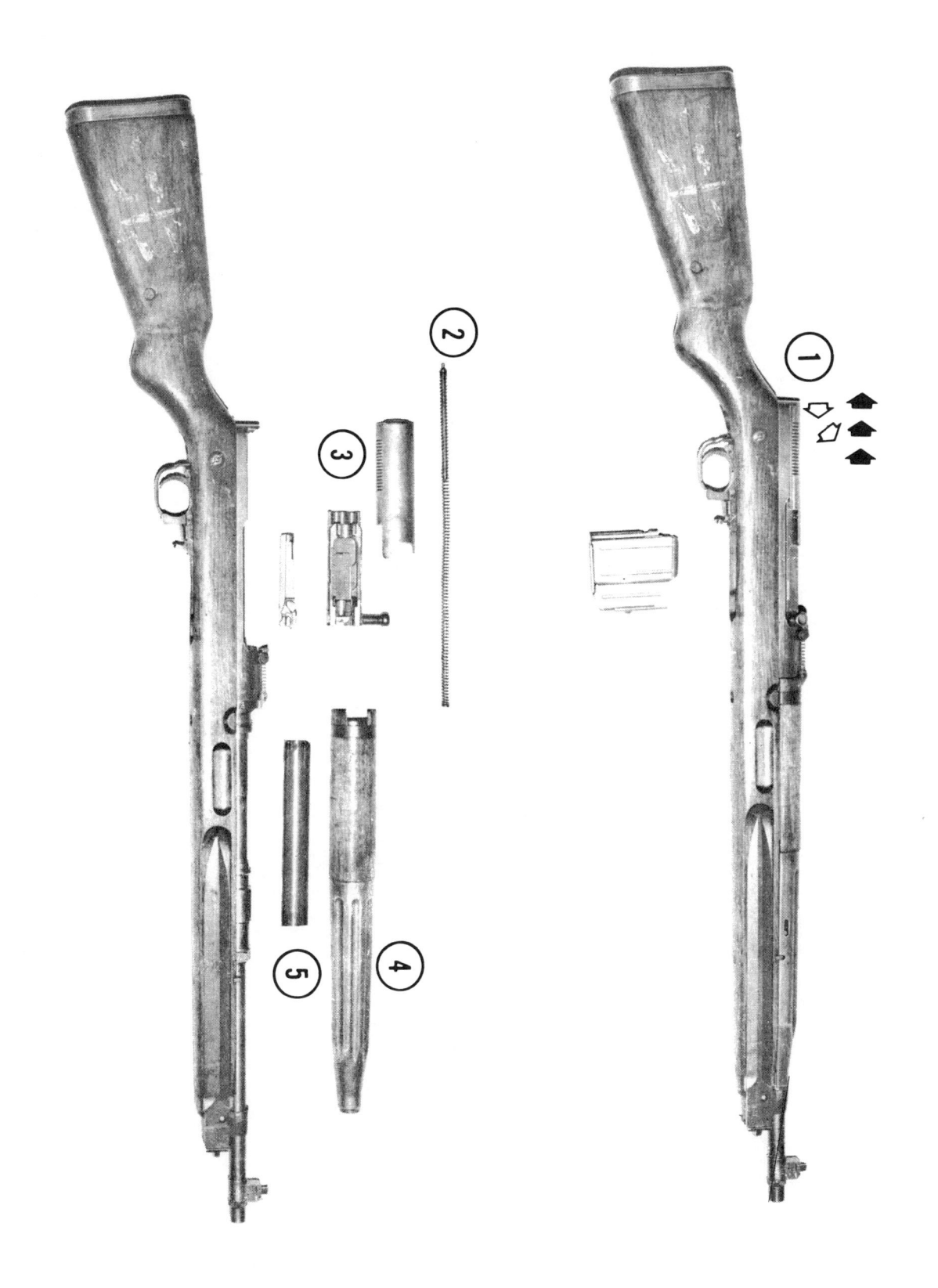

7.62-mm M-52

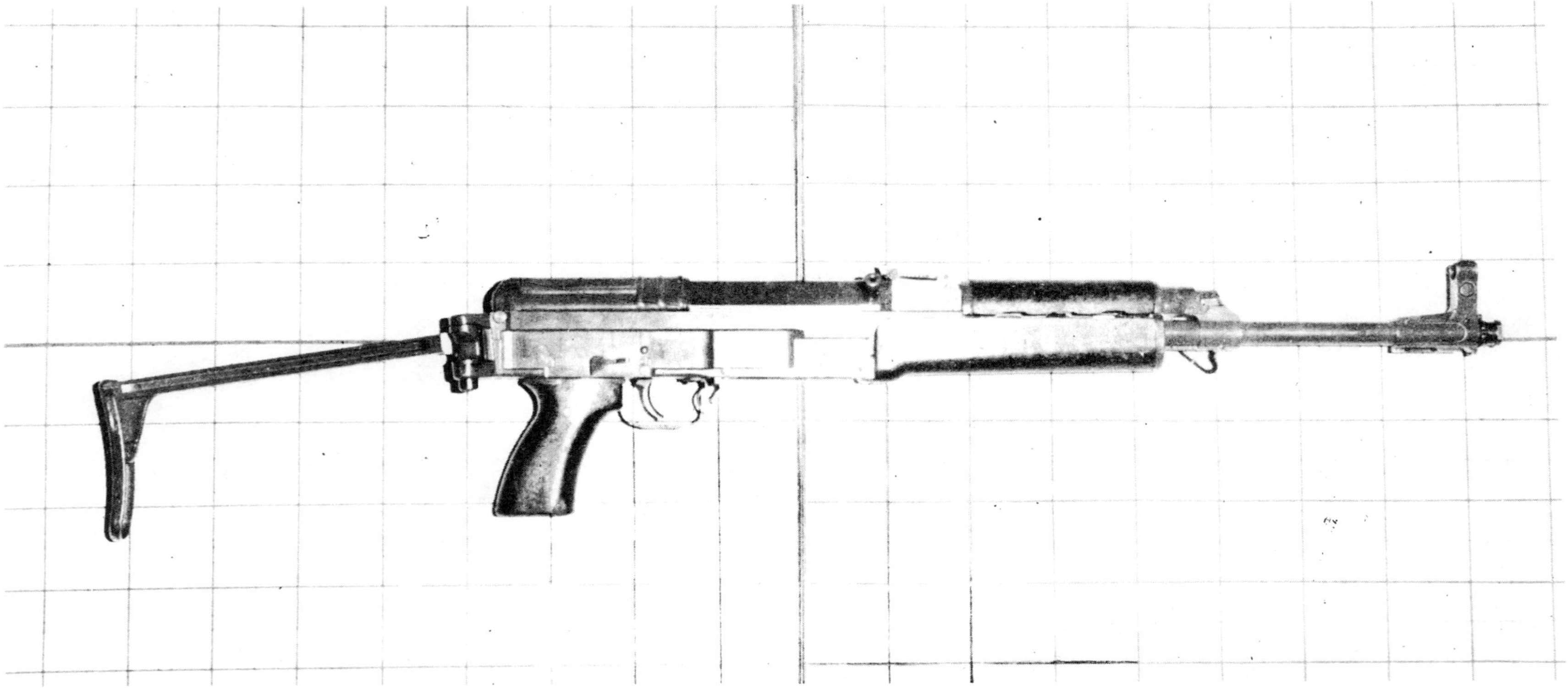

CZECHOSLOVAKIA   7.62-MM SHORT, MODEL 58

RIFLE

CZECHOSLOVAKIA

7.62-mm MODEL 58

The 7.62-mm Model 58 Assault Rifle is the current standard individual weapon of the Czechoslovakian Armed Forces, having replaced the Model 52/57. The Model 52/57 is a slightly modified version of the Czech Model 52 Rifle. Both the Model 58 Assault Rifle and the Model 52/57 Rifle are chambered for the Czech copy of the Soviet M43 short round, designated the Model 57 cartridge. The Model 58 Assault Rifle is similar in appearance and tactical employment to the Soviet AK Assault Rifle though the internal functions differ considerably. This weapon is available in both wooden stock and folding metal stock versions, the folding stock model being issued to parachutist and armor troops.

FUNCTIONING

The model 58 Assault Rifle is a gas-operated, magazine fed, selective fire rifle. With a loaded magazine inserted in the magazine well, the bolt handle is drawn to the rear and released. The slide, carrying the bolt, having been drawn rearward by the bolt handle, is forced forward by the compressed recoil spring. The face of the bolt strips a round from the magazine and chambers it, and the hammer is held to the rear by the sear. This is not a pivoting hammer but a straight-line, linear-travel hammer. The bolt comes to a stop against the rear face of the barrel and the slide and piston continue their forward travel. In the last 3/16 inch of movement of the slide, the locking lugs are cammed down into locking recesses in the receiver. When the trigger is pulled the sear releases the hammer which travels forward to strike the firing pin which in turn strikes the primer. Gas tapped from the barrel impinges against the face of the piston forcing the piston and slide rearward. After 3/16 inch travel of the slide, the locking lugs are cammed up out of the locking recesses in the receiver and the bolt is carried rearward by the slide. If safety/select lever has been set on semi-automatic (the position marked "1") the sear will hold the hammer to the rear and the trigger must be pulled for each shot. If the safety/select lever has been set for full-automatic (the position marked "30") the weapon will continue to fire until the trigger is released or the magazine is empty.

CHARACTERISTIC DATA

Caliber ....7.62-mm (M57 ctdge)
Operation ....Gas
Type of Fire .... Full and semi-auto
Rate of Fire ....800 rpm (Practical 225)
Type of Feed ....Box - 30 rd cap
Weight, empty .... 7.9 lbs
Overall length .... 33.2 in
Effective range ....400 meters
Muzzle velocity ....2,310 fps

FIELD STRIP PROCEDURE

STEP   ACTION

1. Pull Cover Retaining Pin out to the right.
2. Remove the Cover.
3. Slide Bolt Carrier with assembled Bolt and Hammer to the rear, lift up and remove from Receiver.
4. Rotate Hammer to left and remove from Bolt Carrier and remove Bolt and Locking Lugs.
5. Pull Upper Handguard retaining Pin out to the right and remove Upper Handguard.
6. Slide the Gas Piston to the rear, raise the front end up and slide forward to remove from Receiver.

ASSEMBLY PROCEDURE

Assemble in the reverse order. Slide Gas Piston into Receiver from the front. Replace Upper Handguard and Upper Handguard Retaining Pin. Assemble Locking Lugs and Bolt Carrier and attach Hammer. Slide Bolt Carrier with Bolt and Hammer into Receiver. Replace Cover and push Cover Retaining Pin through to the left.

LOADING AND FIRING

To load: Push Safety/Select Lever to the safe position. Insert a loaded Magazine into Magazine Well. Draw the Bolt Handle to the rear and release. The Bolt will chamber a round and the Hammer will be held to the rear by the Sear.

To fire: Push Safety/Select Lever to the type fire desired. Pull the Trigger. If Safety/Select Lever is forward, the weapon will fire semi-automatic and the Trigger must be pulled for each shot. If the lever is set to the rear the weapon will fire full-automatic and will continue to fire until the Trigger is released or the Magazine is empty. When the last round has been fired, the Bolt will remain held open by a Bolt hold-open device.

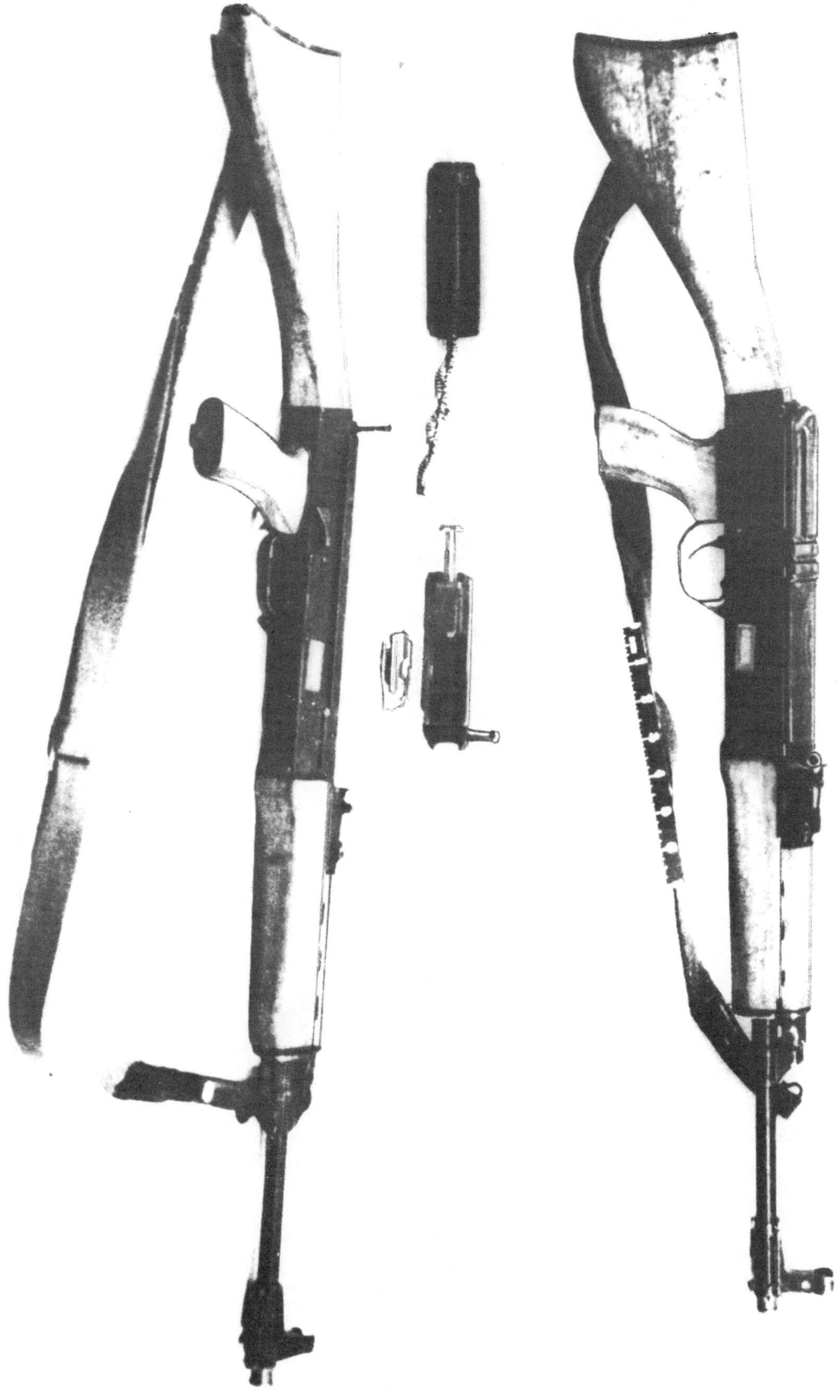

DENMARK 7.62-MM NATO, MADSEN

RIFLE DENMARK

7.62-mm MADSEN ASSAULT RIFLE

The 7.62-mm Madsen Assault Rifle is a gas-operated, magazine fed, selective fire rifle, manufactured by Dansk Industri Syndicat, which makes extensive use of aluminum components in its design. The barrel is attached to a steel barrel extension into which the bolt locks during firing, allowing for the use of an aluminum receiver. The receiver cover, trigger housing, rear sight, magazine and follower, carrying handle, magazine latch, bipod parts, and bayonet sheath are also fabricated from aluminum. The bore and chamber of the barrel are chrome plated. A grenade launcher is an integral machined portion of the muzzle end of the barrel. The gas system is of the long stroke type and the bolt locks in a manner similar to the Soviet AK Assault Rifle (rotating head). This is an extremely well made piece. The design is relatively simple, with only five major subassemblies and can be easily field-stripped without the use of tools. One fault appears to be in the design and attachment of the straight-line stock, which is expected to be improved. The weapon examined and illustrated is a preproduction model and minor changes are expected to be introduced in the final production model.

FUNCTIONING

The Madsen Assault Rifle is a gas-operated rifle which utilizes a bolt carrier, rotating bolt and trigger assembly which are similar in design and operation to comparable components in the Soviet AK Assault Rifle. The recoil spring is positioned around the gas piston, and in this respect pulls the action closed in counter recoil action, rather than pushing the carrier and bolt forward as in conventional design. With a loaded magazine inserted in the magazine well, the bolt handle is drawn to the rear and released. The safety/select lever must be set for type fire desired, it cannot be set on "SAFE" until the hammer is cocked. The bolt carrier and bolt are pulled forward by the driving spring and the hammer is held in the cocked position by the sear. The bolt strips a round from the magazine and chambers it and comes to a stop against the rear face of the barrel. The bolt carrier continues forward for a short distance, while camming surfaces inside the carrier rotate the bolt so that locking lugs on the bolt engage locking recesses in the barrel extension. When the trigger is pulled the sear releases the hammer, the hammer pivots forward to strike the firing pin which in turn strikes the primer. Gas is tapped from the barrel where it enters the gas cylinder to impinge against the face of the gas piston. The rear end of the gas piston is ball shaped and is engaged in a cup shaped opening in the top forward portion of the bolt carrier. The gas piston moves approximately 1/8 inch before the ball shaped end of the piston makes contact with the bolt carrier to move the carrier rearward. As the carrier moves rearward it rotates the bolt into the unlocked position and carries it rearward, over-riding the hammer and striking a buffer in the rear of the receiver cover. The driving spring around the piston then pulls the parts forward to chamber the next round. If the safety/select lever was set for full-automatic, the hammer will be released when the action closes and the weapon will continue to fire until the trigger is released or the magazine is empty.

CHARACTERISTIC DATA

Caliber . . . . .7.62-mm (NATO)
Operation . . . . .Gas
Type of Fire . . . . Full and semi-auto
Rate of Fire . . . . 550 rpm (Practical 150)
Type of Feed . . . . .Box - 20 rd cap
Weight, empty . . . . .10.2 lbs
Overall length . . . . .43 in
Effective range . . . . 540 meters

FIELD STRIP PROCEDURE

STEP   ACTION

1. Swing Barrel Handle down to the left, push forward on the Dismounting Lever, (attached to the Driving Spring Base) rotate Handle half way to vertical (which rotates Driving Spring Base. This will disengage the Receiver Cover.
2. Lift off Receiver Cover.
3. Disconnect Gas Piston from Bolt Carrier.
4. Slide Bolt Carrier and assembled Bolt rearward and lift up out of Receiver.
5. Rotate Handle to the vertical position until Dismounting Lever is up, which disengages the Driving Spring Base. Draw the Handle rearward which will remove the Driving Spring Base, Gas Piston and Driving Spring from the Gas Piston Tube.
6. Lift the Gas Piston Tube and Upper Handguard Assembly from the Barrel.
7. Remove the two Trigger Group Assembly Retaining Pins and disengage Trigger Guard Assembly from Receiver.

ASSEMBLY PROCEDURE

Assemble in the reverse order. Assemble Gas Piston Tube and Upper Handguard to Barrel. Place Trigger Group Assembly into Receiver and replace two Retaining Pins. Assemble Handle to Driving Spring Base, place Driving Spring into Base, insert Gas Piston into Driving Spring, slide assembly into Gas Piston Tube and rotate handle to the left to lock. Assemble Bolt to Carrier, slide into grooves in Receiver push partway forward and engage ball shaped end of Gas Piston into notch in Bolt Carrier. Slide Receiver Cover into place, push forward and rotate Handle down to lock Receiver. Push forward on Dismounting Lever to free Handle and rotate Handle to vertical position.

LOADING AND FIRING

To load: Draw Bolt Handle to the rear and release. Push Safety/Select Lever to "S" ("SAFE"). Insert loaded Magazine into Magazine Well.

To fire: Move Safety/Select Lever to type fire desired, "E" for semi-automatic fire and "A" for automatic fire. Pull the Trigger. The weapon will fire. If Safety/Select Lever is on "E" the Trigger must be pulled for each shot. If set on "A" the weapon will continue to fire until Trigger is released or the Magazine is empty.

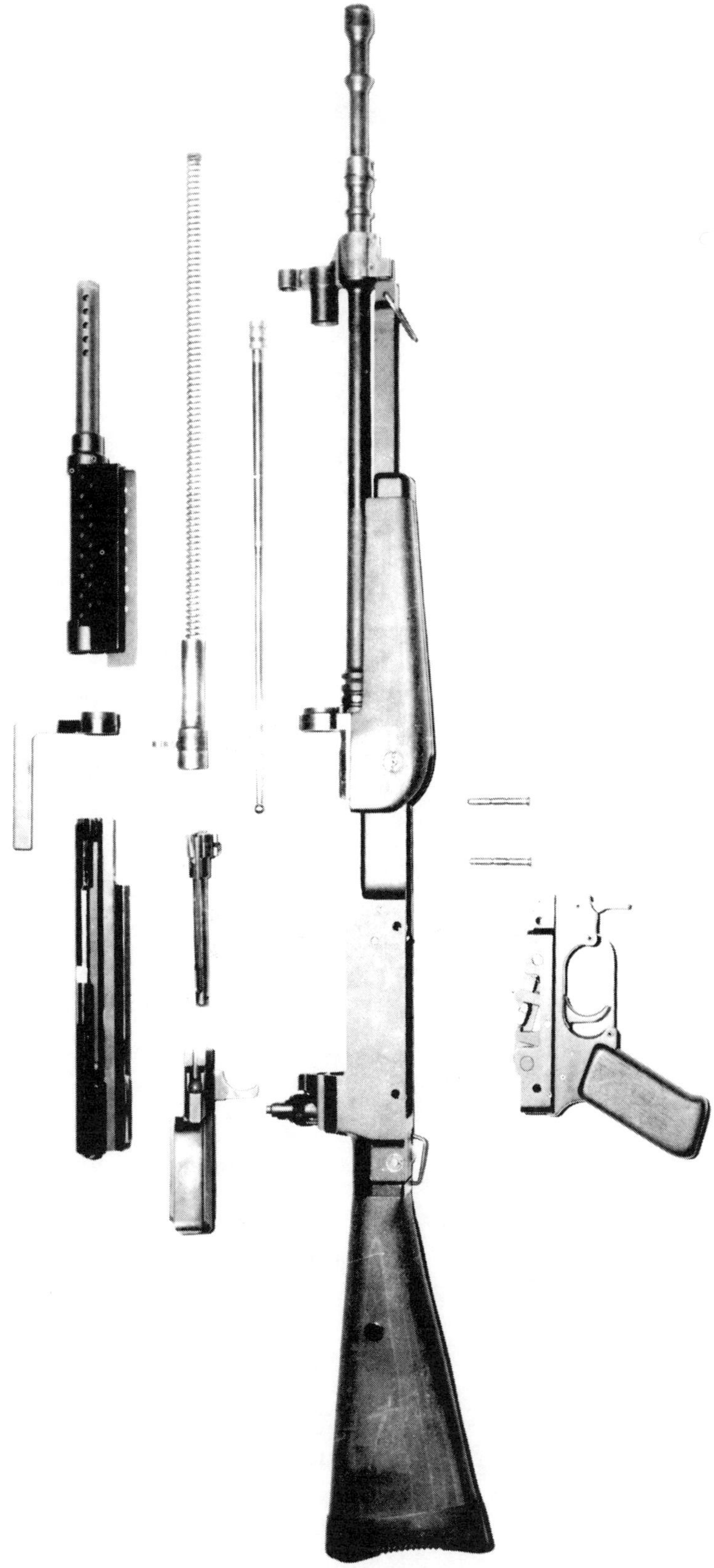

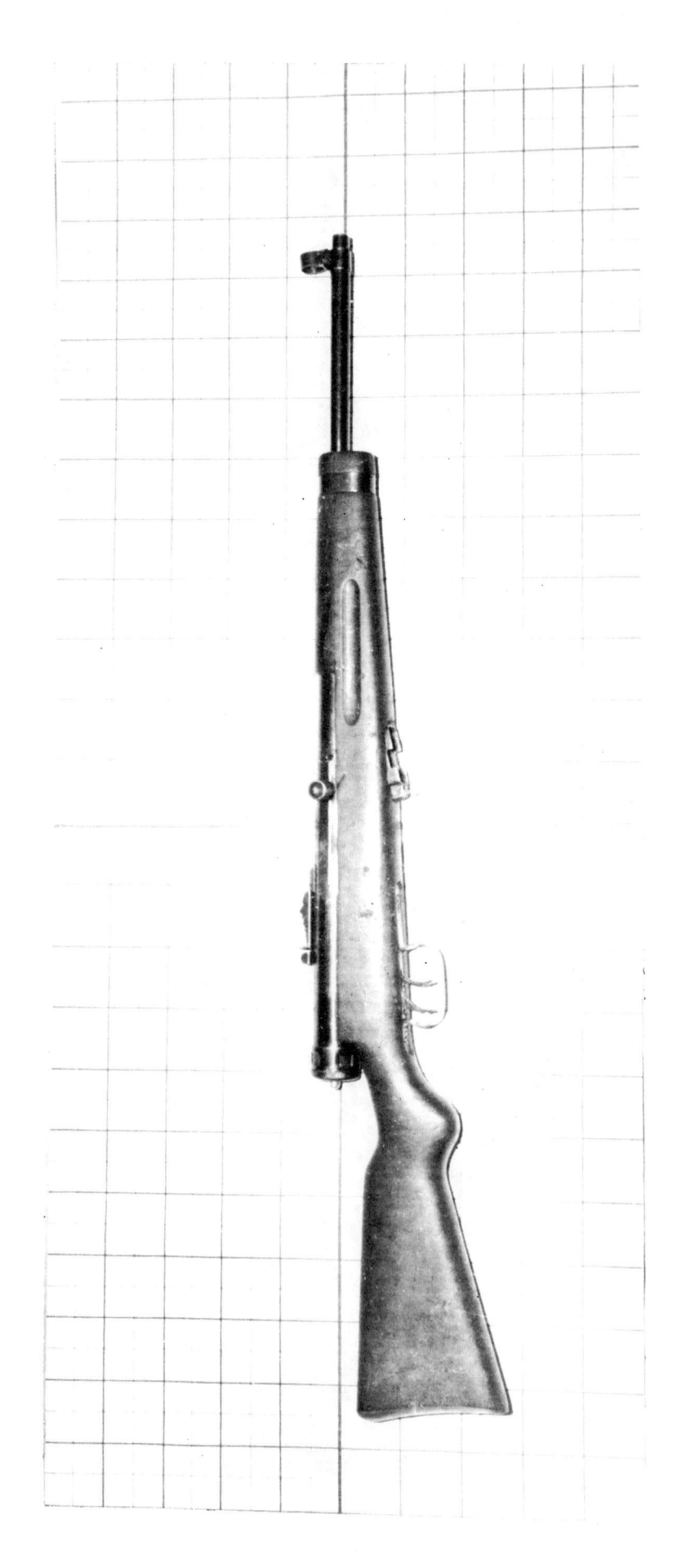

DOMINICAN REPUBLIC .30 CARBINE, MODEL 2

CARBINE   DOMINICAN REPUBLIC

.30 cal CRISTOBAL CARBINE (M-2)

The .30 caliber CRISTOBAL Carbine, Model 2, is a delayed-blowback, magazine-fed, automatic carbine. Designed by a European associated with the Dominican Army technical service after WWII. The weapon is similar in function and appearance to the Beretta Model 38-series submachineguns. The CRISTOBAL is chambered for the U.S. .30 caliber carbine round. This weapon functions on the retarded-blowback of the Beretta weapon. In this retarded-blowback action the bolt is in two pieces. These two pieces, the lightweight bolthead and the heavier rear portion, or striker, are connected by an inertia, or delay lever. The rotational movement of this lever during the initial rearward movement of the recoiling parts, creates for a short time, a mechanical disadvantage which must be overcome before the bolt continues its rearward movement. There is some slight rearward movement of the cartridge case during this initial movement of the bolthead. This movement of the cartridge case during the period of high chamber pressure is facilitated by a fluted chamber. This is a selective fire weapon, but the selection for type of fire desired is accomplished by the use of two triggers. If the forward trigger is pulled, the weapon fires full-automatic. The safety is located on the left side of the receiver, and its action blocks the sear and triggers.

FUNCTIONING

The retarded-blowback action utilized by this weapon is an unusual though simple design. The weapon fires from an open bolt. With a magazine in place, and either of the triggers pulled, the bolt assembly moves forward under impulse of the compressed recoil spring, strips a round from the magazine and chambers it. The delay lever, connecting the heavy rear portion of the bolt to the lighter forward, or bolthead section, must rotate in its traverse hole through the bolt assembly. This movement delays the completion of forward travel of the rear portion until the bolthead is fully forward and the round completely chambered. Upon firing, the cartridge case is thrust back against the bolthead, the delay lever, the lower arm which is bearing against a slot in the bottom of the receiver, is forced to rotate rearward. This movement of the lever, the upper portion of which is bearing against the front of the rear bolt section, tends to force this heavy section rearward. In overcoming the resistance of this heavy rear portion of the bolt assembly, the lever mounted in a traverse hole in the forward bolt section, pushes this lighter section forward against the rear of the barrel, effectively delaying the rearward or opening movement of this piece. After the heavy rear portion of the bolt has completed its maximum free movement it draws the bolthead section back with it. The bolt assembly moving rearward compresses the recoil spring and at its rear most point, depending on which trigger is pulled, the sear will be up to engage the bolt or will be depressed and the bolt will move forward and the firing cycle will be repeated.

CHARACTERISTIC DATA

Caliber .... 30 cal (U.S. Carbine)
Operation .... Retarded-blowback
Type of Fire .... Full and semi-auto
Rate of Fire .... 550-580 rpm (Practical-100)
Type of Feed .... Box 25 & 30 rd cap
Weight, empty .... 7.8 lbs
Overall length .... 37.2 in
Effective range .... 315 meters
Muzzle velocity .... 1,875 fps

FIELD STRIP PROCEDURE

STEP   ACTION

1. Press in on the Receiver Cap Lock and remove the Cap.
2. Remove the Recoil Spring and Bolt Assembly from the rear of the receiver.
3. Remove the cross piece located in the forward section of the Bolt Assembly, remove the Delay Lever, and separate the Bolt.

ASSEMBLY PROCEDURE

Assemble in the reverse order. Place the two parts of the Bolt together, assemble the Delay Lever and place the cross pin into position. Slide the Bolt Assembly into the rear of the Receiver and slide the Recoil Spring in behind it. Assemble the Receiver Cap onto the Receiver and engage the Receiver Cap Lock.

LOADING AND FIRING

To load: Draw the Bolt Handle, located on the right side of the Receiver, to the rear to engage the Bolt with the Sear. Push the Bolt Handle forward. Push the Safety Lever, located on the left side of the Receiver to the rear. The weapon is now on SAFE. Place a loaded Magazine into the Magazine Well and engage. Push Safety forward.

To fire: Pull the Trigger the weapon will fire full or semiautomatic depending on the position of the Select Lever. When the Magazine is empty the Bolt will remain to the rear.

① Cap Lock

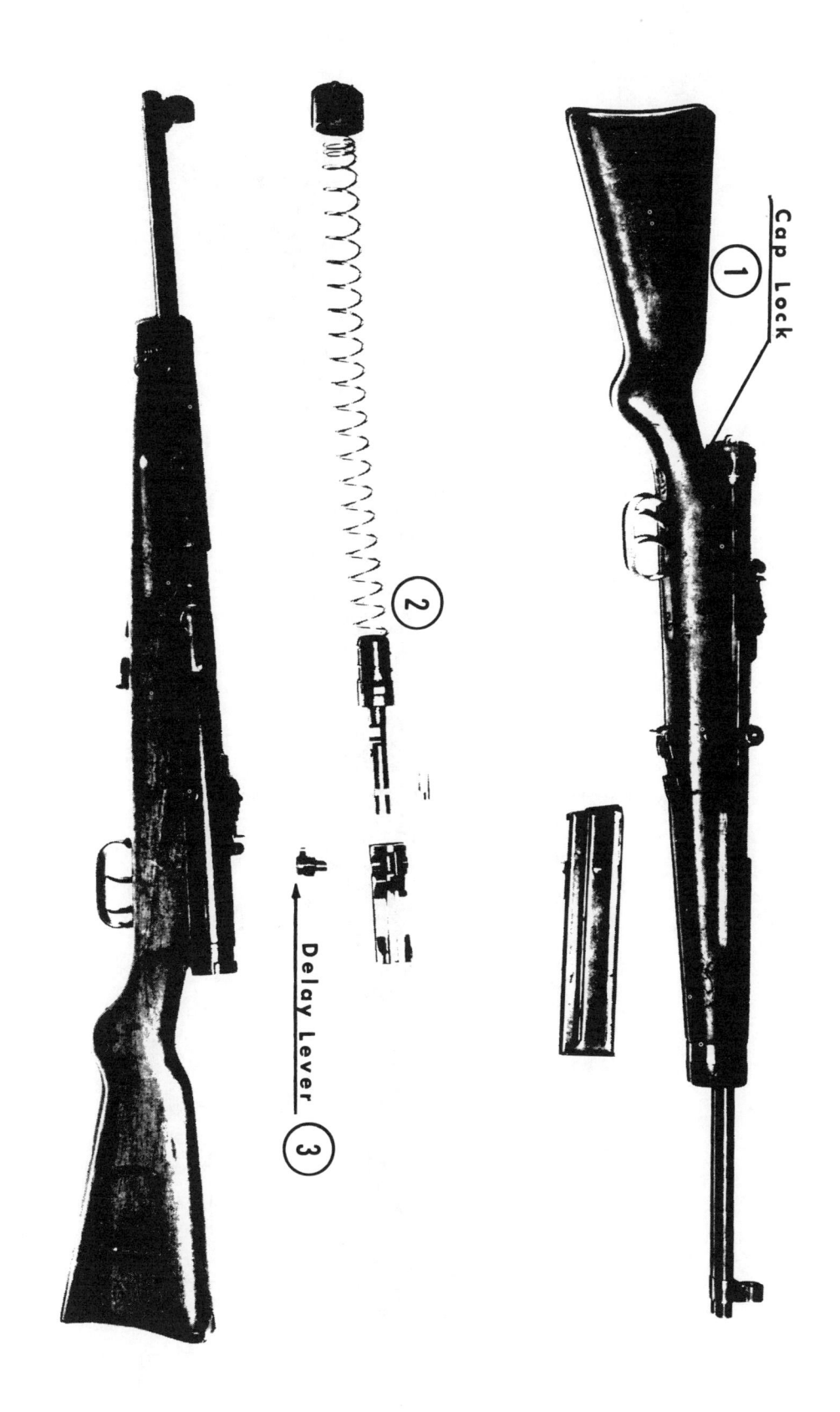

②

③ Delay Lever

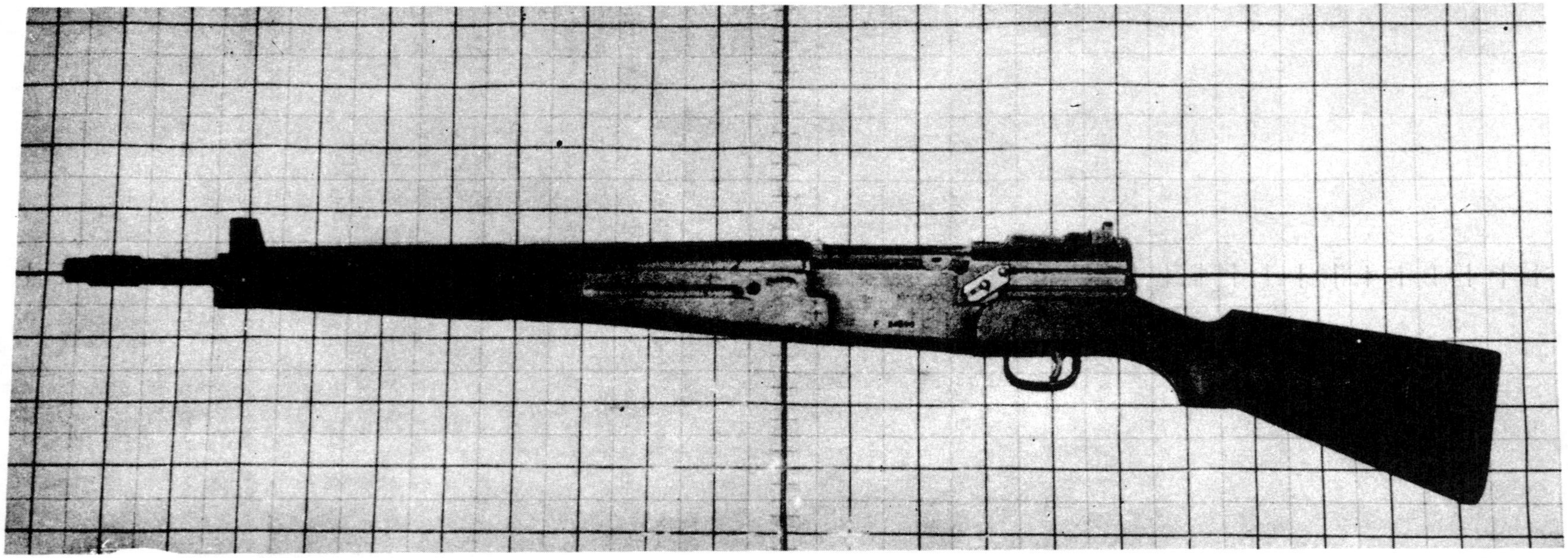

FRANCE   7.5-MM M29, MODEL 1949

RIFLE　　　　　　　　　　　　　　　　　　　　　　　　　　　　　　　　FRANCE

7.5-mm MODEL 1949 (MAS-49)

The French MAS-49 Rifle is a gas-operated, magazine fed rifle which utilizes a direct gas thrust against the bolt carrier to operate the mechanism. This weapon is another example of the French design technique in which the good points of numerous weapons have been incorporated into one system. The bolt is cammed down in front of a shelf in the bottom of the receiver by camming surfaces in the bolt carrier similar to the Soviet Tokarev and Belgian FN actions; the gas piston and cylinder components usually found in gas operated rifles are eliminated, the gas being directed through a gas tube directly against the face of the bolt carrier similar to the Swedish Ljungman system. A grenade launcher is attached to the muzzle of the piece which can be adjusted for range by a worm gear located on the left side of the forward stock band. This weapon is simple to operate and easy to disassemble. The magazine catch is a component part of the magazine, rather than being a part of the weapon, and the magazine can be loaded through the top of the receiver by strip-clips.

FUNCTIONING

This rifle utilizes a direct gas thrust system of operation. With a loaded magazine inserted in the magazine well, or an empty magazine inserted and then loaded through the top of the receiver, the bolt handle is drawn to the rear, drawing the bolt carrier and bolt rearward to override and cock the hammer. The hammer is held to the rear by the sear when the bolt handle is released. The bolt and carrier move forward under impulse of the compressed recoil spring and the bolt strips a round from the magazine and chambers it. The bolt comes to a stop against the rear face of the barrel and the bolt carrier continues its foward movement for 9/16 inch during which time camming surfaces inside the carrier force the rear of the bolt down in front of a shelf in the bottom of the receiver. When the trigger is pulled the sear releases the hammer which pivots forward to strike the firing pin driving it into the primer. Gas is tapped from the barrel into a gas tube mounted above the barrel. The upper forward face of the bolt carrier is drilled to a depth of 7/8 inches to surround the rear of the gas tube when the action is closed. The gas traveling through the gas tube impinges directly against the bolt carrier in the hole in the face of the carrier, driving the carrier rearward. The carrier moves independent of the bolt for 9/16 inches before the bolt is cammed up to unlock by the camming surfaces inside the carrier. The gas tube is still inside of the carrier for an additional 5/16 inches rearward travel as a precaution against gas venting from the rear of the tube. The rearward movement of the bolt and carrier cocks the hammer and the piece is ready to fire again. This weapon fires semi-automatic and the trigger must be pulled for each shot.

CHARACTERISTIC DATA

Caliber .... 7.5-mm (M29 ctdge)
Operation .... Gas
Type of Fire .... Semi-auto only
Rate of Fire .... 40 rpm
Type of Feed .... Box 10 rd cap
Weight, empty .... 10.4 lbs
Overall length .... 43.2 in
Effective range .... 540 meters

FIELD STRIP PROCEDURE

STEP   ACTION

1. Push down on Cover Latch.
2. Push forward on Cover.
3. Lift Cover up and remove rearward off the Receiver, the Recoil Spring exerts pressure on the Cover during this operation.
4. Remove Recoil Spring.
5. Grasp Bolt Handle and pull Bolt Carrier with assembled Bolt rearward and upward. When the dismounting notches line up the Carrier can be lifted up out of the Receiver. Lift Bolt out of Bolt Carrier and remove Firing Pin.

ASSEMBLY PROCEDURE

Assemble in the reverse order. Slide Firing Pin into Bolt and assemble Bolt to Bolt Carrier, engage Firing Pin base into notch in Carrier. Slide Bolt Carrier and assembled Bolt into Receiver. Place Recoil Spring into hole in rear of Bolt Carrier. Slide Buffer Guide and Tube, carried inside of Cover into rear of Recoil Spring, and slide Cover into grooves in Receiver, push forward slightly, and down and then pull to the rear so that Cover Latch engages.

LOADING AND FIRING

To load: Grasp Bolt Handle and draw Bolt to the rear and release. Push Safety Button located on right front of Trigger Guard to "SAFE." The Safety Button cannot be put on "SAFE" unless the Hammer is cocked. Insert loaded Magazine into Magazine Well, and draw the Bolt Handle to the rear and release. Bolt will strip a round from the Magazine and chamber it. If the Magazine is not loaded when inserted into weapon, draw the Bolt Handle to the rear, the Bolt hold-open device will keep the Bolt open. Load the Magazine from the top of the Receiver from five-round strip-clips. When ten rounds have been loaded into the Magazine draw the Bolt Handle to the rear slightly and release. The Bolt will strip a round from the Magazine and chamber it.

To fire: Push Safety Button to "FIRE." Pull the Trigger. The weapon will fire. This weapon fires semi-automatic only and the Trigger must be pulled for each shot.

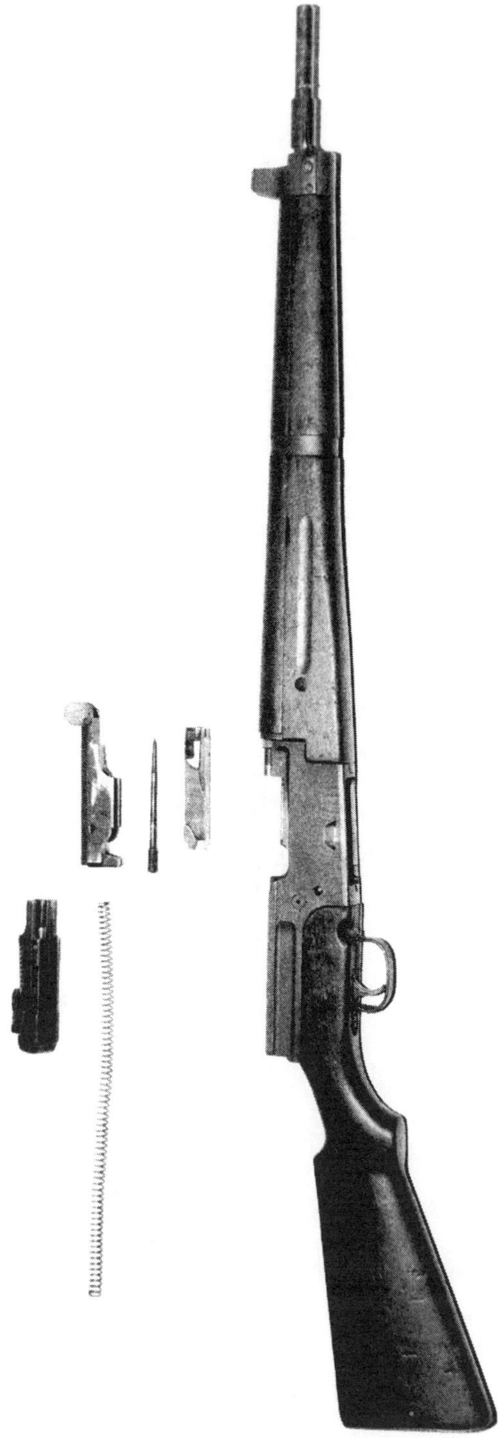

GERMANY 7.92-MM, GEW-43

7.92-mm GEWEHR 43 (GEW43)

The 7.92-mm Gewehr (GEW43) was the last German designed semi-automatic rifle to see action, though limited, in WWII. It is a well-designed weapon though some portions are crudely machined and was apparently so produced with the idea of rapid production, low cost and ready expendability. Various models incorporating minor modifications may be found. The bolt cover is cast and roughly machined and in most models the trigger guard assembly is composed of stamped components. The design readily lends itself to further military development. It combines most of the conventional gas operated rifle principles. The gas is tapped from the top of the barrel and the gas piston is therefore located above the barrel, similar to the Soviet Tokarev rifle. The Tokarev weakness, an easily bent, metal, upper handguard, is eliminated in the GEW 43 by a sturdy wooden upper handguard. Unlike most gas systems, the system utilized in this weapon makes use of two compatible actions. Gas tapped from the barrel enters a gas cylinder, where normally it would then expand against a piston, pushing the piston and action to the rear. In this case, the gas expands against a short tappet-like piston, which imparts this thrust to a separate operating rod. In this respect, the system is somewhat like that of the U.S. .30 caliber Carbine, which makes use of a short stroke piston.

FUNCTIONING

This is a gas-operated semi-automatic rifle. With a loaded magazine in place, the bolt is drawn to the rear and released. The bolt moves forward, strips a round from the magazine and chambers it. When the trigger is pulled the sear releases the hammer and the hammer pivots to strike the firing pin extension in the rear of the bolt which in turn drives the firing pin into the primer. Gas is tapped off the barrel into a chamber located on top of the barrel. The gas passes from the chamber into a cylinder where it impinges against a short, "free" tappet-like piston. This tappet imparts the sharp blow received from the expanding gas to the operating rod, which in turn transmits this motion to the bolt slide. The firing pin is withdrawn from the face of the bolt at the initial movement of the bolt slide. After a short rearward travel of the bolt slide, the firing pin cams the locking lugs in the bolt out of engagement with the locking seats in the receiver, the bolt engaged by the bolt slide moves to the rear with the bolt slide. The operating rod moves forward to its original position under impulse of the operating rod spring, and the bolt and bolt slide having reached the rearmost point of recoil are then forced forward by the compressed recoil spring. A round is stripped from the magazine and chambered. The hammer which has been cammed back by the rearward motion of the recoiling parts is engaged by the sear.

CHARACTERISTIC DATA

Caliber	7.92-mm (Ger Svc)
Operation	Gas
Type of Fire	Semi-auto only
Rate of Fire	30-35 rpm
Type of Feed	Box-10 rd cap
Weight, empty	9.7 lbs
Overall length	44.25 in
Effective range	680 meters

FIELD STRIP PROCEDURE

STEP   ACTION

1. With the chamber empty and the Magazine removed, draw the Bolt Handle to the rear. Holding the Bolt to the rear, push in on the Bolt Slide Lock located at the right rear of the Bolt Slide to lock the Bolt in the open position.
2. Turn the Safety Lever to the right as far as it will go.
3. The Recoil Spring Guide is now projecting from the rear of the Bolt Slide. Push in on the Recoil Spring Guide and raise the rear of the Bolt Slide Assembly up and out of the Receiver. Remove the Bolt Cover from the Bolt Slide Assembly. The Bolt can now be removed from the Bolt Slide by moving the Bolt Slide Lock out of engagement.
4. Remove the Cleaning Rod from beneath the Barrel. Press in on the Forearm Band Locking Spring on the right side of the fore-end and slide the Forearm Cap forward.
5. Remove the Upper Handguard.
6. Pull the Operating Rod to the rear slightly.
7. Remove the Gas Piston and Tappet Piston. Remove the Operating Rod.

ASSEMBLY PROCEDURE

Proceed in the reverse order. Place the Operating Rod in its tunnel in the top of the Receiver. Push the Operating Rod to the rear and assemble the Tappet Piston and the Gas Piston, allow the assembly to move forward. Replace Cleaning Rod. Replace the Upper Handguard and slide the Forearm Cap back into place. Assemble the Bolt to the Bolt Slide and attach the Bolt Cover, lock the Bolt in its rearmost position in the Bolt Slide by pushing in on the Bolt Slide Lock. Assemble the Recoil Spring and Guide to the Bolt Slide Assembly. Place the assembly into the guide groove in the Receiver, slide forward slightly and push down into position. Holding the Bolt Handle, release the Bolt Slide Lock and allow the Bolt to move forward.

LOADING AND FIRING

To load: Place the Safety Lever on "SAFE." Insert a loaded Magazine from the bottom. Pull the Bolt Handle to the rear and release it. The Bolt will move forward, strip a round from the Magazine and chamber it. Turn Safety Lever to the left.

To fire: Pull the Trigger and the weapon will fire.

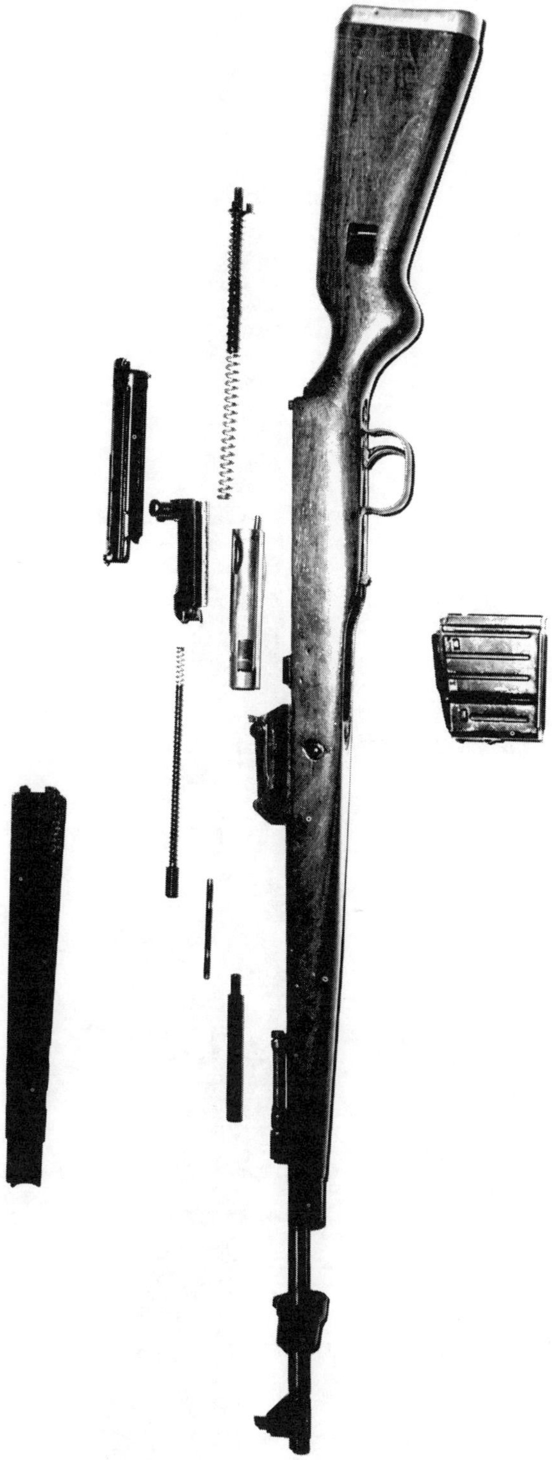

GERMANY 7.62-MM NATO, G3

RIFLE   W. GERMANY

7.62-mm ASSAULT RIFLE (G-3)

The West German G-3 Assault Rifle is a blowback operated, magazine fed weapon which is basically an improved version of the Spanish CETME (Centro de Estudios Technicos de Materials Especiales) Model 58 Assault Rifle. One of the main differences between the G-3 and the Model 58 is in the construction of the bolthead. The G-3 bolthead is designed to function with the full power NATO cartridge while the Model 58 is designed to function with the reduced power cartridge used by Spanish rifles. The weapon functions on the retarded-blowback or delayed-blowback system. The G-3 incorporates many features which make it easily adaptable to mass production. With the exception of the bolt and barrel, most of the parts are stamped and drawn from sheet steel. The weapon has a combination flash hider and grenade launcher fastened to the muzzle. Models are available with bipods and with folding metal stocks.

FUNCTIONING

One unusual design feature of this weapon is the location of the operating handle. This handle is located in the forward end of a tube mounted above the barrel. The handle is spring loaded and folds down out of the way when not in use. With a loaded magazine in place, this handle is flipped up and grasped, pulled sharply to the rear and released. The bolt will move forward and chamber a round. When the trigger is pulled the hammer is released striking the firing pin. The bolt is composed of two pieces, a forward bolthead section containing locking rollers on both sides, and the heavier rear section which has the operating rod extension attached to its forward upper end. The round is chambered and the bolt head comes flush against the breech end of the barrel. The locking is effected by the rollers carried in the bolthead, the rollers engaging in recesses in a fixed breech ring. The rollers are cammed into their locked position by a protrusion on the front of the rear bolt section. Upon firing the rearward thrust on the bolt head tends to cam the rollers out of engagement, but the cam angle is so steep that unlocking is accomplished at a great mechanical disadvantage. The delay in the movement of the bolthead is sufficient to allow the projectile to leave the muzzle before the bolt opens. The bolt moves to the rear, extracting and ejecting the empty case and cocking the hammer. The bolt then moves forward to chamber the next round. If the select lever is on single fire, the trigger must be pulled for each round fired. If the lever is on autofire, the sear will release the hammer and the weapon will continue to fire.

CHARACTERISTIC DATA

Caliber . . . . 7.62-mm (NATO)
Operation . . . . Retarded-blowback
Type of Fire . . . . Full and semi-auto
Rate of Fire . . . . 550-600 rpm (Practical 150)
Type of Feed . . . . Box - 20 rd cap
Weight, empty . . . . 9.5 lbs
Overall length . . . . 40.35 in
Effective range . . . . 540 meters

FIELD STRIP PROCEDURE

STEP   ACTION

1. Remove the two Stock Retaining Pins and remove the Stock.
2. Pivot the Trigger Group down.
3. Slide the Bolt Assembly out of the rear of the Receiver.

ASSEMBLY PROCEDURE

Assemble in the reverse order. Slide the Bolt Assembly into the Receiver. Swing the Trigger Group up into place and slide the Stock onto the rear of the Receiver. Place the two Stock Retaining Pins through the Receiver and Stock.

LOADING AND FIRING

To load: Insert a loaded Magazine. Grasp the Operating Handle, located in the tube above the Barrel, pull it to the rear and release. The Bolt will move forward and chamber the first round when the Operating Handle is released.

To fire: Pull the Trigger, the Hammer will be released and the weapon will fire. If the Select Lever is set for Single fire, the Trigger must be pulled for each shot. If the Lever is set for Automatic, the weapon will fire until the Trigger is released or the Magazine is empty.

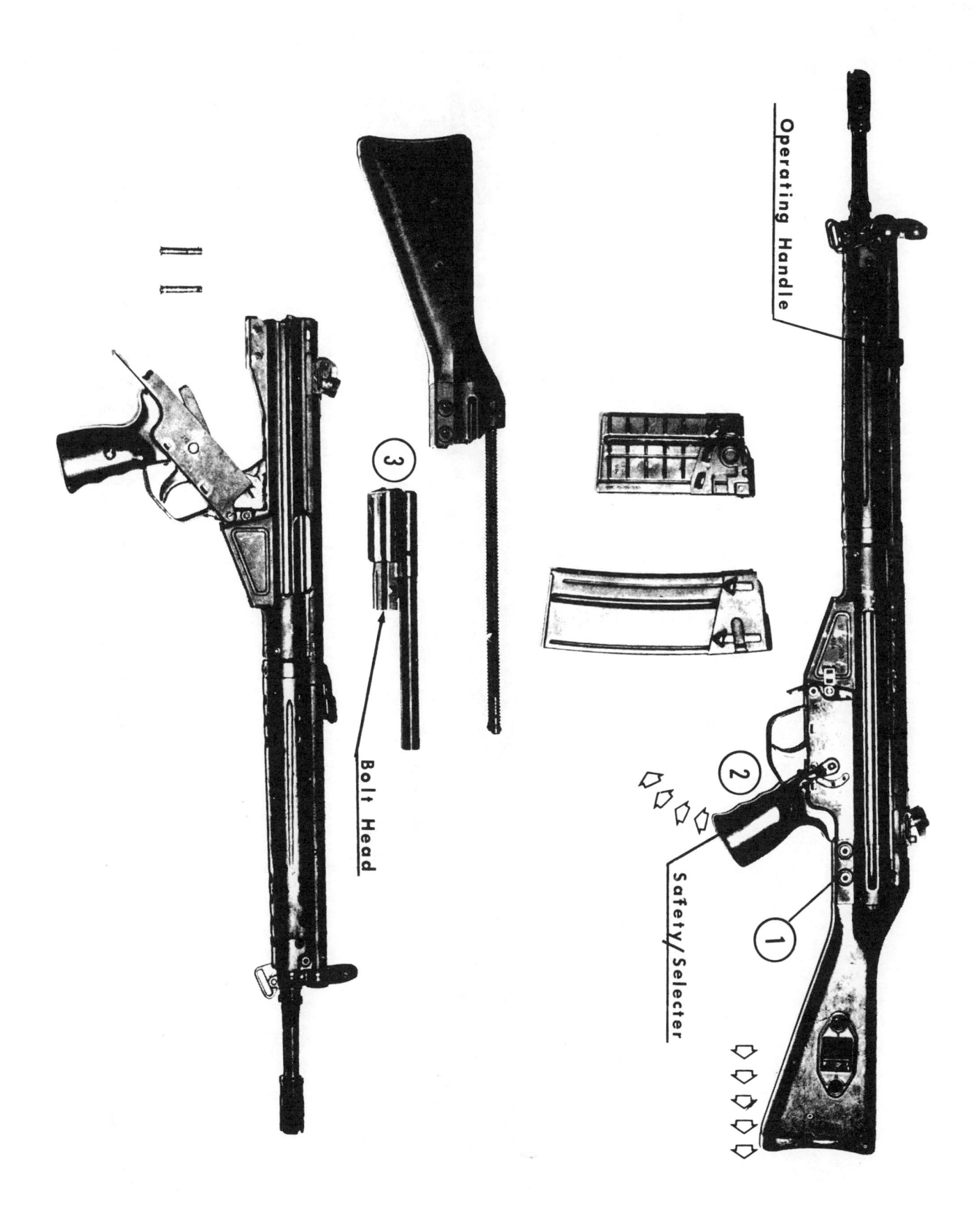

Operating Handle

Bolt Head

Safety/Selecter

① ② ③

97

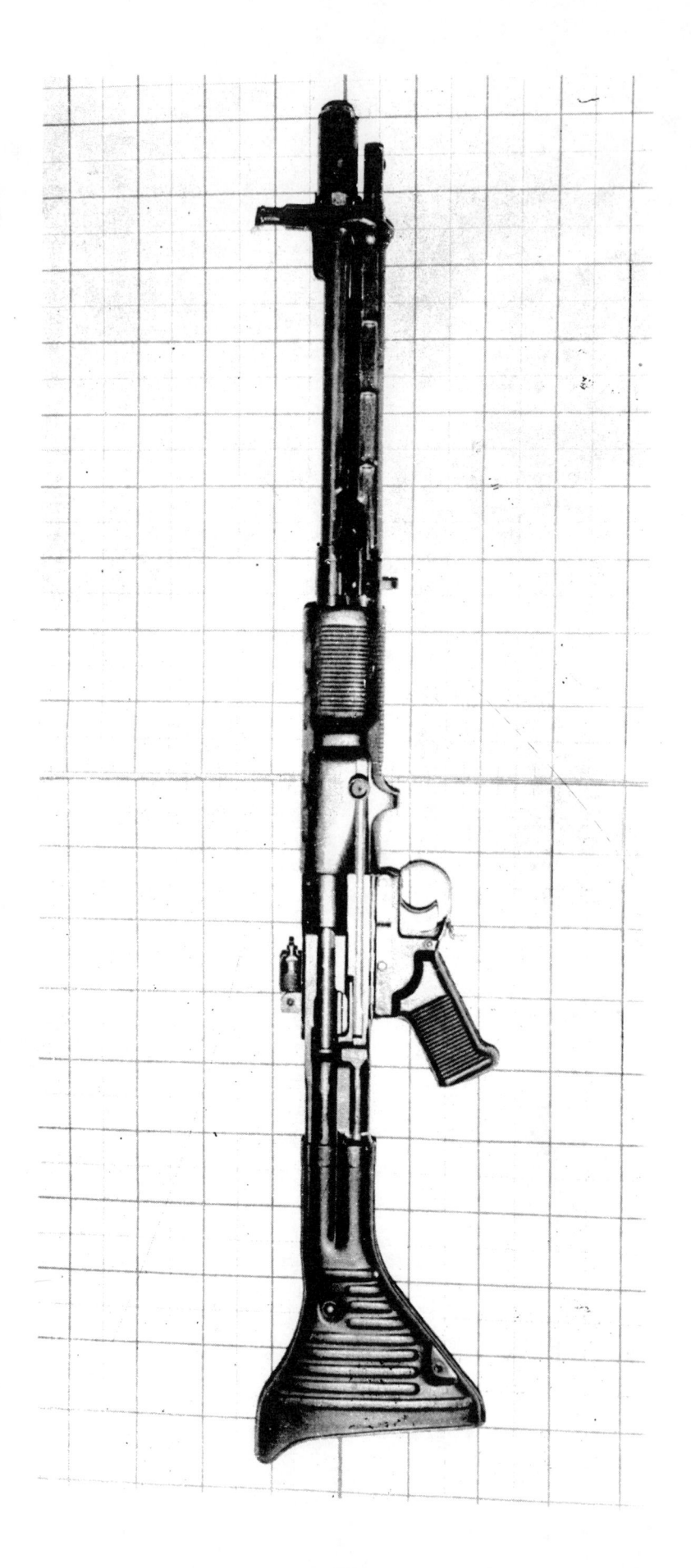

GERMANY 7.92-MM, FG-42--METAL STOCK

RIFLE   GERMANY

7.92-mm FG-42 (FALSCHIRMJAEGER GEWEHR 42)

The German FG-42 Rifle is a gas-operated, magazine fed, selective fire rifle which fires full-automatic from an open bolt and semi-automatic from a closed bolt. This is an exceptionally well designed piece being composed of stamped, machined and plastic components. The bipod which folds up to enclose the lower portion of the barrel; a straight-line stock which contains a buffer unit; an extremely effective muzzle brake/compensator; and a variable gas regulator, are some of the advance design components of this piece. The bolt locking system is similar to the Lewis gun system in that the bolt rides on a stud mounted on top of the rear of the gas piston and is rotated into locking position by the final forward movement of the piston. Manufactured at the Krieghoff Works at Suhl, Germany, it was designed primarily for airborne troops and made its first appearance in the German raid on Crete. Two models, one with a wooden stock and curved pistol grip and the other with a plastic stock and sharply slanted pistol grip, were produced.

FUNCTIONING

This weapon employs a rotating bolt locking system and fires from both an open and closed bolt. The bolt handle is located on the right side of the receiver, the safety and fire select lever is placed on the left side of the trigger housing. The safety is applied only when the bolt is open. With a loaded magazine inserted into the magazine port on the left side of the receiver, the bolt handle is drawn to the rear bringing the gas piston and attached bolt to the rear. A sear bent on the bottom of the piston is engaged by the sear, holding the piston and bolt to the rear if the select lever is set for full-automatic fire. When the trigger is pulled, the sear releases the piston which moves forward under impulse of the compressed recoil spring. The bolt strips a round from the magazine and chambers it. The bolt rides on top of the rear of the piston, a stud on the piston riding in a helical groove machined in the bolt. When the bolt stops against the rear face of the barrel, the piston, which has 2½ inches more to travel before being fully forward, continues to travel, the stud on the piston riding in the groove in the bolt causes the bolt to turn so that locking lugs on the forward end of the bolt engage locking recesses in the receiver to lock the action closed. If the select lever has been set for semi-automatic fire, the action is not held to the rear by the sear, but moves forward to the position where the bolt has chambered a round but has not rotated to lock, and then is engaged by the sear. When the trigger is pulled the sear releases the piston which moves forward 2½ inches to rotate and lock the bolt. In both cases, when the piston reaches its forwardmost position and the bolt is locked, the firing pin is driven into the primer. Gas is tapped from the barrel forcing the piston rearward. The piston moving, rotates the bolt out of locked position and carries it rearward also. Depending on the type fire selected, the piston may be engaged in its rearmost position or in the forward position with the bolt not rotated to lock.

CHARACTERISTIC DATA

```
Caliber ..................................................................7.92-mm
Operation ...................................................................Gas
Type of Fire ..................................................Full and semi-auto
Rate of Fire .....................................................550 rpm (Practical 225)
Type of Feed ..................................................box - 20 and 30 rd cap
Weight, empty ..................................................................10.7 lbs
Overall length ..................................................................39.5 in
Effective range ...............................................................540 meters
```

FIELD STRIP PROCEDURE

STEP   ACTION

1. Press in on Stock Lock and remove Stock.
2. Press in on Buffer Latch, turn Buffer Group 1/4 turn to left and remove.
3. Draw the Bolt Handle to the rear.
4. Remove Bolt Handle.
5. Remove Gas Piston, Bolt and Recoil Spring with Guide from Receiver.

ASSEMBLY PROCEDURE

Assemble in the reverse order. Assemble Recoil Spring and Guide into rear of Gas Piston, and slide assembled Piston, Bolt, Spring and Guide into Receiver. Assemble Bolt Handle into operating slot in Receiver. Lock Buffer Group to rear of Receiver. Slide Stock onto Receiver until Stock Lock engages.

LOADING AND FIRING

To load: Insert a loaded Magazine into the Magazine Port on left side of Receiver. Draw the Bolt Handle to the rear. The Sear will engage the Sear Bent in the rear of the Gas Piston and hold the Bolt to the rear Swing the Safety/Select Lever down to center position to "SAFE" (on plastic stock model). On wooden Stock model push the Safety Lever located near the rear of the Trigger Group Housing to the up position to "SAFE."

To fire: Push the Safety Lever on the wooden Stock model down. Rotate Select Lever to the rear to "D" for full-automatic fire or forward to "E" for semi-automatic fire. On the plastic Stock model swing the Safety/Select Lever forward for semi-automatic fire or rearward for full-automatic fire. Pull the Trigger. The weapon will fire. If set for semi-automatic fire the Trigger must be pulled for each shot. If set for full-automatic fire the weapon will continue to fire until the Magazine is empty or the Trigger is released.

1. Stock Lock
3. Bolt Handle
4.
2. Buffer Group
5.

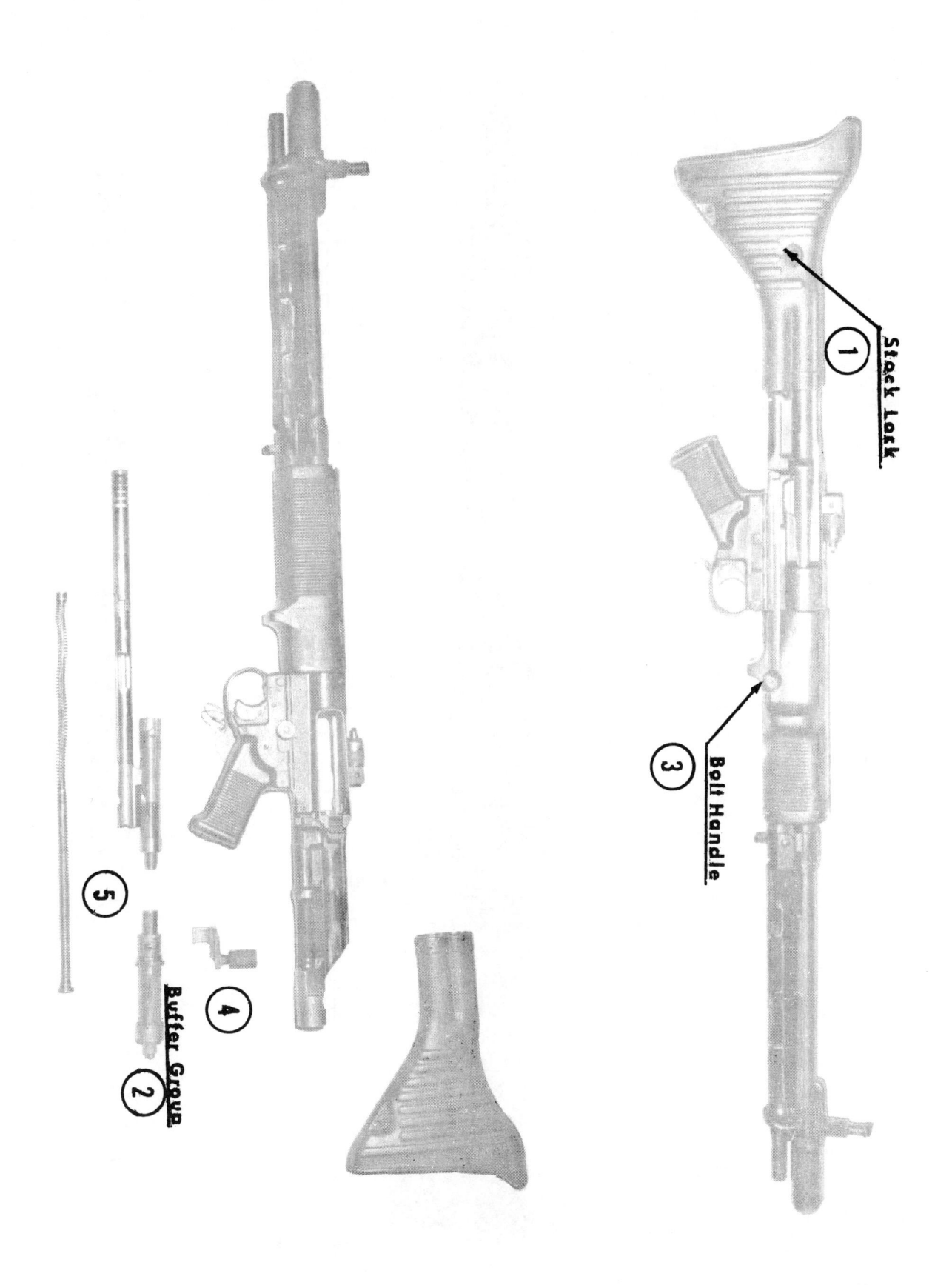

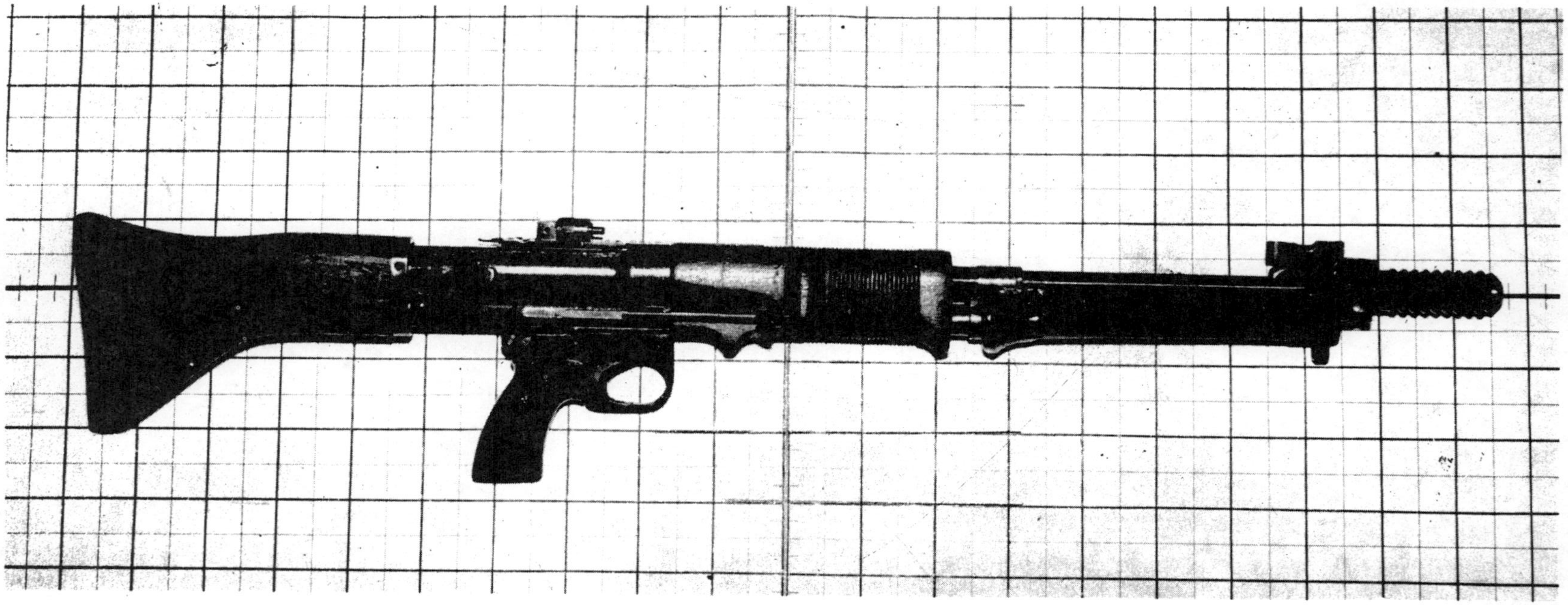

GERMANY   7.92-MM, FG-42 (WOOD STOCK)

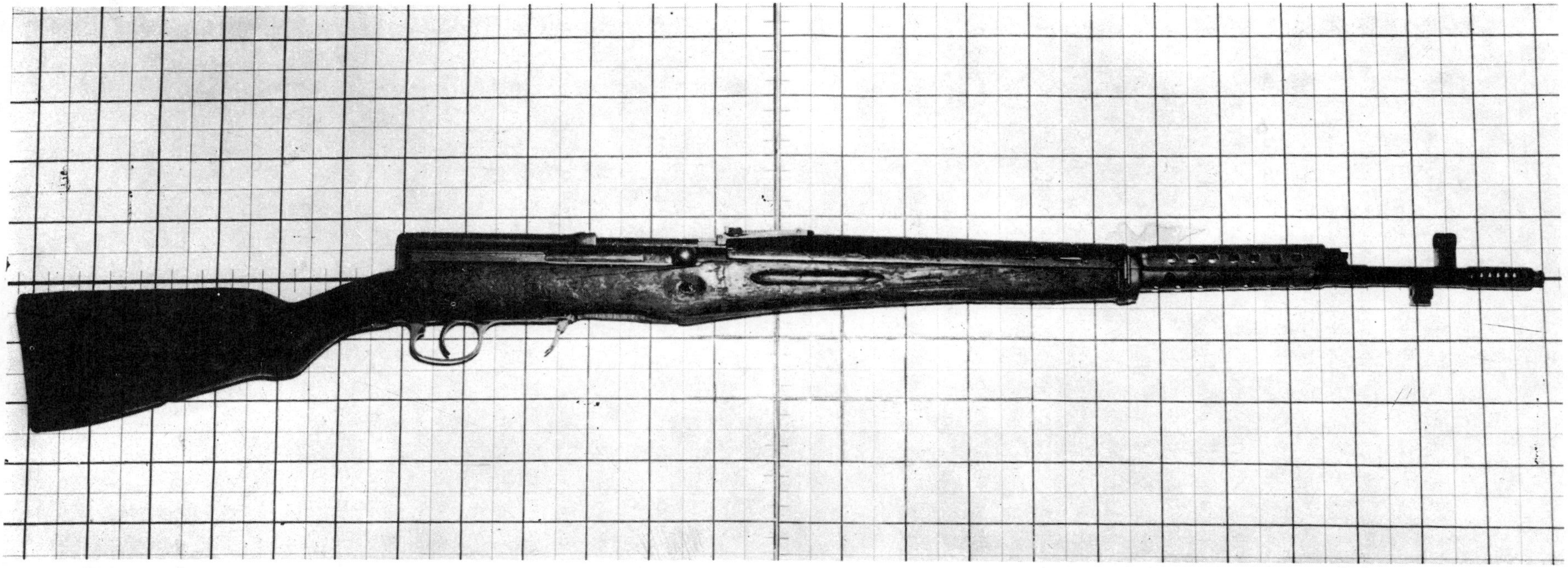

RUSSIA 7.62-MM, MODEL 1940

RIFLE   U.S.S.R.

7.62-mm MODEL 1940 (SVT) (TOKAREV)

The Tokarev Model 1940 (SVT) Semi-automatic Rifle is a gas-operated, magazine fed weapon which was the last of a series of gas operated automatic and semi-automatic rifles produced by the Soviets prior to WWII. The SVT model of the Tokarev was capable of semi-automatic fire only while the AVT model incorporated a modified safety lever, which when pushed to the right, set the piece for semi-auto (SVT model only), and when pushed to the left, set the piece on full-auto. The Tokarev series of rifles, including the M1938SVT, as well as an earlier rifle designed by S. G. Seminor (the M1936AVS) are all distinguished by their flimsyness and difficulty of maintenance. None of these weapons are standard in the Soviet Army, being replaced by the SKS Carbine and the AK Assault Rifle, though they may be found in many countries friendly to the Soviet Bloc. The action is locked by the bolt carrier forcing the rear of the bolt down into locking recesses in the receiver. The gas piston operates on the tappet principle; mounted above the barrel, it delivers a sharp blow to the face of the bolt carrier to unlock the action. This tappet piston system was a major weak point in the design of the weapon since any manhandling of the piece which caused it to damage the upper handguard also damaged this piston causing the piece to malfunction.

FUNCTIONING

The trigger and sear mechanism of the M1940 SVT rifle is relatively simple while the gas piston and related components are quite complex, for this type weapon. With a loaded magazine in place, the bolt handle is drawn to the rear, drawing with it the bolt carrier which contains the bolt and striker mechanism. When the bolt handle is released the carrier and bolt move forward under impulse of the compressed recoil spring, a round is stripped from the magazine and chambered. The bolt stops against the rear face of the barrel while the carrier continues forward for another ¼ inch camming the rear of the bolt down so that locking lugs on the bolt are positioned behind a shoulder in the receiver. The hammer is held in the cocked position by the sear. When the trigger is pulled the sear releases the hammer which pivots forward to strike the firing pin causing it to strike the primer. Gas is tapped from the barrel into a gas cylinder, where it strikes the face of a short gas piston driving it to the rear. The gas piston, connected to a tappet piston, transmits this rearward movement to the tappet piston which in turn forces an operating rod rearward. The operating rod moving in a tunnel beneath the rear sight base transmits this movement as a sharp blow to the forward end of the bolt carrier, starting the carrier to the rear. After ¼ inch of travel the bolt carrier cams the rear of the bolt out of the locking shoulder in the receiver and the bolt and carrier continue to the rear to compress the recoil spring and forcing the hammer back to be held to the rearby the sear. A buffer spring absorbs some of this final rearward movement of the bolt and carrier. The operating rod moves to its forward position under impulse of the operating rod spring. Pulling the trigger will fire the weapon again. The trigger must be pulled for each shot since this is a semi-automatic weapon.

CHARACTERISTIC DATA

Caliber . . . . .7.62-mm (M1908 ctdge)
Operation . . . . .Gas
Type of Fire . . . . semi-auto only
Rate of Fire . . . . 30 rpm
Type of Feed . . . . .Box - 10 rd cap
Weight, empty . . . . 8.2 lbs
Overall length . . . . 48.1 in
Effective range . . . . 540 meters

FIELD STRIP PROCEDURE

STEP   ACTION

1. Turn the Thumb Latch at the rear of the Receiver to the left, push in on the Trigger Group Lock, this will allow the Trigger Group to be removed if necessary.
2. Push the Receiver Cover forward until the Buffer Spring Guide can be pushed down and disengaged from the Receiver Cover.
3. Remove the Buffer Spring and Guide from the rear of the Receiver.
4. Remove the Receiver Cover and the Recoil Spring and guide.
5. Slide the Bolt Carrier and Bolt to the rear, lift up on the Bolt Handle and continue to draw the assembly to the rear until the Carrier and Bolt can be lifted out of the Receiver.
6. Push in on the Front Band Lock and remove the Front Band.
7. Lift off the metal and wooden Handguards.
8. Draw the Tappet Piston to the rear until the front end clears the Gas Piston and then remove the Tappet Piston, forward away from the Operating Rod.
9. Remove the Gas Piston.
10. Remove the Operating Rod and Operating Rod Spring from the tunnel beneath the Rear Sight.

ASSEMBLY PROCEDURE

Assemble in the reverse order. Assemble the Operating Rod and Spring into the tunnel beneath the Rear Sight, slide the Gas Piston over the Gas Cylinder, place the Tappet Piston into position, slide back and mate with the Gas Piston. Assemble the two Handguards and the Front Band. Assemble the Bolt to the Carrier and slide onto the Receiver until the guide grooves line up and the assembly can be attached to the Receiver. Slide the Recoil Spring and Guide into the rear of the Carrier. Assemble the Buffer Spring and Guide to the Recoil Spring Guide and lock into the rear of the Receiver. Assemble the Receiver Cover to the Receiver.

LOADING AND FIRING

To load: Insert a loaded Magazine. Push the Safety Lever located in the Trigger Guard forward. Draw the Bolt Handle to the rear and release it. The Bolt will move forward and chamber a round.

To fire: Push the Safety Lever to the right. Pull the Trigger. The weapon will fire. This is a semi-automatic weapon and the Trigger must be pulled for each shot fired.

106

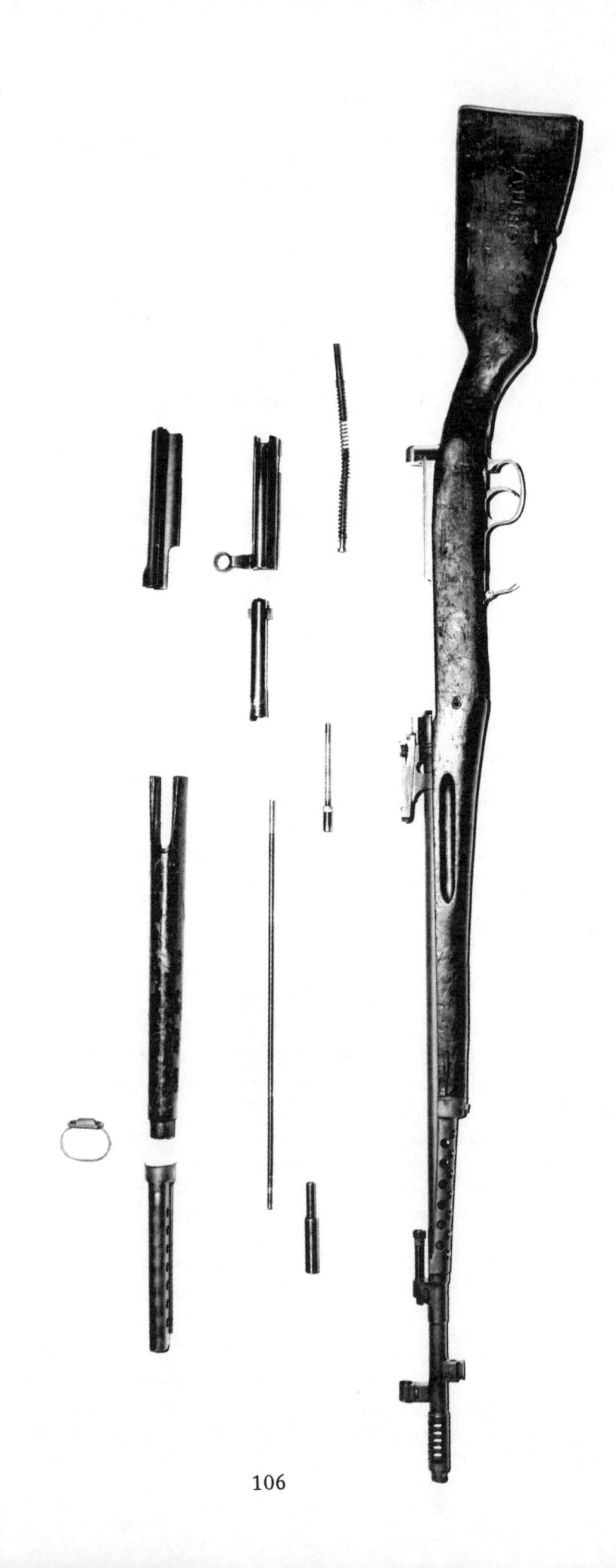

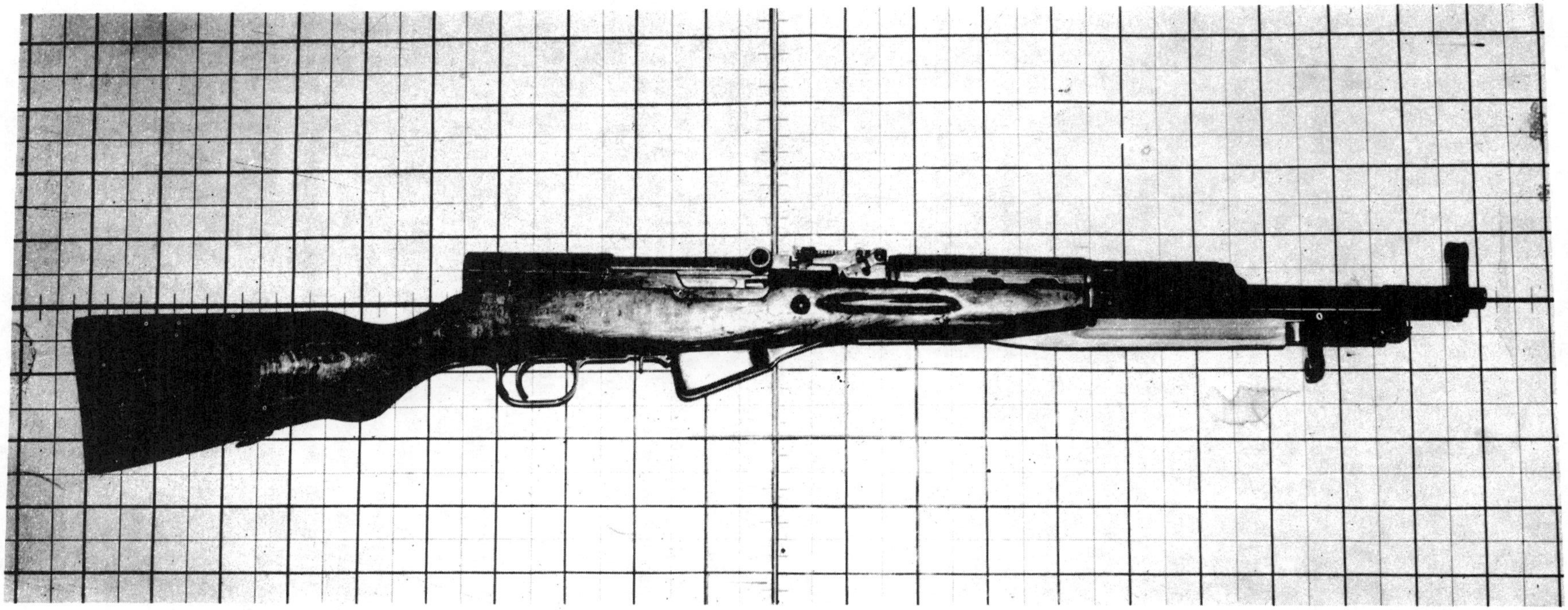

RUSSIA   7.62-MM M43, SKS

CARBINE U.S.S.R.

7.62-MM CARBINE (SKS)

The Soviet 7.62-mm Carbine Model SKS, is a limited standard infantry weapon, which has been replaced in the Soviet Army by the AK-47 Assault Rifle. It is a gas-operated weapon chambered for the Model 43 intermediate cartridge. Although classified as a carbine by the Soviets, it qualifies as a rifle by U.S. standards. The present production model is fitted with a permanently attached folding knife-type bayonet. The SKS is a relatively simple, well-constructed weapon, having two unusual features. First, the magazine is not detachable. When the magazine latch is moved to the rear, the magazine pivots down toward the front through an angle of approximately 30 degrees so that the cartridges can be removed without working them through the chamber. Second, the folding bayonet is permanently attached to the rifle by a large rivet. The rear sight is graduated from 100 to 1,000 meters in 100 meter increments. There is a battle sight elevation setting for 350 meters on the sight leaf. This weapon is manufactured by the CHICOM as the Type 56.

FUNCTIONING

This is a gas-operated, semi-automatic weapon. With the magazine loaded, a round is chambered by drawing the bolt handle to the rear and releasing it. When the trigger is pulled, the trigger arm is pushed forward and pushes the sear forward out of engagement with the hammer. The hammer rotates under the impulse of the hammer spring and strikes the firing pin. As the hammer rotates, the hammer heel lowers the forward end of the disconnector and the forward end of the trigger arm. The trigger arm is disengaged from the sear and the sear returns to the rear position. The firing pin strikes the primer. After the bullet passes the gas port in the barrel, the gases, entering the gas cylinder, exert pressure on the piston and the bolt carrier is moved to the rear by the piston rod. The bolt carrier moving to the rear raises the rear of the bolt which disengages the bolt locking surface from the receiver lug, and brings the bolt to the rear. Extraction and ejection of the case takes place at this time. The rearward movement of the bolt cocks the hammer, and the sear under the action of the sear spring is positioned to engage the hammer. The bolt having reached its rearmost position, compresses the recoil spring and the piston and piston rod return to the forward position under the action of the piston rod spring. The bolt moves forward, the bolt carrier lowers the rear of the bolt as it approaches the breech, and the bolt locking surface is positioned in front of the receiver locking lug. The bolt, in lowering, has depressed the protruding front end of the disconnector. The hammer is thus disengaged from the disconnector and is held in the cocked position by the sear. The bolt, in completing its forward movement, strips a round from the magazine and chambers it. The trigger must be released before it can be pulled to fire the next round.

CHARACTERISTIC DATA

Caliber .... 7.62-mm (M43 ctdg)
Operation .... Gas
Type of Fire .... Semi-auto only
Rate of Fire .... 30 rpm
Type of Feed .... Fixed box - 10 rd cap
Weight, empty .... 8.2 lbs
Overall length .... 40.16 in
Effective range .... 470 meters
Muzzle velocity .... 2,411 fps

FIELD STRIP PROCEDURE

STEP   ACTION

1. With the weapon empty and the Magazine unloaded, swing the Safety down to "Off."
2. Rotate the Cover Retaining Pin upward as far as it will go.
3. Push in slightly on the Receiver Cover and pull the Cover Retaining Pin to the right as far as it will go. Remove the Cover from the Receiver.
4. Remove the Recoil Spring Assembly from the Bolt Carrier.
5. Pull back on the Bolt Handle, sliding the Bolt Carrier and Bolt to the rear.
6. Lift the assembled Bolt Carrier and Bolt from the Receiver and remove the Bolt from the Bolt Carrier.

ASSEMBLY PROCEDURE

Proceed in the reverse order. Assemble Bolt to Bolt Carrier, place in Receiver, and slide forward. Assemble Recoil Spring Assembly into rear of Bolt Carrier. Place Receiver Cover onto Receiver, push forward slightly and push Cover Retaining Pin through the Receiver to the left. Turn the Receiver Cover Pin down.

LOADING AND FIRING

To load: Push the Safety Lever up. Pull back on Bolt Handle; Bolt and Bolt Carrier will be held to the rear by the Bolt-hold-open device. Place one end of the ten-round charger into the charger guide, which is machined into the top forward edge of the Bolt Carrier. Push down on the cartridges until all the cartridges are loaded into the Magazine. Remove the empty charger. Pull back slightly on the Bolt Handle and release it. Bolt and Bolt Carrier will now move forward and chamber a round.

To fire: Push Safety to "Off." Pull the Trigger, weapon will fire for each pull of the Trigger until the Magazine is empty.

4
3
6

Cover Retaining Pin
2
1
Safety
5
Bolt Handle

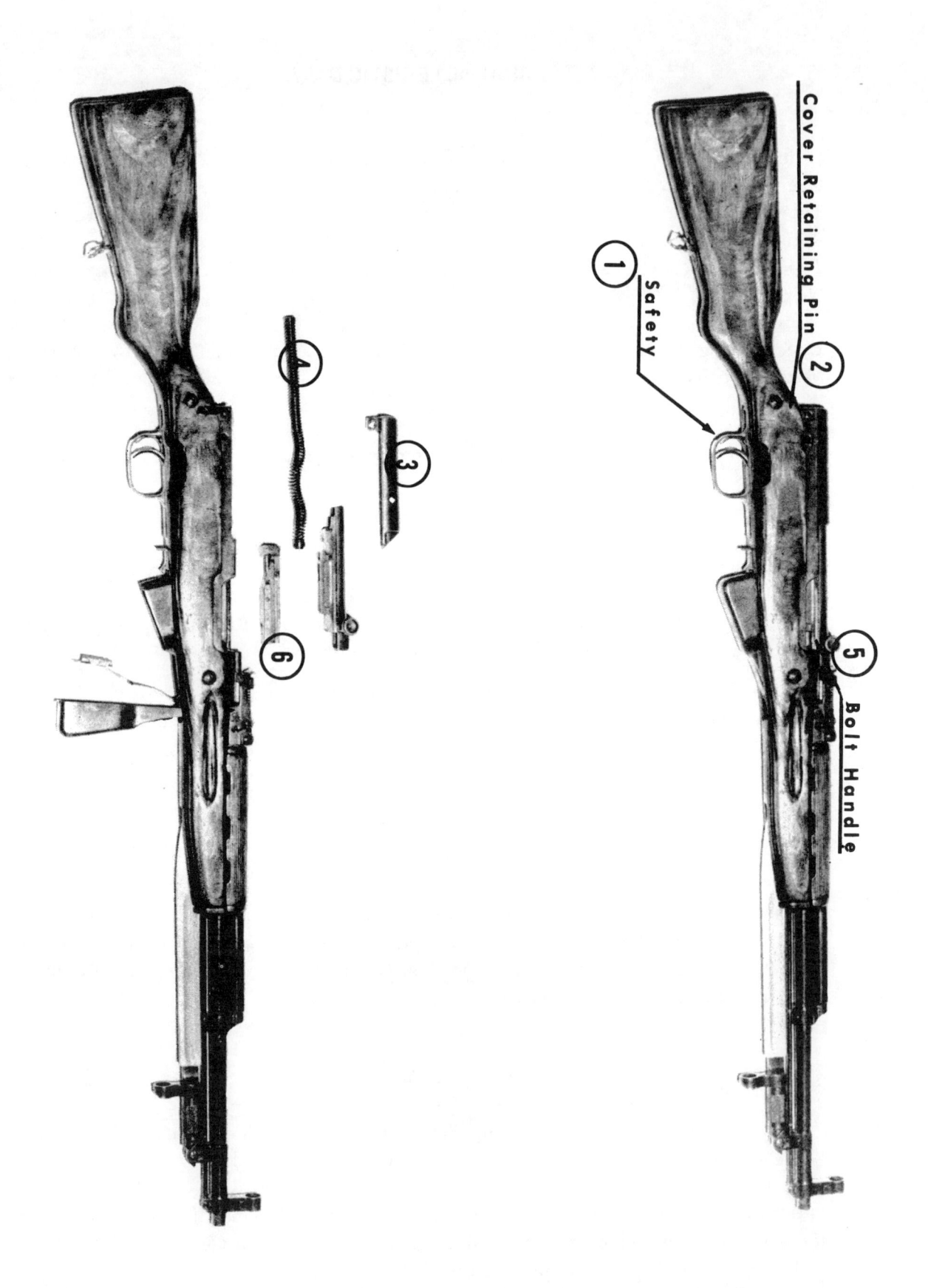

RUSSIA 7.62-MM M43, AK

RIFLE   U.S.S.R.

7.62-mm AK (KALASHNIKOV)

The Soviet 7.62-mm AK Assault Rifle is a gas-operated, selective fire weapon, which is chambered for the Soviet M1943 cartridge. Classed as an assault rifle rather than a submachinegun, it fires a rifle-type intermediate round. It is much more accurate than true submachineguns such as the Sten, Uzi, U. S. M3A1, MAT-49, etc., which fire pistol ammunition. This is an extremely well made weapon, being constructed almost completely of machined components rather than stampings and is produced in two versions, one with a wooden stock, the other with a folding metal stock. A modification of this weapon, which incorporates a longer barrel, bipod, and drum type magazine into its design is replacing the RPD light machinegun. The barrel on all the AK models and modifications is chrome plated and locking is accomplished by a rotating bolt. The Chinese Communist production model of this weapon is designated the Type 56.

FUNCTIONING

The AK Assault Rifle is a magazine fed weapon, which fires from a closed bolt position utilizing a rotating bolt locking system. The safety/select lever is located on the right side of the receiver above the trigger guard. With this lever in its uppermost position the weapon is on "SAFE;" with the lever halfway down, the weapon is set for semi-automatic fire. With a loaded magazine in place, the bolt handle is drawn to the rear drawing the bolt carrier and piston with the attached bolt to the rear, overriding and cocking the hammer and compressing the recoil spring. When the bolt handle is released, the bolt carrier and bolt move forward, the face of the bolt strips a round from the magazine and chambers it. The face of the bolt strikes the rear face of the barrel and its forward movement is stopped, the bolt carrier continues forward and cam surfaces in the bolt carrier acting on lugs on the bolt, rotate the bolt to the right, locking lugs on the head of the bolt engage locking recesses in the receiver and the hammer is ready to be released. If the select lever is set for semi-automatic fire when the trigger is pulled, the semi-automatic sear and disconnector pivot, the hammer is released striking the firing pin which in turn strikes the primer. Gas is tapped from the barrel into the gas cylinder to impinge against the piston. The piston and bolt carrier move to the rear, the cams in the carrier rotate the bolt to unlocked position and the carrier and bolt continue to the rear pivoting the hammer rearward where it is engaged by the disconnector and held to the rear. The trigger must be pulled for each shot. If set for full-automatic, a full-automatic disconnector on the bolt carrier strikes the full-automatic sear, rotating it to release the hammer and the hammer pivots forward to strike the firing pin. The firing cycle continues until the trigger is released or the magazine is empty. There is no bolt hold-open device on this weapon, when the magazine is empty the bolt will be in the closed position.

CHARACTERISTIC DATA

Caliber . . . . .7.62-mm (M43 ctdge)
Operation . . . . .Gas
Type of Fire . . . . Full and semi-auto
Rate of Fire . . . . 600 rpm (Practical 225)
Type of Feed . . . . .Box - 30 rd cap
Weight, empty . . . . 10.6 lbs
Overall length . . . . 34.2 in
Effective range . . . . 470 meters
Muzzle velocity . . . . 2,342 fps

FIELD STRIP PROCEDURE

STEP   ACTION

1. Push in on the Recoil Spring Guide which protrudes from the rear of the Receiver.
1a. At the same time the Recoil Spring Guide is pushed in raise up on the Receiver Cover and remove it from the Receiver.
2. Push the Recoil Spring Guide in as far as it will go and lift it up and out of the Receiver with the Recoil Spring.
3. Slide the Bolt Carrier, Bolt and Piston rearward until they can be lifted up and out of the Receiver.
4. Turn the Bolt head until the lugs on the Bolt align with the cam grooves in the Carrier, slide the Bolt rearward until it disengages and then slide it forward and out of the Bolt Carrier.
5. Pivot the Handguard Lock up.
6. Disengage the Handguard from the Receiver and lift it up and off of the Barrel.

ASSEMBLY PROCEDURE

Assemble in the reverse order. Slide Handguard into position and pivot the Handguard Lock down to engage. Assemble the Bolt to the Bolt Carrier and slide the assembled Bolt and Carrier into the Receiver. Slide the Recoil Spring and Recoil Spring Guide into the rear of the Bolt Carrier, push forward until the rear of the Guide clears the rear of the Receiver, and push down to engage the rear of the Receiver. Slide the Receiver Cover into place, push in on the Recoil Spring Guide and push the Receiver Cover down to lock.

LOADING AND FIRING

To load: Insert a loaded Magazine. Push Safety Lever on right side of Receiver up to "SAFE." Draw the Bolt Handle to the rear and release it. The Bolt will move forward and chamber a round.

To fire: Push Safety Lever to type of fire desired. Pull the Trigger. The weapon will fire. If the Select Lever is set all the way down the weapon will fire semi-automatic and the Trigger must be pulled for each shot. If the Select Lever is set in the mid-position the weapon will fire full-automatic fire and will continue to fire until the Trigger is released or the Magazine is empty.

1. Recoil Spring Guide
1a.
2.
3.
4.
5. Handguard Lock
6.

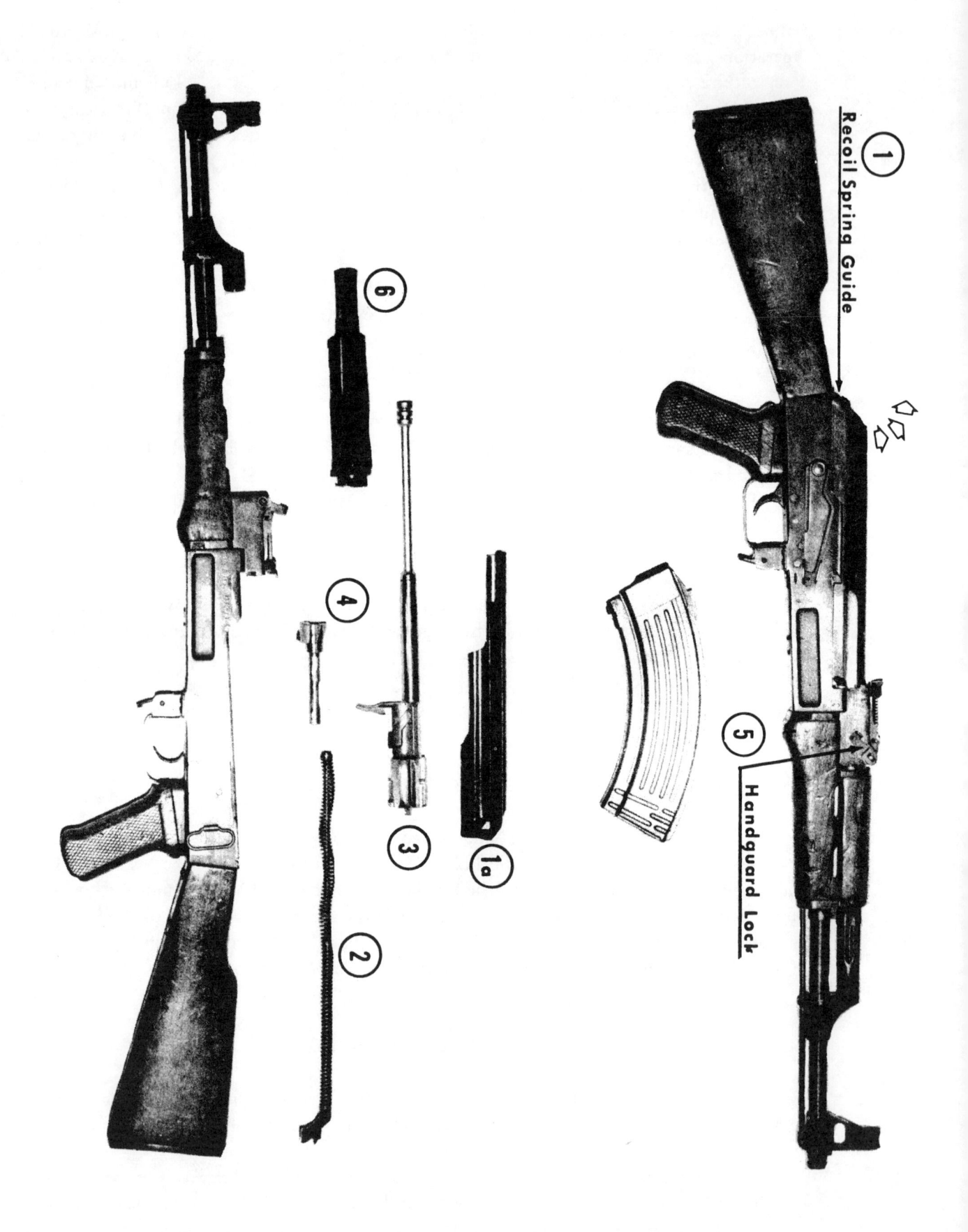

114

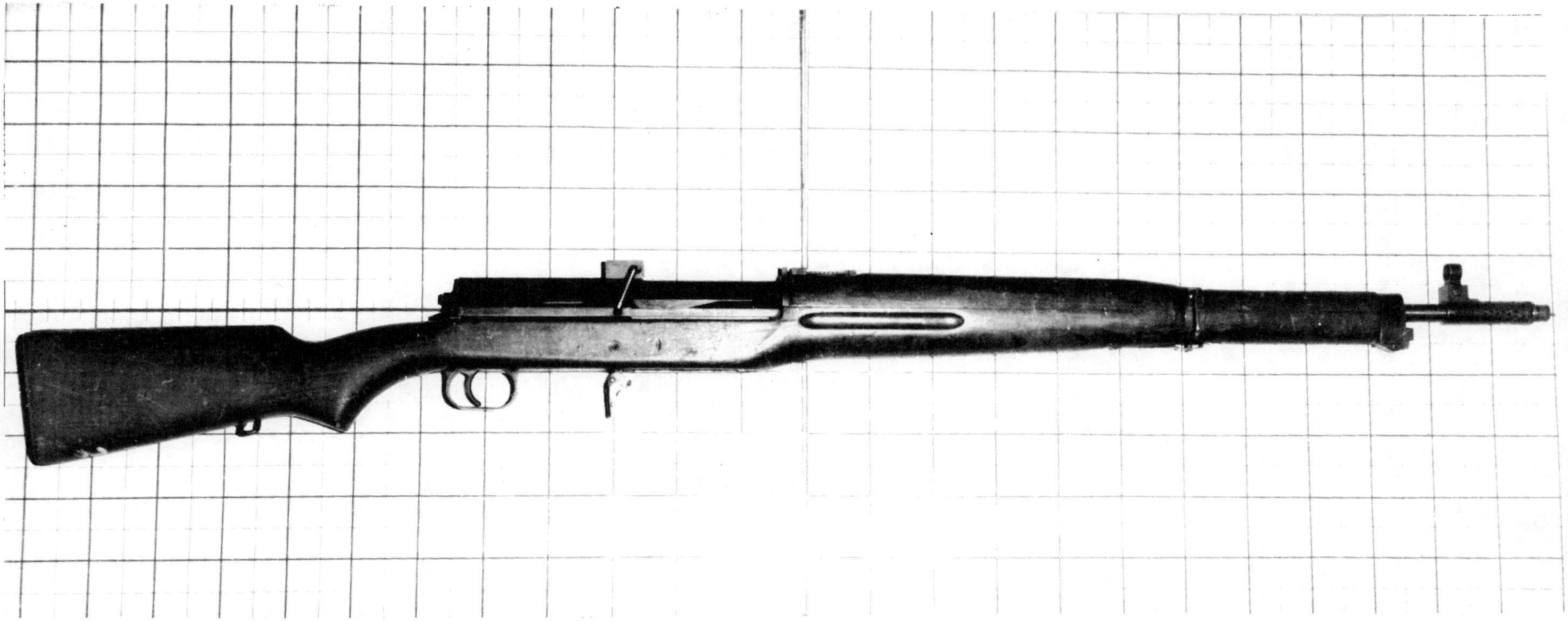

SWEDEN 6.5-MM, AG42B

RIFLE   SWEDEN

6.5-mm AG42B (LJUNGMAN)

The 6.5-mm Ljungman Rifle is a gas-operated, magazine fed rifle which utilizes a direct thrust gas system similar to the French MAS-49 Rifle. This rifle, designed by the Swedish engineer Ljungman, is also produced by the Madsen plant in Denmark as well as an Egyptian arms production firm where it is known as the "Hakim." These weapons differ in only minor points; the Swedish version has the top of the barrel slotted at the muzzle to act as a compensator; the Egyptian version (illustrated) has a compensator/flash suppressor attached to the muzzle; the Madsen model utilized a ventilated upper handguard. The Madsen model also modified the gas system by winding the gas tube around the barrel in order to (theoretically) produce a delay in opening the bolt. The Egyptian version uses a straight gas tube similar to the AG42B model since the Madsen design was not too successful. Madsen produced the weapon in a number of calibers, the Egyptian "Hakim" model was chambered for the 7.92-mm round.

FUNCTIONING

With a loaded magazine inserted in the magazine well, the receiver cover is grasped by the diagonal grooves on both sides of the cover, the cover is pushed forward to engage the bolt carrier, then drawn to the rear and released. The cover must be brought fully to the rear so that the bolt carrier latch is released by striking the back plate to unlock the carrier from the cover, allowing the carrier and bolt to move forward. The bolt strips a round from the magazine and chambers it. The carrier continues forward for a short distance, camming surfaces inside the carrier forcing the rear of the bolt down in front of a shelf in the receiver. The hammer which has been forced to pivot rearward when the bolt overrides it, is engaged by the sear and held in the cocked position. The face of the carrier has a short tubular extension on it which encloses the rear face of the gas tube when the carrier is fully forward. When the trigger is pulled, the sear releases the hammer and the primer is struck by the firing pin. Gas is tapped from the barrel into a gas cylinder and then directly into the gas tube. The gas in this tube impinges directly against the face of the carrier, starting the carrier rearward. After a short rearward movement (7/16 inch), the cams in the carrier raise the rear of the bolt and the bolt is carried to the rear by the carrier, compressing the recoil spring and then moving forward to chamber the next round. This is a semi-automatic weapon and the trigger must be pulled for each shot. The safety lever is located on the back plate and when pushed on "SAFE" the bolt is not released during the manual loading action, the carrier remaining to the rear with the cover. When the safety is turned to "FIRE," the cover must be drawn to the rear slightly to unlock the carrier, allowing it to move forward with the bolt to chamber a round.

CHARACTERISTIC DATA

Caliber 6.5-mm
Operation . . . . .Gas
Type of Fire . . . . .Semi-auto only
Rate of Fire . . . . 30 rpm
Type of Feed . . . . .Box - 10 rd cap
Weight, empty . . . . 10.3 lbs
Overall length . . . . 48.2 in
Effective range . . . . 580 meters

FIELD STRIP PROCEDURE

STEP   ACTION

1. Move Safety Lever between "SAFE" and "FIRE" position (vertical).
2. Slide Back Plate up and remove.
3. Move Cover rearward off of Receiver. Remove Recoil Spring and Guide.
4. Slide Carrier and Bolt to the rear, tilt to the left and lift Carrier and Bolt from Receiver.
5. Unscrew Upper Band screw and slide upper Band forward, slide Sling Swivel Band forward. Remove Upper Handguard.
6. Remove Trigger Housing screws and lift Receiver and Barrel Assembly from the Stock Assembly. Remove Trigger Housing from Stock Assembly.

NOTE: Steps 5 and 6 do not need to be performed for normal cleaning.

ASSEMBLY PROCEDURE

Assemble in the reverse order. Assemble Trigger Housing, Barrel, and Receiver to Stock Assembly and replace Trigger Housing screws. Assemble Upper Handguard, slide Sling Swivel Band and Upper Band back into place. Assemble Bolt to Carrier and slide into Receiver. Place Recoil Spring and Guide into rear of Carrier, and engage rear of Spring with Back Plate stud. Slide Cover onto Receiver from the rear, slide forward slightly, and assemble Back Plate to rear of Receiver. Move Safety Lever to "SAFE."

LOADING AND FIRING

To load: This weapon may be loaded by inserting a loaded Magazine into the Magazine Well or by loading an empty Magazine from the top of the Receiver by 5-round strip-clips. With a loaded Magazine in place, turn the Safety Lever to "SAFE," draw the Cover forward to engage the Carrier and then draw to the rear and release. The action will stay open.

To fire: Turn the Safety Lever to "FIRE," draw the Cover to the rear slightly, the Carrier will unlock from the Cover and move forward, the Bolt will strip a round from the Magazine and chamber it. Pull the Trigger. The weapon will fire. This weapon fires semi-automatic only and the Trigger must be pulled for each shot.

118

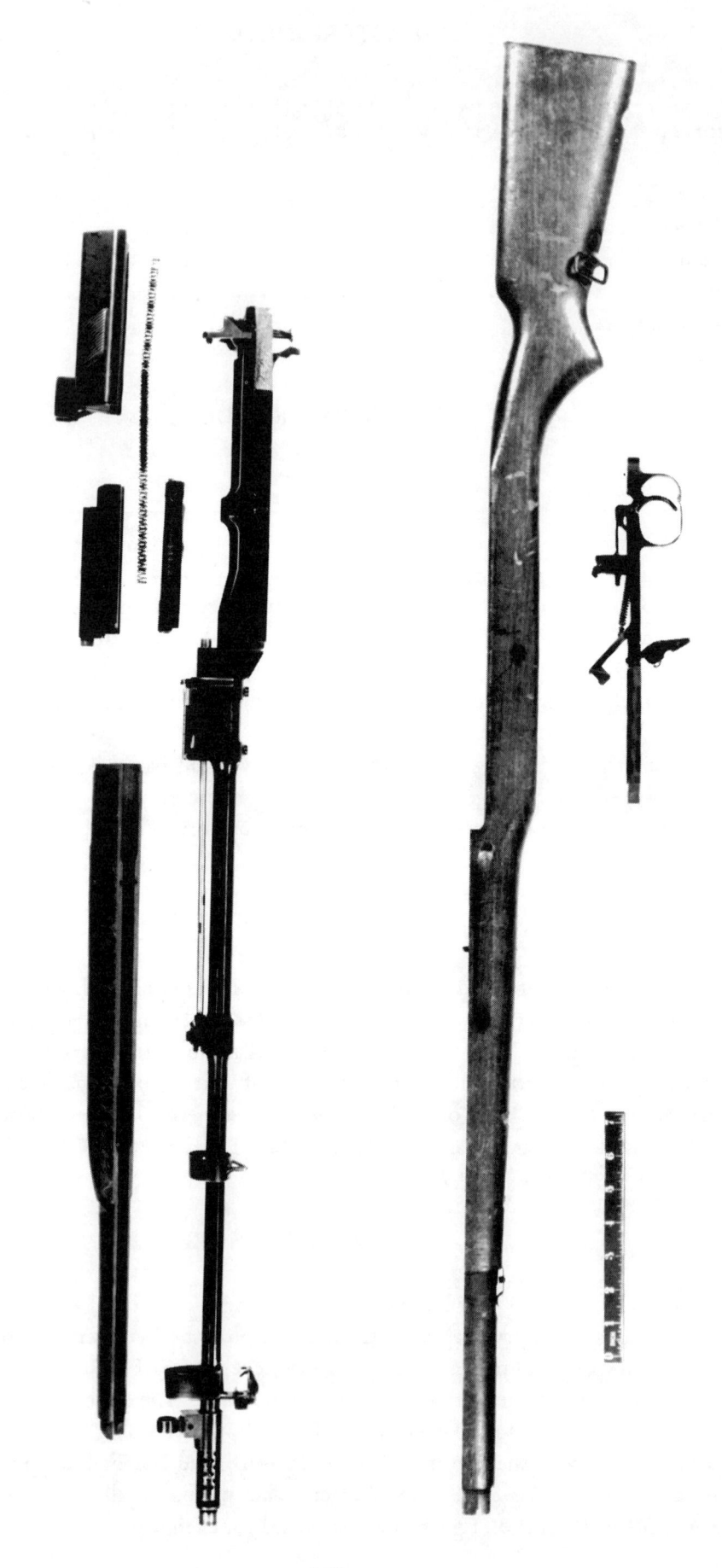

SUBMACHINEGUNS

SECTION III

There is no small arm in the world today which rose to such immediate fame during WWII, and is slated to be even more famous in the future, than the weapon designated as a submachinegun. In broad general terms a submachinegun may be described as a shoulder fired arm, air cooled, magazine-fed, chambered for pistol ammunition and capable of full-automatic fire. Because of the size of the ammunition used, most submachineguns are light, compact, easy to handle and simple to maintain. Almost all recently designed submachineguns (post 1950) weigh less than eight pounds, are capable of selective fire (full and semi-automatic), fire at a rate of 450 to 550 rounds per minute and are designed in such a manner that certain components may be folded or telescoped to decrease the overall length of the piece when required.

A submachinegun, because of the fact that it fires a pistol round, should not be confused with full-automatic firing pistols which are termed machine pistols. Such pistols, and there are many, were normally designed as conventional semi-automatic pistols. The change lever for converting to full-automatic fire and the detachable shoulder stock were usually added as modifications in the hopes of increasing tactical capability. (Usually a waste of time.) In Europe, weapons which fire pistol ammunition, have been, and in some countries still are, referred to as "machine pistols". In the United Kingdom, submachineguns were habitually referred to as "Machine carbines". Both are misnomers by factual definition. The U.K. has accepted this fact in regard to their "machine carbine" and many European arms manufacturers who have introduced new models of this type arm into the field since 1950 have dropped the term "machine pistol".

All modern submachineguns are distinguished by compactness, simplicity, ease of manufacture and minimal maintenance. Being chambered for relatively low powered ammunition there is no need for a complex bolt locking system. The round is small enough so that magazines containing as many as fifty rounds may be used. Recoil is light, eliminating a space wasting buffer system. Stress and strain on moving components is negligable, allowing for the use of metal and plastic stampings in construction. Manufacture can be accomplished with non-specialized tooling and maintenance can be carried out with a minimum of skill and equipment. Perhaps the most important point, one being viewed by every country in the world, is that the submachinegun is ideally suited to in-fighting, jungle warfare, street combat or any other shooting engagement which calls for movement, firepower and suprise.

The submachineguns covered in this handbook represent a very small fraction of hundreds of submachineguns which have been produced in usable quantities. Most of the successful systems are discussed including weapons which were manufactured by the millions as well as some pieces that could well reach the million mark in the near future. The reader may well encounter all the weapons in this handbook or copies or design derivations thereof--an understanding of the arms discussed in this section should lay the ground work for an understanding of all such pieces that may be encountered.

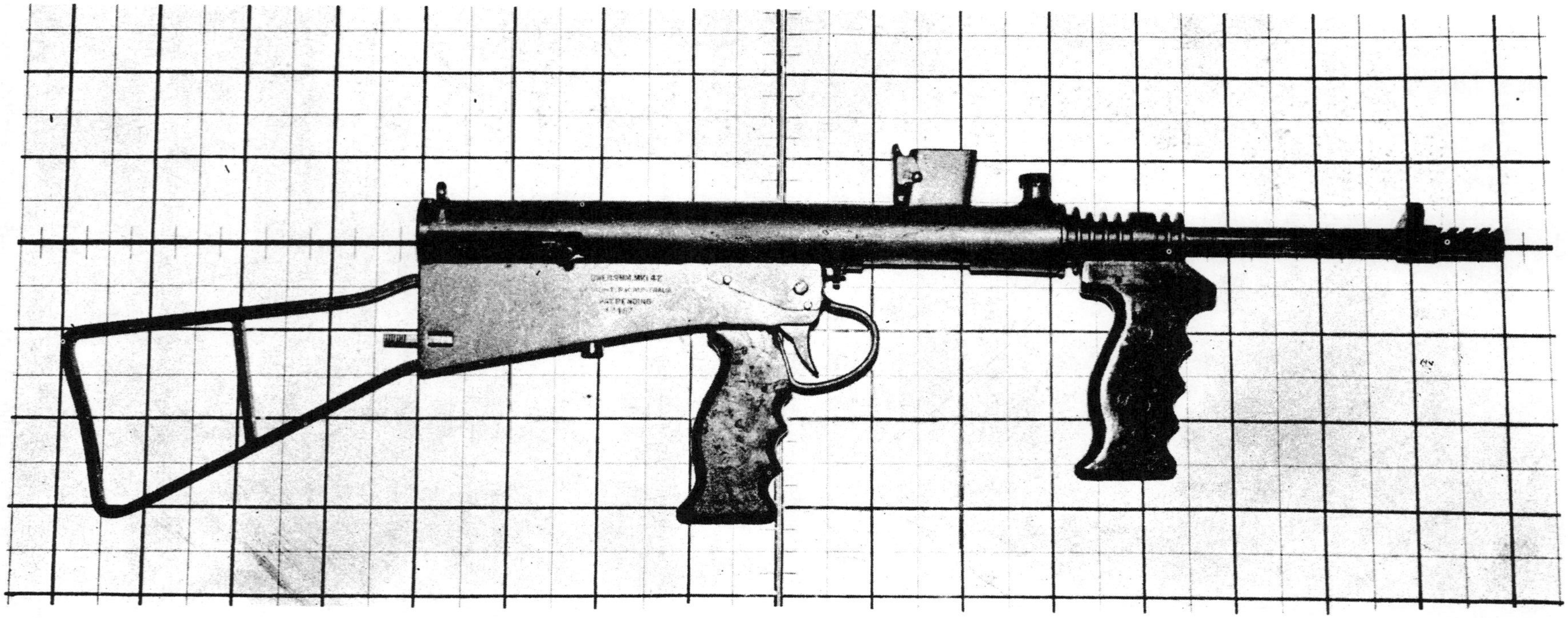

AUSTRALIA 9-MM, MARK 1/42

SUBMACHINEGUN   AUSTRALIA

9-mm SUBMACHINEGUN, OWEN

The 9-mm Australian Owen submachinegun is a straight blowback, magazine fed submachinegun which closely resembles the British Sten gun series of weapons. This machinegun incorporates a compensator at the muzzle, cooling fins near the breech end of the barrel, top magazine feed, and front and rear pistol grips. It has a quick-change barrel which is held in place by a simple spring-loaded plunger through the top of the receiver forward of the magazine well. Due to the top feed system, the front and rear sights are offset to the right. This is a cheap, reliable weapon which has been replaced by the Australian designed F1 (Aust) submachinegun. The Owen may be found with a wooden butt stock or as the two versions illustrated; closed trigger group housing and skeleton stock; open trigger group housing and solid metal stock. An unusual design feature of this weapon is the lack of an ejector in the receiver or bolt. The ejector is contained in the magazine. Because of this, only the Owen magazine can be used.

FUNCTIONING

This is an efficient, durable, simple-to-operate submachinegun. The bolt is rather heavy, the firing pin is a machined protrusion on the face of the bolt, the recoil spring is relatively light and the fire selection is activated by a simple lever which regulates the trigger position. With a loaded magazine in place, the bolt is drawn to the rear and held in place by the sear. When the trigger is pulled, the sear releases the bolt which moves forward under impulse of the compressed recoil spring, strips a round from the magazine, chambers it and fires it. The bolt moves to the rear under impulse of the gases generated in the chamber by the discharging cartridge, and is engaged by the sear if the select lever has been set for single shot fire. If the select lever is set for full-automatic, the sear is held down out of engagement position with the bolt and the bolt will move forward and the firing cycle will be repeated.

CHARACTERISTIC DATA

Caliber	9-mm
Operation	Blowback
Type of Fire	Full and semi-auto
Rate of Fire	600 rpm (Practical-125)
Type of Feed	Box - 32 rd cap
Weight, empty	9.7 lbs
Overall length	32.1 in
Effective range	270 meters

FIELD STRIP PROCEDURE

STEP   ACTION

1. Press down on Stock Catch and remove Stock.
2. Pull up on Barrel Lock and remove Barrel to the front.
3. Pull out on Bolt Handle Dismounting Plunger and disengage Handle from Bolt.
4. Tilt Receiver forward and remove Bolt and Recoil Spring from Receiver.

ASSEMBLY PROCEDURE

Assemble in the reverse order. Slide Bolt and Recoil Spring into Receiver. Engage Bolt Handle to Bolt. Pull up on Barrel Lock, slide Barrel into front of Receiver and release Lock. Attach Stock.

LOADING AND FIRING

To load: Turn Select Lever located on left side of Trigger Housing Group to "SAFE." Insert loaded Magazine in Magazine Housing. Pull Bolt Handle to the rear until Sear engages Bolt.

To fire: Turn Select Lever to type of fire desired. Pull the Trigger. If Select Lever is on "Single Shot" the Trigger must be pulled for each shot fired. If Select Lever is on "Rapid" or automatic fire, the weapon will continue to fire until the Trigger is released or the magazine is empty.

123

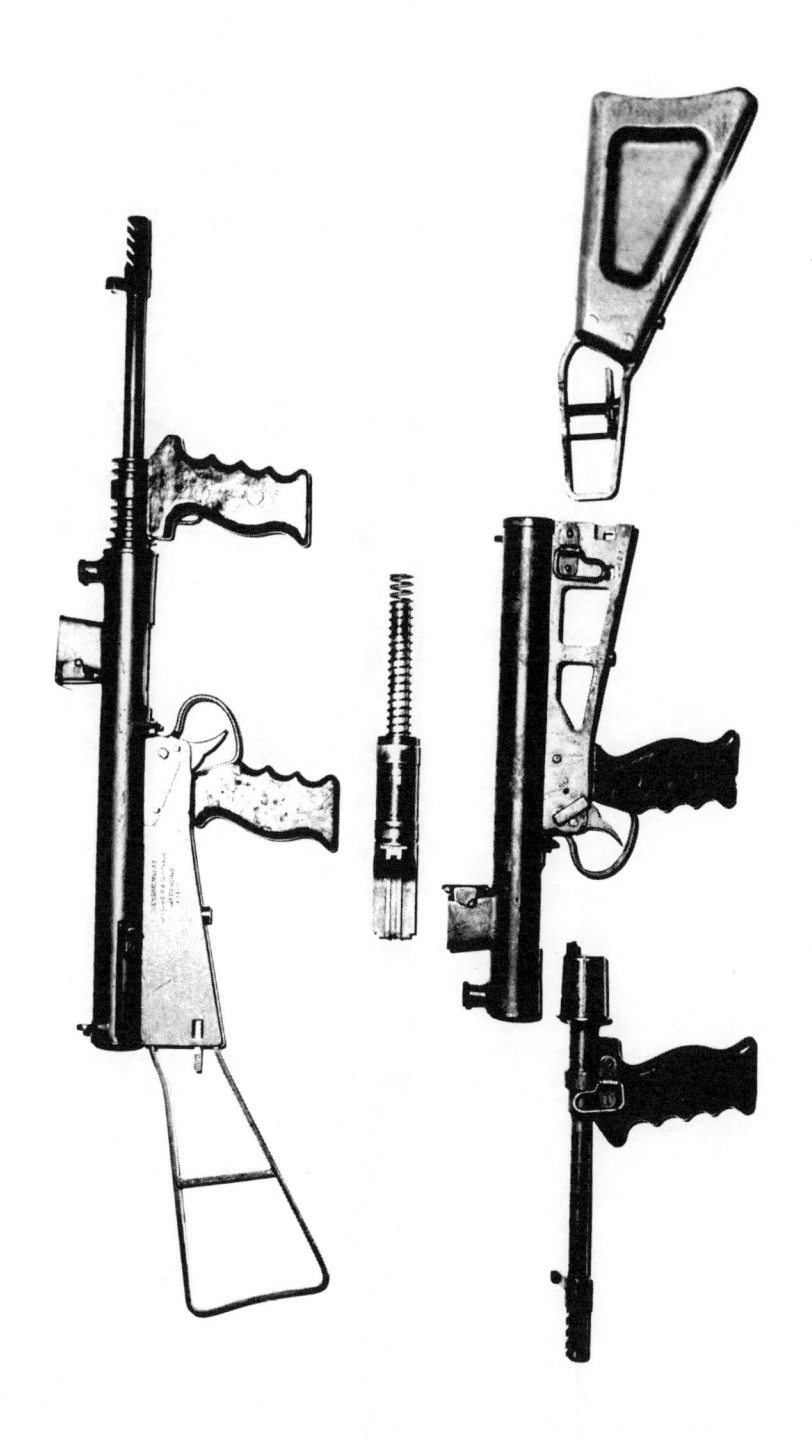

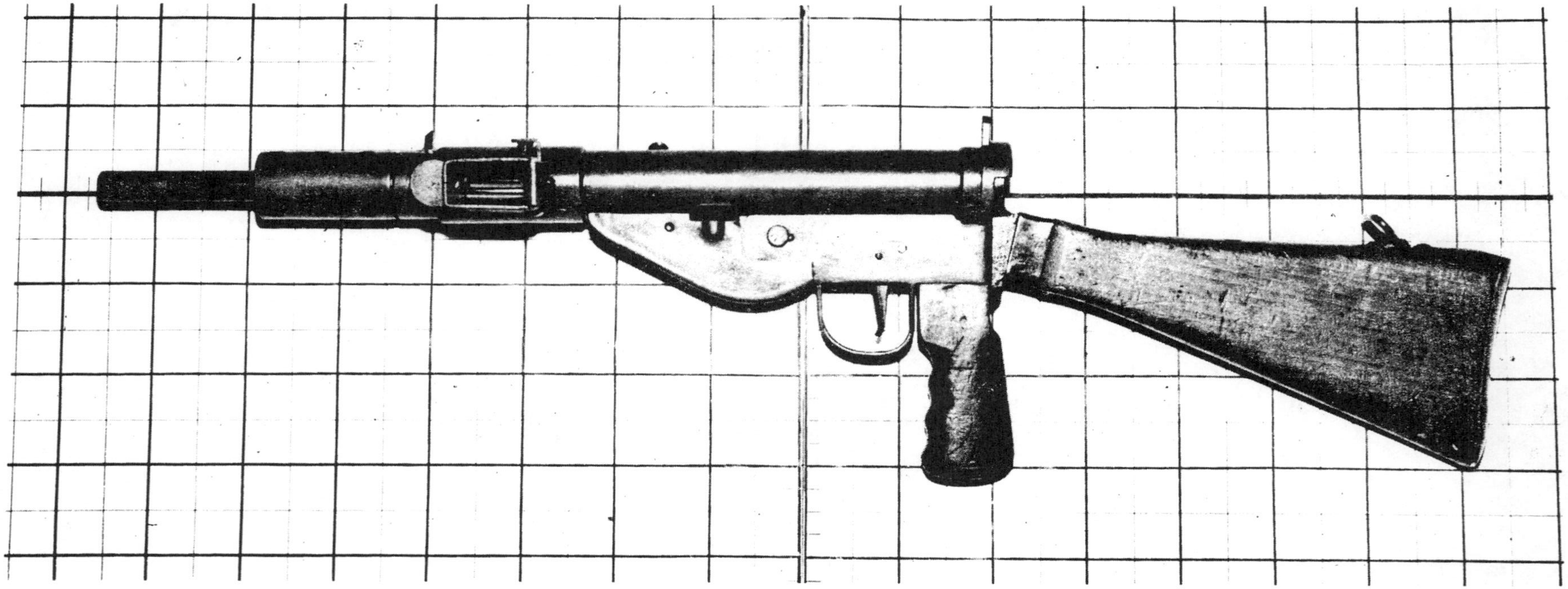

GREAT BRITAIN   9-MM, MARK V STEN

SUBMACHINEGUN   GREAT BRITAIN

9-mm MARK V (STEN)

The 9-mm Mark V STEN Submachinegun represents the final major modification to the STEN series of submachineguns. Introduced in 1944, it was first issued to British airborne units but was later issued to all units of the British Armed Forces. Various models of the Famous STEN gun were produced starting with the Mark I in June 1941. This weapon is noted for its simplicity of design, manufacture and maintenance. Hundreds of thousands of these STEN guns were manufactured not only by the allied nations of WWII, but by Germany and Nationalist China. Of the different Marks (Models) produced, almost all had interchangeable parts so that in many instances a model will be encountered that poses an identification problem. Stocks of one model may be found assembled to receivers of quite a different model, while barrels of the various models are quite often switched between models. The piece illustrated for instance, while basically the Mark V STEN, has a barrel from the Mark II model. Early models of the Mark V had wooden foregrips and some models had a trapdoor in the butt plate. Regardless of which model of the STEN gun is encountered it is in all respects an efficient, reliable and rugged weapon, which does the job for which it was designed so that it could be unlocked from its side-feeding position and rotated around to the bottom of the receiver so that the magazine housing sleeve effectively covered the ejection port to keep out dust and dirt. Over two million Mark II STEN guns were manufactured between 1942 and 1944.

FUNCTIONING

The STEN gun is a straight blowback weapon firing from an open bolt. The fire select button is a "push-through" button located above and forward of the trigger guard in the trigger group housing. The safety is a simple notch cut in the rear portion of the bolt handle retracting slot into which the bolt handle is engaged when the bolt is drawn to the rear. With a loaded magazine inserted, the bolt is drawn to the rear where it is engaged by the sear and held to the rear. Pulling the trigger releases the bolt and the bolt moves forward under impulse of the compressed recoil spring, strips a round from the magazine, chambers it and fires it. The bolt moves to the rear and if the fire select button is pushed to the right, the sear will engage the bolt and the trigger must be pulled for each shot. If the fire select button is pushed to the left the weapon will fire full-automatic and will continue to fire until the trigger is released or the magazine is empty.

NOTE: The Mark IIS is a modified version of the Mark II with a silencer attached. The Mark VI STEN gun is the Mark V STEN with a silencer attached. It is recommended that both of these weapons be fired semi-automatic only.

CHARACTERISTIC DATA

Caliber 9-mm
Operation .... Blowback
Type of Fire .... Full and semi-auto
Rate of Fire .... 600 rpm (Practical 125)
Type of Feed .... Box - 32 rd cap
Weight, empty .... 8.7 lbs
Overall length 30.2in
Effective range .... 150 meters

FIELD STRIP PROCEDURE

STEP   ACTION

1. Press in on the Recoil Spring Cap which protrudes from the Receiver Cap and slide the Stock Assembly down off the Receiver.
2. Press in on the Recoil Spring Cap and rotate the Cap until it disengages from the Receiver and remove the Receiver Cap, Recoil Spring Cap and Recoil Spring.
3. Draw the Bolt Handle to the rear to the Safety Notch in the Bolt Handle slot, turn the Handle to disengage it from the Bolt and slide the Bolt out the rear of the Receiver.
4. Unscrew the Barrel Retaining Sleeve and remove it and the Barrel from the Receiver.

ASSEMBLY PROCEDURE

Assemble in the reverse order. Slide the Barrel into the front of the Receiver and assemble the Barrel Retaining Sleeve over the Barrel and screw onto the Receiver. Slide the Bolt into the rear of the Receiver, attach the Bolt Handle to the Bolt and slide the Bolt forward. Assemble the Recoil Spring, Recoil Spring Cap and Receiver Cap into the rear of the Receiver and turn the Recoil Spring Cap to engage the Receiver. Slide the Stock Assembly partially onto the Receiver, push in on the Recoil Spring Cap and slide the Stock Assembly up the rest of the way.

LOADING AND FIRING

To load: Insert a loaded Magazine into the Magazine Housing and push it in until it locks into place. Push the Fire Select Button to the type of fire desired. Draw the Bolt to the rear and raise the Bolt Handle into the Safety Notch. NOTE: The Bolt can be locked in its forward position by pushing the bolt handle through the bolt to engage a hole in the opposite side of the receiver. To fire: Disengage the Bolt Handle from the Safety Notch. Pull the Trigger. The weapon will fire. If the Select Button is set for semi-automatic fire, "R" for Repetition, the Sear will engage the Bolt and the Trigger will have to be pulled for each shot. If the Select Button is set for full-automatic, "A" for Automatic, the weapon will continue to fire until the Trigger is released or the Magazine is empty.

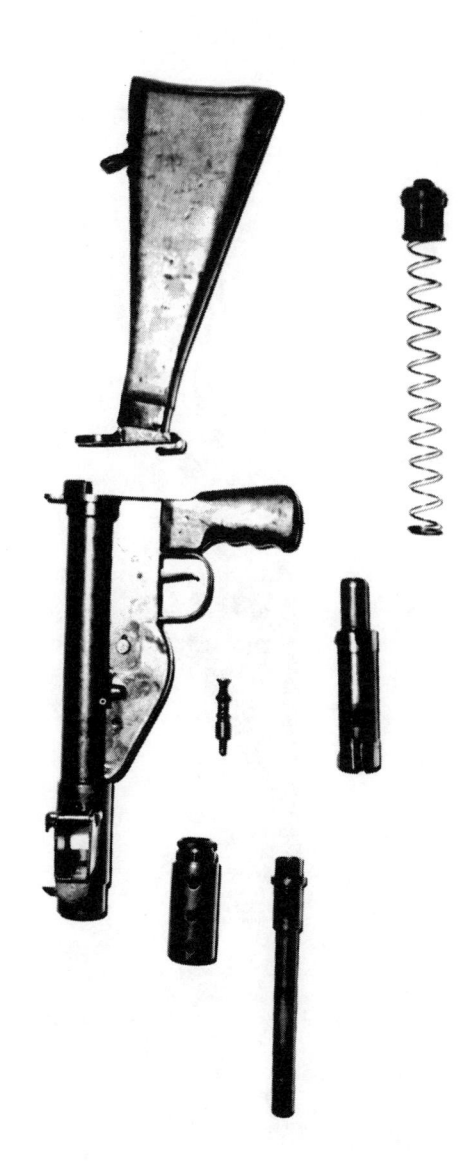

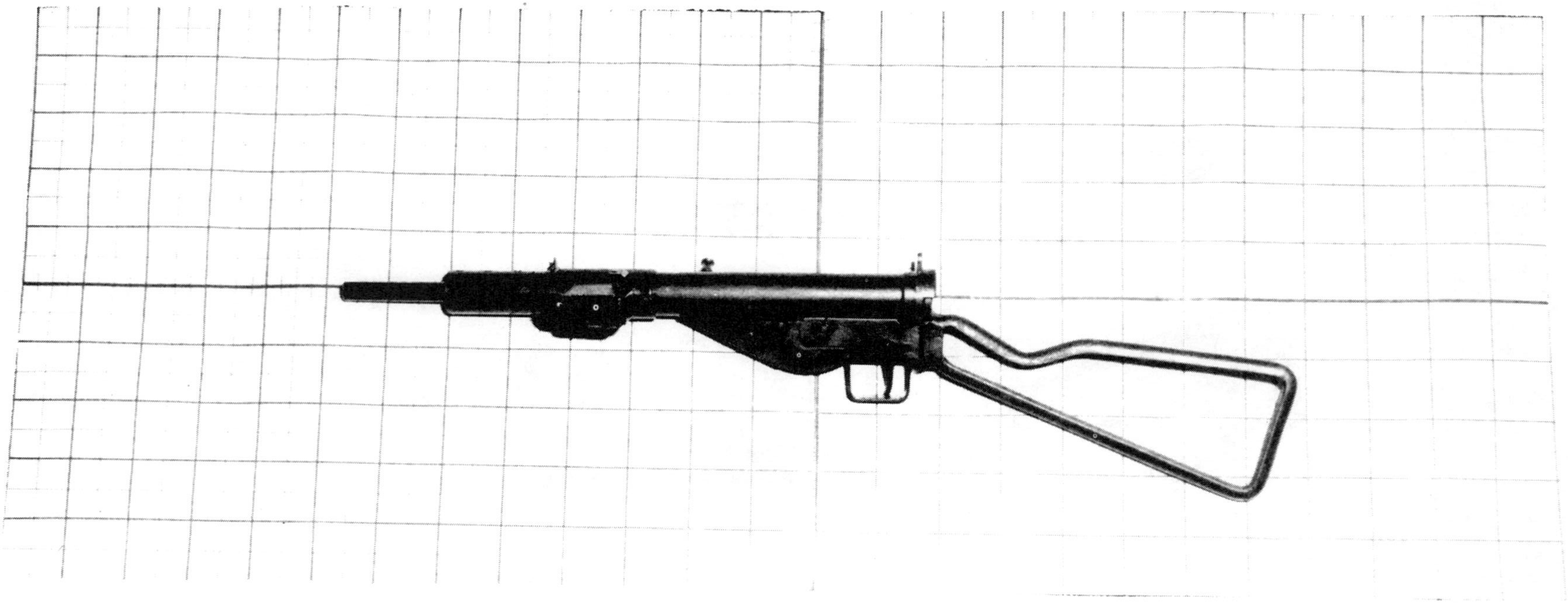

GREAT BRITAIN   9-MM, MK II STEN

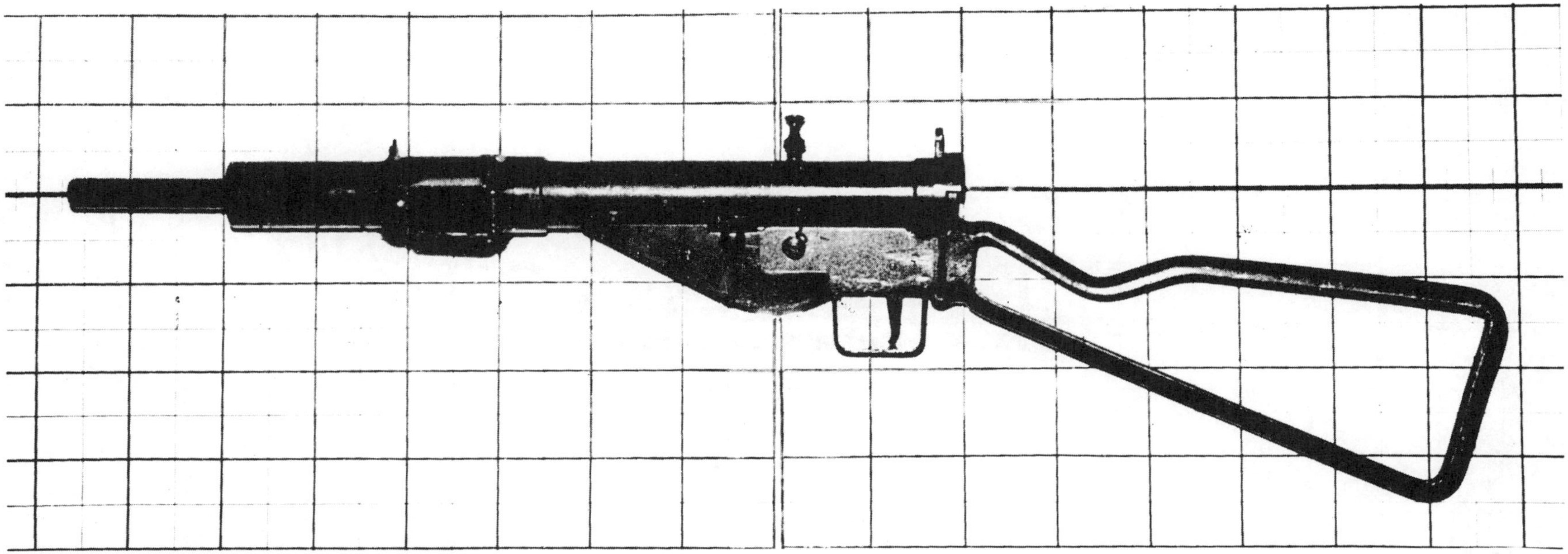

COMMUNIST CHINA 9-MM, COPY OF MK II STEN

CZECHOSLOVAKIA   7.62-MM, MODEL 24

SUBMACHINEGUN — CZECHOSLOVAKIA

7.62-mm MODEL 24

The Czechoslovakian Model 24 Submachinegun superseded the Czech Model 23 submachinegun being adopted in 1952 when the manufacture of the Model 23 ceased. This is an extremely compact, efficient weapon which utilizes the system where the bolt surround the barrel and the magazine is inserted into the pistol grip. The bolt surrounds the barrel when in the forward position for a distance of 6.2 inches. This enables the weapon to utilize a relatively long barrel (11.2 inches) and also places the chamber sufficiently far to the rear of the receiver to allow the magazine to be inserted into the pistol grip, rather than forward of the trigger guard, as is generally the case in submachineguns. This original design was produced in a wooden stock version as the Model 23 and a metal folding stock version as the Model 25. Both of these early models were chambered for the 9-mm Parabellum round. Designed in 1948 by Holek, more than 100,000 were manufactured by mid-1950. Production of these models ceased in 1952 when production of the models-24 and 26 began. These later models were identical to the earlier models with the exception of the caliber which was changed to the Soviet 7.62-mm pistol round, though loaded to velocities 20% greater than that of the Soviet round (approximating that of the U.S. .30 caliber carbine round). Other minor changes were made; the rear sight was redesigned; an additional sling loop was attached to the stock bracket; and the pistol grip redesigned to accomodate the 7.62-mm magazine. The Model 24 is the wooden stocked version while the Model 26 is the metal folding stock version. The Israeli Uzi submachinegun is very similar in design; utilizing a bolt which surrounds the barrel when forward and utilizing the pistol grip as a magazine housing.

FUNCTIONING

The Czech Model 24 Submachinegun is a straight blowback weapon which fires from an open bolt. The safety is located behind the trigger and locks the bolt in either the open or closed position. In the forward position, the bolt handle automatically engages a notch in the forward end of the bolt handle retracting slot to lock the bolt in the forward position. The type of fire, full or semi-automatic is controlled by pressure applied to the trigger. A half-pull of the trigger will deliver semi-automatic fire; a full pull on the trigger will result in full-automatic fire. With a loaded magazine inserted in the pistol grip, the bolt handle is drawn to the rear where the bolt is engaged by the sear. Pulling the trigger releases the bolt which moves forward, strips a round from the magazine, chambers it and fires it. The bolt moves to the rear compressing the recoil spring, if the trigger has been pulled only half-way, the sear will engage the bolt and hold it open. If the trigger has been pulled fully to the rear the sear remains out of engagement with the bolt and the firing cycle will be repeated until the trigger is released or the magazine is empty.

CHARACTERISTIC DATA

Caliber 7.62-mm
Operation .... Blowback
Type of Fire .... Full and semi-auto
Rate of Fire .... 600 rpm (Practical 175)
Type of Feed .... Box - 32 rd cap
Weight, empty .... 7.2 lbs
Overall length .... 26.9 in
Effective range .... 225 meters
Muzzle velocity ....1,850 fps

FIELD STRIP PROCEDURE

STEP   ACTION

1. Push in on the button in the center of the Receiver Cap, turn the Cap.
1a. Remove the Receiver Cap.
2. Draw the Bolt Handle to the rear and remove the Bolt with the attached Recoil Spring, Recoil Spring Guide, and Bolt Guide.
3. Using the face of the Bolt as a disassembly tool, unscrew the Barrel Locking Collar from the front of the Receiver.
4. Slide the Barrel forward out of the Receiver.

ASSEMBLY PROCEDURE

Assemble in the reverse order. Slide the Barrel into the front of the Receiver. Slide the Barrel Locking Collar over the Barrel and screw onto the front of the Receiver using the face of the Bolt to tighten it into place. Slide the Bolt Assembly into the rear of the Receiver. Screw the Receiver Cap onto the rear of the Receiver.

LOADING AND FIRING

To load: Draw the Bolt to the rear. Push the Safety Lever located behind the Trigger to the right to lock the Bolt to the rear. Place a loaded Magazine into the Pistol Grip.

To fire: Push the Safety Lever to the left. Pull the Trigger. The weapon will fire. If the Trigger is pulled half-way to the rear the weapon will fire semi-automatic and the Trigger must be pulled for each shot. If the Trigger is pulled fully to the rear the weapon will fire full-automatic and will continue to fire until the Trigger is released or the Magazine is empty.

NOTE: A Magazine loading device is built into the right side of the forearm. A strip clip of eight rounds is placed in the track of the loading device. The Magazine lips are aligned with the track and the Magazine is pushed forward. The ammunition is stripped from the strip clip into the Magazine. The strip clip is removed from the feeding track and a new one put into place and the process is repeated until the Magazine is loaded.

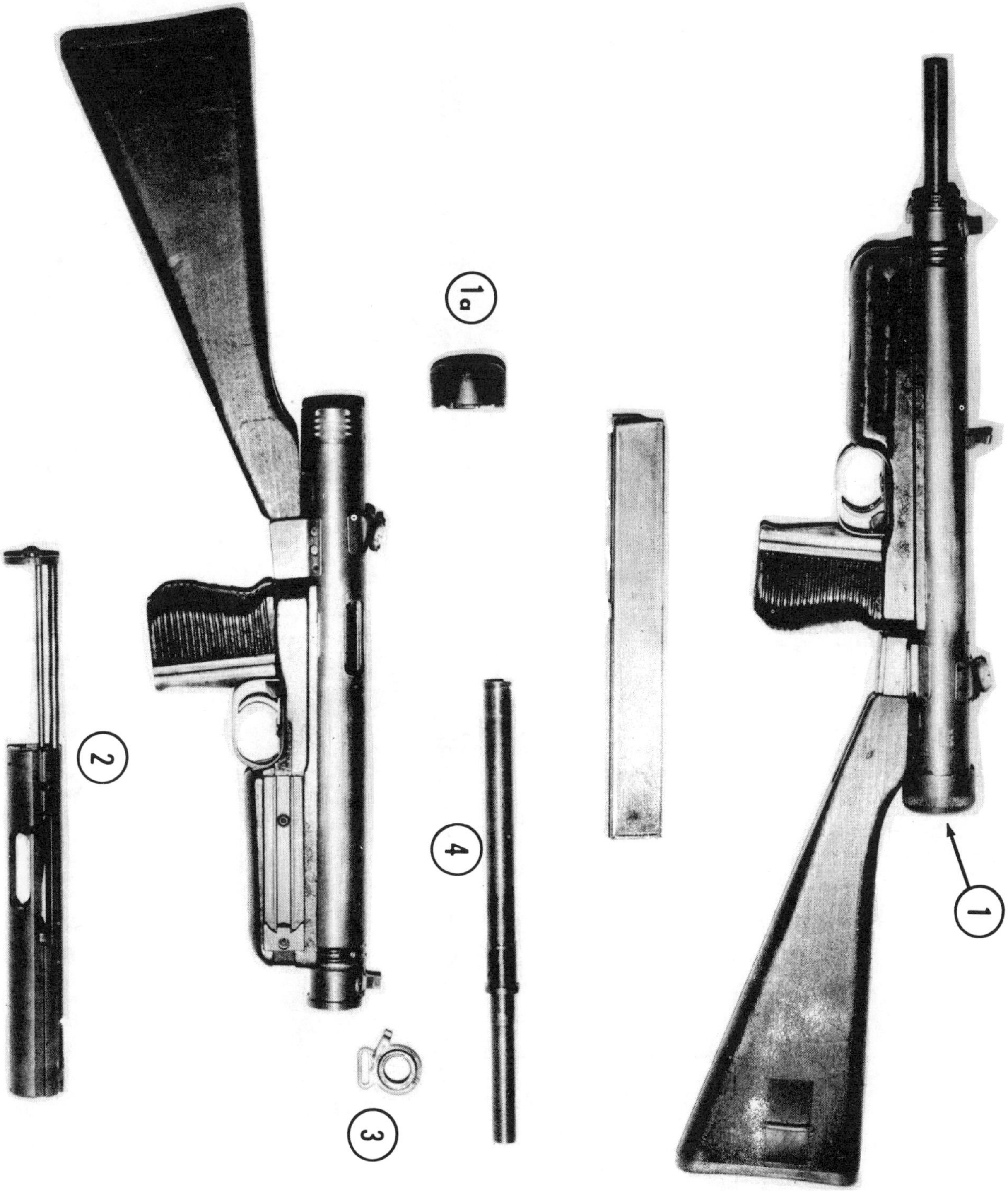
1a
2
3
4
1

7.62-mm M-24

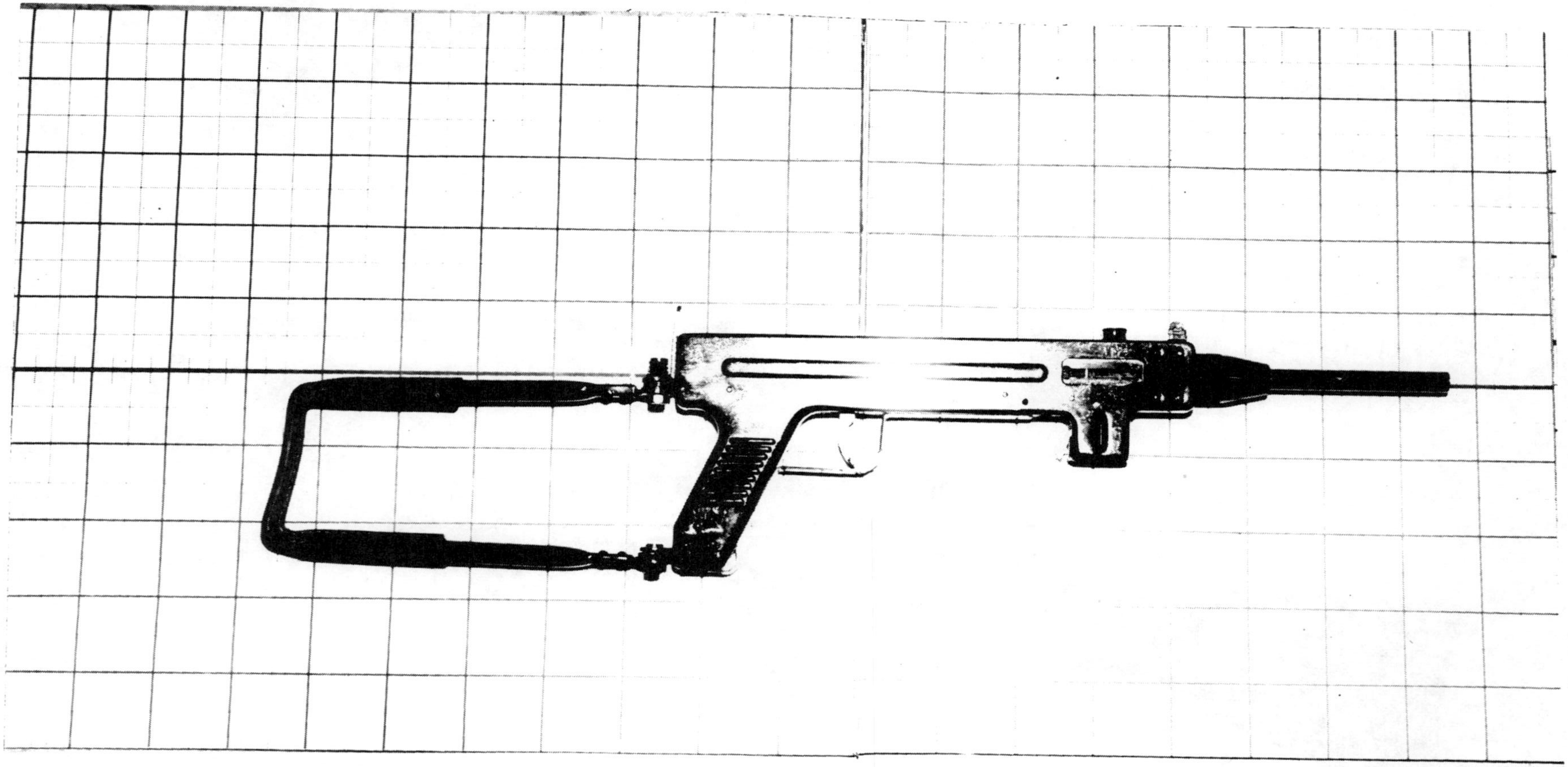

DENMARK 9-MM, MODEL 1950

SUBMACHINEGUN   DENMARK

9-mm MADSEN SUBMACHINEGUN (M-50)

The 9-mm M-50 Submachinegun is an extremely simple, well-made weapon. It incorporates low cost production features, sturdiness and simplicity of disassembly, seldom found in weapons of this type. The receiver is a complete two-piece stamping, hinged together at the rear for ease of take-down. The stock is one of the most rigid types available and the weapon can be fired as easily with the stock folded as it can with the stock unfolded. A rather unusual feature is the addition of a " grip safety" positioned just behind the magazine housing. As in most submachineguns, the magazine housing is utilized in firing as a fore-grip. In gripping the housing in firing, this vertically positioned lever must be pressed forward. Should the firer's grip on the magazine housing be released during firing, the lever automatically blocks the path of the bolt.

FUNCTIONING

This is a simple blowback weapon firing from an open bolt. With the bolt in the forward position and a loaded magazine inserted, the bolt handle on the top of the receiver is pulled to the rear. The bolt is held in this position until the trigger is pulled. When the trigger is pulled, the sear (trigger rod) is pulled down out of engagement with the bolt and the bolt moves forward under the impulse of the compressed recoil spring. The bolt strips a round from the magazine, chambers and fires it. If the safety lever behind the magazine housing is not pressed forward, the upper lip of the lever will engage a notch on the lower forward portion of the bolt and prevent it (the bolt) from moving forward to fire.

CHARACTERISTIC DATA

Caliber 9-mm
Operation .... Blowback
Type of Fire .... Full-auto only
Rate of Fire .... 460 rpm (Practical-125)
Type of Feed .... Box - 32 rd cap
Weight, empty .... 7.1 lb
Overall length .... 30.7 in (stock extended)
Effective range .... 225 meters

FIELD STRIP PROCEDURE

STEP   ACTION

1. Unscrew the Barrel Nut and remove.
2. Fold the Stock to its closed position. Lay the weapon on its right side. Grasp the Sling Swivel and pull up. The left side of the Receiver will pivot open on the hinge at the rear of the Receiver.
3. Lift out the Barrel.
4. Push the Operating Spring Guide forward slightly, lift up and remove the Operating Spring and the Guide from the Receiver.
5. Lift the Bolt out of the Receiver.

ASSEMBLY PROCEDURE

Proceed in the reverse order. Position the Bolt in the Receiver. Assemble the Operating Spring Guide to the Operating Spring and assemble to the Bolt. Place the Barrel in position. Close the left side of the Receiver onto the right side. Slide the Barrel Nut onto the Barrel and screw into place.

LOADING AND FIRING

To load: Draw the Bolt to the rear. Push the Safety Button, located on the left side of the Receiver above the Trigger, to the rear. This locks the Trigger Rod. Insert a loaded Magazine into the well. The Stock may be unfolded or left folded.

To fire: Push the Safety Button forward to "Fire" position. Grasp the Magazine Well with the left hand. NOTE: A "Grip Safety" lever is located just behind the Magazine Well. It must be pressed with the hand gripping the Magazine Well in order for the weapon to fire. Pull the Trigger. The weapon will fire. This weapon fires automatic only, there is no selection system for semi-automatic fire. It fires from an OPEN BOLT. Do not allow the Bolt to move forward with a loaded Magazine in the weapon unless it is intended to fire the weapon.

3
5
4
2
Operating Spring Guide
1
Barrel Nut

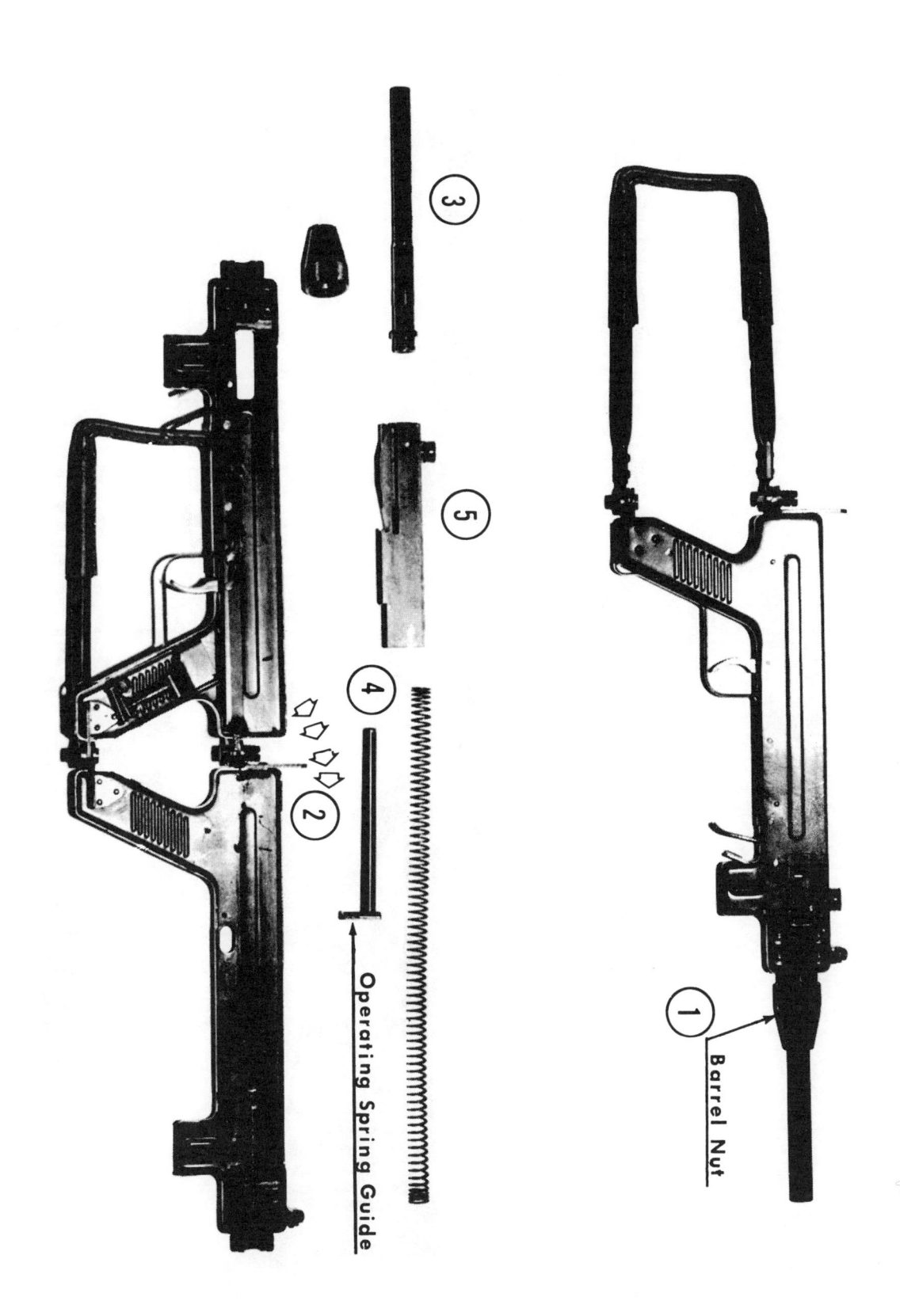

9-mm M1950

FINLAND 9-MM, MODEL 1931

SUBMACHINEGUN   FINLAND

9-mm M1931 (SOUMI)

The 9-mm SOUMI Submachinegun is a well made, though relatively heavy, submachinegun used by most of the Scandinavian countries. Designed by the Finnish arms designer, Lahti, who also designed the Model L-35 pistol which bears his name, (The Finnish L-35 Pistol is known as the Model 40 Pistol in Sweden.) it was adopted by the Finnish Armed Forces in 1931. It was produced at the Finnish arms factory of Oy Tikkakoski Ab and is sold commercially under SOUMI license by Husqvarna in Sweden; Hispano Suiza in Switzerland; and Madsen in Denmark. The Swedish model is designated the m/37-39 and has a slightly shorter barrel than the Model 1931; the Swiss model is known as the MP 43/44 and incorporates a bayonet lug to accept the standard Swiss bayonet: Madsen produced the weapon in Denmark with a series designation of P.2 or P.5. Design work and prototypes of the SOUMI date to as early as 1922 evolving to the 1926 model chambered for the 7.65-mm cartridge. This Model 1926 was extensively modified and has reached production as the present Model 1931. The weapon is completely machined, utilizes a reduced diameter bolt, and incorporates a bolt handle which remains stationary while the bolt is moving during firing. Various types of Magazines were designed and used with the SOUMI submachinegun; 20- and 50-round box magazines and 40- and 71- round drum magazines. Since the mid-1950's this weapon has been modified to accept the Swedish 36-round magazine used with the Swedish M/45B (Carl Gustaf) Submachinegun.

FUNCTIONING

The SOUMI Submachinegun is a straight blowback weapon. With a loaded magazine inserted in the magazine well, the bolt handle located beneath the receiver cap is pulled to the rear and released. The bolt is held to the rear by the sear. The fire select button located just ahead of the trigger guard may be pushed forward for full-automatic fire or positioned to the rear for semi-automatic fire. The safety lever is a sliding bar located in front of the trigger guard. With the safety set on "FIRE" (forward) and the fire select button set for the type fire desired, the trigger is pulled, the sear releases the bolt, the bolt moves forward under impulse of the compressed recoil spring, strips a round from the magazine, chambers it and fires it. The bolt moves to the rear and if the select button is set for semi-automatic, the sear will engage the bolt holding it to the rear and the trigger must be pulled for each shot. If the select button is pushed forward for full-automatic fire the sear will remain out of engagement and the weapon will continue to fire as long as the trigger is held back or until the magazine is empty.

CHARACTERISTIC DATA

Caliber 9-mm
Operation .... Blowback
Type of Fire .... Full and semi-auto
Rate of Fire .... 900 rpm (Practical 250)
Type of Feed .... Box-20, 36, 50 rd cap Drum - 40, 71 rd cap
Weight, empty .... 11.5 lbs
Overall length .... 34.2 in
Effective range .... 300 meters

FIELD STRIP PROCEDURE

STEP   ACTION

1. Draw the Bolt Handle slightly to the rear and unscrew the Receiver Cap.
1a. Remove the Receiver Cap and Recoil Spring.
2. Draw the Bolt Handle to the rear and remove the Bolt. Allow the Bolt Handle to move forward.
3. Pivot the Barrel Jacket Lock down, twist Barrel Jacket to the left and remove from the Receiver.
3a. Slide the Barrel forward out of the Receiver.

ASSEMBLY PROCEDURE

Assemble in the reverse order. Assemble the Barrel to the Receiver. Slide the Barrel Jacket over the Barrel and twist onto the Receiver. Push the Barrel Jacket Lock down. Slide the Bolt into the rear of the Receiver. Assemble the Receiver Cap and Recoil Spring into the Receiver and screw the Receiver Cap on. For the last few turns of the Receiver Cap, pull back on the Bolt Handle so that the Receiver Cap may be screwed down firmly.

LOADING AND FIRING

To load: Push the Safety Lever to the rear to put the weapon on "SAFE." Insert a loaded Magazine into the Magazine Well. Pull the Bolt Handle to the rear and release. The Bolt will be held to the rear by the Sear. Set the Fire Select Button to the type fire desired. Forward for full-automatic and centered for semi-automatic fire.

To fire: Push the Safety Lever forward to "FIRE." Pull the Trigger. The weapon will fire. If set for semi-automatic fire the Trigger must be pulled for each shot. If set for full-automatic fire the weapon will continue to fire until the Trigger is released or the Magazine is empty.

Receiver Cap
1
3
Barrel Jacket Lock
3a
2
1a

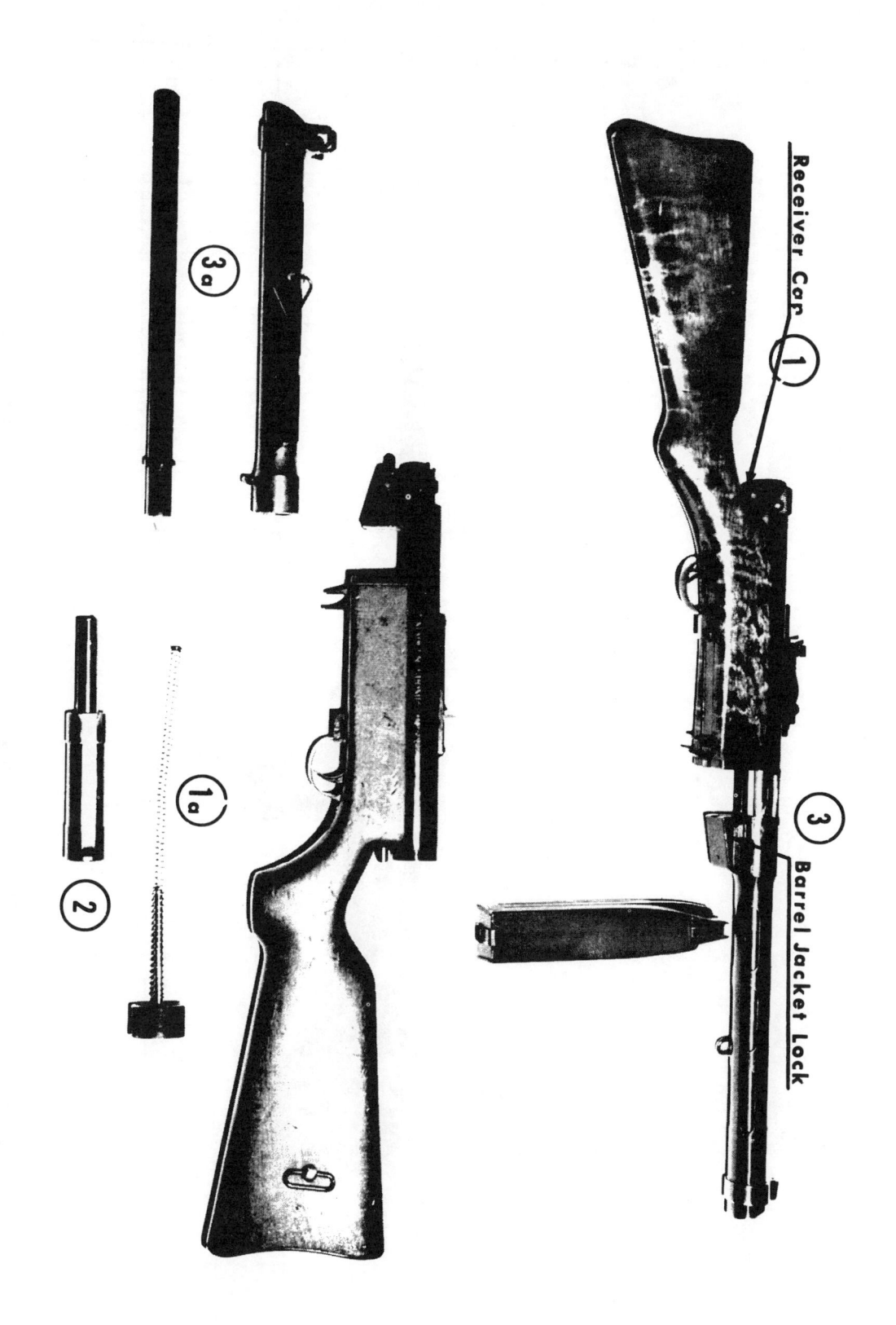

9-mm M 1931

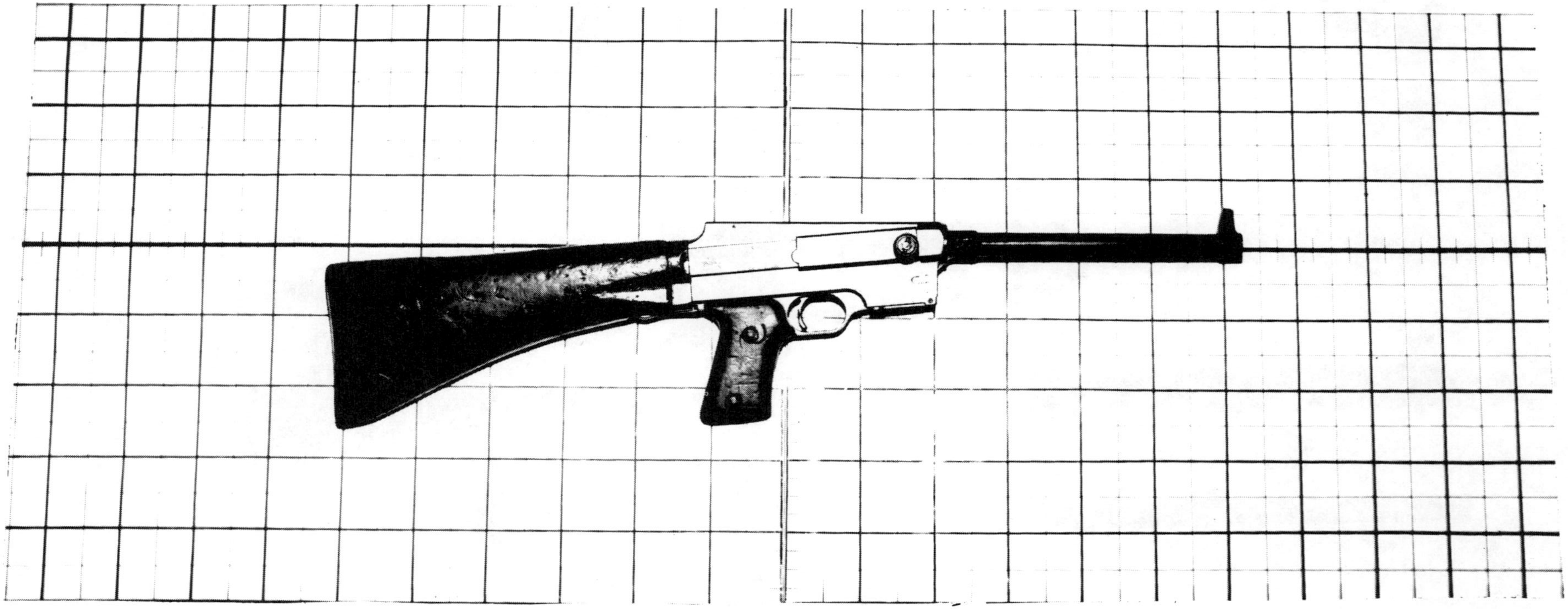

FRANCE 7.65-MM LONG, MAS-38

SUBMACHINEGUN   FRANCE

7.65-mm M-38 (MAS-38)

The 7.65-mm MAS-38 submachinegun was the official standard submachinegun of the French Army at the start of WWII. Other models of this weapon exist with minor modifications, notably separate firing pin design and one version with a tubular stock. The piece fires the French Model 1935 pistol round, a relatively underpowered round which is not to be confused with the 7.65-mm round which is identical with the .32 Colt Automatic Pistol cartridge. This is a straight blowback submachinegun with no unusual design features. Worthy of note is a safety system incorporated in the weapon. The trigger folds forward and up and when in this position, cannot be pressed to fire the weapon. If the bolt is cocked to the rear ready to fire, it cannot be released until the trigger is deliberately unfolded to firing position. If the bolt is forward and the trigger is pivoted up, a lever mounted to bear against the upper forward edge of the trigger, is forced up into a notch in the bolt, effectively preventing the bolt from being drawn to the rear to the cocked position until the trigger is deliberately unfolded.

FUNCTIONING

The 7.65-mm MAS-38 is a straight blowback submachinegun. With a loaded magazine placed in the magazine well and the bolt drawn to the rear, the bolt is engaged by the sear and held to the rear until the trigger is pulled. The recoil spring in this weapon is contained in a tube in the stock, thus accounting for the rather short receiver length of the piece. The bolt does not travel in a straight line, longtitudinal to the axis of the bore, but travels at a slightly downward angle. This slight downward angle of the bolt travel theoretically imparts a hesitation to the rearward bolt movement. When the trigger is pressed, the sear releases the bolt which travels forward, stripping a round from the magazine, chambering it and firing it. Movement of the bolt to the rear extracts and ejects the round in a normal manner, and if the trigger is pressed, the action of loading and firing is repeated until the trigger is released.

CHARACTERISTIC DATA

Caliber	7.65-mm
Operation	Recoil
Type of Fire	Full-auto only
Rate of Fire	580 rpm (Practical 125)
Type of feed	Box-32 rd cap
Weight, empty	7.1 lbs
Overall length	24.9 in
Effective range	125 meters

FIELD STRIP PROCEDURE

STEP   ACTION

1. With the Magazine removed, pull the Trigger and allow the Bolt to go forward. Press in on Butt-Catch located beneath the forward end of the Butt and twist the Butt to the right, remove to the rear.
2. Press the Trigger and slide the Triggerguard Assembly to the rear.
3. Remove the Bolt and Recoil Spring from the Receiver to the rear.

ASSEMBLY PROCEDURE

Proceed in the reverse order. Slide the Bolt and Recoil Spring into the Receiver. With the Trigger pressed to the rear, slide the Triggerguard Assembly onto the Receiver. Slide the Butt over the Recoil Spring, push forward and twist to lock onto the Receiver.

LOADING PROCEDURE

To load: Draw the Bolt to the rear. Pivot the Trigger forward and up. Place a loaded Magazine into the magazine well, making sure it is locked in place. Unfold the Trigger down into the firing position.

To fire: Press the Trigger, the Bolt will be released, move forward, chamber and fire a round. This action will continue until the Magazine is empty or the Trigger is released.

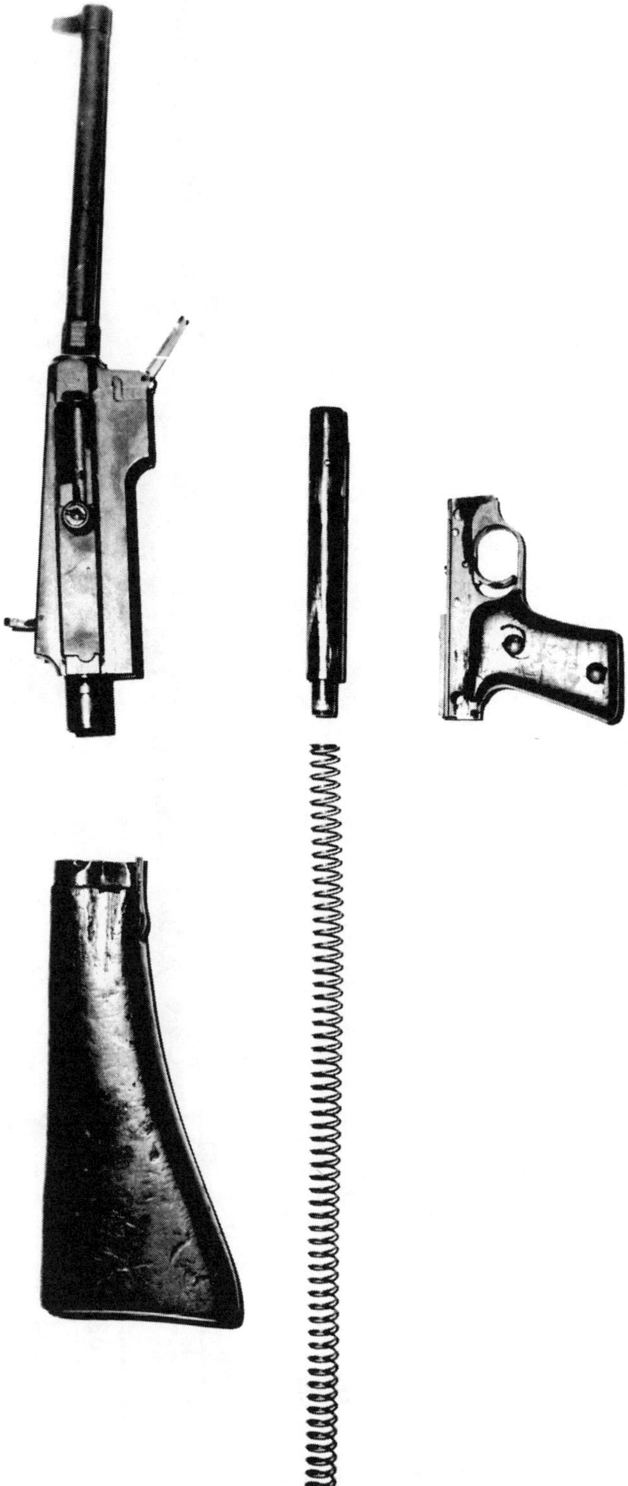

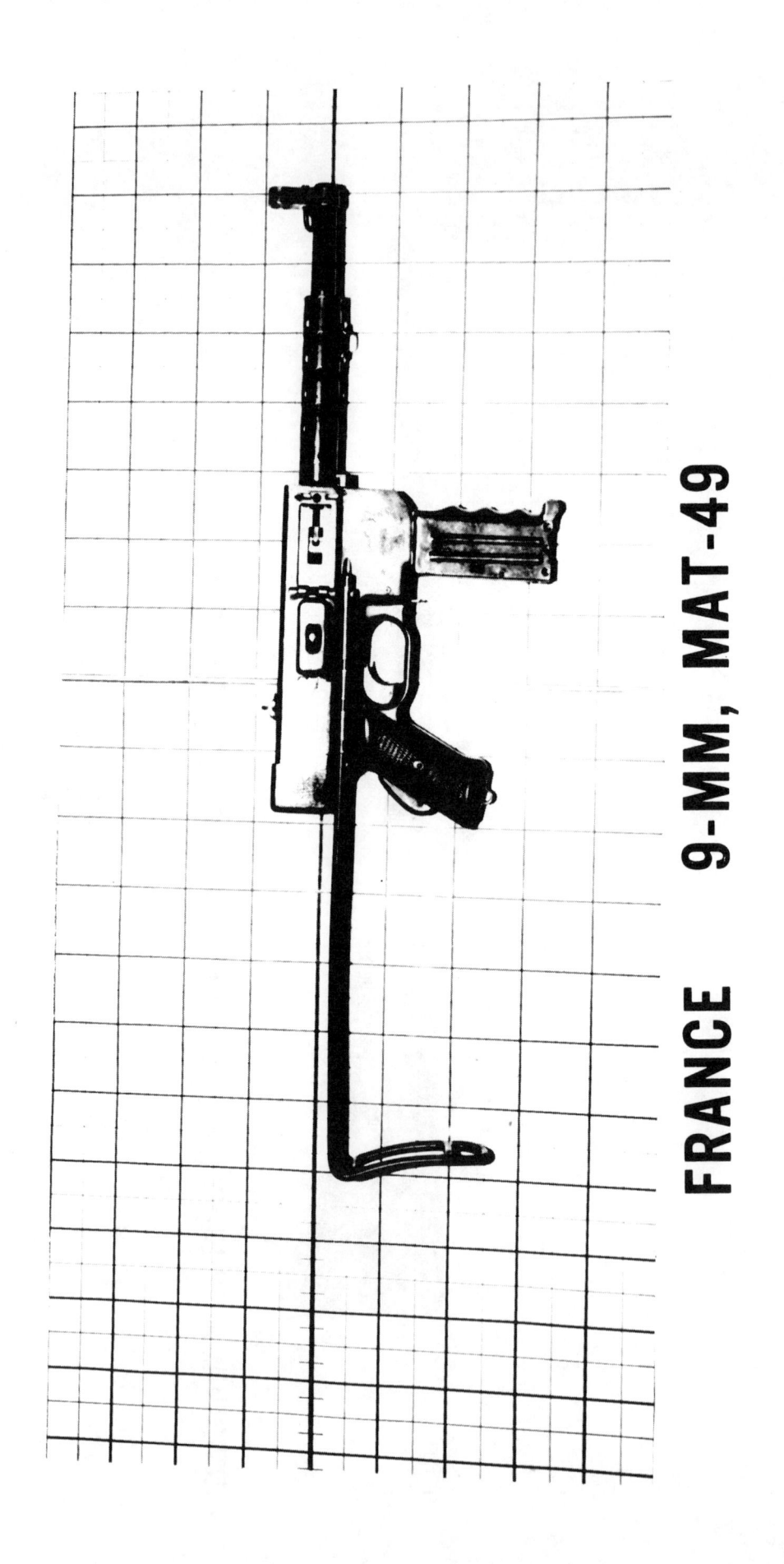

FRANCE 9-MM, MAT-49

SUBMACHINEGUN   FRANCE

9-mm SUBMACHINEGUN M1949 (MAT 49)

The 9-mm M1949 Submachinegun is manufactured by the Manufacture Des Armes, Tulle (MAT) and is gradually replacing the earlier 7.65-mm MAS 38 Submachine gun. This submachinegun has seen extensive service in Indo-China and Algeria. The weapon design makes extensive use of stampings, and is in general, very well made. Two rather unusual (for a submachinegun) features are incorporated into the design of the piece. One is a folding magazine housing, which swings forward and up, to engage a bracket on the bottom of the barrel jacket; this makes the weapon handy for airborne and armored troops. The other feature is a grip safety, which precludes the accidental discharge of the piece if dropped. The ejection port has a cover, which automatically opens when the bolt is moved in either direction.

FUNCTIONING

This is a straight blow-back operated submachinegun, firing from an open bolt. With the magazine housing pivoted down and locked, a magazine is inserted. The bolt handle is drawn to the rear and the bolt engages the sear. The ejection port cover is now open. Squeezing the grip safety and pulling the trigger fires the weapon.

NOTES TO REMEMBER

1. This weapon can be carried with a loaded magazine in the magazine housing and the housing swung up and locked into place against the barrel jacket. When bringing the magazine housing down into vertical position, make sure that the magazine housing lock, located on the underside of the trigger housing, engages the magazine housing firmly.

2. The weapon will not fire unless the grip safety is completely depressed.

3. With the magazine housing up and locked, and the wire stock fully telescoped, this is an extremely compact arm. It can be effectively concealed beneath a person's clothing, being only 15½ inches long and less than half of that dimension wide.

CHARACTERISTIC DATA

Caliber 9-mm
Operation . . . . Blowback
Type of Fire . . . . Full-auto only
Rate of Fire . . . . 600 rpm (Practical-125)
Type of Feed . . . . Box-32 rd cap
Weight, empty . . . . 8.5 lbs
Overall length (stock extended) . . . . 28.2 in
    (retracted) . . . . 18.3 in
Effective range . . . . 225 meters

FIELD STRIP PROCEDURE

STEP   ACTION

1. After Removing the Magazine, push forward on the Magazine Housing Lock and rotate Magazine Housing forward and up slightly.
2. Push in on Trigger Housing Lock.
3. Swing the Barrel and Receiver up away from the Trigger Housing.
4. Remove the Bolt, Recoil Spring and Guide from the Receiver.
5. Press the Stock Release Catch in.
6. Remove the Stock by pull to the rear.

Step two and three should be performed simultaneously. Step five and six should be performed simultaneously.

ASSEMBLY PROCEDURE

Proceed in the reverse order except that the Stock may be assembled to the Trigger Housing after the weapon has been assembled. Place the Recoil Spring and Guide into the Bolt and assemble to the Barrel and Receiver Assembly. Place the rear of the Barrel and Receiver Assembly into the guide at the rear of the Trigger Housing. Swing down into position firmly until Trigger Housing Lock engages. Adjust Magazine Housing up or down.

LOADING AND FIRING

To load: With the Bolt forward and the Ejection Port Cover down, insert a loaded Magazine into the Magazine Housing. If the housing is in the horizontal position, swing it down to the vertical. Make sure the Magazine Housing Lock engages. Make sure the Magazine Catch is engaged.

To fire: Pull the Bolt Handle (located on the left side of the Receiver) to the rear. The Bolt will remain to the rear, since this weapon fires from an open bolt. The Ejection Port Cover will now be open. Push the Bolt Handle to its forward position. Grasp the grip firmly and insure the Grip Safety is squeezed in. Pull the Trigger. The weapon will fire until the Trigger is released or the Magazine is empty.

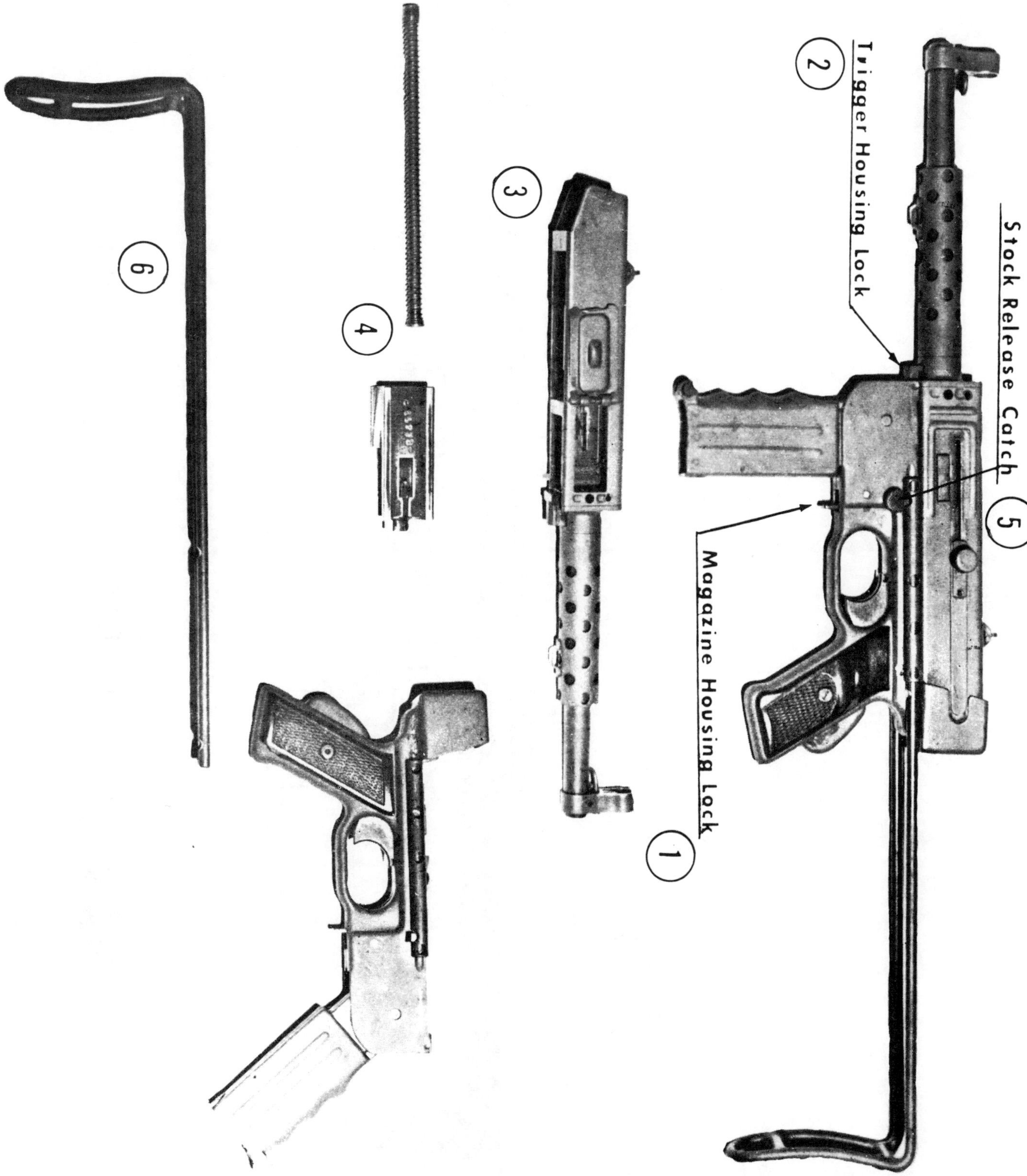

1
2
Trigger Housing Lock
3
4
5
Stock Release Catch
6
Magazine Housing Lock

9-mm MAT-49

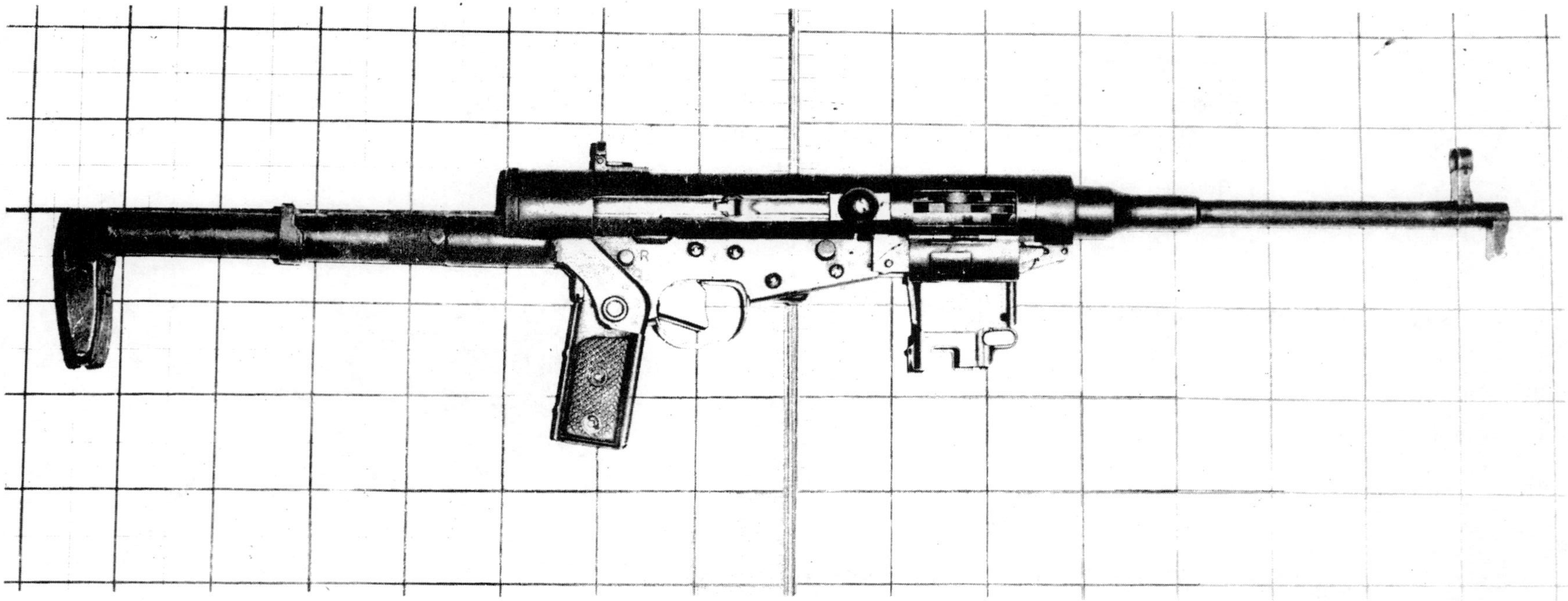

FRANCE 9-MM, "UNIVERSAL"

SUBMACHINEGUN   FRANCE

9-mm "UNIVERSAL" (HOTCHKISS)

The French 9-mm "Universal" Submachinegun is a blowback operated, magazine fed weapon which utilizes a hammer and complex firing pin cocking system. Many features incorporated in the design of this weapon are unusual and extremely complicated. Produced by the Hotchkiss firm located in Paris, France, in 1949 it was originally intended for police work and was capable of semi-automatic fire only. Later modifications included a full-automatic fire capability. The weapon is designed for compactness - stock and magazine housing fold up from the bottom and the barrel can be telescoped into the receiver when not in use. The advantages of such compactness are more than offset by the disadvantages of complex stamping and machining operations involved in manufacture. The unusual bolt design utilizes a striker cocking and locking system, the striker being locked until the bolt is fully forward, and then being struck by the hammer when the trigger is pulled. Totally unnecessary in a simple blowback weapon. This weapon was used to a limited degree by the French in Indochina and a small quantity were purchased by Venezuela in 1950.

FUNCTIONING

This is a straight blowback weapon which fires full and semi-automatic from a closed bolt. With a loaded magazine in place, the bolt handle is drawn to the rear and released. The bolt moves forward under impulse of the compressed recoil spring, strips a round from the magazine and chambers it. The firing pin is cocked during the rearward movement of the bolt and a firing pin safety lock engages the firing pin and blocks any movement of the firing pin until the bolt is fully forward. This firing pin safety lock is cammed out of engagement with the firing pin as the round is chambered. Pulling the trigger releases the hammer, the hammer pivots forward and strikes the firing pin release lever, the firing pin moves forward to strike the primer and the bolt moves rearward. The bolt overrides the hammer and the firing pin is cocked and the firing pin safety lever engages the firing pin. If the select lever is set for semi-automatic fire the trigger must be pulled for each shot. If set for full-automatic fire, the weapon will continue to fire until the trigger is released or the magazine is empty.

CHARACTERISTIC DATA

Caliber	9-mm
Operation	Blowback
Type of Fire	Full and semi-auto
Rate of Fire	650 rpm (Practical 175)
Type of Feed	Box - 32 rd cap
Weight, empty	7.7 lbs
Overall length, stock extended	30.6 in
stock & bbl retracted	17.2 in
Effective range	175 meters

FIELD STRIP PROCEDURE

STEP ACTION

1. Pivot Stock down slightly, turn Receiver Cap and remove Cap.
2. Pull Pistol Grip down and to the rear and remove Trigger Group Housing and Stock Assembly.
3. Remove Recoil Spring.
4. Remove Bolt Assembly from rear of Receiver in the following manner:
NOTE 1 — Press in on Firing Pin Release Lever.
NOTE 2 — Press Bolt Lock inward.
NOTE 3 - Slide Bolt out rear of Receiver until Bolt Lock clears Receiver, press Cocking Lever to Cock Firing Pin and slide Bolt out of Receiver.

ASSEMBLY PROCEDURE

Assemble in the reverse order. With Firing Pin Cocked, slide Bolt into Receiver. Assemble Recoil Spring onto Bolt. Attach Trigger Group Housing and pivot up. Place Receiver Cap onto Receiver and turn to lock.

LOADING AND FIRING

To load: Push Safety/Select Lever to "SAFE." Draw Bolt Handle to the rear. Insert loaded Magazine into Magazine Well.

To fire: Place Safety/Select Lever to type fire desired. Push Bolt Handle forward. Pull the Trigger. The weapon will fire. If the fire Select Lever is set for semi-automatic fire the Trigger must be pulled for each shot. If the fire Select Lever is set for full-automatic fire the weapon will continue to fire until the Trigger is released or the Magazine is empty.

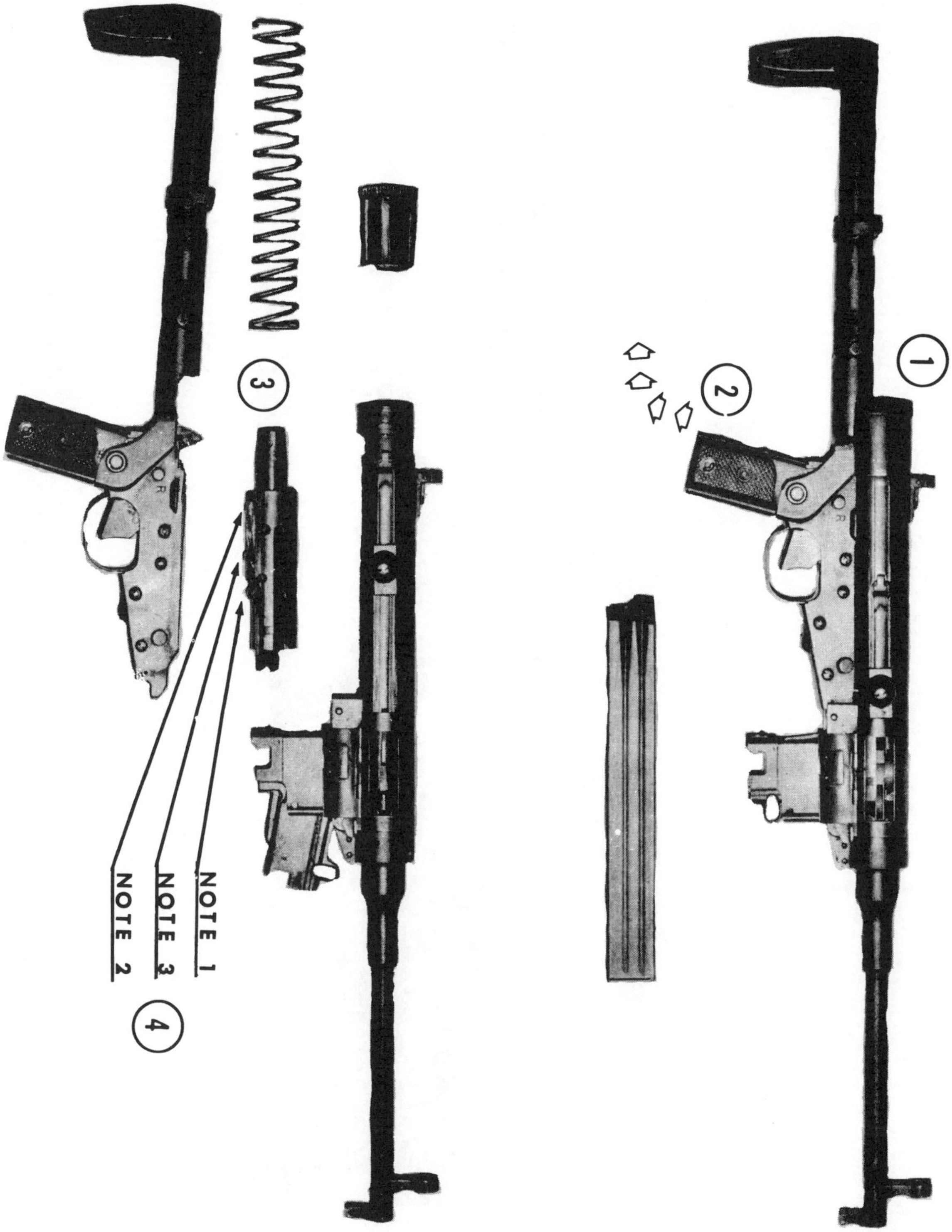
1
2
3
4
NOTE 1
NOTE 3
NOTE 2

9-mm "Universal"

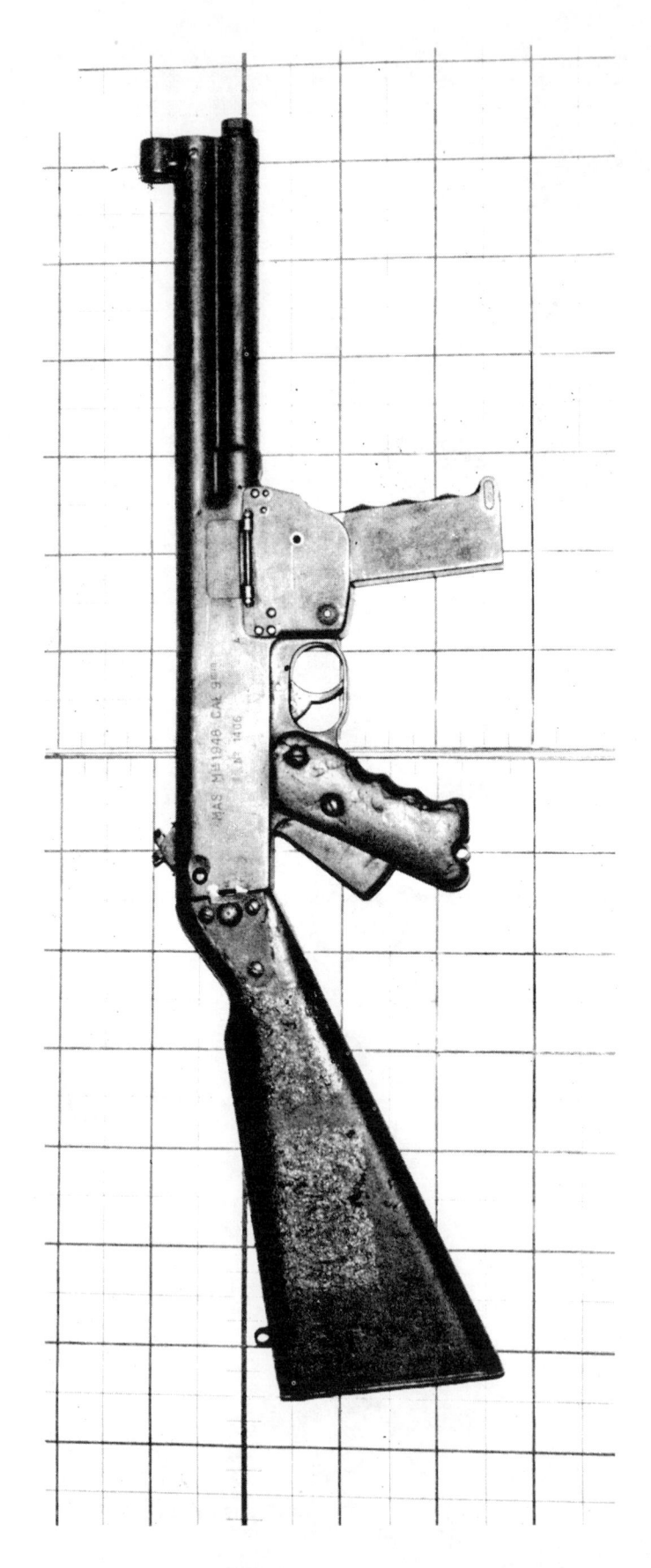

FRANCE   9-MM, M1948 TYPE C4

SUBMACHINEGUN   FRANCE

9-mm M1948 TYPE C4 (MAS)

The French MAS M1948 Type C4 Submachinegun is the fourth of a series of submachineguns designed and produced by the French MAS Arsenal during 1947 and 1948. The weapon incorporates a number of unusual features which stress the French design aims of compactness and ease of manufacture, though the bolt system, a so-called retarded blow-back system, is unnecessarily complex in view of the pistol round for which the piece is chambered. The wooden stock folds to lie against the left side of the receiver and the magazine housing pivots forward so that the magazine is positioned below the barrel when not in use. The bolt handle is located on the left side of the bolt extension housing, above the barrel, to the rear of the front sight. The bolt is composed of two pieces; a heavy cylindrical bolt extension, which houses the recoil spring and guide in its rear portion, and which connects with the bolt handle at its forward end; and the bolt proper, which is attached beneath the rear end of the extension. The firing pin is affixed to the rear of the extension enclosed by the bolt. A vertically positioned lever is carried in the bolt; its upper end in contact with the extension and its lower end in contact with a shelf in the receiver when the action is fully closed. When the weapon is fired, the so-called retardation or hesitation of the movement of the bolt is caused by this lever being forced to pivot, due to the rearward thrust of the bolt. The upper portion of this lever engaging the heavy extension, must overcome not only the weight of this extension but the resistance of the recoil spring contained in the extension. By the time the lever pivots, the lower portion which is in contact with the receiver being thrust forward and the upper portion which is in contact with the extension being rotated rearward, the bullet has left the muzzle and the action can open safely.

FUNCTIONING

With a loaded magazine inserted in the magazine well, the bolt handle is drawn to the rear and then pushed forward, the bolt is engaged by the sear and held to the rear. A grip safety is located at the rear of the pistol grip and must be pressed before the bolt can be released. Pull the trigger, the bolt will move forward, strip a round from the magazine and chamber it. The face of the bolt stops against the breech end of the barrel and the bolt extension continues to move forward, the firing pin carried in the extension strikes the primer. As the bolt starts to move rearward, the lever carried in the bolt acting against the shelf in the receiver and the heavy extension, causes a slight delay in opening of the action. If the trigger has been pulled slightly to the rear the weapon will fire semi-automatic; if the trigger has been pulled fully to the rear the weapon will fire full-automatic.

CHARACTERISTIC DATA

Caliber	9-mm
Operation	Retarded Blowback
Type of Fire	Full and semi-auto
Rate of Fire	550 rpm (Practical 175)
Type of Feed	Box - 32 rd cap
Weight, empty	6.5 lbs
Overall length	25.4 in
Effective range	225 meters

FIELD STRIP PROCEDURE

STEP   ACTION

1. Unlatch Stock and fold to the left.
2. Remove Receiver Pin.
3. Remove Trigger Guard Group by pulling down.
4. Tilt rear of Receiver down and remove Bolt, Bolt Extension and attached Recoil Spring Guide.

ASSEMBLY PROCEDURE

Assemble in the reverse order. Slide Bolt Extension with attached Recoil Spring, Recoil Spring Guide and Bolt into the Receiver. Place Trigger Guard Group into position and replace Receiver Pin. Unfold Stock.

LOADING AND FIRING

To load: The Grip Safety, if it is not pushed in, will lock the Bolt in either the closed or open position. Insert a loaded Magazine into the Magazine Housing. Draw the Bolt Handle to the rear and push forward. The Bolt will remain held to the rear by the Sear. Grip the Piston Grip, squeezing in on the Grip Safety.

To fire: With the Grip Safety firmly squeezed, pull the Trigger. If the Trigger is pulled only partially to the rear, the weapon will fire semi-automatic only and the Trigger must be pulled for each shot. If the Trigger is pulled fully to the rear, the weapon will fire full-automatic and will continue to fire until the Trigger is released or the Magazine is empty.

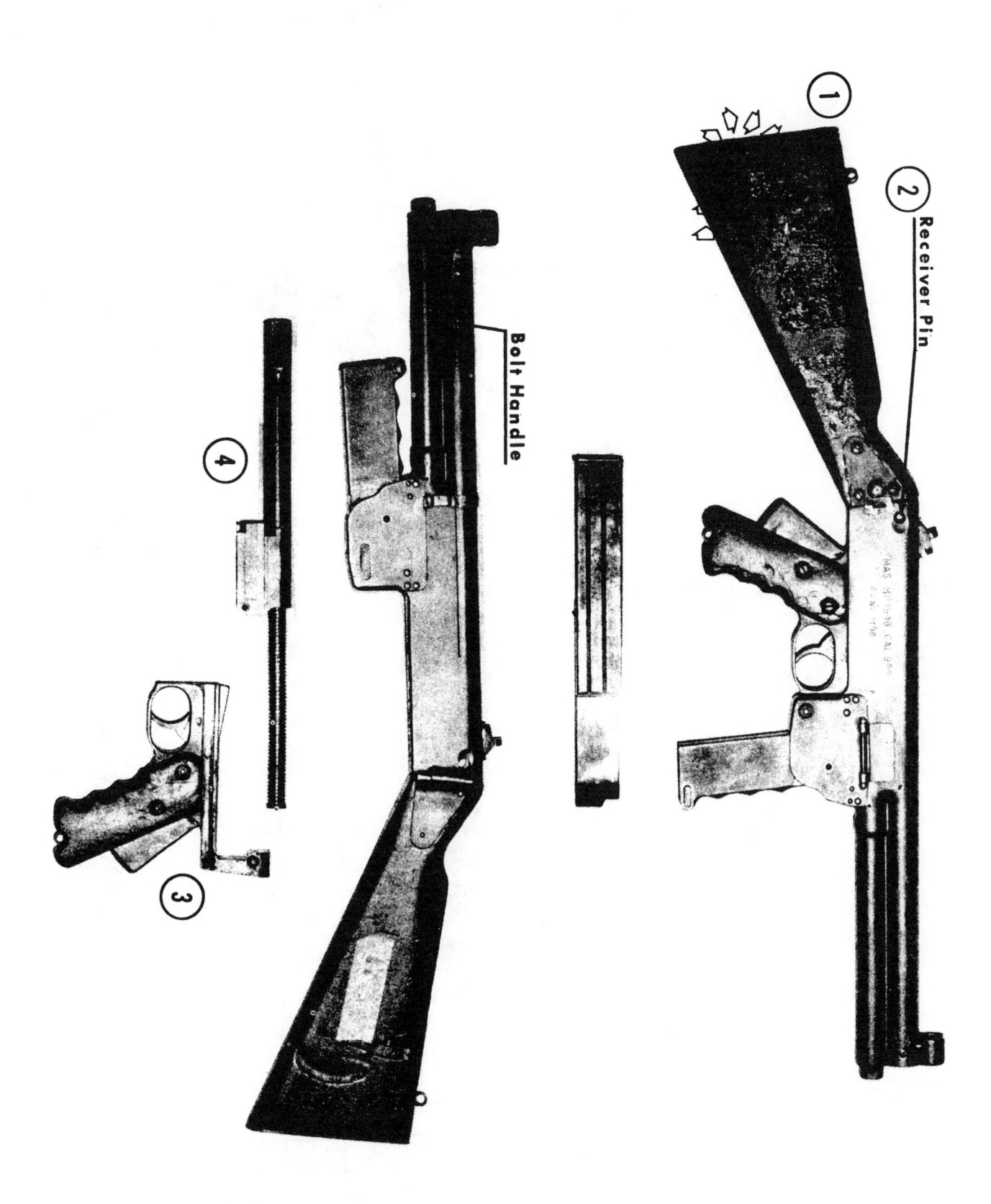

Bolt Handle

①
② Receiver Pin
③
④

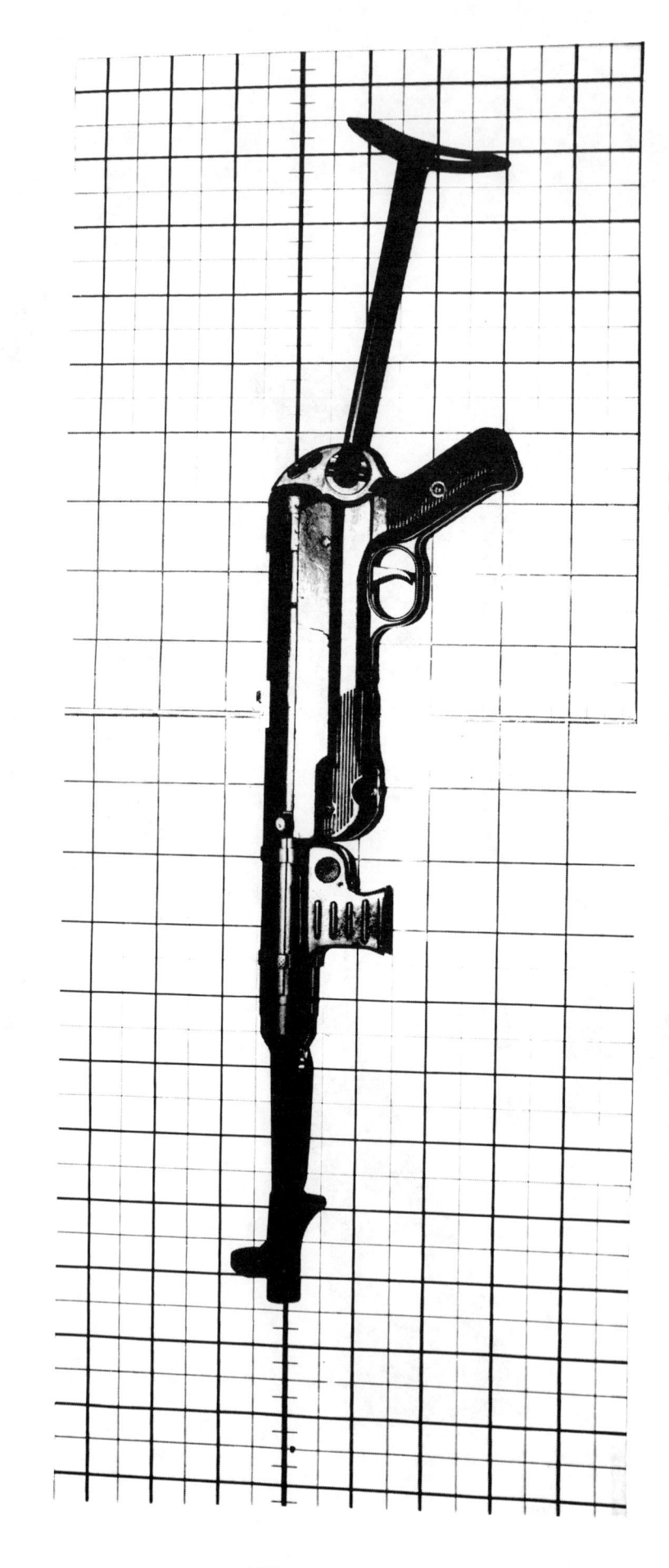

GERMANY 9-MM, MP-40

SUBMACHINEGUN   GERMANY

9-mm MASCHINENPISTOLE 40 (MP 40)

The German 9-mm MP 40 is a true submachinegun (firing a pistol caliber round) as compared to other weapons designated Maschinenpistole - as in the case of the MP 43 which was classed by the Germans as a Machine Carbine, though tactically employed as a submachinegun and assault rifle. The MP 40 was a modification of the earlier MP 38, often called the Schmeisser Parachute Model, and eventually supplanted all other types of submachineguns in the German Army. A later modification of the MP 40 was the wooden-stocked MP 41 which saw limited production and use. The MP 40 was developed by the Haenel factory at Suhl, Germany and is distinguished by the fact that steel and plastic is utilized throughout its construction.

FUNCTIONING

This is a straight blowback weapon which fires from an open bolt. The bolt should not be allowed to move forward with a loaded magazine in place unless it is intended to fire the piece. With a loaded magazine in place and the bolt held open by the sear, the trigger is pulled to release the bolt. The sear, through a linkage with the trigger, pivots down out of engagement with the sear-bent in the bolt. The bolt; under the impulse of the recoil spring and the compressed buffer spring, which are housed in a three-piece, telescoping, recoil spring and buffer spring tube assembly; moves forward, strips a round from the magazine and chambers it. The firing pin, a separate unit projecting from the forward end of the first (large) recoil spring tube and under tension from the recoil spring, functions essentially the same as a fixed firing pin, protruding from the face of the bolt as the round is chambered and firing the round at the same time the extractor snaps over the rim of the chambered cartridge. The firing pin is spring loaded by the recoil spring to allow some flexibility of movement of the tip of the firing pin when the bolt enters the ejection phase. As the bolt moves to the rear after firing, the large diameter buffer spring housed in the combined recoil spring and buffer spring housing assembly, cushions the final recoil movement of the bolt at its rearmost position. Due to this buffer system, this weapon has a very "soft" recoil and is relatively easy to hold for short burst firing. The bolt is held to the rear by the sear if the trigger has been released. If the trigger is still held back, the bolt will move forward after completing its recoil motion, and the firing cycle is repeated until the magazine is empty.

CHARACTERISTIC DATA

```
Caliber ................................................................ 9-mm
Operation ........................................................ Blowback
Type of Fire ............................................... Full-auto only
Rate of Fire ................................... 530 rpm (Practical-150)
Type of Feed ....................................... Box-32 rd cap
Weight, empty ............................................... 8.2 lbs
Overall length, stock folded .............................. 24.9 in
         Stock extended ................................... 35.1 in
Effective range ............................................ 270 meters
```

FIELD STRIP PROCEDURE

STEP   ACTION

1. Remove the Magazine and allow the Bolt to slide forward by pulling the Trigger. Pull the Receiver Lock down and turn to lock in open position. The stock may be folded or unfolded for disassembly.
2. Grasp the Magazine Housing with one hand; grasp the Pistol Grip with the other hand, pull the Trigger and twist the Pistol Grip to the right and pull to the rear. The Frame Group will slide out of engagement with the Receiver.
3. Draw back slightly on the Bolt Handle and remove the Recoil Spring Housing and Firing Pin Assembly from the rear of the Receiver.
4. Pull the Bolt Handle to the rear and out of the Receiver, this removes the Bolt Assembly which is attached to the Handle.

ASSEMBLY PROCEDURE

Proceed in the reverse order. Slide the Bolt into the Receiver and push forward. Slide the Recoil Spring Housing and Firing Pin Assembly into the rear of the Receiver so that it enters the Bolt. Slide the Frame Group onto the Receiver and twist down and to the left. Pull out slightly on the Receiver Lock, turn and release.

LOADING AND FIRING

To load: With the Bolt to the rear and the Bolt Handle locked in the Safety Notch at the rear of the Bolt Handle slot, insert a loaded Magazine into the Magazine Housing.

To fire: Pull the Bolt Handle down out of engagement with the Safety Notch. NOTE: This weapon fires from an open bolt. The Bolt should not be allowed to move forward with a loaded Magazine inserted unless it is intended to fire the weapon. Pull the Trigger. The weapon will fire, full-automatic only, until the Magazine is empty or the Trigger released.

9-mm MP 40

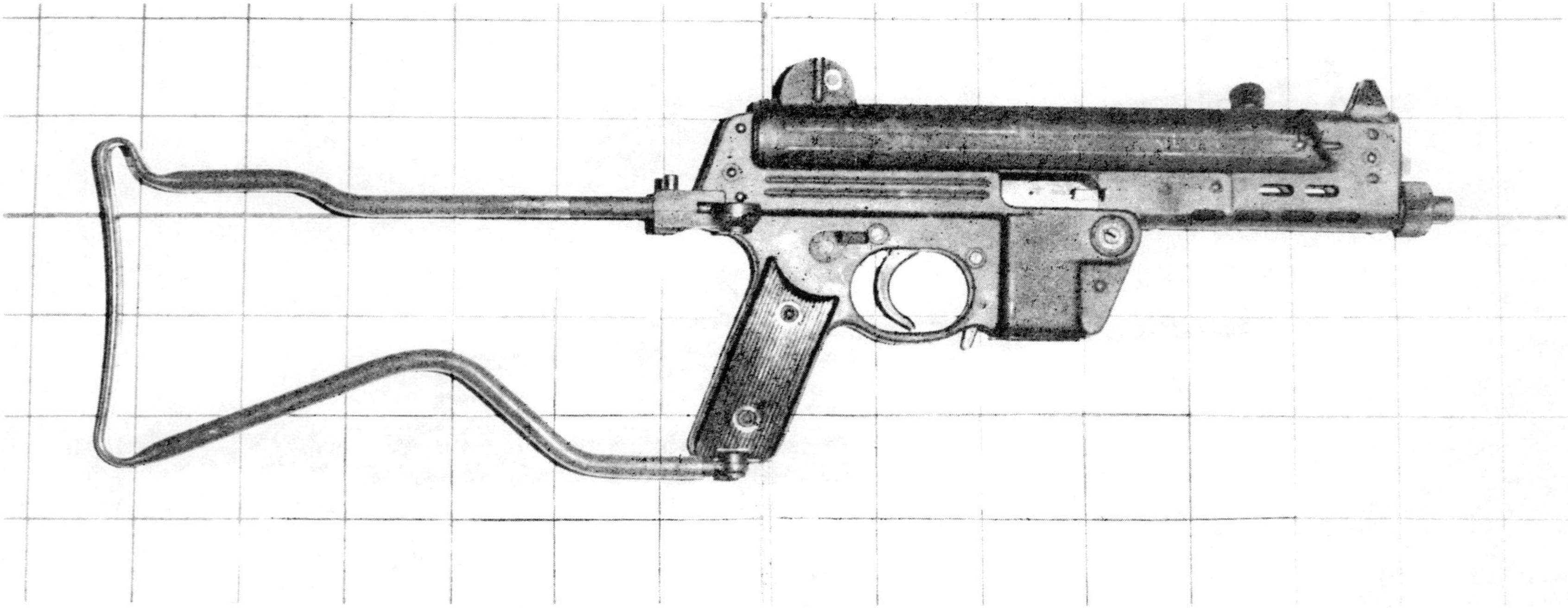

GERMANY   9-MM, MPK

SUBMACHINEGUN   GERMANY

9-mm MPK (WALTHER)

The Walther 9-mm MPK Submachinegun was introduced on the commercial market in 1963. There are two basic models of this series of Walther submachineguns, the MPL (Lang) and the MPK (Kurz); which are identical in all respects except for their length. The MPK is a simple, reliable, effective submachinegun which utilizes a stamped receiver and a heavy, forward-balanced bolt system. The bolt is composed of a heavy, cylindrical upper body and a light breech-block lower body. The upper body is drilled to accomodate the recoil spring and recoil spring guide. The guide is supported at both ends in the receiver and supports the movement of the bolt as well as guiding the recoil spring. The cylindrical upper body is machined in such a manner that only a small portion of the body, at the front and rear, contacts the inside of the receiver during movement. The lower breech-block body of the bolt is the portion of the bolt that strips the round from the magazine, chambers and fires it. Some models of the MPK have a two-position safety lever, one position for "SAFE" and the other for "FIRE," full-automatic fire only. Other models have a three-position safety/select lever, in which the weapon can be put on "SAFE" at "S," semi-automatic fire at "E" and full-automatic fire at "D." The folding stock can be folded to either side of the weapon.

FUNCTIONING

With a loaded magazine inserted into the magazine well, the bolt handle is drawn to the rear and then pushed forward. The bolt moves independently of the bolt handle, though the bolt handle can be locked to the bolt if it becomes necessary to manually clear the piece due to a jam. The bolt will remain to the rear held by the sear. If the safety has been put on "SAFE" the sear cannot release the bolt. With the safety set to "FIRE," the trigger is pulled, the bolt moves forward under impulse of the compressed recoil spring, strips a round from the magazine, chambers it and fires it. If the select lever is set for full automatic, the weapon will continue to fire until the trigger is released or the magazine is empty. If the select lever has been set for semi-automatic, the sear will engage the bolt and the trigger must be pulled for each shot. A special safety device is built into this weapon: If the bolt handle is released during cocking, before the sear engages the bolt, a special lever will stop the bolt before it can strip a round from the magazine and chamber it; this same lever locks the trigger so that the bolt handle must be pulled to the rear to disengage the bolt from this safety device.

CHARACTERISTIC DATA

Caliber 9-mm
Operation .... Blowback Type of Fire Full and semi-auto
Rate of Fire .... 550 rpm (Practical 150)
Type of Feed .... Box - 32 rd cap
Weight, empty .... 6.2 lbs
Overall Length, stock folded .... 14.8 in
Effective range .... 175 meters

FIELD STRIP PROCEDURE

STEP   ACTION

1. Push Receiver Pin out as far as it will go from right to left.
2. Remove Receiver from Trigger Group Assembly.
3. Tilt the rear of Receiver down and slide the Bolt, Recoil Spring and Recoil Spring Guide out the rear of the Receiver.
4. Push the Barrel Lock up and unscrew the Barrel Locking Nut.
4a. Remove the Barrel Locking Nut.
5. Remove Barrel from the front of the Receiver.

ASSEMBLY PROCEDURE

Assemble in the reverse order. Slide Barrel into front of Receiver. Slide Barrel Locking Nut over Barrel and screw onto Receiver. Assemble the Bolt, Recoil Spring and Recoil Spring Guide into the rear of the Receiver. Assemble the Trigger Group Assembly to the Receiver and push the Receiver Pin through the Receiver from left to right.

LOADING AND FIRING

To load: Pivot Safety/Select Lever to the rear to "SAFE." Insert a loaded Magazine into the Magazine Well. Draw the Bolt Handle to the rear and push forward, the Bolt will be engaged by a Sear and remain to the rear.

To fire: Push the Safety/Select Lever to the type fire desired. Pull the Trigger. The weapon will fire. If the Safety/Select Lever is set for "E" (semi-automatic) the Trigger must be pulled for each shot fired. If the Lever is set for "D" (full-automatic) the weapon will continue to fire until the Trigger is released or the Magazine is empty.

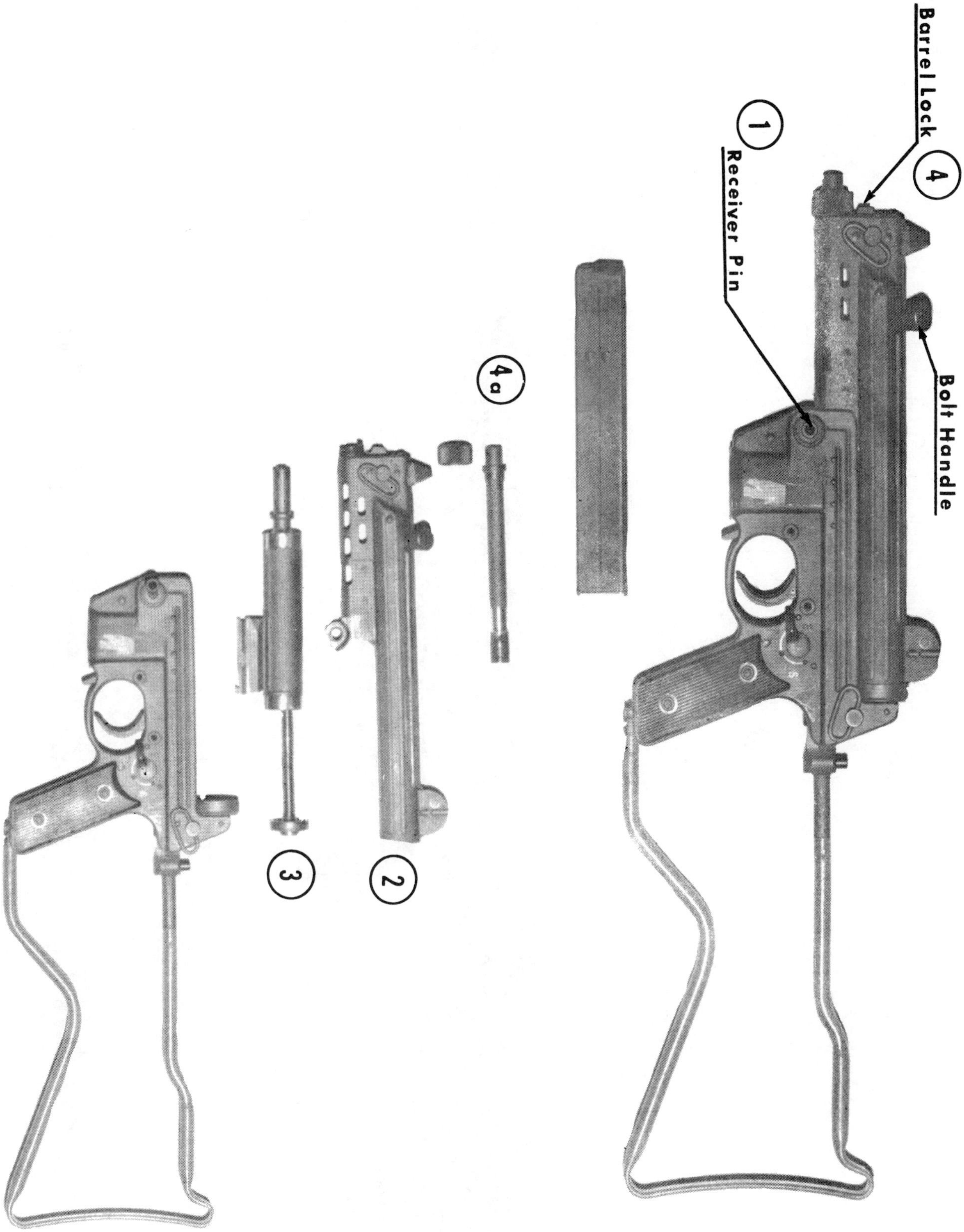
Barrel Lock
1
Receiver Pin
4
Bolt Handle
4a
3
2

9-mm MPK

GERMANY 7.92-MM SHORT, MP-43

SUBMACHINEGUN   GERMANY

7.92-mm MASCHINENPISTOLE 43 (MP 43)

The 7.92-mm MP 43 is one of a series of Machine Carbines developed by Germany during WWII and is the production model most often encountered. Based strongly on the Walther Machine Carbine 42 (MKb 42), two versions were produced, the MP 43 and the MP 43/1. Later the nomenclature was changed to MP 44 and in December 1944 it was again redesignated as the Sturmgewehr 44 (StG 44). By January 1944, 14,000 MP 43s were in the hands of the German Army. Production reached 5,000 a month by February 1944. The weapon was the outgrowth of German desire to produce an effective Machine Carbine firing a special intermediate size cartridge. This weapon will not chamber the standard German 7.92-mm rifle round but is designed to fire the 7.9-mm Pistolenmunition-43, later changed to "Kurz Patrone-43." Starting in the summer of 1942 extensive field tests between the Haenel and Walther machine carbine designs were carried out. These tests continued through the fall and winter of 1942. In the spring of 1943 the Walther design was rejected in favor of the Haenel. With the Haenel selected for service issue, it was modified and simplified for mass production. The original Haenel striker system was replaced with the internal hammer system previously found on the Walther MKb 42. The gas cylinder was simplified, the bayonet lug was eliminated and a new stacking pin was introduced. The Schmeisser hook-in-receiver-safety was eliminated in preference to the mechanical safety found in the Walther system.

FUNCTIONING

This is a gas-operated, semi- and full-automatic weapon. When the round is fired, gas is tapped from the barrel into the gas cylinder where it impinges against the face of the gas piston. Attached to the rear of the gas piston is the bolt carrier assembly. As the gas piston moves to the rear (approximately 7/16") the claw on the underside of the bolt carrier engages a mating claw on the upper rear surface of the bolt. Continuation of this movement lifts the rear of the bolt 3/32" to disengage it from its locked position and carries it to the rear. Upon completion of its rearward travel, the gas piston and bolt carrier, under the impulse of the compressed recoil spring, (with the bolt still engaged) moves forward. When the bolt face strikes the chamber, the piston and carrier continue forward for a small distance and cam the rear of the bolt down into a locked position. Pulling the trigger now releases the hammer which strikes the cylindrical striker assembled in the underhang extension of the bolt which in turn drives the "free floating" firing pin into the cartridge primer. In automatic firing the selector serves to cam an auxiliary operating bar into contact with an auxiliary sear. In semi-automatic firing the selector bar disconnects the auxiliary operating bar from the auxiliary sear.

CHARACTERISTIC DATA

Caliber ....7.92-mm Short
Operation ....Gas
Type of Fire .... Full and semi-auto
Rate of Fire ....800 rpm (Practical-250)
Type of Feed ....Box -30 rd cap
Weight, empty .... 8.2 lbs
Overall length .... 36.7 in
Effective range ....480 meters

FIELD STRIP PROCEDURE

STEP　　　　　　　　　　　　ACTION

1. With the Chamber empty and the Magazine removed, push the Locking Pin through the Receiver from the right side. Hold the Stock firmly.
2. Pull the Stock off to the rear, and remove the Recoil Spring.
3. Pull the Trigger and swing the Trigger Group Assembly down.
4. Pull back on the Bolt Handle to bring the Piston and Bolt Carrier Assembly and Bolt to the rear.
5. Slide the Piston and Bolt Carrier Assembly with the attached Bolt out the rear of the Receiver. Disengage the Bolt from the Bolt Carrier.

In step 2, the Stock must be held firmly since it is under slight tension of the Recoil Spring.

ASSEMBLY PROCEDURE

Proceed in the reverse order. Mate the claws on the top of the Bolt with the claws on the underside of the Bolt Carrier and slide the assembly into the Receiver. Assemble the Recoil Spring into the Receiver. Swing the Trigger Group Assembly up into place, aline the Stock with the Recoil Spring and the rear of the Receiver and push the Stock forward into assembled position. Push the Locking Pin through the Receiver.

LOADING AND FIRING

To load: This weapon fires from a closed Bolt. Push the Safety Lever up to "SAFE." Insert a loaded Magazine into the Magazine Well. Draw the Bolt Handle to the rear and release. The Bolt will travel forward, strip a round from the Magazine and chamber it. Push the fire selector button to the type fire desired -- push to the right for full-automatic; to the left for semi-automatic -- push Safety Lever down.

To fire: Pull the Trigger. The Sear will release the Hammer, the Hammer will rotate forward to impinge against the Firing Pin and the weapon will fire. If the select button is on semi-auto the Trigger must be pulled for each shot. If the select button is on automatic, the weapon will fire until the Trigger is released or the Magazine is empty.

COMPARISON OF MP-43 SERIES WEAPON (ABOVE), AND SOVIET AK-47 (BOTTOM)

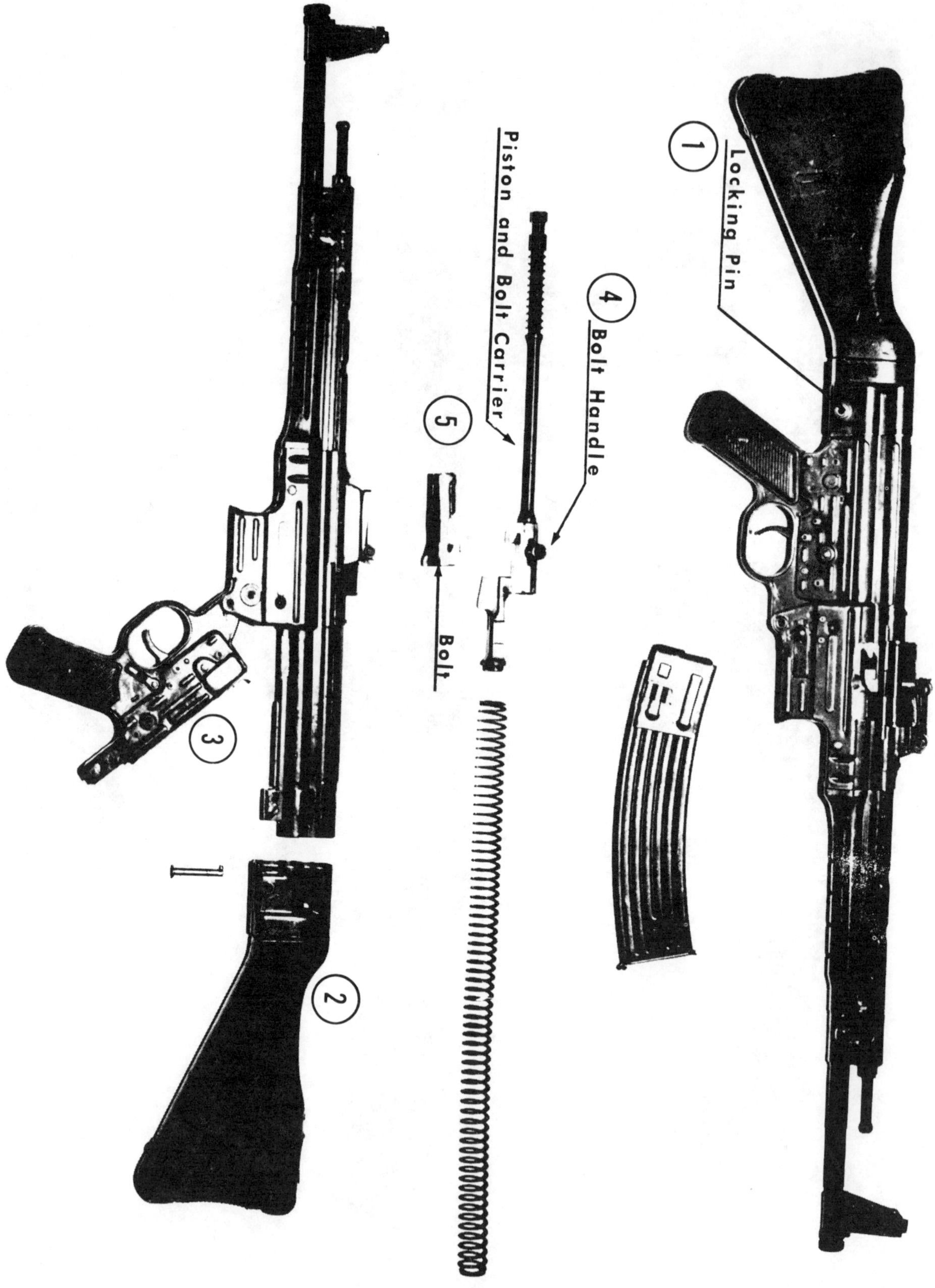
1
Locking Pin
Piston and Bolt Carrier
4
Bolt Handle
5
Bolt
3
2

7.92-mm MP-43

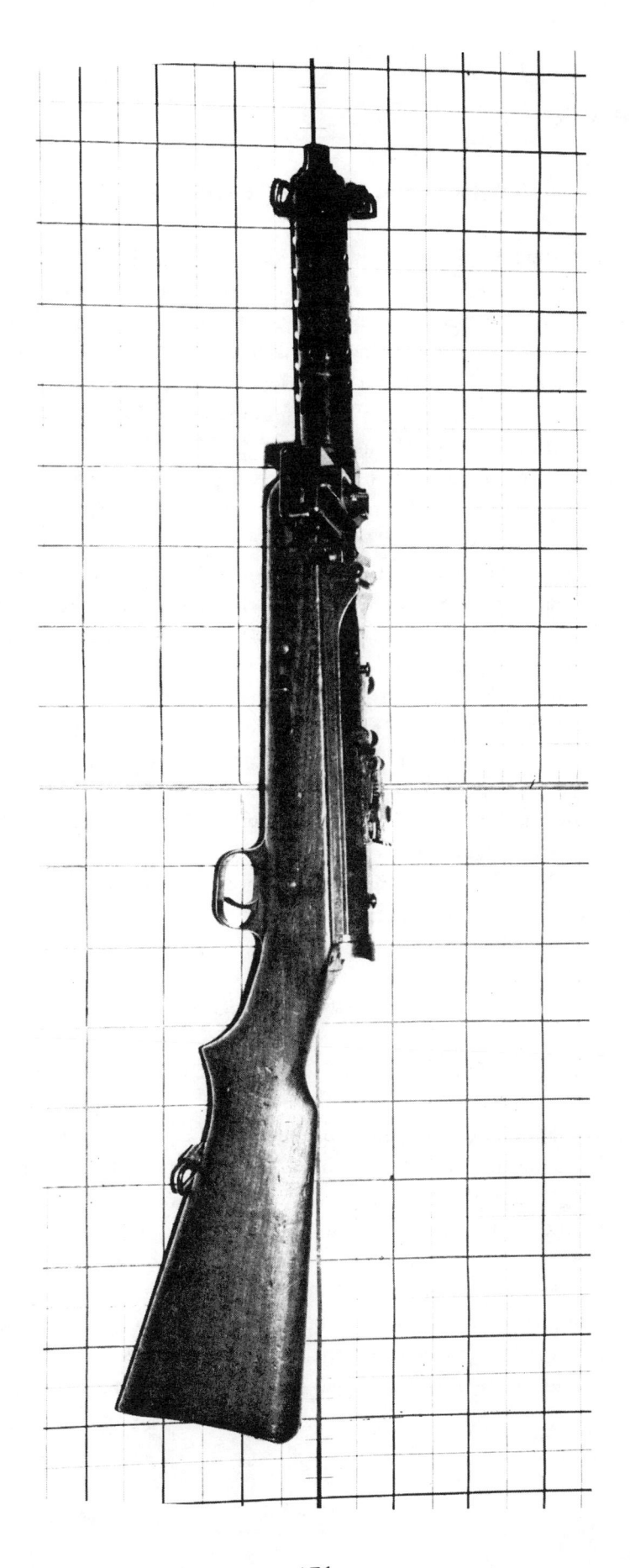

GERMANY   9-MM, STEYR-SOLOTHURN

SUBMACHINEGUN   GERMANY

9-mm MP 34 (o) (STEYR-SOLOTHURN)

The 9-mm Steyr-Solothurn Submachinegun was originally produced by the Steyr-Daimlar-Puch firm in Steyr, Austria. The first models produced were designated the Model 1930 and were adopted by the Austrian Police. The Austrian Army adopted the weapon in 1934 and this model was designated the MP 34 (o). This model was chambered for the 9-mm Mauser and 9-mm Steyr cartridge and after 1939 production models of this weapon were chambered for the 9-mm Parabellum round. The 9-mm Parabellum model was used by German units during WWII and was also purchased by Portugal in this caliber and given the Portugese designation of m/42. The weapon chambered for the 9-mm Mauser cartridge was used primarily by Austrian troops during the war. The piece chambered for the 9-mm Parabellum round has a small magazine housing than do those chambered for the 9-mm Mauser and Steyr round, thus magazines for the different calibers are not interchangeable. This same weapon, designated the S1-100 is sold commercially through offices in Zurich, Switzerland. This is a straight blowback weapon, extremely rugged and well made, being completely machined and is one of the finest examples of the state-of-the-art in submachinegun design encountered today. One noteworthy point is the magazine loading device built into the magazine housing. This enables the firer to load magazines from a strip clip by simply repositioning the empty magazine into the bottom of the magazine housing and stripping the cartridges into it through a loading device built in the top of the magazine housing. Models of the weapon marked MP 34 (o) are chambered for the 9-mm Steyr cartridge; models marked MP (o) are designed to fire the 9-mm Mauser round; models chambered for the 9-mm Parabellum cartridge are designated the P.M. Steyr M/42 or are marked with German Army acceptance-proof marks.

FUNCTIONING

The Steyr-Solothurn Submachinegun is a straight blowback weapon which fires from an open bolt. The safety slide is located on the top of the receiver in front of the rear sight and the fire select button is positioned on the left side of the stock between the trigger guard and the magazine housing. With a loaded magazine in place the bolt is drawn to the rear. The sear will engage the bolt and hold it open. When the trigger is pulled the sear releases the bolt, the bolt moves forward under impulse of the compressed recoil spring contained in the stock, a round is stripped from the magazine, chambered and fired. The bolt moves to the rear and if the fire select is set to the rear exposing the letter "E" (for semi-automatic) the sear will engage the bolt and the trigger must be pulled for the next shot. If the select button is pushed forward exposing the letter "D" (for full-automatic) the weapon will continue to fire until the trigger is released or the magazine is empty.

CHARACTERISTIC DATA

Caliber . . . . 9-mm Steyr, Parabellum,
. . . . Mauser and 7.63-mm Mauser
Operation . . . . Blowback
Type of Fire . . . . Full and semi-auto
Type of Fire . . . . Full and semi-auto
Rate of Fire . . . . 500 rpm (Practical 175)
Type of Feed . . . . Box - 30 rd cap
Weight, empty . . . . 9.5 lbs
Overall length . . . . 33.2 in
Effective range . . . . 300 meters

FIELD STRIP PROCEDURE

STEP   ACTION

1. Push down on the Receiver Lock Button located forward of the Receiver Lock, push in on the Receiver Lock and raise the Cover. This Cover comprises the whole top of the Receiver with the exception of the feedway.
2. Grasp the Bolt Handle and pull the Bolt to the rear until the reduced diameter portion of the Bolt clears the feedway, lift front of the Bolt up and pull the Bolt forward from the Receiver with the attached Recoil Spring Strut.
3. Open the trapdoor located in the Butt, turn the Recoil Spring Plug ¼ turn to the right and remove the Recoil Spring Plug, Recoil Spring and Recoil Spring Guide from the Stock.

ASSEMBLY PROCEDURE

Assemble in the reverse order. Place the Recoil Spring with Guide and Plug into the Stock and lock into place. Slide the Bolt into the Receiver, making sure the Recoil Spring Strut engages the Recoil Spring Guide Head, and push the Bolt rearward until the reduced diameter portion clears the feedway, then drop into place and allow it to move forward. Close the Cover and latch securely.

LOADING AND FIRING

To load: Push the Safety Slide forward to "SAFE." Insert a loaded Magazine in the Magazine Housing. Draw the Bolt Handle to the rear to open the Bolt. The Sear will engage the Bolt and hold it open.

To fire: Push the Safety Slide rearward to "FIRE." Set the Select Button to type of fire desired. Pull the Trigger, the weapon will fire. If set for semi-automatic, the Trigger must be pulled for each shot fired. If set for full-automatic, the weapon will fire until the Trigger is released or the Magazine is empty.

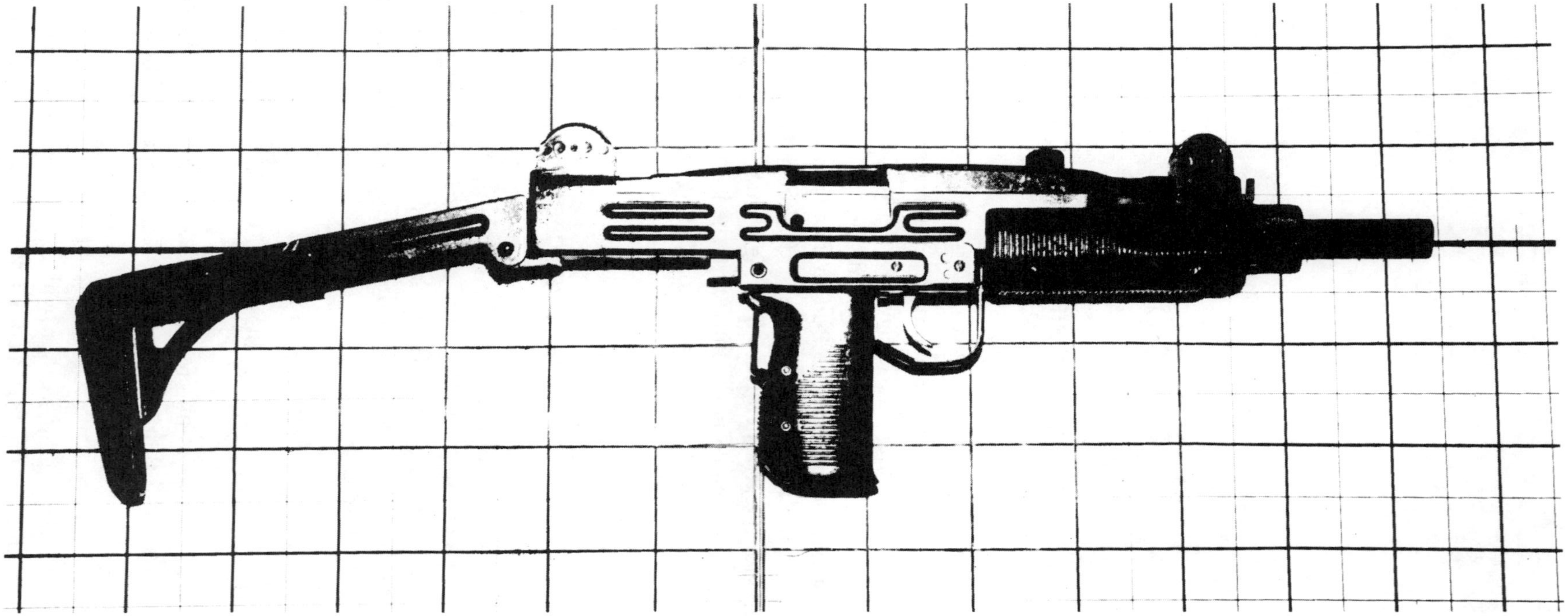

ISRAEL 9-MM, NO 2 MK A

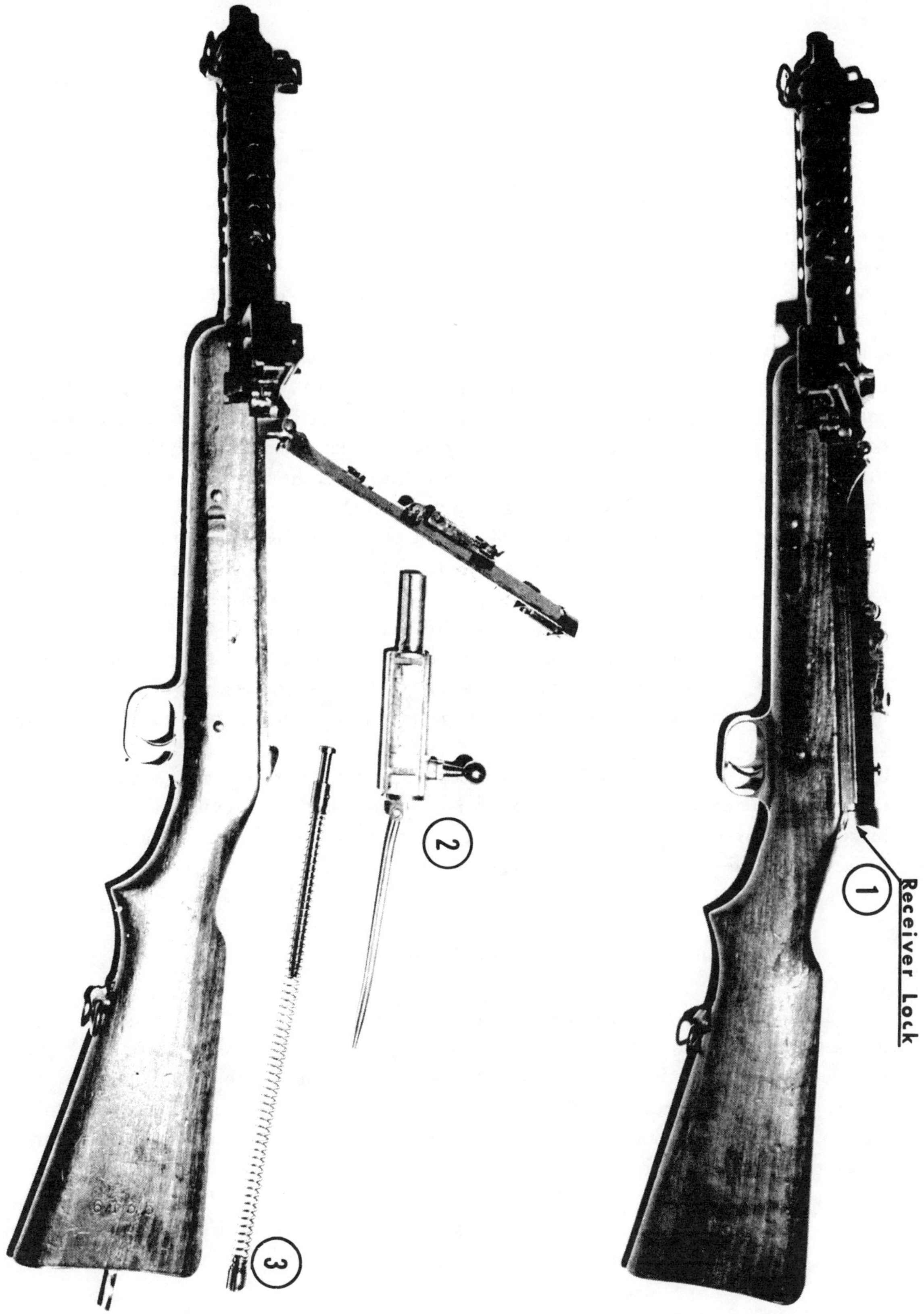
2
3
1
Receiver Lock

9-mm MP-34

SUBMACHINEGUN   ISRAEL

9-mm UZI SUBMACHINEGUN (Mk2 ModA)

The 9-mm UZI Submachinegun is an extremely compact weapon, utilizing metal stamped parts and plastics in its construction. Designed by Major Uziel Gal, it is the standard submachinegun of the Israeli Army, and has been adopted by the West German Army as well as the Armies of Peru and the Netherlands. The weapon embodies a number of unconventional features with more than normal emphasis being placed on safety of handling and balance. The receiver is rectangular in shape, composed of stampings with plastics being utilized in the construction of the forearm and pistol grip. There are no external moving parts when the weapon is fired. The cocking handle located on top of the receiver, moves to the forward position after the bolt is cocked to the rear. Two major design advantages of this weapon are the bolt system; hollowed out to surround the barrel for the major length of the bolt; and the location of the magazine well which is in the pistol grip. Both of these features tend to balance the piece very well and shortens the overall receiver length considerably. While this weapon utilizes a straight blowback system, the bolt due to its length, is heavy enough to function properly with the 9-mm cartridge. In being hollowed out to telescope the barrel, the actual travel of the bolt is quite short. The magazine being placed in the pistol grip eliminates a major fault encountered in using the magazine as a forward hand grip, as is the case in many submachineguns; an eventual malfunction of the magazine catch or deformation of the magazine itself. The weapon has a conventional safety, a sliding button type, which blocks the trigger when pushed to the rear, but also utilizes a grip-safety in the grip which blocks the sear if not pressed in when firing. Two more features worthy of note are the quick removable barrel (unscrewing the barrel nut lock makes the barrel easily removable), and the telescoping metal stock which when folded forward gives the weapon an overall length of slightly over 17 inches.

FUNCTIONING

The 9-mm UZI submachinegun is a straight blowback weapon. With a loaded magazine in place, the bolt is drawn to the rear by operating the cocking handle located on the top of the receiver. The bolt is held to the rear by the sear and the cocking handle, being released, moves to its forward position. After pushing the select lever to either full-auto or semi-auto position the piece is ready to fire. The grip safety must be squeezed in when gripping the pistol grip. Pulling the trigger releases the sear and the bolt moves forward, chambers a round and fires it. The bolt moves to the rear, overriding the sear. If the selector is set for full-auto, the sear will not engage and the bolt will move forward for a firing cycle. If the selector is set for semi-auto the bolt will remain held to the rear by the sear until the trigger is pulled again.

CHARACTERISTIC DATA

Caliber	9-mm
Operation	Blowback
Type of Fire	Full and semi-auto
Rate of Fire	550-600 rpm (Practical-125)
Type of Feed	Box-25, 32, 40 rd cap
Weight, empty	8.2 lbs
Overall length	Stock extended 26.2 in
	Stock folded 17.3 in
Effective range	225 meters
Muzzle velocity	1,325 fps

FIELD STRIP PROCEDURE

STEP   ACTION

1. Press the Cover Latch to the rear.
2. Raise the Cover and remove it from the Receiver.
3. Raise the Bolt, from the front, and remove it with the Recoil Spring, forward out of the Receiver.
4. Press in on the Barrel Nut Lock.
5. Unscrew the Barrel Retaining Nut and remove the Barrel.
6. Remove the Trigger Group Retaining Pin and disassemble the Trigger Group from the Receiver.

ASSEMBLY PROCEDURE

Assemble in the reverse order. Assemble the Trigger Group to the Receiver and put the Trigger Group Retaining Pin in place. Assemble the Recoil Spring and Guide to the Bolt and slide into the Receiver. The Barrel and Barrel Retaining Nut may be assembled to the Receiver either before or after the Bolt is placed in the Receiver. Lock the Cover into place on the top of the Receiver.

LOADING AND FIRING

To load: Draw the Cocking Handle, located on the top of the Receiver, to the rear until the Bolt is engaged by the Sear. Release the Handle and it will move to the forward position. Push the Safety Button to the rear to "SAFE". Insert a Magazine in the Pistol Grip.

To fire: Push the Safety Button forward to fire, to either the full or the semi-automatic position. Grip the Pistol Grip firmly to depress the Grip Safety, pull the Trigger. The weapon will fire. If the Select Button is on semi-auto, the Trigger must be pulled for each shot. If the Select Button is on auto, the weapon will fire until the Trigger is released or the Magazine is empty.

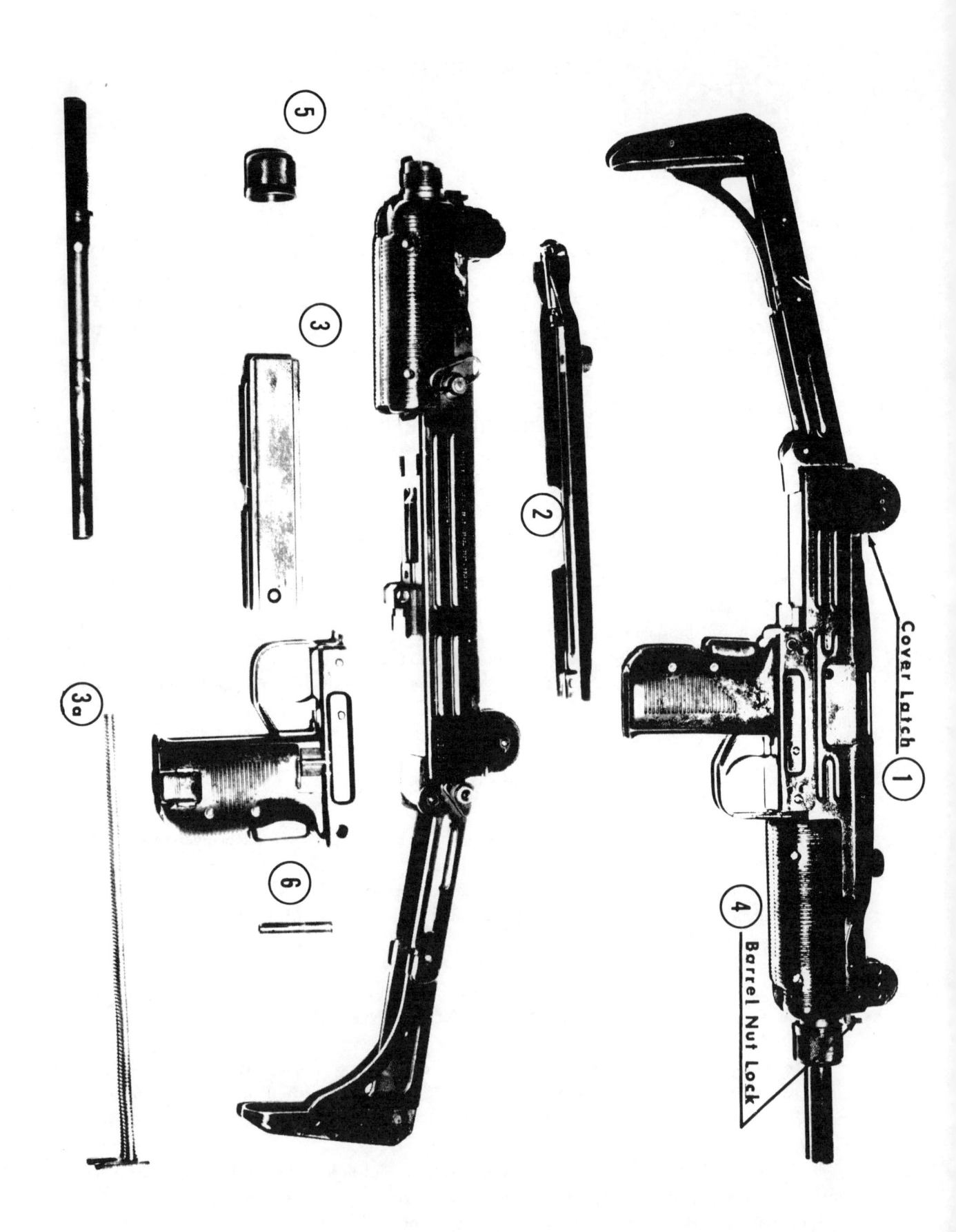

9-mm No. 2 MK A

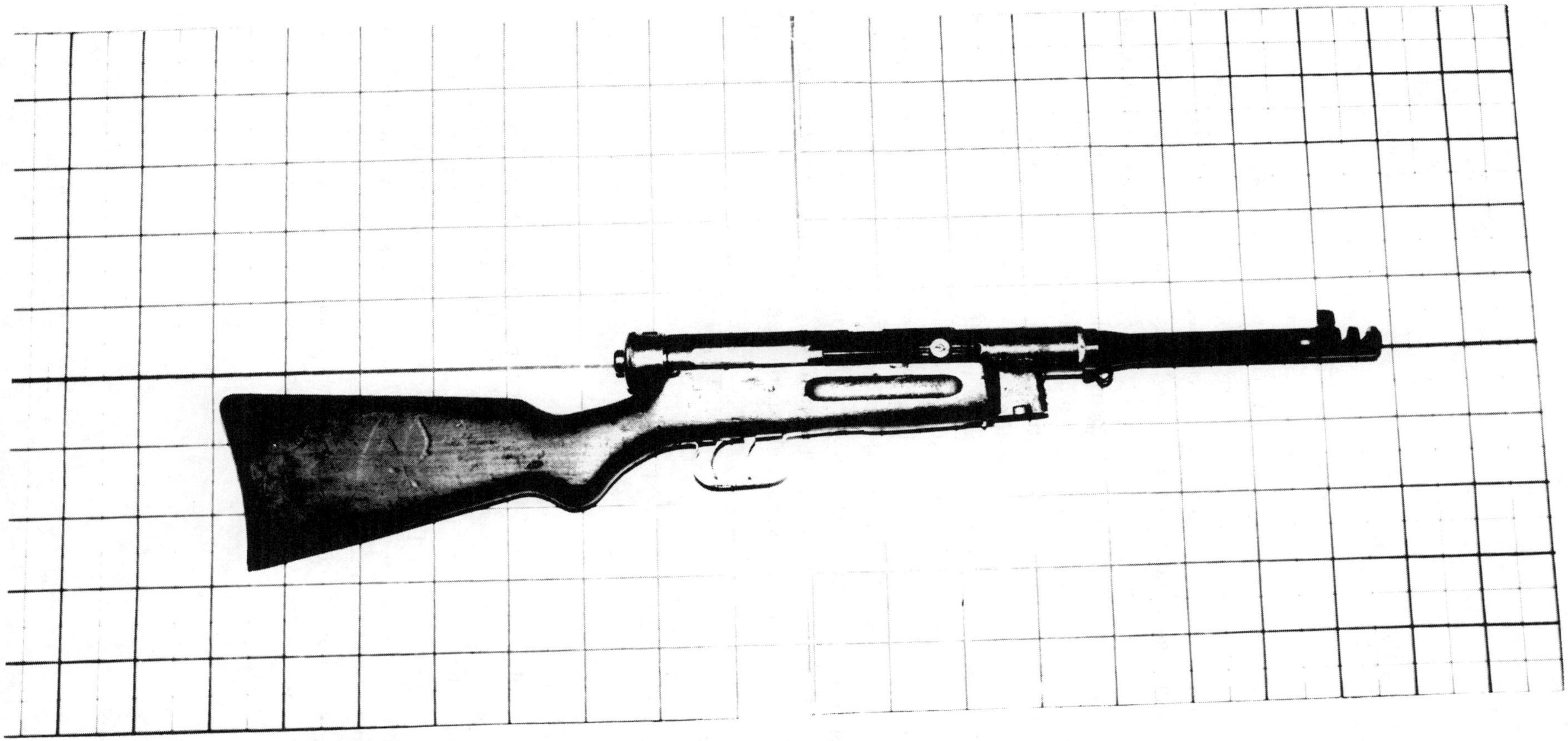

ITALY 9-MM, MODEL 38/42

SUBMACHINEGUN   ITALY

9-mm MODEL 38/42 (BERETTA)

The 9-mm Beretta Model 38/42 Submachinegun was designed by Marengoni in 1942 and was manufactured by the firm of Pietro Beretta, Gardone Valtrompia, Brescia, Italy. The Model 38/42 is a simplified version of the Beretta Model 1938A and Beretta Model 1 Submachineguns and although designed in 1942 it did not go into full production until mid-1943. The earlier weapon, the Model 1928A utilized a barrel jacket for cooling and appeared with a number of various compensator designs. The Model 1 was designed without a barrel jacket, had a simple two-slot compensator and a folding metal stock. The Model 38/42 retained the good points of both of these earlier weapons which include a fluted barrel for cooling (later production models have a smooth barrel), a simple compensator, the wooden rifle stock of the 1938A model, a modified, fixed firing pin bolt and the double trigger system for fire selection. The 38/42 was used by German and Italian units during the latter part of WWII and Rumania purchased some from the Beretta factory in 1944. A later, more simplified model, (Model 38/49) produced at the Beretta factory has been purchased by a number of countries. All the various models of the Beretta submachinegun are efficient, capable weapons, easy to maintain and somewhat more accurate due to stock design and balance, than the average submachinegun.

FUNCTIONING

The 9-mm Beretta Model 38/42 Submachinegun is a straight blowback weapon which fires from an open bolt. Fire selection is determined by a double trigger system. A pivoting safety lever is located on the left side of the receiver above the trigger guard. With a loaded magazine inserted in the magazine well, the bolt handle is drawn to the rear. At its rearmost position the bolt is engaged by the sear and held to the rear and the bolt handle with its attached dust cover may be pushed forward. The bolt handle does not move with the bolt during firing. When either the front or rear trigger is pulled, the bolt is released by the sear and moves forward under impulse of the compressed recoil spring, stripping a round from the magazine, chambering it and firing it. The bolt moves to the rear and if the front trigger (semi-automatic fire) has been pulled the sear will engage the bolt and the trigger must be pulled for each shot. If the rear trigger was pulled (full-automatic fire) the sear will not engage the bolt and the weapon will continue to fire until the trigger is released or the magazine is empty.

CHARACTERISTIC DATA

Caliber	9-mm
Operation	Blowback
Type of Fire	Full and semi-auto
Rate of Fire	550 rpm (Practical 200)
Type of Feed	Box - 20 & 40 rd cap
Weight, empty	9.7 lbs
Overall length	31.6 in
Effective range	250 meters

FIELD STRIP PROCEDURE

STEP   ACTION

1. Push in on the Recoil Spring Guide which protrudes from the center of the Receiver Cap and turn the Cap ¼ turn to the left.
2. Remove the Receiver Cap, Recoil Spring Guide and Recoil Spring.
3. Draw the Bolt Handle to the rear and remove the Bolt and Internal Recoil Spring Guide.

ASSEMBLY PROCEDURE

Assemble in the reverse order. Slide the Bolt into the rear of the Receiver. Place the Internal Recoil Spring Guide into the front end of the Recoil Spring and assemble the Recoil Spring and both Recoil Spring Guides into the Receiver. Slide the Receiver Cap over the end of the Receiver, push in on the Recoil Spring Guide and turn the Receiver Cap to lock into place.

LOADING AND FIRING

To load: Push the Safety Lever to "SAFE." Draw the Bolt Handle to the rear until the Bolt is engaged by the Sear and then push the Bolt Handle forward again. Insert a loaded Magazine into the Magazine Well.

To fire: Push the Safety Lever to "FIRE." Pull the Trigger. The weapon will fire. If the front Trigger has been pulled the weapon will fire semi-automatic and the Trigger must be pulled for each shot. If the rear Trigger was pulled the weapon will fire full-automatic. It will continue to fire until the trigger is released or the Magazine is empty.

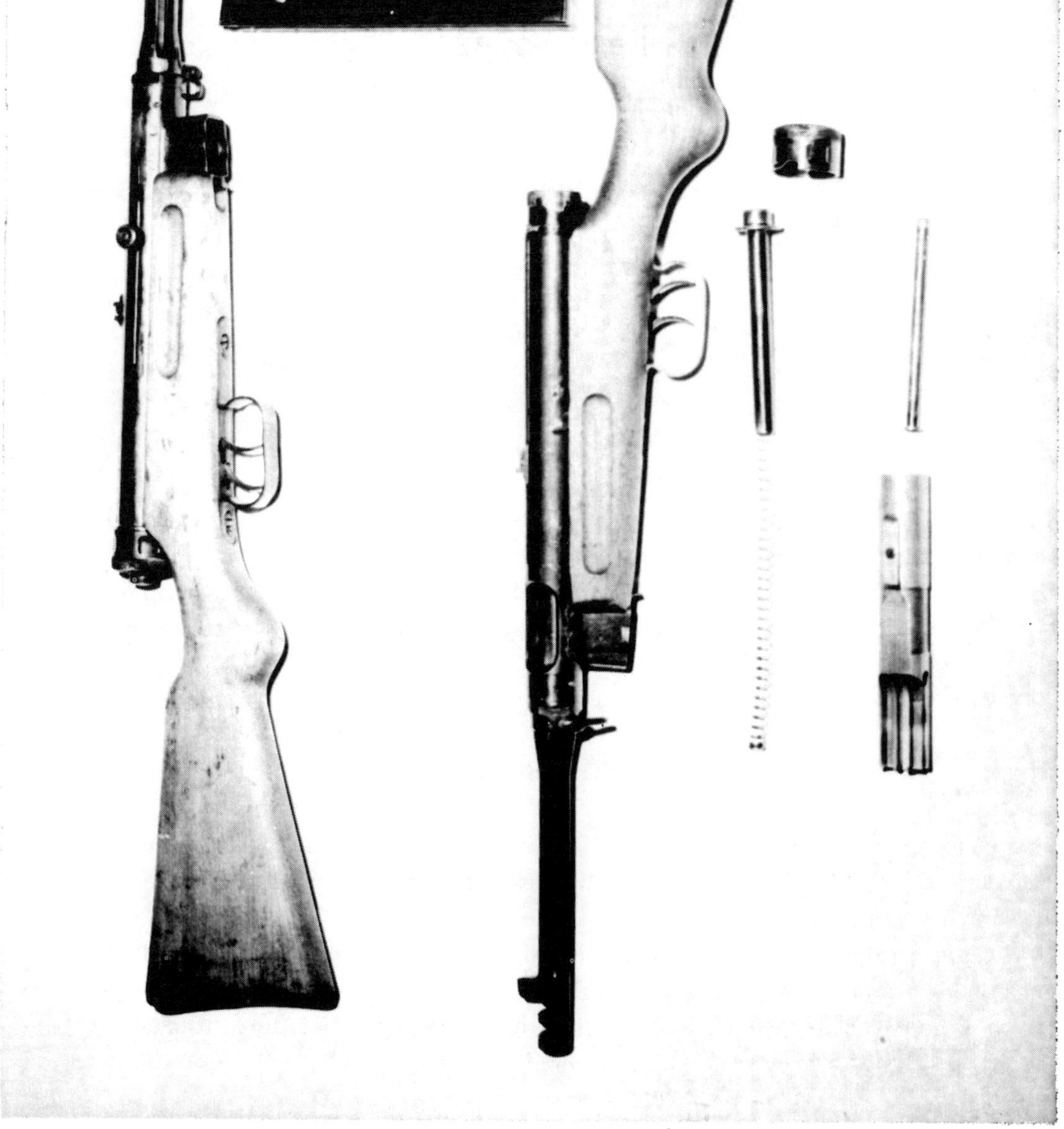

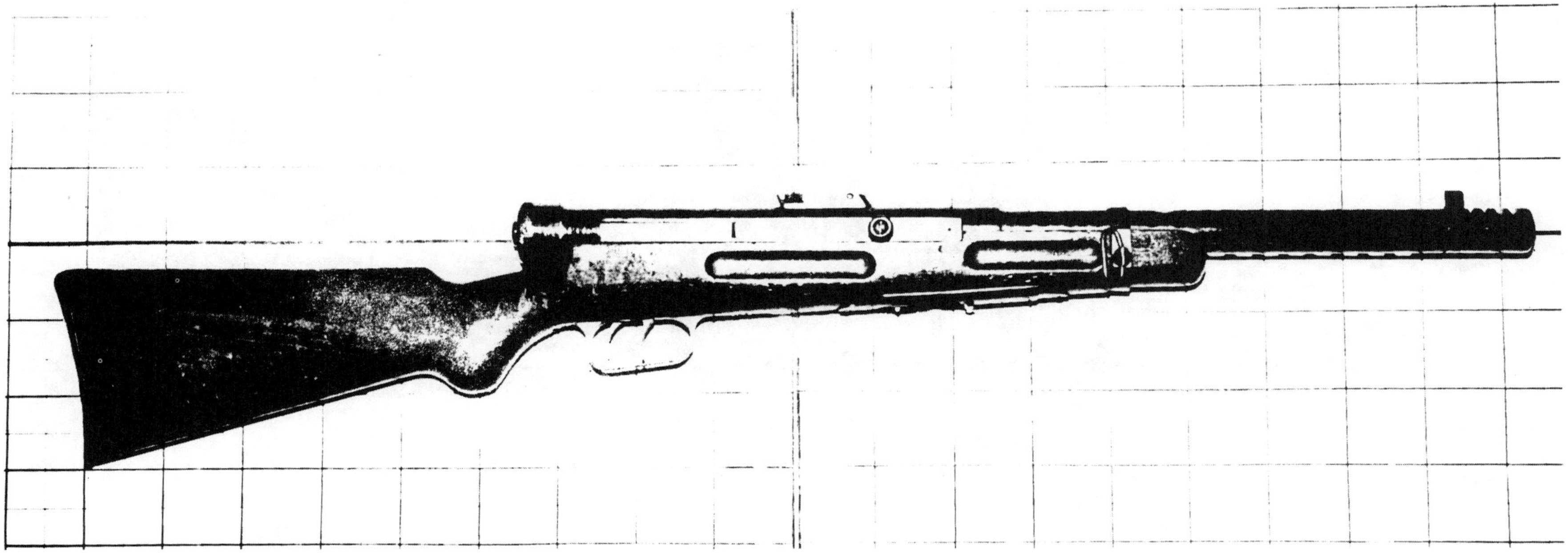

ITALY   9-MM, MODEL 1938A

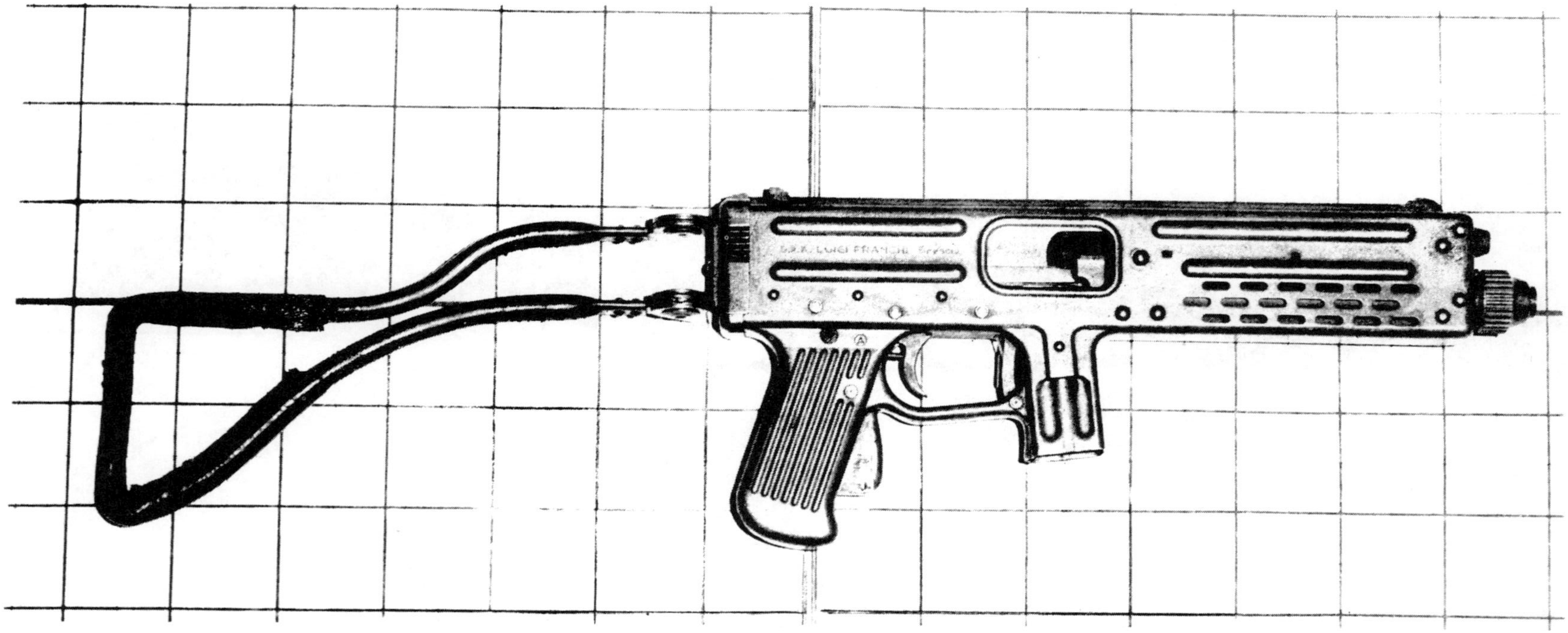

ITALY   9-MM, LF-57

SUBMACHINEGUN   ITALY

9-mm LF-57 (FRANCHI)

The 9-mm LF-57 Submachinegun is manufactured by the Italian firm, Luigi Franchi, located in Brescia, Italy. A prototype of this piece was produced by the Franchi firm in 1956 as the LF-56 and after minor modifications appeared as the LF-57. This weapon is composed of a completely stamped receiver, the receiver being made in two halves which are held together at a seam extending the length of the receiver. The bolt, barrel, recoil spring and guide as well as some smaller components are the only parts machined. The weapon utilizes a bolt design which is becoming increasingly popular in the submachinegun design field; a heavy bolt extension is carried above and forward of the bolt proper which provides the weight needed to keep the action closed and yet does not require a long receiver. The forward end of this bolt extension is contacted by the bolt handle to open the bolt. After the bolt has been drawn to the rear by the bolt handle, the bolt handle is forced forward by a bolt handle return spring. Thus the bolt moves independent of the bolt handle during firing. The stock folds to the right side of the weapon. The only safety device on this piece is a grip safety located in the front strap of the pistol grip. This grip safety must be pushed in before the bolt can be drawn to the rear and it must also be squeezed before the trigger will release the sear to fire the weapon.

FUNCTIONING

The LF-57 is a straight blowback weapon which fires full and semi-automatic. With a loaded magazine in place, the grip safety is squeezed and the bolt handle is drawn to the rear and released. The bolt will be held to the rear while the bolt handle returns to its forward position under the impulse of a bolt handle return spring. To fire the weapon the grip safety must be squeezed at the same time that the trigger is pulled. The bolt will move forward strip a round from the magazine, chamber it and fire it. The fire select button is a push-through button located above the grips. Pushing the button on the side marked "A" (right side of Receiver) will cause the weapon to fire full-automatic. Pushing the button the side marked "S" (left side of receiver) will cause the weapon to fire semi-automatic. Some models of this weapon may be found without the fire select button and are capable of full-automatic fire only.

CHARACTERISTIC DATA

```
Caliber ................................................................. 9-mm
Operation ........................................................... Blowback
Type of Fire ................................................. Full-auto only
Rate of Fire ................................... 500 rpm (Practical 175)
Type of Feed ................................... Box - 20 & 40 rd cap
Weight, empty .................................................... 7.1 lbs
Overall length, stock folded ............................... 15.9 in
Effective range ............................................. 200 meters
```

FIELD STRIP PROCEDURE

STEP   ACTION

1. Fold open the Stock.
2. Grasp Stock, pull Back Plate Latch located on top of Back Plate to the rear and slide Back Plate up off of Receiver.
3. Remove Recoil Spring and Recoil Spring Guide.
4. Tilt rear of Receiver down and remove Bolt Assembly.
5. Unscrew Barrel Lock Nut and Remove Nut and Barrel.

ASSEMBLY PROCEDURE

Assemble in the reverse order. Slide Barrel into front of Receiver and screw Barrel Lock Nut to Receiver. Slide Bolt Assembly into rear of Receiver. Assemble Recoil Spring and Recoil Spring Guide into Bolt. Slide Back Plate with attached Stock down onto Receiver making sure the Back Plate Latch engages.

LOADING AND FIRING

To load: Squeeze the Grip Safety in by grasping the Pistol Grip firmly. Draw the Bolt Handle to the rear and release. The Bolt will remain held to the rear by the Sear. Insert a loaded Magazine into the Magazine Housing. Release the Grip Safety and the weapon is on "SAFE".

To fire: Grasp the Pistol Grip firmly, squeezing in on the Grip Safety. Pull the Trigger and the weapon will fire. If the fire select button has been pushed from right to left, the weapon will continue to fire until the magazine is empty or the trigger is released. If the button has been pushed from left to right, the Trigger must be pulled for each shot.

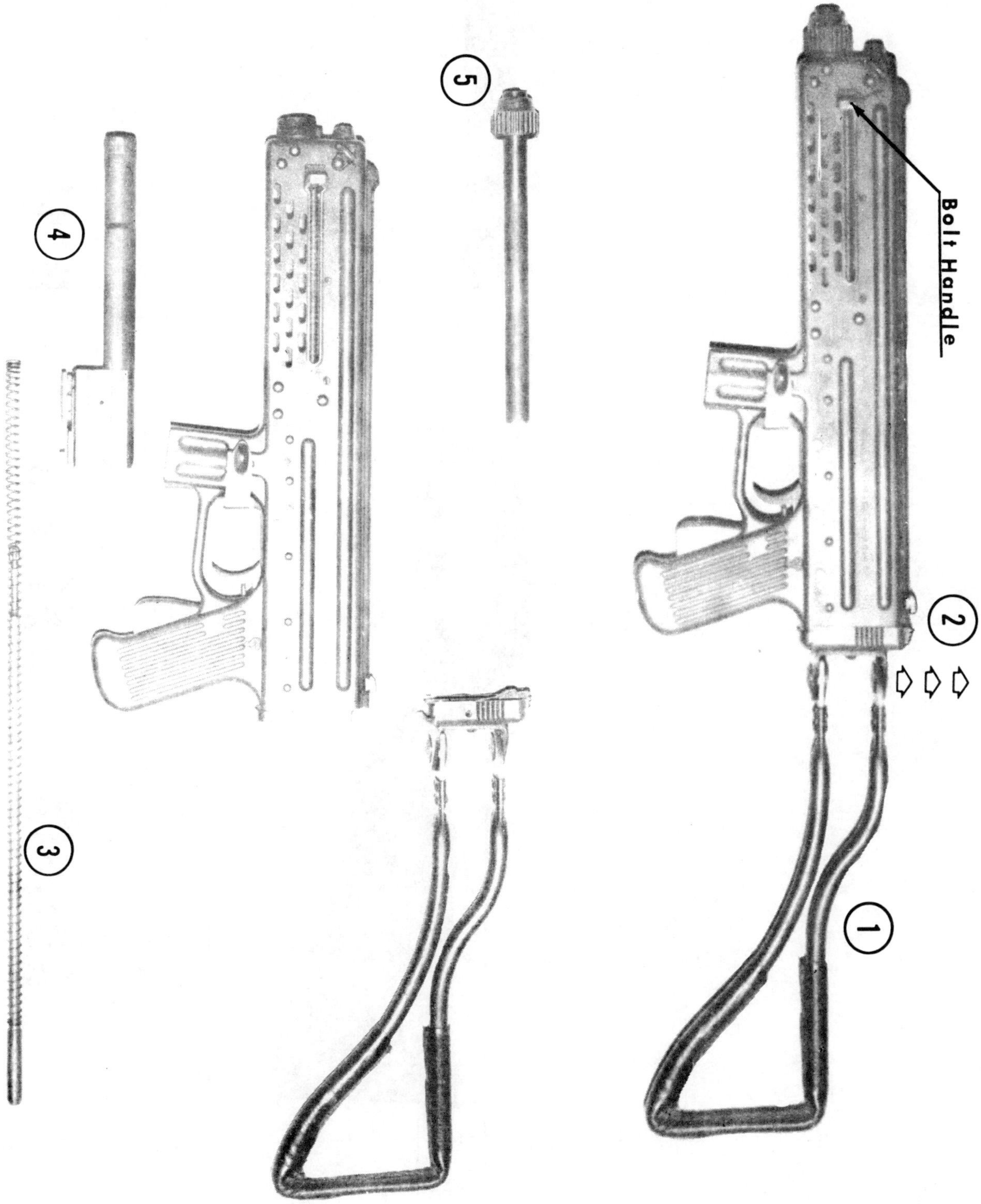
5
4
3
2
1
Bolt Handle

9-mm LF-57

RUSSIA   7.62-MM, PPSH-41

SUBMACHINEGUN   U.S.S.R.

7.62 - mm PPSh-41 (SHPAGIN)

The Soviet PPSh-41 Submachinegun was designed by George S. Shpagin and was officially adopted by the Soviet Army in 1941. It replaced the Degtyarov series of submachineguns and is presently obsolete in the Soviet Union but may be found in most of the Satellite and Communist Bloc armies. It is an extremely simple, inexpensive weapon, composed mainly of stampings; the bolt and barrel being the only major machined components in the weapon. As a straight blowback weapon it has an extremely high rate of fire. Due to a relatively ineffective compensator, the muzzle climbs rapidly in full-automatic fire and there is considerable muzzle blast. It fires from an open bolt, the barrel is chrome-plated, and a so-called buffer is positioned in the rear of the receiver. The original Soviet weapon is designed to accept a 71 round drum magazine as well as a 35 round box magazine. Some models produced by Communist China, the Type 50, will handle only the box magazine; the Hungarian copy, the M48 and the Iranian copy, the M22, will function with both the box and the drum magazines. The North Korean copy, the Model 49, will accept only the 71 round capacity drum magazine.

FUNCTIONING

The PPSh-41 submachinegun is a straight blowback submachinegun which fires from an open bolt. The weapon is put on safe by pushing a sliding stud on the bolt handle into a notch in either the front or rear portion of the bolt handle retracting slot in the receiver. The bolt can be locked in this manner in either the open or closed position. The fire select lever is located ahead of the trigger inside the trigger guard. Pushed forward, the weapon will fire full-automatic, drawn to the rear, the disconnector functions to release the sear allowing it to engage the bolt and semi-automatic fire is achieved. With a loaded magazine inserted the bolt is drawn to the rear. Pull the trigger, releasing the bolt. The bolt moves forward under impulse of the compressed recoil spring, strips a round from the magazine, chambers it and fires it. The bolt moves to the rear and if the fire select lever is set for semi-automatic the sear will engage the bolt and hold it open. The trigger must be pulled for each shot. If the select lever is set for full-automatic the sear will not engage the bolt and the weapon will continue to fire until the trigger is released or the magazine is empty.

CHARACTERISTIC DATA

Caliber .... 7.62-mm (7.63-mm Mauser)
Operation .... Blowback
Type of Fire .... Full and semi-auto
Rate of Fire .... 900 rpm (Practical-175)
Type of Feed .... Box - 35 rd cap
.... Drum - 71 rd cap
Weight, empty .... 8.7 lbs
Overall length .... 33.2 in
Effective range .... 200 meters

FIELD STRIP PROCEDURE

STEP   ACTION

1. Push in on the Receiver Lock located at the rear of the Receiver and pivot the top of the Receiver up.
2. Pull the Bolt Handle to the rear slightly and lift the Bolt and the attached Recoil Spring, Recoil Spring Guide and Buffer up and out of the Receiver.

ASSEMBLY PROCEDURE

Assemble in the reverse order. Assemble the Bolt with assembled Recoil Spring, Guide and Buffer into the Receiver. Pivot the top of the Receiver down until the Receiver Lock engages.

LOADING AND FIRING

To load: Draw the Bolt to the rear and push the Safety Slide in to engage the rear Safety Notch in the Bolt Handle retracting slot. Insert a box or drum Magazine into the Magazine Well from the bottom. Push the Fire Select Lever forward, for full-automatic fire or rearward for semi-automatic fire.

To fire: Pull the Safety Slide out of the Bolt Handle retracting slot. Pull the Trigger. The weapon will fire. If the Fire Select Lever is set for semi-automatic the Trigger must be pulled for each shot. If the Select Lever is set for full-automatic the weapon will continue to fire until the Trigger is released or the Magazine is empty.

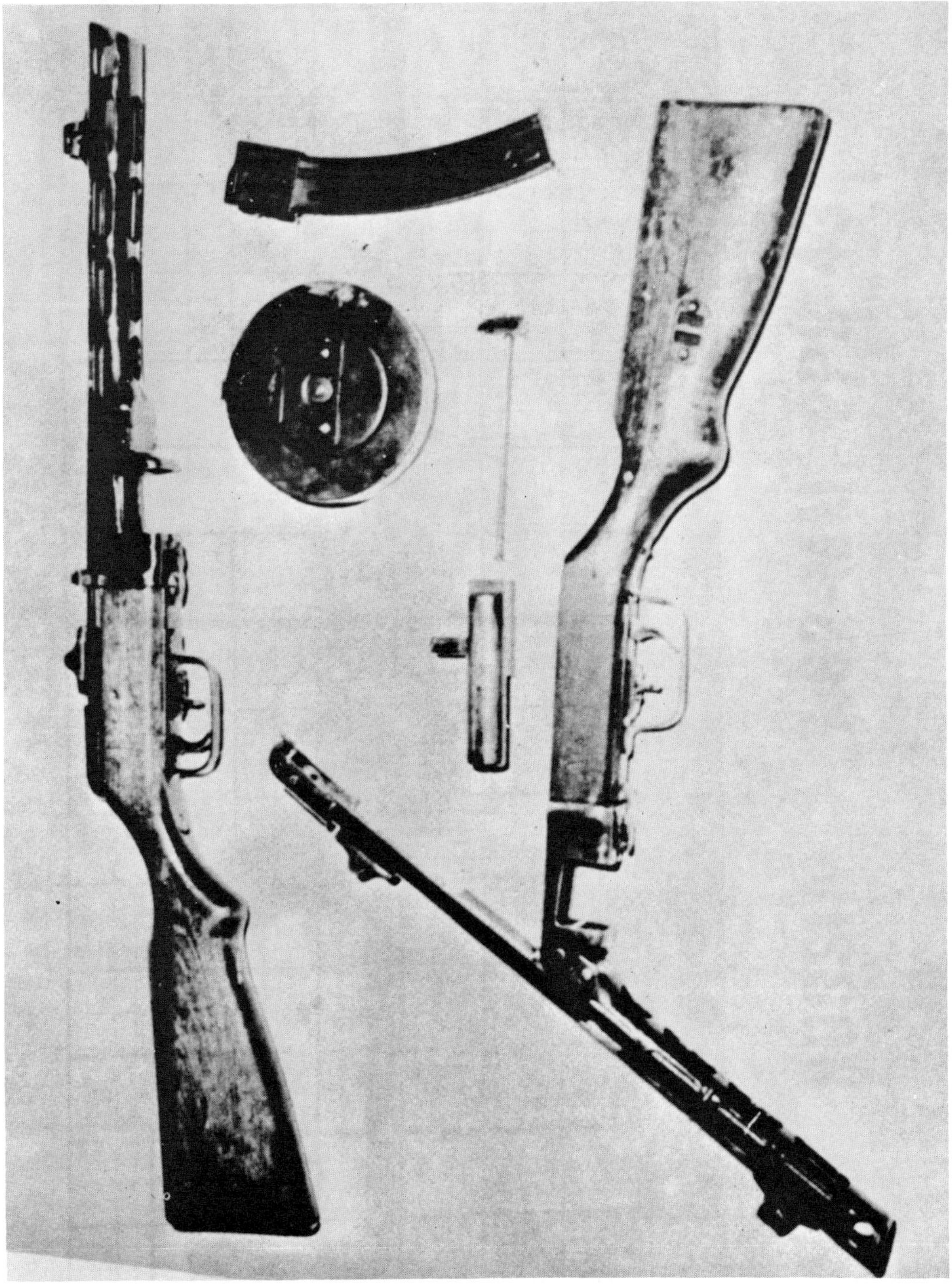

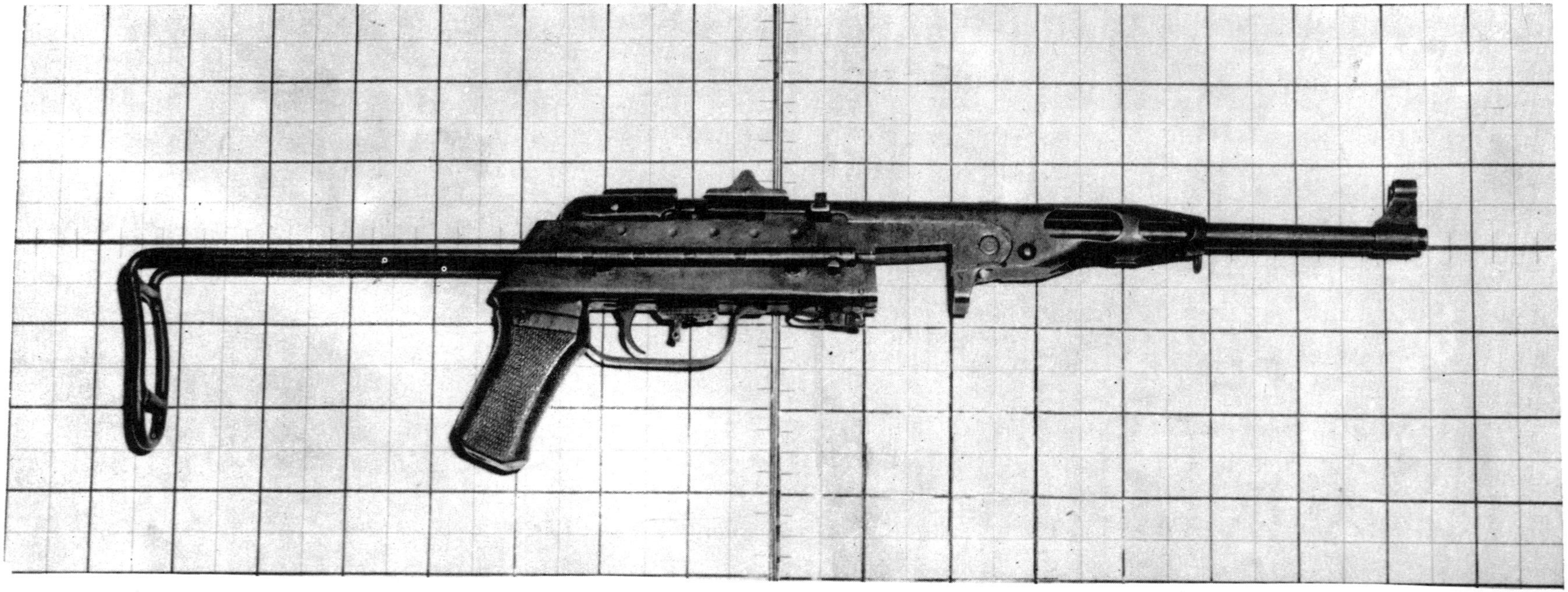

VIET CONG 7.62-MM, VIET CONG MODIFIED K-50

RUSSIA 7.62-MM, PPS-43

SUBMACHINEGUN   U.S.S.R.

7.62-mm PPS-43 (SUDAREV)

The Soviet PPS–43 Submachinegun is a modification of the PPS–42 Submachinegun which was designed by A. I. Sudarev in 1942. The early model was produced in Leningrad, the initial assembly line output being issued to Soviet troops defending the city of Leningrad against the German blockade. Field tested directly from the factory, the PPS–42 was modified slightly and standardized in 1943 as the PPS–43. This weapon is composed entirely of stampings with the exception of the bolt, barrel, recoil spring with guide and some minor components. The only non-metal portion of the piece are the pistol grips and the fiber buffer plate. The weapon fires full-automatic only from an open bolt. An unusual design feature is the lack of a fixed ejector. The forward end of the recoil spring guide projects through the face of the bolt when the bolt is in full recoil thus ejecting the empty case from the receiver. A combination muzzle brake/compensator is attached to the forward end of the barrel jacket and is relatively ineffective due to the high rate of fire and lightness of the piece, accomplishing little more than increasing the muzzle blast. The metal stock folds up and over the top of the receiver making this an extremely compact, easy-to-handle weapon. It is manufactured by the Chinese Communist as the Type 43; a wooden stocked version is manufactured by Poland as the M1943/52.

FUNCTIONING

The 7.62-mm PPS–43 is a straight blowback weapon which fires full-automatic only. The safety lever is located on the right side of the forward portion of the trigger guard. With a loaded magazine inserted in the magazine well the bolt is drawn to the rear where the sear engages it and holds it open. Pushing forward on the safety lever will lock the bolt in this position. (The safety lever may also be set on "SAFE" with the bolt forward.) Pulling the safety lever to the rear will unlock the bolt. Pull the trigger, the sear releases the bolt, the bolt moves forward, strips a round from the magazine, chambers it and fires it. The bolt moves to the rear and if the trigger is still held to the rear, the firing cycle will be repeated until the magazine is empty or until the trigger is released.

CHARACTERISTIC DATA

```
Caliber ..................................................7.62-mm (7.63-mm Mauser)
Operation ............................................................Blowback
Type of Fire ...................................................Full-auto only
Rate of Fire ...........................................700 rpm (Practical 150)
Type of Feed ..............................................Box - 35 rd cap
Weight, empty ...................................................7.2 lbs
Overall length, stock folded ......................................24.2 in
Effective range ...............................................175 meters
```

FIELD STRIP PROCEDURE

STEP   ACTION

1. Push in on the Receiver Lock located at the rear bottom edge of the Receiver and pivot the lower part of the Receiver down.
2. Pull the Bolt Handle to the rear slightly and lift the Bolt and attached Recoil Spring, Recoil Spring Guide and Buffer up and out of the Receiver. The Recoil Spring, Guide and Buffer may be disconnected from the Bolt.

ASSEMBLY PROCEDURE

Assemble in the reverse order. If the Recoil Spring, Guide and Buffer have been disconnected from the Bolt, assemble them to the Bolt. Assemble the Bolt with assembled Recoil Spring, Guide and Buffer into the Receiver. Pivot the lower part of the Receiver up until the Receiver Lock engages.

LOADING AND FIRING

To load: Draw the Bolt to the rear and push the Safety Lever forward to "SAFE." Insert a loaded Magazine into the Magazine Well.

To fire: Pull the Safety Lever to the rear. Pull the Trigger. The weapon will fire until the Trigger is released or the Magazine is empty.

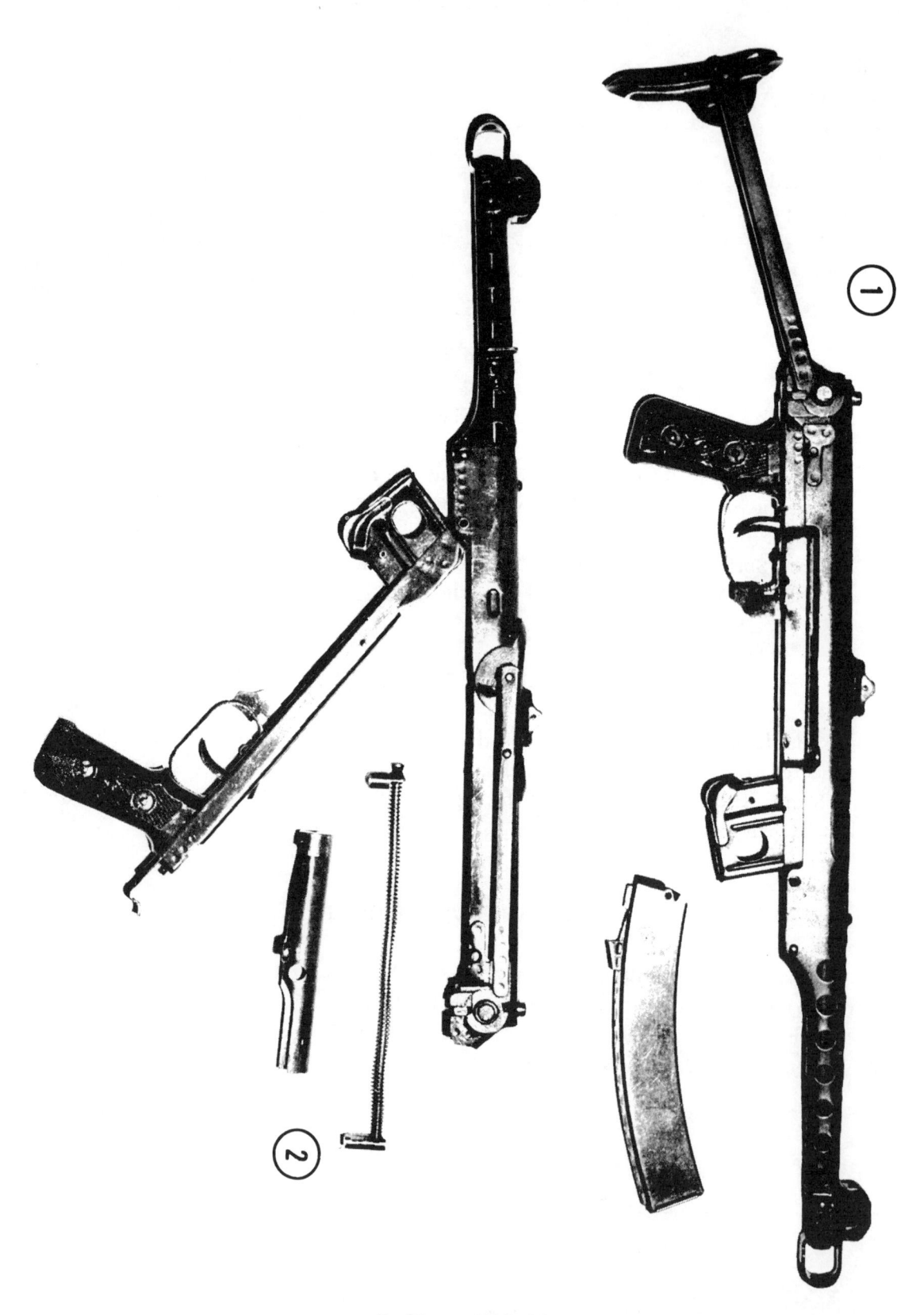

7.62-mm PPS-43

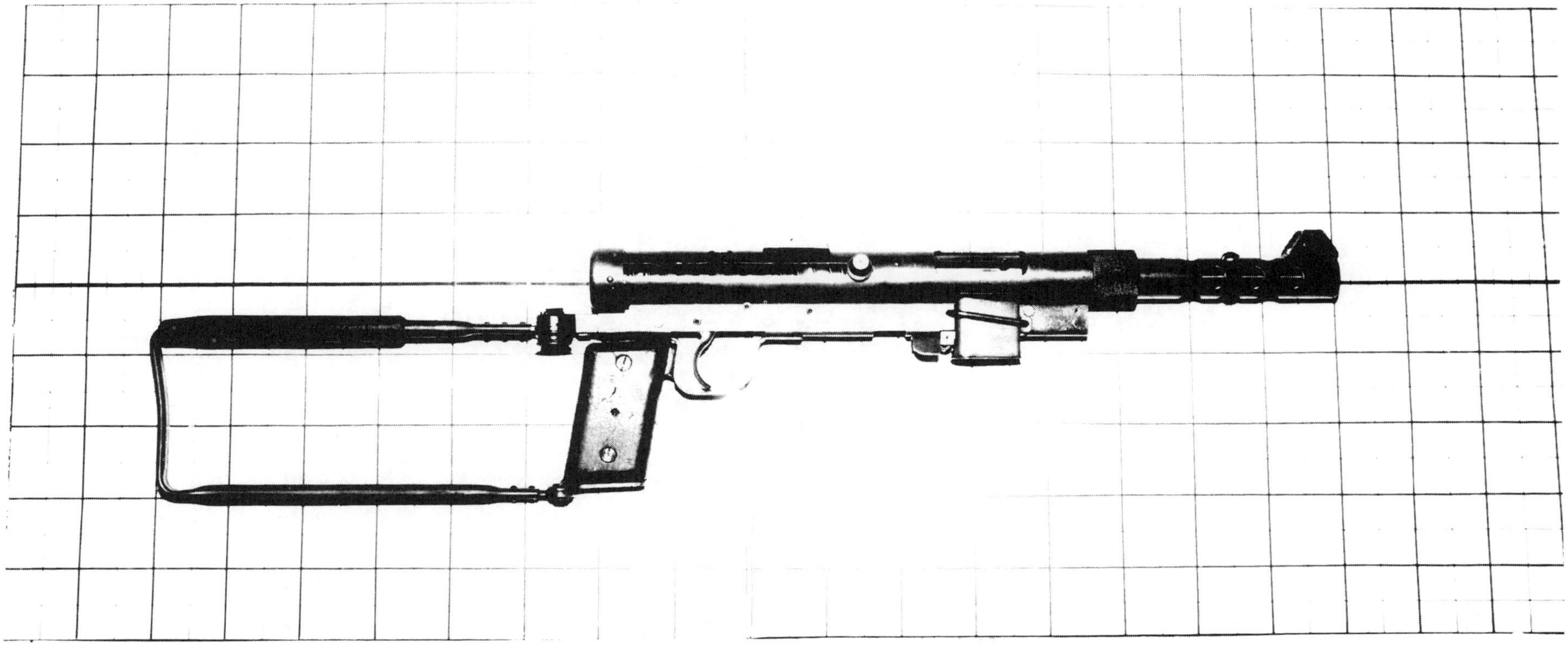

SWEDEN 9-MM, M45B

SUBMACHINEGUN   SWEDEN

9-MM SUBMACHINEGUN (Carl Gustaf) (M45B)

The 9-mm M45B Submachinegun was developed in 1944 and 1945 by the Carl Gustaf Geversfaktori, located in Elkilstune, Sweden. This weapon has been in production in Sweden since 1945 and many hundreds of thousands have been manufactured both for local consumption and for export. It is the current standard submachine gun in the Swedish Army. The original M45 submachine gun was made to utilize the 50-round SOUMI box magazine. After the early 1950s the heavy 50-round magazine was discarded in favor of the new 36-round type, developed in the late 1940s. The M45 model illustrated, is distinguished from the early M45 models by the magazine housing which is pinned in place and may be removed to accommodate the larger SOUMI magazine if the need arose. Later models of the M45B, produced after the 36-round magazine became available in large quantities, has a permanently attached (riveted) magazine housing and thus cannot be converted to receive the SOUMI 50-round magazine. The M45B model is sold commercially under the trade name of "Carl Gustaf" and has been adopted and produced by Egypt since the early 1950s.

FUNCTIONING

The basic design of the M45 has not changed since its introduction in 1945. It is an extremely sturdy and durable weapon and fires from the open-bolt position in a straight blow-back operation. It is made, in most part, of heavy stampings and the folding stock is one of the strongest and best designed of all the various types used on submachine guns. The bolt can be safetied in either the forward or rearward position. With the bolt to the rear, engaged by the sear, a loaded magazine is inserted. When the trigger is pulled, the bolt moves forward, stripping a round from the magazine, chambering it and firing it. Action is repeated until the trigger is released or the magazine is empty. The rate of fire has been purposely held low so that the weapon can be fired single-shot by proper trigger manipulation.

NOTES TO REMEMBER

This weapon fires a special hi-velocity 9-mm Parabellum cartridge, designated the 9-mm Model 39B. It has a much heavier jacket structure and therefore serves as an effective armor-piercing round. Since the Model 39B develops higher pressure, it is forbidden to be used in other 9-mm caliber weapons.

Hold the Receiver Cap firmly when removing in disassembly. The Operating Spring pushes very strongly against the Cap.

CHARACTERISTIC DATA

Caliber	9-mm Parabellum
Operation	Blowback
Type of Fire	Full-auto only
Rate of Fire	600 rpm (Practical-100)
Type of Feed	Box M45 - 50 rds
	M45B - 36-50 rds
	M45B - late model - 36 rds
Weight, empty	6.1 lbs
Length, stock extended	31.8 in (retracted - 21.7 in)
Effective range	270 meters

FIELD STRIP PROCEDURE

STEP   ACTION

1. Press the Magazine Release lever and remove the Magazine.
2. Press in on the plug in the center of the Receiver Cap, turn the Cap counterclockwise, and carefully remove the Cap.
3. The Operating Spring and Bolt may now be withdrawn from the rear of the Receiver.
4. With a hard object, push in on the Barrel Jacket Nut Catch and unscrew the Barrel Jacket Nut which surrounds the rear of the Barrel.
5. The Barrel and Barrel Jacket may now be removed from the front of the Receiver.

ASSEMBLY PROCEDURE

Proceed in the reverse order. Place the Barrel into the front end of the Receiver. Slide the Barrel Jacket down over the Barrel and screw the Barrel Jacket Nut onto the Receiver. Slide the Bolt into the rear of the Receiver, assemble the Operating Spring to the Bolt. Place the Receiver Cap over the end of the Operating Spring, push until it envelopes the rear of the Receiver, and turn clockwise.

LOADING AND FIRING

To load: Pull the Bolt to the rear by the Bolt Handle (located on the right side of the Receiver) and engage the Bolt Handle in the Safety Notch by moving it up. Insert a loaded Magazine into the Magazine Housing.

To fire: Disengage the Bolt Handle from the Safety Notch. Pull the Trigger. The weapon will fire until the Trigger is released or the Magazine is empty.

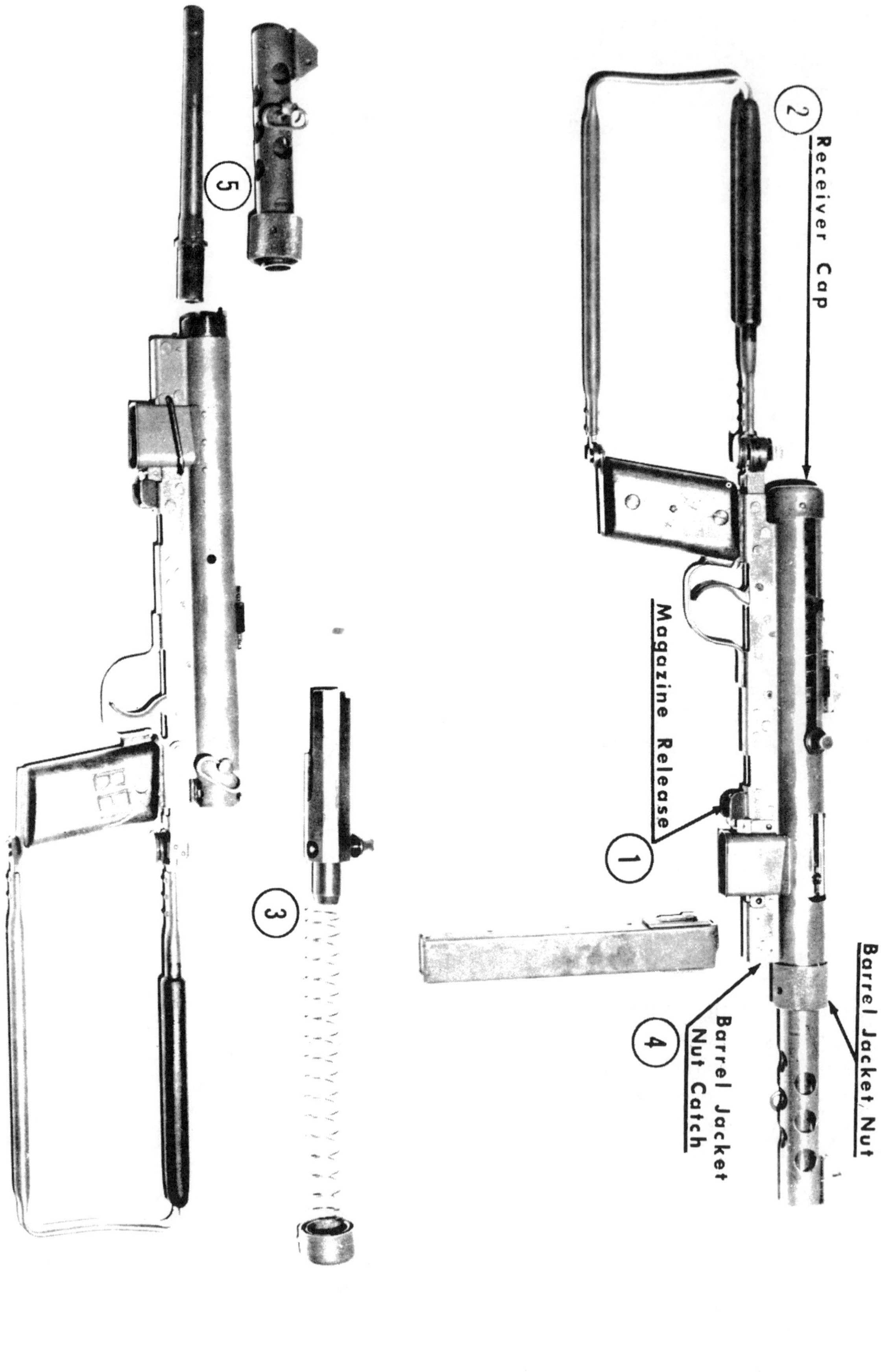
5
2
Receiver Cap
Magazine Release
1
3
4
Barrel Jacket
Nut Catch
Barrel Jacket Nut

9-mm M45B

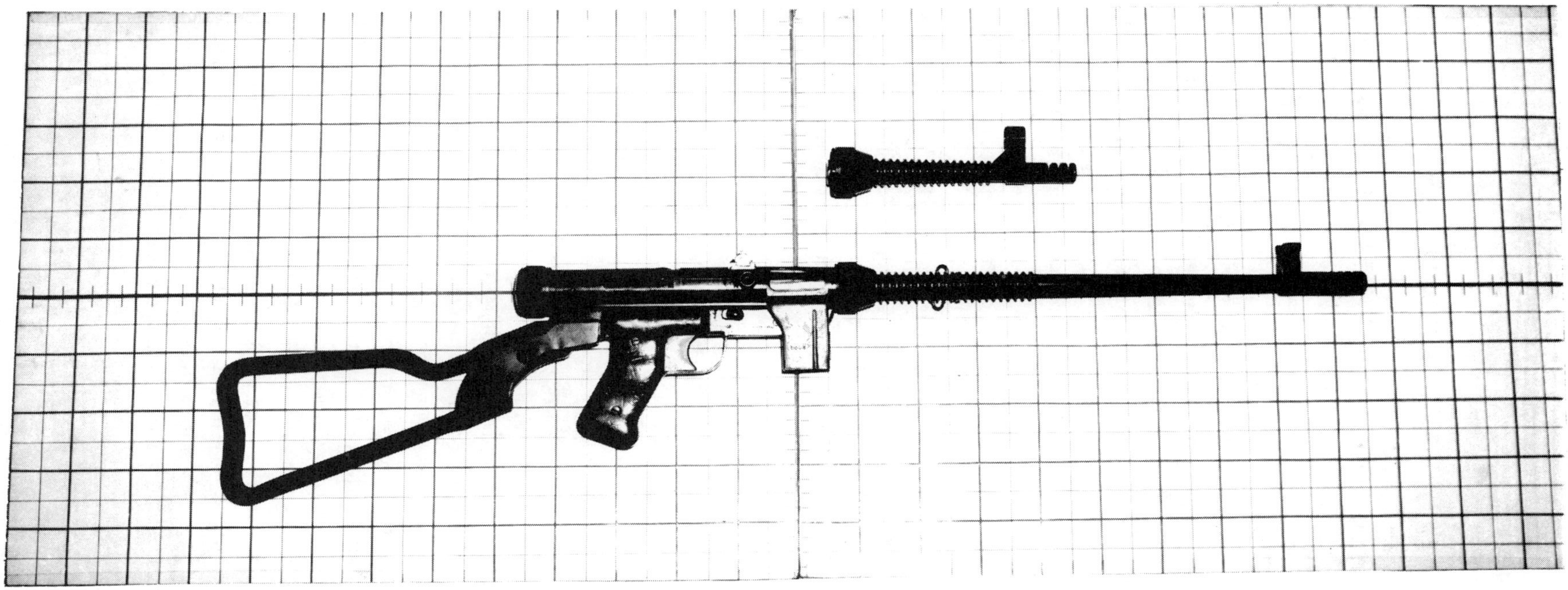

SWITZERLAND 9-MM, F.V. MK 4

9-mm "REXIM" F.V. MK 4

The Swiss F.V. MK 4 submachinegun is a blowback operated magazine fed weapon which fires from a closed bolt. Developed in early 1950 and officially introduced in 1953 by the firm of Rexim S A of Geneva, Switzerland, it was originally designated the "FAVOR" after the designer, Colonel Favier. Five thousand weapons were manufactured at the Spanish arsenal, La Coruna under the sponsorship of the Swiss firm. During 1954 and 1955 the weapon was demonstrated to prospective Middle East buyers but was turned down as being too complicated. In 1956 Spain tested the weapon but also refused to buy, favoring simpler and cheaper Spanish designed arms. In 1957 the Rexim firm went bankrupt and the Spanish arsenal offered the MK 4 for sale as the "La Coruna." This weapon was produced in various models, distinguished mainly by the different barrel lengths. The unusual bolt design which utilized a separate hammer and a telescoping system of recoil and buffer springs improved accuracy though its design and assembly created unnecessary machine operations. The closed bolt firing also increased the possibility of a "cook-off." A number of unusual features made this an excellent piece notwithstanding its lack of acceptance and included a compensator, a combination bolt handle locking sleeve and ejection port cover, a quick detachable barrel and a quick removable stock. Several thousand weapons were manufactured and they may be encountered in any part of the world.

FUNCTIONING

This is a rather complicated blowback operated submachinegun. Firing from a closed bolt it utilizes a "U" shaped yoke which functions between the hammer and the firing pin. With a loaded magazine inserted, the fire-select/safety lever is moved from "SAFE" (G) to the type fire desired; "C" for semi-automatic and "R" for full-automatic fire. The bolt handle is drawn to the rear and then released; the hammer is held by the sear, the bolt moves forward and chambers a round. When the trigger is pulled the hammer moves forward under impulse of the compressed recoil/buffer spring and strikes the yoke which is carried on the forward end of the telescoping spring guide. The yoke strikes the rebounding firing pin which is carried inside the bolt functioning the primer. When the bolt moves to the rear it pushes the telescoping spring guide and hammer rearward compressing the recoil/buffer spring. As the bolt moves forward to chamber the next round, the hammer is held to the rear by the sear. If the select lever is set for semi-automatic fire the trigger must be pulled to allow the hammer to move forward. If the select lever is set for full-automatic fire, the bolt trips the sear release lever when it chambers a round, which in turn releases the hammer and allows the hammer to move forward. This cycle is repeated until the trigger is released.

CHARACTERISTIC DATA

Caliber 9-mm
Operation .... Blowback
Type of Fire .... Full and semi-auto
Rate of Fire .... 600 rpm (150 practical)
Type of Feed .... Box - 32 rd cap
Weight, empty .... 8.3 lbs (8" bbl)
Overall length .... 27.2 in (8" bbl)
Effective range .... 135 meters (8" bbl)
.... 240 meters (18" bbl)

FIELD STRIP PROCEDURE

STEP · ACTION

1. Press Stock Release and remove Stock.
2. Press in on Receiver Cap lock and unscrew Receiver Cap.
3. Draw Bolt Handle to rear until it lines up with the dismounting notch and remove Bolt Handle from the Receiver.
4. Remove Telescoping Spring Guide and Springs with Hammer and Yoke assembly from the rear of the Receiver.
5. Slide Bolt from rear of Receiver, remove Firing Pin and Spring.
6. Unscrew Barrel Lock Nut and remove Barrel.
7. Lift Ejection Port Cover Sleeve from top of Receiver.

ASSEMBLY PROCEDURE

Assemble in the reverse order. Place Ejection Port Cover Sleeve on top of Receiver. Slide Barrel into front of Receiver and screw Barrel Lock Nut on. Assemble Firing Pin and Spring into Bolt. Attach forward end of Telescoping Spring Guide with Yoke, Hammer and Recoil Spring assembly to rear of Bolt. Slide complete assembly into Receiver and align Bolt Handle Hole in Bolt with Bolt Handle dismounting notch. Assemble Bolt Handle through dismounting notch into Bolt. Screw Receiver Cap to rear of Receiver. Assemble Stock to Receiver.

LOADING AND FIRING

To load: Draw Bolt Handle to the rear and engage Bolt Handle Locking Sleeve around Bolt Handle. Set Fire-Select/Safety Lever to "G". Insert loaded Magazine into Magazine Well.

To fire: Disengage Bolt Handle Locking Sleeve from Bolt Handle and allow Bolt to move forward and chamber a round. Move Fire-Select Lever to type of fire desired. Pull the Trigger. The weapon will fire. If the Select Lever has been set for semi-automatic fire, "C", the Trigger must be pulled for each shot. If the Select Lever has been set for full-automatic fire, ("R"), the weapon will continue to fire until the Trigger is released or the Magazine is empty.

MACHINEGUNS

SECTION IV

Historical records indicate that the Gatling Gun was one of the first successful mechanical machineguns. Invented by Richard J. Gatling, it was operated by a hand crank which caused the gun to load, cock, fire, extract and eject and reload. Later models were motor driven and attained the exceptional rate of fire of 3,000 rounds per minute. Today's successful counterparts are the M61, 20-mm "Vulcan" Cannon and the 7.62-mm "Mini-gun", both of which operate on the multi-rotating barrel system and are capable of firing at rates in excess of 7,000 rounds per minute.

These weapons are of course not true machineguns. The machinegun by definition is a weapon capable of automatically loading and firing a round of ammunition, extracting the fired case from the barrel and ejecting it from the mechanism, positioning a new cartridge for loading and loading and firing this round. This cycle being repeated until action by the firer, or lack of ammunition, causes it to cease. Basically, a machinegun is a weapon in which all the mechanical functions are caused to operated by the gun itself, with the exception of the initial manual effort of positioning the ammunition for the first shot and pulling the trigger. The machinegun, as it has been encountered since WWI, may be defined as a weapon chambered for a rifle caliber cartridge, air cooled or water cooled, utilizing some form of mount (as contrasted to being completely hand held), fed from a belt, box, drum, pan, stripclip, hopper, etc., capable of full-automatic fire and able to attain a rate of fire (dependent on design) of from 350 to 2,000 rounds per minute. Many machineguns are capable of semi-automatic fire as well as full-automatic fire; are adaptable to more than one type of mount; may incorporate a design feature which enables it to be fed from either a belt or box (or a pan)magazine or a box or drum magazine, by repositioning minor components; and in the case of many late models are becoming one-man weapons.

The few machineguns which are covered in this handbook represent a broad cross-section of successful machinegun designs. Some may be considered obsolescent but represent such a truly unusual system that the fact that they saw extensive action by various countries is worthy of note. Others which are covered are such fine examples of the gun designers (and manufacturers) art that they will be around for many years to come. Still others represent design and production ingenuity of exceptional quality and the ideas may be "picked up" and exploited in the future by countries who do not want to spend the Research and Development time and money to breed a new arm. All in all, the Special Forces Soldier will find some of these weapons in almost any corner of the world. The various systems discussed here should prepare him for surprises and if he is surprised by something new, he should let the right people know.

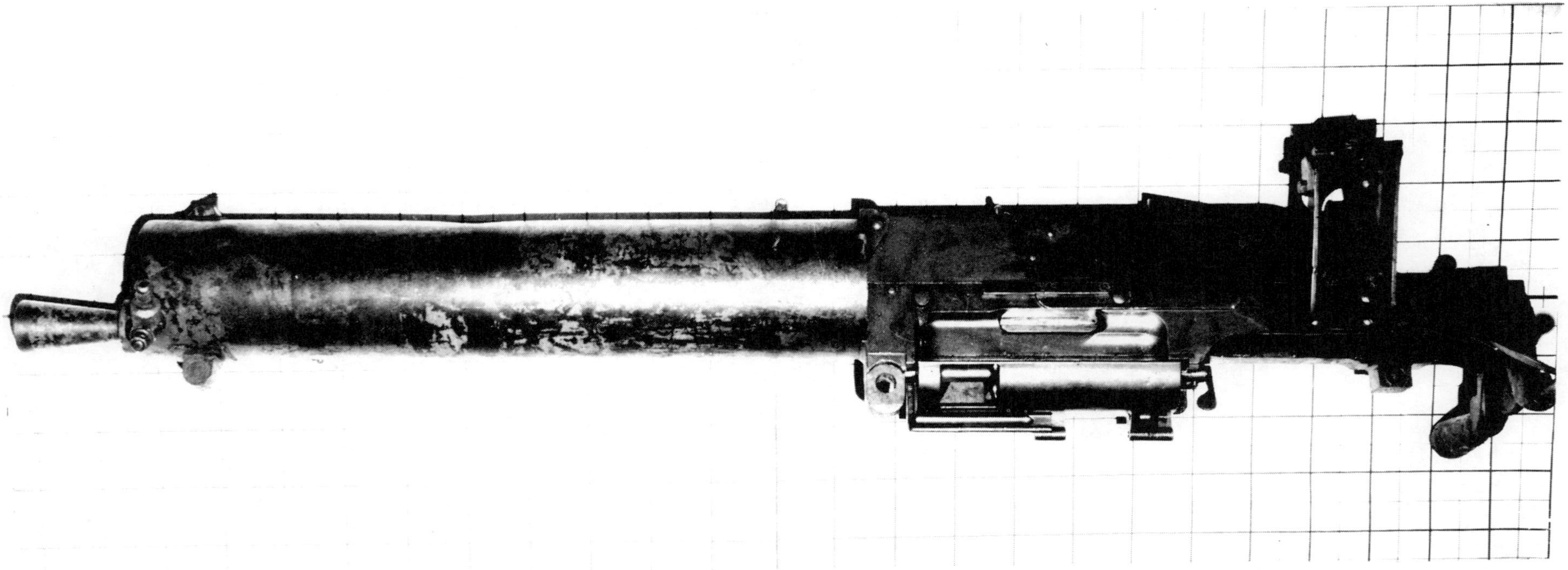

AUSTRIA   8-MM, MODEL 07/12

MACHINEGUN   AUSTRIA

8-mm MODEL 07/12

The Austrian Schwarzlose Model 07/12 Machinegun is a heavy water-cooled machinegun which is one of the first successful retarded blowback system machineguns to be produced. Invented by Andreas W. Schwarzlose in 1902, it was produced by the Steyr Firm in 1905. Both the Model 1905 and the later modified version the Model 1907 utilized an oil pump device to lubricate the cases as they entered the chamber. The Model 1912 which followed was considerably modified and the oil pump system was eliminated. In all of these models the action is never truly locked, being held closed against chamber pressure by the weight of the recoiling parts as well as a complex toggle system which created a mechanical disadvantage to be overcome by the recoiling parts. The barrel on this weapon is relatively short, since the bullet had to be out of the bore before the action opened and the action was held closed only by a heavy breechblock, a toggle system and a heavy recoil spring. This weapon saw extensive use in WWI and was used by a number of countries during WWII in various calibers.

FUNCTIONING

This weapon utilizes a retarded blowback system to hold the breech closed during the moment of firing. With a loaded belt inserted in the feedway and the crank handle operated three times to chamber a round, the trigger is pulled. The trigger bar releases the firing pin and under the impulse of the heavy, dual purpose recoil spring, it is forced forward to strike the primer. As the cartridge case in the barrel moves back against the face of the breech block, the breech block starts to move rearward. The breech block is connected to an elbow joint arm which is in turn connected to another arm which is pivot-pinned to the receiver. When the action is closed these two arms are almost parallel to each other, the fulcrum of movement being in a nearly horizontal plane. The movement of the breech block is thus transmitted to the receiver through the arm pinned to the receiver for a short length of time before the arms start to move through the opening arc. This hesitation plus the weight of the breech block and the extremely heavy recoil spring keep the action closed until the bullet has left the muzzle of the short barrel. The forward movement of this heavy recoil spring in forcing the firing pin against the primer also contributes some momentary opening resistance to the movement of the breech block. This weapon fires full-automatic only and the firing cycle will be repeated until the trigger is released or the belt is empty.

CHARACTERISTIC DATA

Caliber	8-mm
Operation	Retarded blowback
Type of Fire	Full-auto only
Rate of Fire	400 rpm (Practical 225)
Type of Feed	Belt - 100 rd cap
Weight, w/mount	102 lbs
Overall length	49.3 in
Effective range	2,180 meters

FIELD STRIP PROCEDURE

STEP   ACTION

1. Push Cover Latch to the left, push Locking Lug on Cover above feedway to unlock and raise Cover.
2. Rotate Back Plate Lock to the right.
3. Stand weapon up on the Back Plate end, place feet on Spade Grips, turn weapon counterclockwise to unlock Back Plate and raise weapon up carefully off of the Back Plate against pressure of the very strong Recoil Spring.
4. Remove Recoil Spring and Guide Plug from Receiver.
5. Remove Breech Block with attached Elbow Joint, Striker Assembly and Crank Assembly from Receiver through the top. Remove Striker Assembly from Breech Block.

ASSEMBLY PROCEDURE

Assemble in the reverse order. Assemble Striker Assembly into Breech Block, slide Breech Block into Receiver and assemble Crank Assembly to Receiver and Breech Block. Slide Recoil Spring and Guide Plug into Receiver and carefully stand weapon on end. Raise weapon up far enough to assemble Recoil Spring and Guide Plug into Receiver, position Back Plate under end of Receiver, mating Recoil Spring to Back Plate. Carefully lower the weapon down onto the Back Plate against tension of the Recoil Spring. Hold the Spade Grips with the feet and turn the Receiver until Back Plate is locked to Receiver.

LOADING AND FIRING

To load: Insert the tag end of a loaded belt into the feed guide opening on the right side of the feedway, up over the Feed Sprocket and pull through as far as possible. Operate the Crank Handle and the belt will be engaged by the Feed Sprocket and will be held by the Holding Pawl. Operating the Crank Handle again will position the first round in the belt for feeding. Operating the Crank Handle for the third time will draw a round from the belt and chamber it ready for firing.

To fire: A Safety Catch is located in the center of the Back Plate beneath the paddle-shaped Trigger. Push the Safety Catch to the left and push in on the Trigger. The weapon will fire full-automatic until the Trigger is released or the belt is empty.

Feed Mechanism

Back Plate Latch ②

Crank

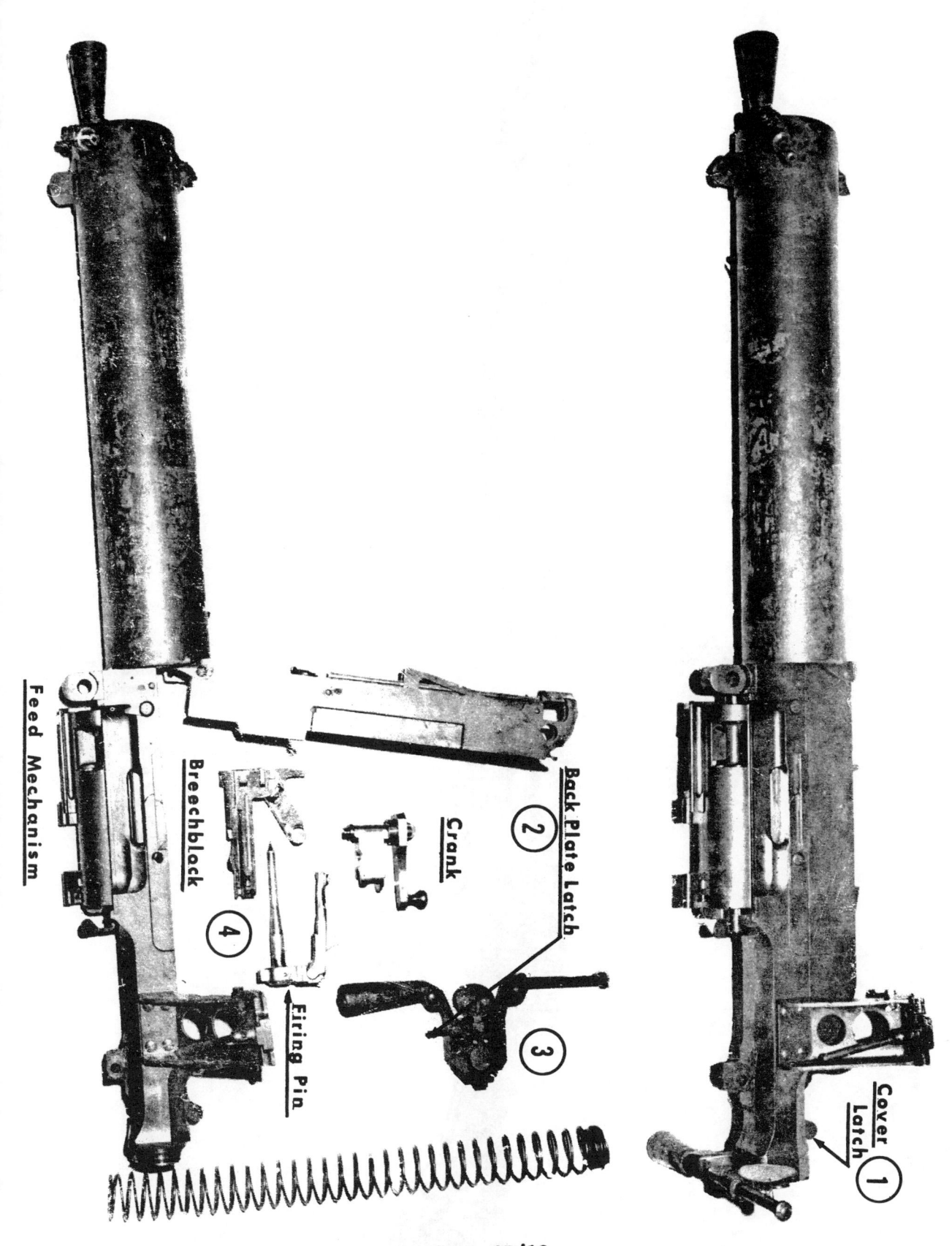

Breechblock

④

Firing Pin

③

Cover Latch ①

8-mm 07/12

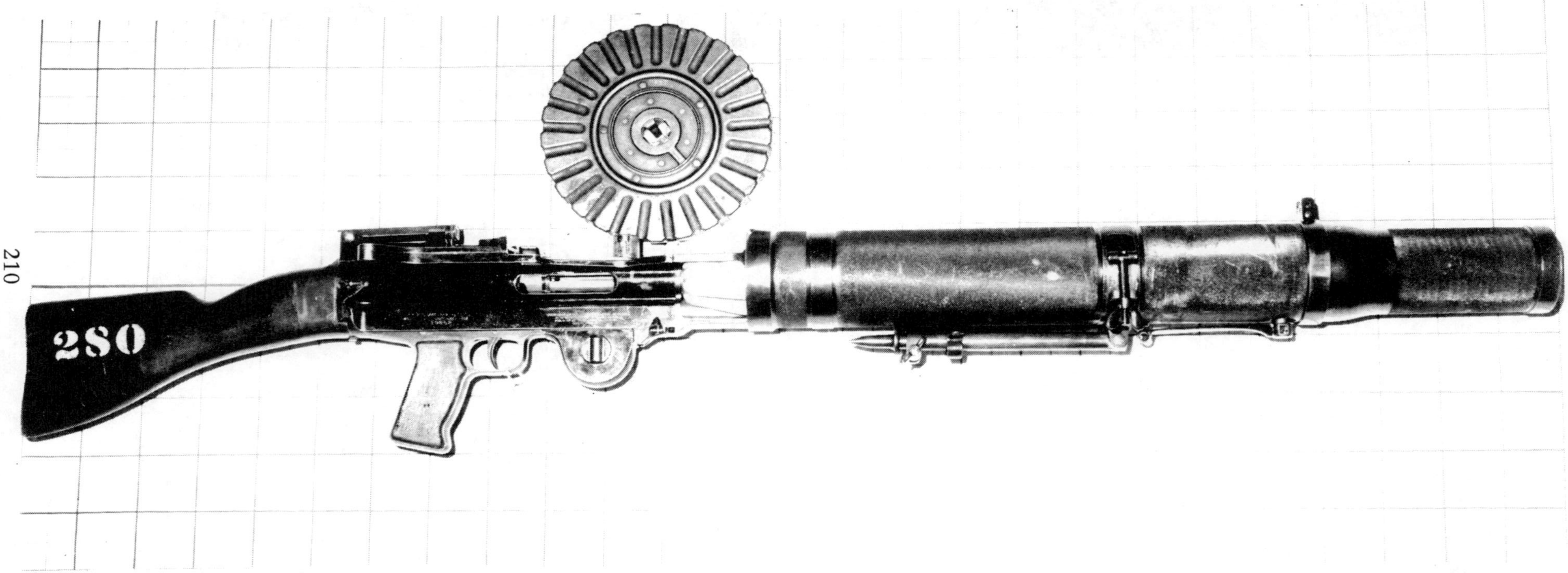

GREAT BRITAIN .303, LEWIS

MACHINEGUN   GREAT BRITAIN

.303 LEWIS M1911

The M1911 Lewis Machinegun is a gas-operated, pan fed machinegun which utilizes a unique return spring device (rack and pinion), an air cooling jacket, and a rotating bolt locking system. Invented by Samuel N. McClean, developed by Colonel I.N. Lewis, it was produced by Birmingham Small Arms Company of England and Savage Arms Corporation of the U.S. during WWI. Developed as an infantry ground machinegun it was successfully adopted to aircraft use, being mounted on British aircraft in 1914. More than a dozen countries have used the Lewis gun, the Japanese faithfully copying the weapon during WWII. The U. S. model of this piece is chambered for the .30-06 cartridge. The air-cooling system consists of a flanged aluminum radiator surrounding the full length of the barrel covered by a jacket. In theory, gases leaving the muzzle of the barrel (the muzzle is approximately 6 inches in from the end of the jacket) suck air the length of the aluminum radiator. The radiator being in contact with the barrel draws heat from the barrel and is cooled by the passing air. This weapon must be unloaded very carefully since even with the pan removed, one round of ammunition remains in the feed system and must be removed manually.

FUNCTIONING

This is a gas-operated machinegun in which the bolt rides on a stud (which carries the firing pin) on the upper rear portion of the gas piston. The bolt is rotated into lock and unlock position by a curved slot in the bolt which the stud engages. This system is similar to the U.S. M60 machinegun. With a loaded pan (pans are designed to carry 47- or 96-rounds) mounted on the magazine post, the bolt handle is drawn to the rear, drawing the bolt and piston rearward where the sear bent on the bottom of the piston is engaged by the sear. The recoil spring on this weapon is a heavy coil spring similar to a clock spring which is wound inside of a toothed gear, the complete unit being contained inside a housing located beneath the receiver ahead of the trigger group. The bottom rear portion of the gas piston has a toothed rack machined into it. The teeth of this rack engage the teeth of the spring loaded gear. As the bolt is drawn rearward, the rack on the piston engaging the gear, revolves the gear, winding the clock-like spring inside the gear. When the trigger releases the sear, the spring unwinding against its wound-up tension, drives the piston forward due to the meshing of the teeth in the rack and gear. The bolt strips a round from the magazine and chambers it, the piston conton continues to move and the stud on the piston which is engaged in the curved slot in the bolt causes the bolt to turn so that locking lugs on the bolt engage recesses in the receiver. The firing pin on the top of the stud strikes the primer. Gas is tapped from the barrel to impinge against the face of the piston driving the piston rearward, unlocking the bolt and the feed post on the bolt swings the feed arm to position the next cartridge for feeding.

CHARACTERISTIC DATA

Caliber 303
Operation . . . . .Gas
Type of Fire . . . . Full-auto only
Rate of Fire . . . . 600 rpm (Practical 250)
Type of Feed . . . . .Pan - 47 rd cap
Weight, empty . . . . 28.3 lbs
Overall length . . . . 50.6 in
Effective range . . . . 1,870 meters

FIELD STRIP PROCEDURE

STEP   ACTION

1. Push in on Stock Latch and turn Butt to left and remove.
2. Pull Trigger and draw Trigger Group slightly to the rear until the Pinion Housing drops forward.
3. Draw Trigger Group rearward off the Receiver.
4. Draw Bolt Handle to the rear and remove from Receiver and grasp rear of Bolt and slide Bolt and Gas Piston out of rear of Receiver. Lift Bolt off rear of Piston.
5. Draw Feed Cover to the rear slightly.
5a. Raise up on Feed Cover and remove from Receiver.
6. Disconnect Feed Arm Latch and lift Feed Arm off Receiver.

ASSEMBLY PROCEDURE

Assemble in the reverse order. Engage Feed Arm onto Feed Arm post and engage Feed Arm Latch. Replace Feed Cover. Assemble Bolt to rear of Piston and slide Piston and Bolt into the Receiver. Replace Bolt Handle. Slide Trigger Group part way onto Receiver, swing Pinion Housing up and push Trigger Group completely forward. Engage Stock to rear of Receiver and turn to lock.

LOADING AND FIRING

To load: Place a loaded 47-round pan Magazine onto the Magazine Post, rotate Magazine slightly to insure Magazine Catch engages the Magazine. Rotate Magazine to right until resistance is encountered. Draw Bolt Handle to the rear. Raise Safety Lever Arm up to engage Bolt Handle.

To fire: Draw Bolt Handle slightly to the rear and push down on Safety Lever Arm. Pull the Trigger. The weapon will fire. This weapon fires full-automatic only and will continue to fire until the Trigger is released or the Magazine is empty.

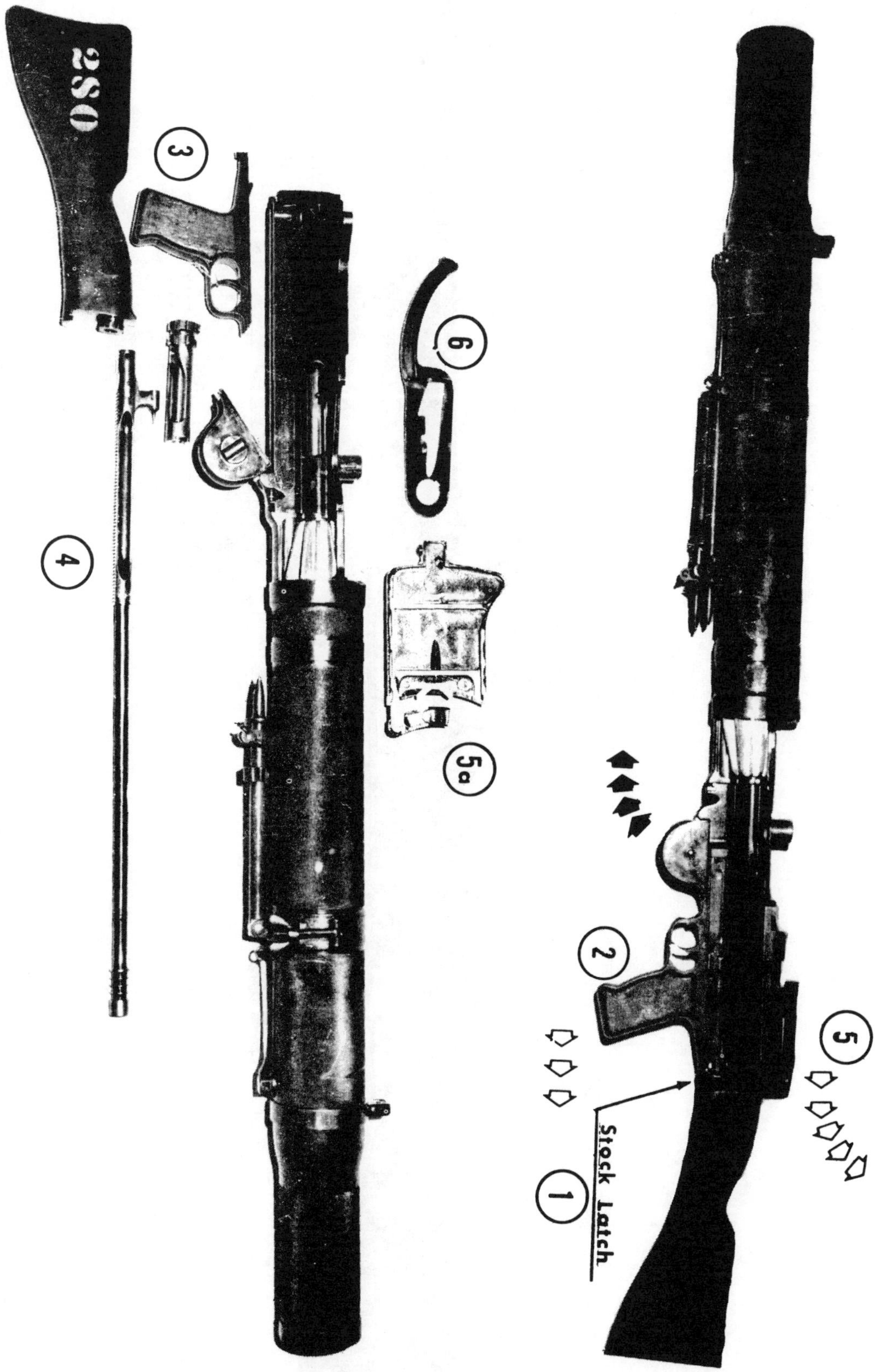
3
6
4
5a
2
5
1
Stock Latch

.303 Lewis

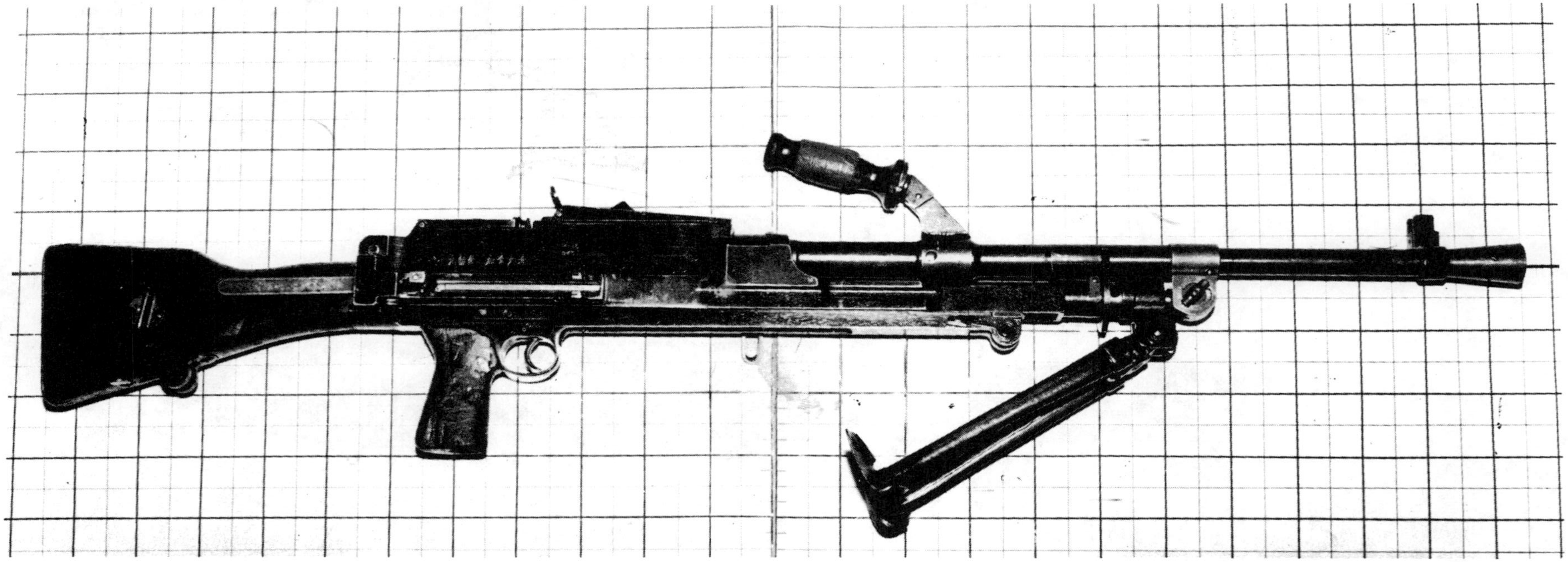

NATIONALIST CHINA 7.92-MM, MARK 2 BREN

LIGHT MACHINEGUN   NATIONALIST CHINA

.30 Caliber MACHINEGUN Type 41

The caliber .30 Type 41 LIght Machinegun is a direct copy of the British Mark II Bren Gun of WWII fame. The Mark II Bren Gun was manufactured by the Canadian Inglis firm for the Chinese Nationalists during WWII. The Canadian model was chambered for the 7.92-mm round and differs from the Type 41 in receiver length which is 4-3/4 inches longer than the Type 41. The Type 41 went into production in Formosa in 1952. The weapon, though chambered for .30 caliber, can be converted to fire 7.92-mm ammunition simply by changing barrels. The Bren gun, one of the most famous light machineguns of WWII, used by many armies throughout the world even today, was developed by the British from the Czechoslovakian Brno ZB LMG. The British were licensed by ZB to manufacture the gun and in 1937 the Enfield Government Arms Plant produced the first guns. By September 1939 production figures reached 400 a week. During WWII the Bren gun was manufactured in very large numbers in both England and Canada. While this weapon is essentially a one-man machinegun to be used from a bipod mount or fired from the hip in moving assault fire. It may be quickly converted to a heavy machinegun by mounting on a tripod mount. This tripod can also be converted to an AA mount and effective AA fire can be delivered against low-flying aircraft. For all general purposes it is intended to be fired single-shot, a round fired for each pull of the trigger in the manner of a semi-automatic rifle. The normal rate of automatic fire, however, is 5 or 6 rounds a burst for five bursts or 1 magazine. A well-trained operator can deliver as many as 150 shots, or 5 magazines in a minute. A spare barrel is issued with each gun and the ease of barrel change is one of the important features of this weapon.

FUNCTIONING

This is a gas-operated, semi- and full-automatic weapon, fed from a thirty round box magazine mounted on the top. With a loaded magazine in place and the bolt drawn to the rear, the trigger is pulled and the bolt travels forward, chambering a round and firing it. THIS WEAPON FIRES FROM AN OPEN BOLT - THE BOLT SHOULD NEVER BE ALLOWED TO MOVE FORWARD WITH A MAGAZINE IN PLACE UNLESS IT IS INTENDED TO FIRE THE WEAPON. Gas is tapped from the barrel near the muzzle, enters the gas cylinder and impinges on the gas piston. The gas piston moves rearward and the bolt which rides on the top-rear of the piston assembly is cammed down out of engagement with locking recesses in the top of the receiver. As the piston and bolt recoil together the recoil spring housed in the stock is compressed. The rearward movement of the piston is stopped by a buffer group also housed in the stock. If the fire selector is set for semi-automatic fire, the sear will rise up and engage the sear notch at the rear of the piston assembly, holding the piston and bolt in the rearmost position. If set for full-automatic fire, the sear will remain in the down position as long as the trigger is held back.

CHARACTERISTIC DATA

Caliber	.30 M2
Operation	Gas
Type of Fire	Full and semi-auto
Rate of Fire	350-600 rpm (Practical-150)
Type of Feed	Box-30 rd cap
Weight, unloaded	23.8 lbs
Overall length	45.7 in
Effective range	1,620 meters

FIELD STRIP PROCEDURE

STEP   ACTION

1. With the Magazine removed and the Bolt drawn to the rear, unlatch the Barrel Nut Catch and swing it up.
2. Grasp the Carrying Handle on the Barrel and slide the Barrel forward.
Pull the Trigger and holding the Cocking Handle, ease the Bolt forward.
3. Push the Locking Pin, located at the upper rear of the Receiver, through the Receiver from right to left.
4. Holding the Receiver with one hand, grasp the Pistol Grip and slide the Butt Group to the rear and off the Receiver.
5. Give a sharp rearward jerk to the Cocking Handle and the Piston Assembly and Bolt will move to the rear far enough to be grasped and pulled out. Tilting the rear of the Receiver down slightly will assist in this operation. Remove the Bolt from the Piston Assembly by sliding it to the rear and lifting it up.
6. Disengage the Cocking Handle from the slot in the Receiver and remove.

ASSEMBLY PROCEDURE

Proceed in the reverse order except that the Barrel may be assembled to the Receiver as the first step. Engage the Bolt to the rear of the Piston Assembly and slide into the Receiver. Place the Cocking Handle in its slot in the Receiver. Tilt the Receiver forward to allow the Piston and Bolt to slide forward. Mate the grooves on the Butt Group with the grooves on the Receiver and slide the Butt Group all the way forward. Assemble the Locking Pin into the Receiver and tap through.

LOADING AND FIRING

To load: Latch a full Magazine into its well in the top of the Receiver. Set the Select Lever to "S" (safe). Draw the Cocking Handle to the rear and push forward again. Move the Select Lever to the type of fire desired.

To fire: Pull the Trigger; depending on the position of the Select Lever the weapon will fire single-shot or full-automatic.

NOTE: The weapon illustrated is the Canadian manufactured Mark II Bren, made for Nationalist China during WWII.

7.92-mm Mk 2

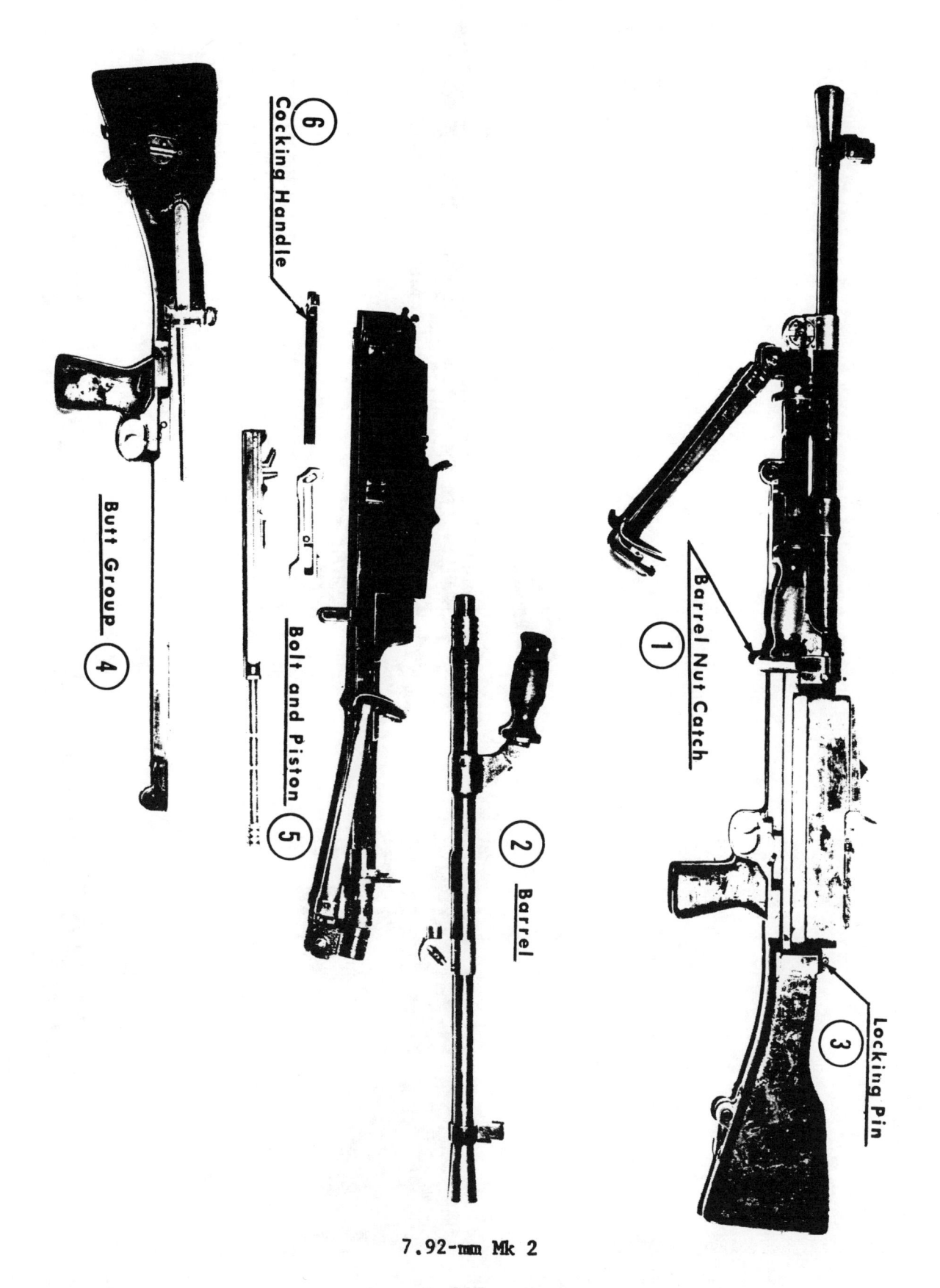

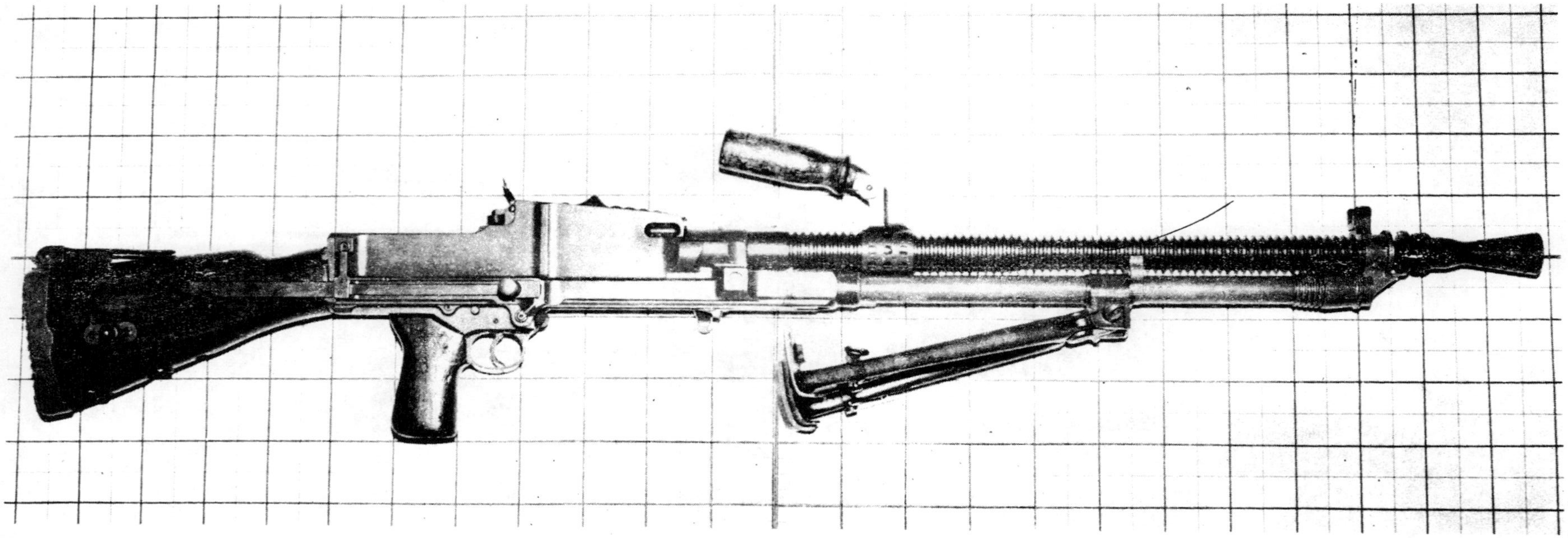

CZECHOSLOVAKIA 7.92-MM, ZB30

MACHINEGUN   CZECHOSLOVAKIA

7.92-mm ZB 30 (BRNO)

The Czech ZB30 Light Machinegun is rated as one of the best light machineguns in the world. It may be tactically employed as a squad automatic rifle or as a company light machinegun. The only drawback encountered in either case is the limited ammunition supply dictated by the small 20 round capacity magazine, though a trained gunner is capable of firing 7 to 8 magazines in one minute. The ZB Works that produced this weapon was established in Brno in 1922. The original design derived from a study of successful automatic weapons, the prototype being produced in 1924 and the first production model, designated the ZB26, being produced in 1926. Modifications of the ZB26 resulted in 1930 with the production of the ZB30 light machinegun. This piece may be encountered in any part of the world. The reliable, though simple bolt locking system and the quick-change barrel are two of its more notable points. The famous British Bren gun was developed from the ZB30 light machinegun in 1935.

FUNCTIONING

The ZB30 is a gas-operated, magazine fed light machinegun which incorporates a quick-change barrel into its design. The bolt riding on a beveled post at the rear of the slide is cammed up into a locked position as the slide reaches its formost point of travel. With a loaded magazine inserted into the top of the receiver, the bolt handle, located on the right side of the receiver is drawn to the rear and then pushed foward. The bolt handle does not move with the bolt during firing. The sear bent in the bottom of the slide is engaged by the sear and the slide and attached piston and bolt are held to the rear. When the trigger is pulled the sear releases the slide which moves forward under impulse of the compressed recoil spring which is contained in the stock. The bolt strips a round from the magazine and chambers it. As the face of the bolt comes to a stop against the rear face of the barrel, the slide continues to move forward a distance of 3/4 of an inch, the cam surface on the rear top of the slide forcing the rear of the bolt up into a locking recess in the top of the receiver; the center post of the slide strikes the firing pin which in turn strikes the primer. Gas is tapped from the barrel into a gas cylinder where it impinges against the face of the gas piston driving it rearward. The piston and slide move to the rear 3/4 of an inch when the rear cam surface of the center post on the slide pulls the rear of the bolt down out of the locking recess in the top of the receiver and carries it rearward. If the safety/select lever is set for full-automatic this action will continue until the trigger is released or the magazine is empty. If set for semi-automatic fire the slide will be engaged by the sear at its rearmost position and the trigger must be pulled for each shot.

CHARACTERISTIC DATA

```
Caliber ................................................................7.92-mm
Operation ................................................................Gas
Type of Fire ................................................ Full and semi-auto
Rate of Fire ...................................... 600 rpm (Practical 120)
Type of Feed ........................................... Box - 20 rd cap
Weight, empty ............................................... 22.2 lbs
Overall length ................................................ 47.9 in
Effective range ........................................... 1,620 meters
```

FIELD STRIP PROCEDURE

STEP   ACTION

1. Raise up on Barrel Nut Catch and slide Barrel forward from Receiver.
2. Remove two Stock and Trigger Group Assembly Retaining Pins and slide assembly rearward from Receiver.
3. Remove Piston, Slide and Bolt from rear of Receiver.
4. Slide Bolt to the rear on the Slide until front end of Bolt disengages from Slide and lift up off of Slide.

ASSEMBLY PROCEDURE

Assemble in the reverse order. Slide Bolt onto the Slide from the rear. Slide Piston, Slide and Bolt into Receiver. Assemble Stock and Trigger Group Assembly onto rear of Receiver and replace Retaining Pins. Slide Barrel into front of Receiver and turn Barrel Nut Catch down to lock.
NOTE: Barrel may be assembled as the first step in assembly.

LOADING AND FIRING

To load: Insert loaded Magazine into top of Receiver. Swing Safety/Select Lever into the vertical ("SAFE") position. Draw the Bolt Handle to the rear and push forward. Bolt will remain held to the rear by the Sear.

To fire: Push the Safety/Select Lever to the type fire desired, rearward for semi-automatic fire and forward for full-automatic fire. Pull the Trigger. The weapon will fire. If set for full-automatic fire the Trigger must be pulled for each shot. If set for full-automatic fire the weapon will continue to fire until the Trigger is released or the Magazine is empty.

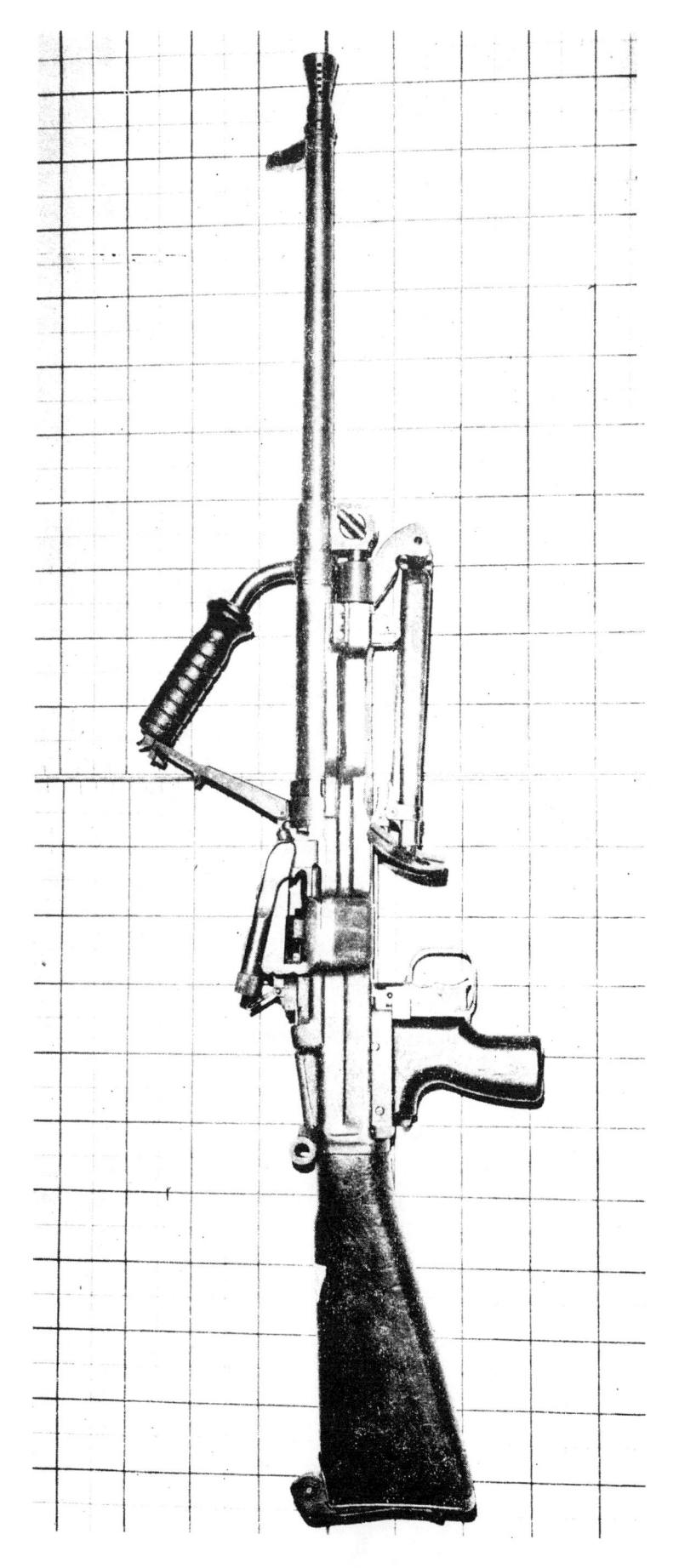

CZECHOSLOVAKIA 7.62-MM, MODEL 1952

MACHINEGUN   CZECHOSLOVAKIA

7.62-mm MODEL 52

The Czech 7.62-mm Model 52 Light Machinegun is a gas-operated, dual feed weapon which fires full and semi-automatic from an open bolt. This piece can be fed from either a 25-round box magazine or a 100-round non-disintegrating metallic belt without changing feed components. The Model 52 has been replaced by a slightly modified version, the 52/57. The Model 52 is chambered for the Czech intermediate cartridge (Model 52 cartridge) while the Model 52/57 is chambered for the Czech copy of the Soviet M43 round (Model 57 cartridge). The Model 52/57 has now been replaced by the Model 59 General Purpose Machinegun in the Czechoslovakian Armed Forces. The Model 52 is an exceptionally well made, versatile weapon, though quite complex to produce due to the high quality machine work required in fabricating the feed block assembly and the receiver. The fire selection system utilizes a double trigger mechanism, the upper half of the trigger delivering semi-automatic fire while pressing the lower half will result in full-automatic fire.

FUNCTIONING

This is a gas-operated weapon in which the bolt is carried on a camming stud mounted on the rear of the slide. With a belt positioned in the feedway, or a box magazine mounted in the magazine well, the pistol grip assembly is unlocked by pushing down on the pistol grip latch and drawing the complete pistol grip assembly rearward until the sear engages the sear bent in the bottom of the slide. (If the grip assembly is already to the rear it must be pushed forward to engage the slide and then drawn to the rear.) When the trigger is pulled the sear releases the slide and the slide carrying the bolt on its upper rear portion moves forward under impulse of the recoil spring contained in the stock, the bolt strips a round from the belt (or magazine) and chambers it. The bolt comes to a stop against the rear face of the barrel and the slide continues to move forward during which time the camming surface of the stud on which the bolt is being carried cams the rear of the bolt into locking recesses in the receiver and the forward face of the stud strikes the firing pin driving it into the primer. Gas is tapped from the Barrel to impinge against the piston which is a forward extension of the slide. The piston moves rearward forcing the slide to the rear during which time the slide cams the bolt down out of locked position and carries it rearward. If the upper portion of the trigger has been pulled (semi-automatic fire) the disconnector is tripped by forward movement of the slide and the sear is raised to engage the slide and the trigger must be pulled for each shot. If the lower portion of the trigger was pulled the weapon will fire full-automatic.

CHARACTERISTIC DATA

Caliber	7.62-mm (M52 ctdge)
Operation	Gas
Type of Fire	Full and semi-auto
Rate of Fire	1,1000 rpm with belt (Practical-350)
Type of Feed	Box - 25 rd cap
	Belt - 100 rd cap
Weight, empty	18.3 lbs
Overall length	41.1 in
Effective range	1,620 meters

FIELD STRIP PROCEDURE

STEP ACTION

1. Press in on Recoil Spring Cap located in Butt of Stock and turn counterclockwise.
2. Remove Cap, Recoil Spring and Guide from Stock.
3. Raise Magazine Port Cover, use Cover as a handle, turn down to right to disengage the Barrel Lock.
4. Grasp Barrel Handle and draw the Barrel forward out of the Feed Block Assembly.
5. Turn Bipod Assembly up and disengage from Receiver.
6. Grasp the Feed Block Assembly which contains the Bolt, Slide and Piston, draw to the rear until the Piston is clear of the Gas Cylinder, lift up and off from the Receiver.
7. Remove Bolt, Slide and Piston from the rear of the Feed Block Assembly and disengage the Bolt from the Slide.
8. The Pistol Grip Assembly may be slide forward off of the Receiver if necessary.

ASSEMBLY PROCEDURE

Assemble in reverse order. If Trigger Group Assembly has been removed, slide onto Receiver and lock into place. Place Bolt over locking cam stud on Slide and assemble Slide, Bolt and Piston into Feed Block Assembly. Assemble Feed Block Assembly onto Receiver. Slide Bipod Assembly onto forward end of Receiver and turn down to lock. Slide Barrel into forward end of Feed Block Assembly and turn Magazine Port Cover up to engage Barrel Lock. Assemble Recoil Spring, Guide and Cap into Stock through Butt.

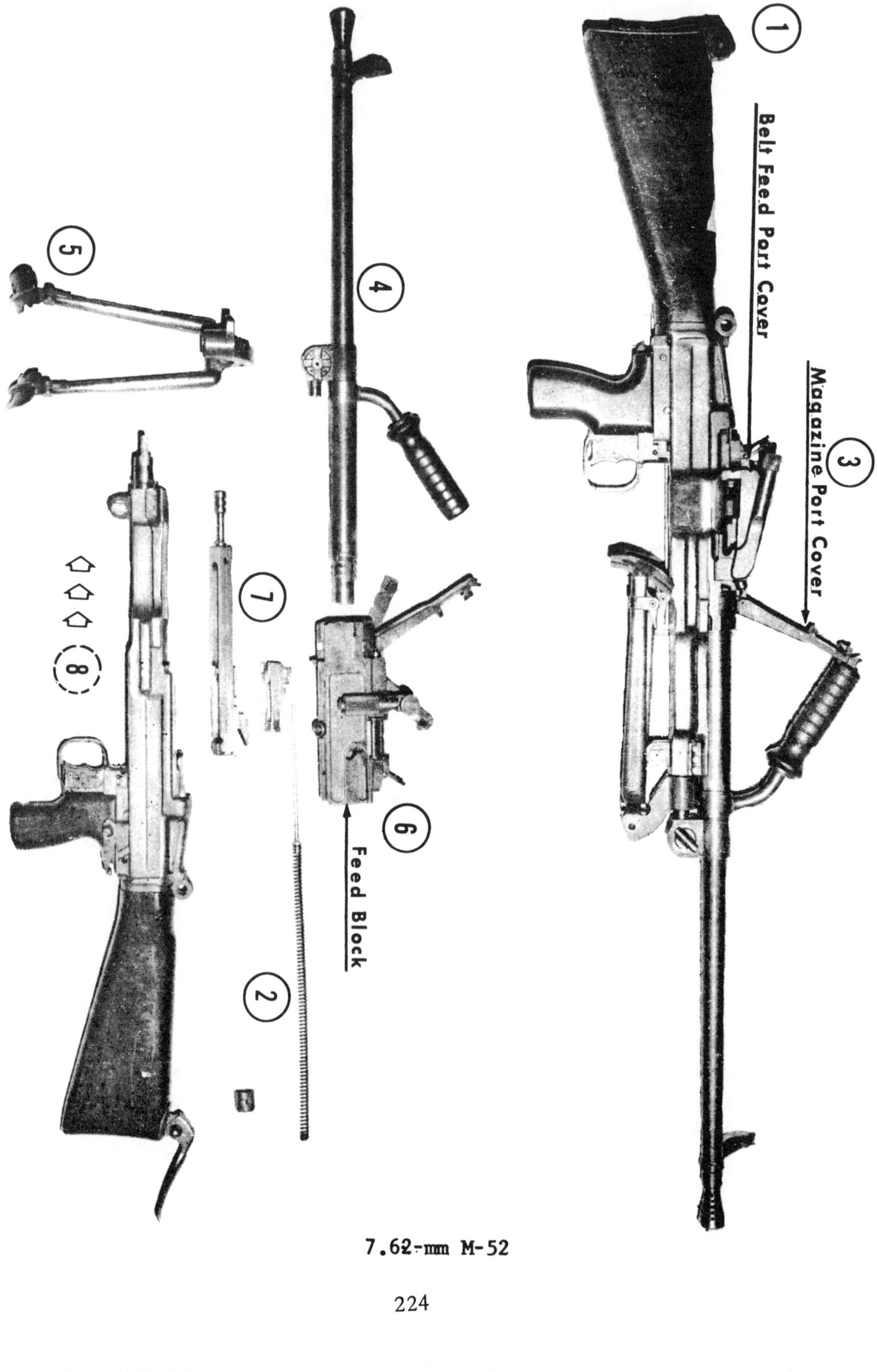
1
Belt Feed Port Cover
3
Magazine Port Cover
4
5
7
8
6
Feed Block
2

7.62-mm M-52

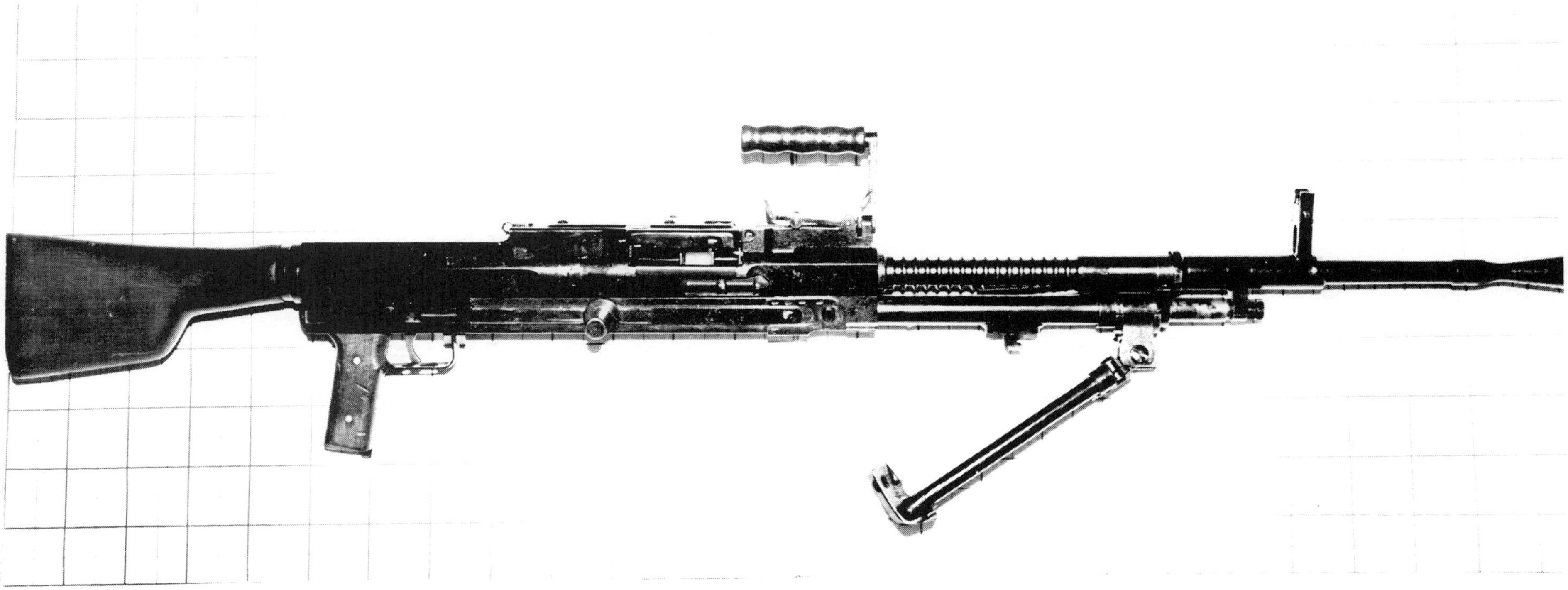

DENMARK 7.62-MM NATO, MADSEN/SAETTER

MACHINEGUN   DENMARK

7.62-mm MACHINEGUN (Madsen/Saetter)

The Danish Madsen/Saetter machinegun is available in calibers from 6.5-mm to 8-mm. This is a gas-operated, belt fed machinegun which can be fired from a bipod, tripod or from the hip. Three models of the ground version have been developed as well as a tank model. A heavier model, .50 caliber, exists in prototype. This is an extremely well de- signed and well made weapon, somewhat more sophisticated than the average weapon being encountered today. A majority of the components are machined, though the machining consists generally of simple turning operations. A lighter model has been developed by Dansk Industri Syndicat which can be mounted on a modified, light tripod. It is available chambered for the 7.62-mm NATO cartridge.

FUNCTIONING

The Madsen/Saetter is a gas-operated, belt fed, bipod or tripod mounted light machinegun. The weapon fires full-automatic only. With a loaded belt in place in the feedway, the operating handle, located on the right side of the trigger housing group, is drawn to the rear. This action draws the bolt carrier with the assembled bolt and gas piston to the rear compressing the recoil spring located in the stock. The sear engages a stud located on the rear bottom of the carrier. The bolt is contained in the forward portion of the carrier. Locking wedges are attached to the rear of the bolt and protrude through slots on either side of the carrier to engage recesses in the receiver when the action is locked. Pulling the trigger draws the sear down out of engagement with the rear of the carrier. The carrier and assembled bolt and gas piston move forwardunder impulse of the compressed recoil spring. A round is stripped from the belt and chambered. The bolt stops against the rear of the barrel and the carrier, continuing its forward movement causes the striker through the face of the bolt to impinge on the cartridge primer. Gas is tapped from the barrel through the gas cylinder housing and impinges against the face of the gas piston. The rear of the piston is attached to the front of the carrier and as the carrier starts to the rear the strikerextension moves back with it, allowing the striker which is spring loaded, to withdraw into the face of the bolt. Rearward movement of the striker extension also allows the locking wedges to be cammed out of engagement in the locking recesses in the receiver. A lever located in the top rear of the receiver is engaged by the carrier, the rearward movement of the carrier pivots it from left to right swinging the belt fed pawl located in the cover also from left to right. This action draws the belt into the feedway, positioning the next cartridge for chambering. The rear of the carrier strikes a buffer mechanism in the butt stock and is held to the rear by the sear if the trigger has been released. If the trigger is still held to the rear, the weapon will continue to fire.

CHARACTERISTIC DATA

Caliber	6.5-mm to 8-mm
Operation	Gas
Type of Fire	Full-auto only
Rate of Fire	750-800 rpm (est) (Practical-450)
Type of Feed	Belt - 50 rd cap
Weight, empty	25.2 lbs
Overall length	38.2 in w/flash hider
Effective range	1,890 meters

FIELD STRIP PROCEDURE

STEP   ACTION

1. With the Bolt forward, press in on Butt Stock Latch located at rear of Trigger Housing Group, turn Butt stock 90 degrees.
2. Pull Butt Stock to the rear.
3. Pivot Trigger Housing Group down and detach from Receiver.
4. Raise Cover and grasping Belt Feed Pivot Stud at the top rear of the Carrier, draw the Carrier to the rear. Disengage the Gas Piston from the front end of the Carrier.
5. Tilt the front of the Receiver up and allow the Carrier with assembled Bolt to slide out of the rear of the Receiver.
6. Swing the Barrel Dismounting Handle out to the left to unlocking position. Swing the Barrel Dismounting Handle up and draw the Barrel forward out of the Receiver.
7. Remove the Cover and Feedway Pin and remove the Cover and Feedway. Lift the Belt Feed Lever Housing from the top rear of the Receiver and remove the Belt Feed Lever.
8. Unscrew the Gas Cylinder Retaining Nut from the forward end of the Cylinder and remove the Gas Cylinder.

ASSEMBLY PROCEDURE

Assemble in the reverse order. Place the Gas Cylinder in the Gas Cylinder Housing and screw the Gas Cylinder Nut in place. Assemble the Belt Feed Lever and Housing to the top of the Receiver. Assemble the Cover and Feedway and replace the Cover Pin. Slide the Barrel into the front of the Receiver and turn handle down to lock. Fold the Barrel Dismounting Handle in. Slide the Carrier and assembled Bolt into the rear of the Receiver, push it forward until the Gas Piston can engage the front of the Carrier. Assemble the Gas Piston in the Gas Piston Tube and engage the rear of the Piston with the Carrier. Swing the Trigger Housing Group up, push the Butt Stock into place and turn down to lock.

LOADING AND FIRING

To load: Push the Safety to "SAFE." Raise the Cover and lay the belt in the Feedway. Close the Cover. Draw the Bolt Handle to the rear.
To fire: Push the Safety to "OFF." Pull the Trigger. This is a full-automatic weapon and it will continue to fire as long as the Trigger is held to the rear.

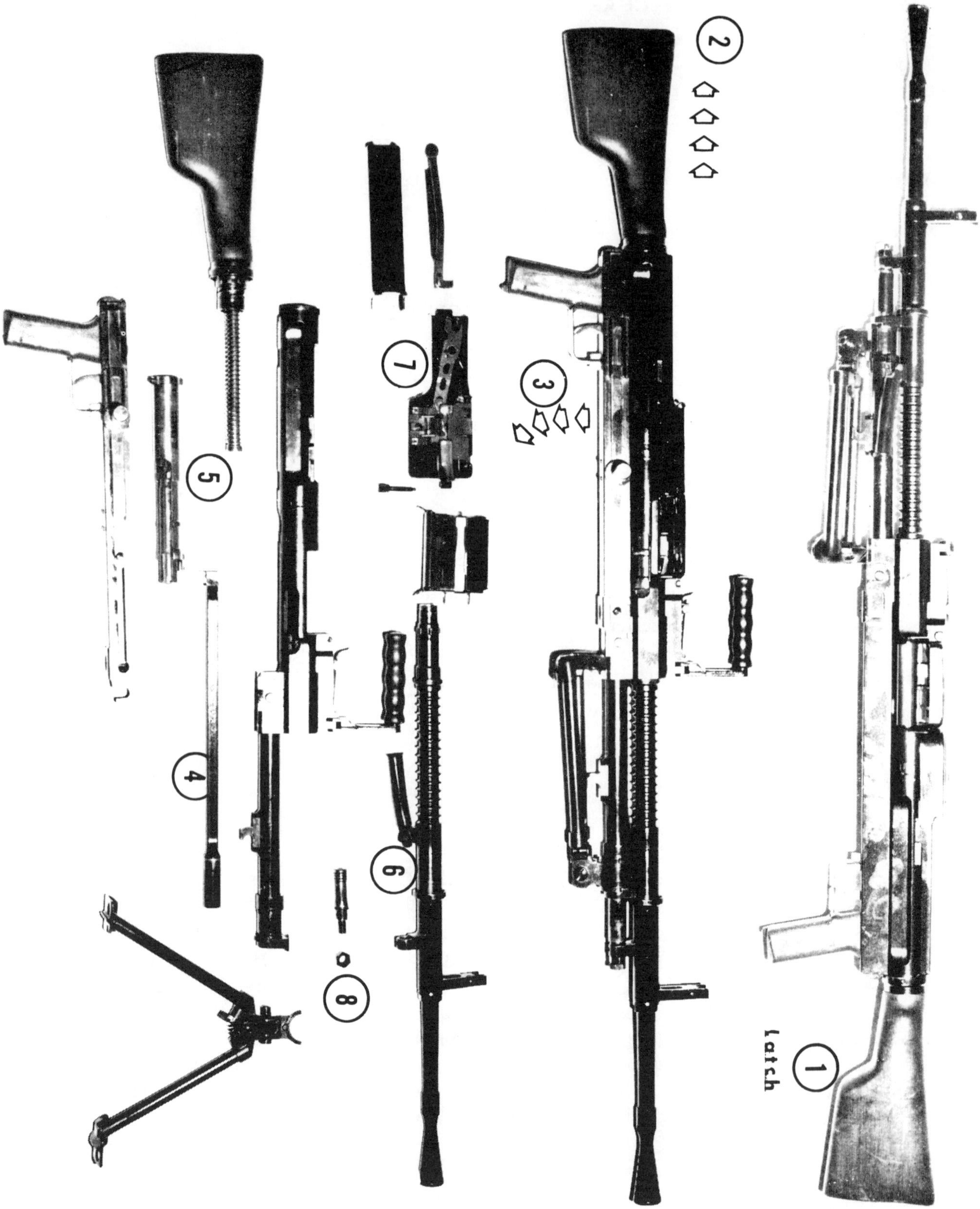

2
3
7
5
4
6
8
1
latch

7.62-mm Madsen/Saetter

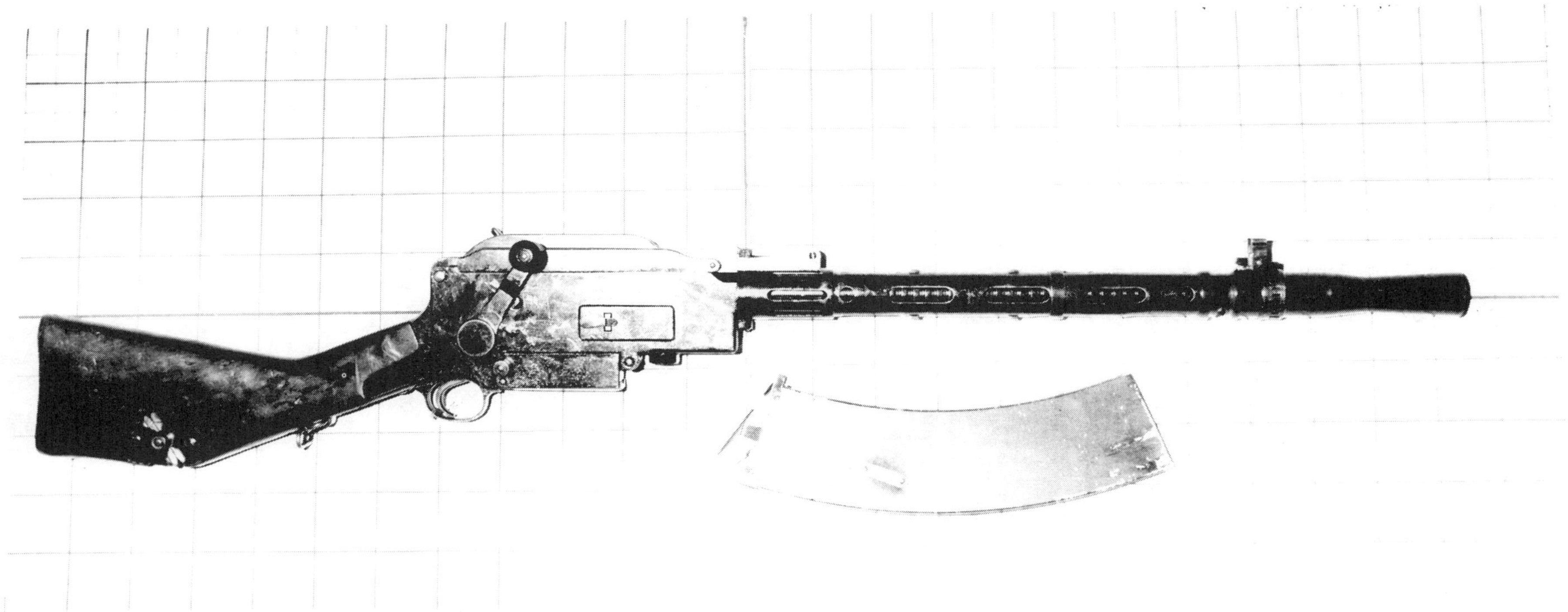

DENMARK 8-MM, MADSEN

MACHINEGUN   DENMARK

8-mm MADSEN LIGHT

The 8-mm Madsen Light Machinegun is a gas-operated weapon of the "long-recoil" type and is the only machinegun in use today which does not utilize a reciprocating bolt system. This machinegun is, and has been, used by more countries than any comparable arm of this type. More than 35 countries have utilized this weapon from 1908 through WWII. The system used in this model is the only "non-ramming" action used in machineguns. The breech block (bolt) does not move in a straight line but rather pivots from its rear to make way for rounds from the magazine, the rounds being pushed into the chamber by a rammer-arm, the breech block then swings up to seal the breech. It is an unusual and efficient arm, and it is expected to be seen for many years to come.

FUNCTIONING

This is a long-recoil type weapon. In this system the barrel recoils a distance equal to the length of the cartridge before unlocking, extraction of the fired case takes place during this recoil phase and as the counterrecoil stroke takes place a new round is positioned and fed into the barrel while the breech is closed by the breech block. With a magazine inserted in the magazine well, positioned on the upper left side of the receiver, the crank handle is drawn to the rear. When the trigger is pulled, the trigger nose releases the recoil arm. The recoil arm under impulse of the compressed recoil spring contained in the stock is forced forward forcing the recoiling parts (breech block, barrel extension and barrel) forward, the recoil arm trips the sear releasing the hammer and the hammer pivots forward to strike the firing pin. As the recoiling parts move forward the front of the pivoting breech block working through a switch plate inside the receiver is cammed down to expose the chamber and the feed arm forces the first cartridge in the distributor feedway into the barrel. The breech block following the switch plate guides now moves up to close the breech as the hammer strikes the firing pin. As the action moves to the rear in recoil, the ejector/extractor is tripped rearward to flip the cartridge out of the barrel and down through the bottom of the receiver. The hammer is cocked, the breech block pivots down to make way for the next round. The feed arm pivots forward to ram the next round into the barrel and the action is repeated until the trigger is released or the magazine is empty if the select lever has been positioned for full-automatic fire. If set for semi-automatic fire the recoiling parts are held to the rear until the trigger is pulled again.

CHARACTERISTIC DATA

Caliber	8-mm, 6.5-mm, 7.7-mm and 7.92-mm
Operation	Recoil
Type of Fire	Full and semi-auto
Rate of Fire	450 rpm (Practical 125)
Type of Feed	Box - 25, 30 & 40 rd cap
Weight, empty	24.7 lbs
Overall length	44.7 in
Effective range	1,270 meters

FIELD STRIP PROCEDURE

STEP   ACTION

1. Remove the Retaining Pin from the upper rear side of the Receiver which allows the Cover to open and pivot the Stock and Trigger Group Assembly down.
2. Reach into the rear of the Receiver and grasp the Feed Arm Axis Bar and draw the recoiling parts and Barrel Assembly to the rear out of the Receiver.
3. Remove the Breech Block Bolt, pull the Feed Arm to the rear and tilt the Breech Block up out through the top of the Barrel Extension Assembly.

ASSEMBLY PROCEDURE

Assemble in the reverse order. Assemble the Breech Block into the Barrel Extension and replace the Breech Block Bolt. Slide assembled recoiling parts into the Receiver. Swing the Stock and Trigger Group Assembly up, close the Cover and replace the Retaining Pin.

LOADING AND FIRING

To load: Place the Safety/Select Lever on "SAFE." Insert a loaded Magazine into the Magazine Well on the upper left hand side of the Receiver and latch into place.

To fire: Move the Safety/Select Lever to the type of fire desired. Draw the Crank Handle to the rear and release. The action will remain open. Pull the Trigger, the action will move forward and the weapon will fire. If the Safety/Select Lever is set for semi-automatic fire the Trigger must be pulled for each shot. If set for full-automatic the weapon will continue to fire until the Trigger is released or the Magazine is empty.

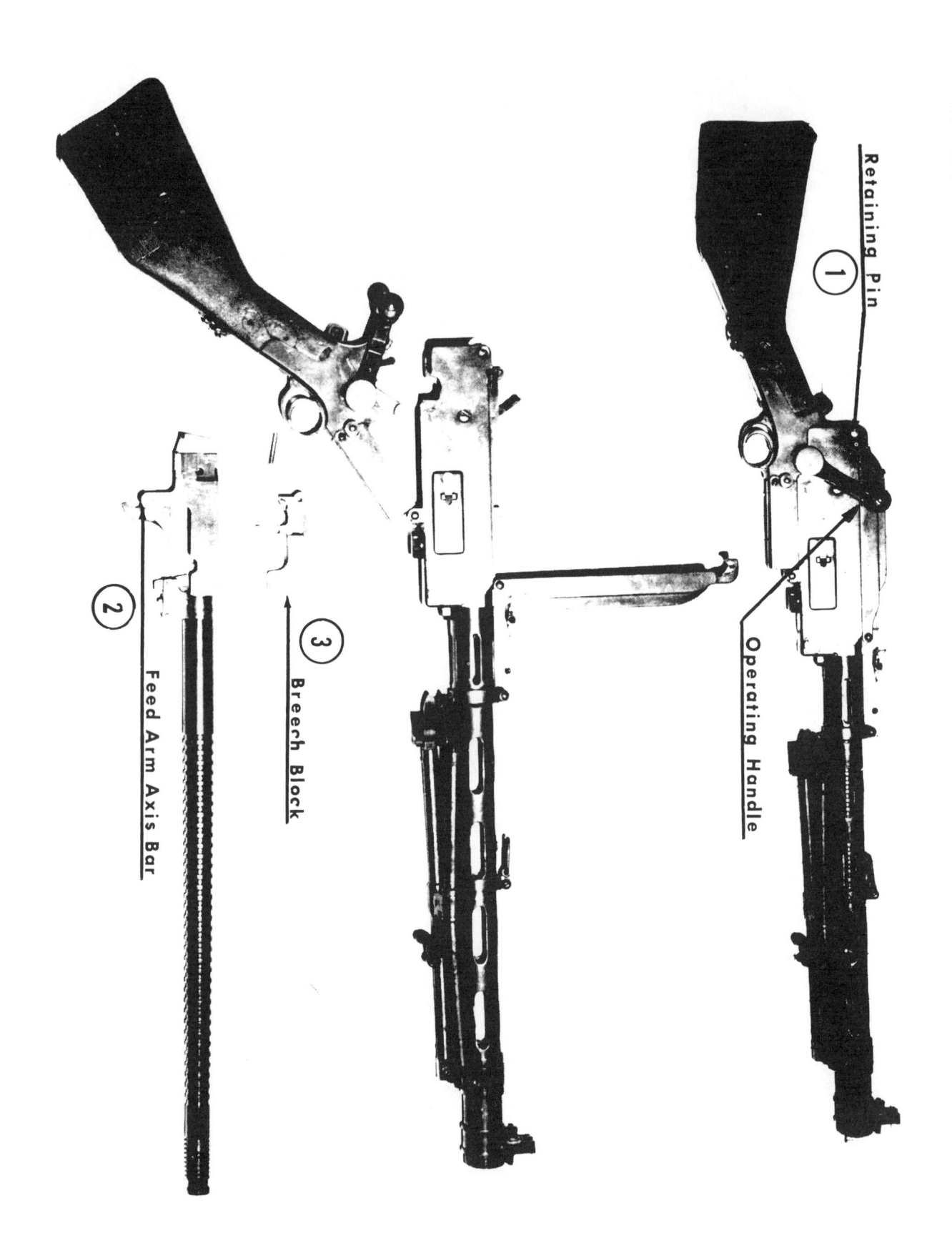

1. Retaining Pin
2. Feed Arm Axis Bar
3. Breech Block

Operating Handle

8-mm Madsen

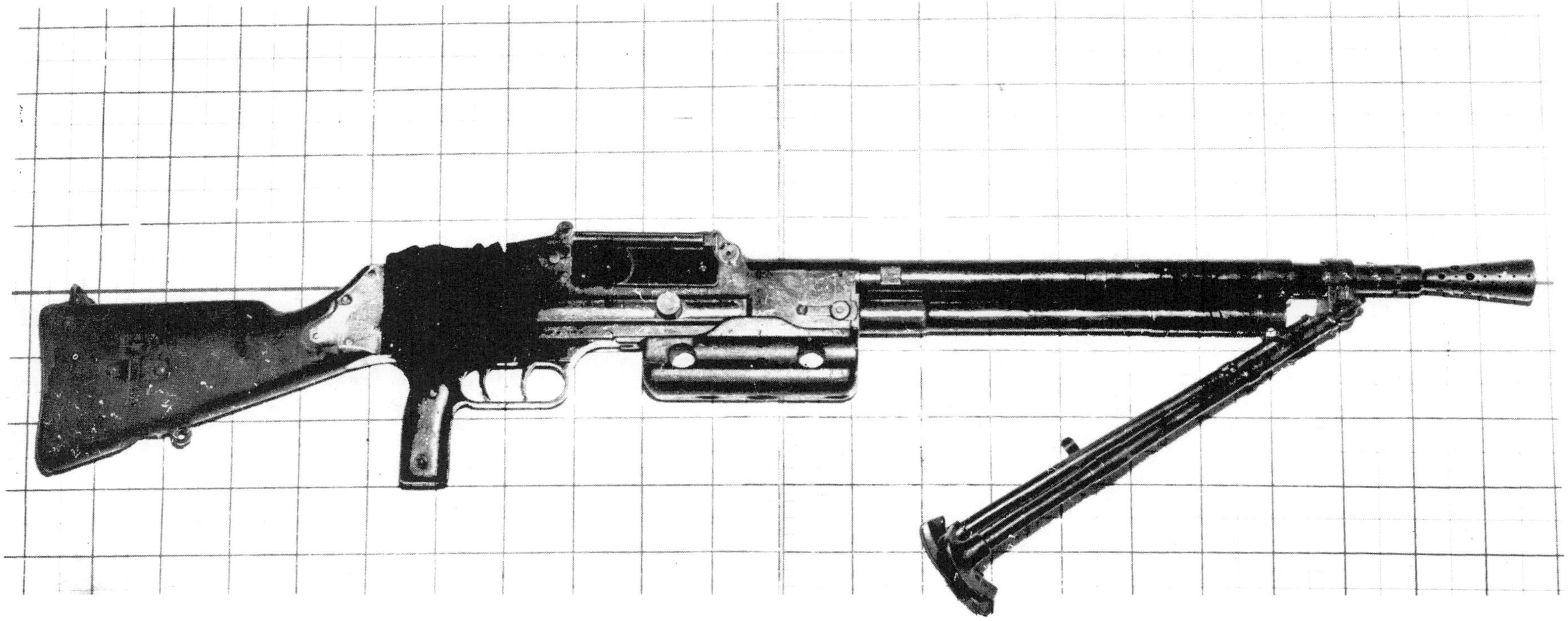

FRANCE 7.5-MM M29, MODEL 1924/29

MACHINEGUN   FRANCE

7.5-mm MACHINEGUN M1924/29

The French 7.5-mm M1924/29 Machinegun (Chattelerault) is a gas-operated, magazine fed, light machinegun, which would normally be classed as an automatic rifle by the U.S. This weapon was adopted by the French in 1924 though the prototype actually appeared in 1921. The standard rifle type cartridge at the time of the introduction of this piece was the 8-mm rimmed round. In order to avoid the feeding difficulties encountered when rimmed rounds are fed from a box magazine, this weapon was chambered for a newly designed 7.5-mm rimless round. Special models of this rifle were made prior to WWII for adaption to fixed aircraft installation. The same basic system was adapted to a heavy machinegun design for use in tanks, armored cars, and fixed defense positions. This machinegun, the M1931A was fed from either a horizontal box magazine or a side-mounted drum holding 150 rounds. While new small arms have appeared in the French service (the M1950 pistol, M1949/56 rifle and the M1952) no provision has been made to produce a new automatic rifle or as this weapon is referred to by the French, a light machinegun.

FUNCTIONING

This is a gas-operated, magazine fed, automatic rifle, incorporating a locking system very similar to that used in the U.S. Browning Automatic Rifle (BAR). This is a selective fire weapon, the type of fire selected by the use of two separate triggers. With a loaded magazine in place, the bolt handle is pulled to the rear to open the bolt. The bolt remains to the rear with the slide and gas piston, the bottom of the rear of the slide being engaged by the sear. Upon pulling the trigger, the sear releases the slide and the assembled slide and bolt move forward, strip a round from the magazine and chambers it. When the bolt comes to a stop against the barrel, the slide continues to move forward. This final movement of the slide forces the rear of the bolt up into a recess in the top of the receiver through a link and at the same time, the striker carried by the slide, impinges against the primer. Gas passes from a port in the barrel into a gas cylinder and expands forcefully against the forward end of the gas piston. The piston and slide start to the rear, the link brings the rear of the bolt down out of engagement in the top of the receiver, and the assembly moves straight to the rear. The recoiling parts strike a buffer system housed in the stock. This weapon incorporates a rate-of-fire reduction mechanism in the stock to slow the rate of fire.

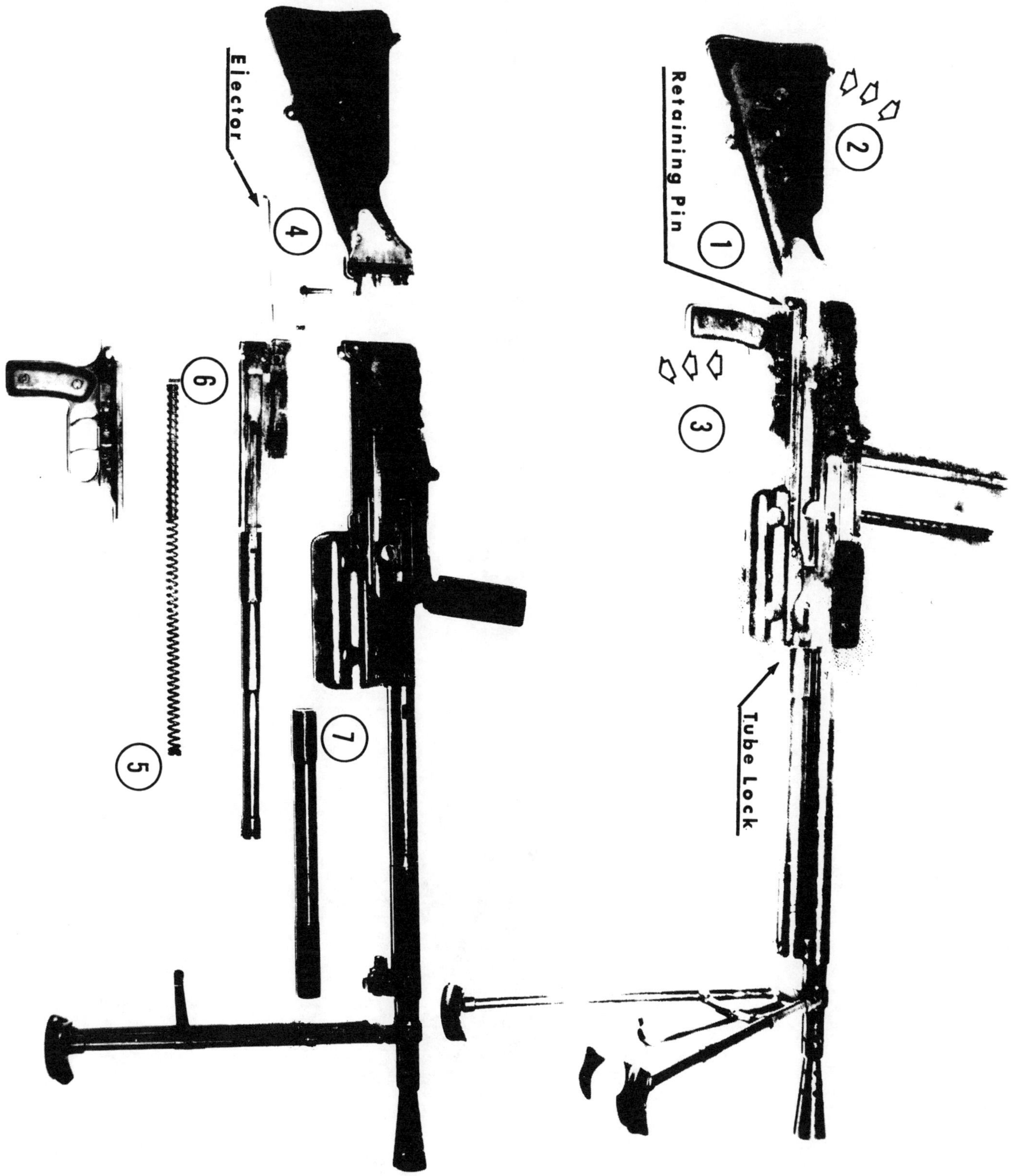
Retaining Pin
Tube Lock
Ejector
1
2
3
4
5
6
7

7.5-mm M24/29

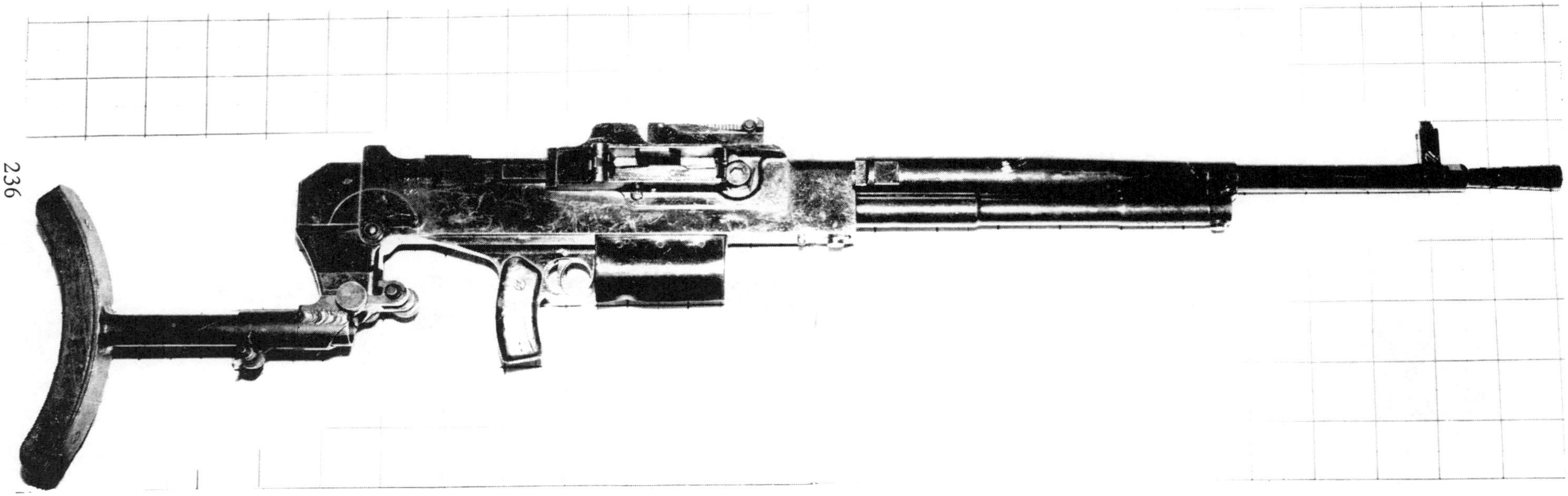

FRANCE 7.5-MM M29, MODEL 1931A

CHARACTERISTIC DATA

Caliber	7.5-mm
Operation	Gas
Type of Fire	Full and semi-auto
Rate of Fire	550 rpm (Practical-175)
Type of Feed	Box - 25 rd cap
Weight, empty	20.5 lbs
Overall length	42.5 in
Effective range	1,620 meters

FIELD STRIP PROCEDURE

STEP   ACTION

1. Remove Stock Retaining Pin.
2. Swing Stock up and disengage from Receiver.
3. Swing Triggerguard down and forward and disengage from Receiver.
4. Pull head of Ejector from slot in Receiver and remove.
5. Disengage Recoil Spring Guide and remove with Recoil Spring.
6. Slide the Piston and Slide with assembled Bolt from rear of Receiver.
7. Turn Gas Cylinder Tube Lock to "O" and remove Gas Cylinder Tube.

ASSEMBLY PROCEDURE

Assemble in the reverse order. Engage Gas Cylinder Tube and lock into place. Assemble Ejector into Receiver. Assemble Bolt to Slide and slide assembly into Receiver. Slide Recoil Spring and Guide into Slide and engage rear of Guide with Receiver. Swing the Triggerguard up into place. Attach Stock and Pivot down. Assemble Retaining Pin to Stock and Receiver.

LOADING AND FIRING

To load: Draw the Bolt Handle to the rear. Swing the Safety located on right side of Trigger Guard into "SAFE." Place loaded Magazine into top of Receiver. Place Safety on "FIRE."

To fire: Press the Trigger; the Bolt will move forward, chamber a round and fire it. If the front Trigger has been pulled the weapon will fire one shot. The Trigger will have to be pulled for each shot. If the rear Trigger has been pulled, the weapon will fire as long as the Trigger is held back or until the Magazine is empty.

MACHINEGUN FRANCE

7.5-mm MACHINEGUN M1931A

The French 7.5-mm M1931A Machinegun is a gas-operated, magazine fed machinegun which functions in a manner very similar to the French M1924/29 Light Machinegun. This is basically a heavy version, classed by the French as a "tank and fortress model" of the Light "Chatellerault" (M1924/29) machinegun. This weapon, originally designed for mounting in armored vehicles, was later modified for mounting on the U.S. caliber .30 M2 machinegun tripod. Near the end of WWII the French developed the MAS M1945 tripod mount for the weapon. Though adapted for a ground role, this weapon is usually en- countered in armored vehicles. The M1931A utilizes a very heavy barrel since it was designed for sustained fire employment and thus has no quick-change capability. It is fed from two types of magazines. Both magazines attach to the right side of the piece. A standard box magazine holding 36 rounds is generally encountered. A drum type, 150-round magazine, was designed for the tactical sustained fire role. This machinegun has no safety lever or device to lock the firing mechanism. When unloading, after the magazine is removed, a round will remain in the feedway. Since the weapon fires from an open bolt, releasing the bolt even with the magazine removed, will chamber and fire the round remaining in the feedway.

FUNCTIONING

This is a gas-operated machinegun which fires from an open bolt. With a loaded magazine in place, pull the operating handle to the rear to open the bolt. The bolt attached to the top of the slide by a link, will remain to the rear with the slide, the bottom of which has been engaged by the sear. The recoil Spring has been compressed by this action. Pulling the trigger will release the slide, the slide will move forward carrying the bolt, a round will be stripped from the magazine and chambered. The face of the bolt comes to a stop against the rear of the barrel and the rear of the bolt is forced up by its link connection with the slide into a recess in the top of the receiver. Continued forward movement of the slide, which carries the firing pin, causes the firing pin to impinge against the cartridge primer and fires the round. Gas tapped from a port in the barrel enters the gas cylinder and strikes the gas piston attached to the forward end of the slide. The piston and slide with attached bolt, move to the rear, pulling the top rear of the bolt down out of engagement with the recess in the top of the receiver. The recoil spring is compressed and the bottom of the slide is engaged by the sear and held to the rear. The weapon will continue to fire if the trigger is held to the rear and the sear is unable to engage the slide.

CHARACTERISTIC DATA

Caliber . . . . .7.5-mm rimless
Operation . . . . .Gas
Type of Fire . . . . Full-auto only
Rate of Fire . . . . 750-770 rpm (Practical-350)
Type of Feed . . . . .Box - 36 rd cap
. . . . Drum - 150 rd cap
Weight, empty . . . . 30.1 lbs
Overall length . . . . 40.6 in
Effective range . . . . 1,850 meters

FIELD STRIP PROCEDURE

STEP　　　　　　　　　　　　ACTION

1. With the weapon empty and the Bolt forward, press in on the Backplate Catch, rotate it 90 degrees and remove the Recoil Spring and Guide.
2. Remove the Backplate Retaining Pin.
3. Pull the Backplate off to the rear.
4. Remove the Trigger Group.
5. Remove the Slide and Piston Assembly with attached Bolt out the rear of the Receiver.
6. Turn the Gas Cylinder Tube Lock and remove the Gas Piston Tube.

ASSEMBLY PROCEDURE

Assemble the weapon in the reverse order. Place the Gas Piston Tube into position and engage. Assemble the Bolt to the Slide and Piston Assembly and slide into the Receiver. Assemble the Trigger Group to the Receiver, press the Backplate into place and assemble the Backplate Retaining Pin to the Receiver and Backplate. Slide the Recoil Spring and Guide into the hole in the rear of the Backplate, push in and turn 90 degrees to engage.

LOADING AND FIRING

To load: Pull the Operating Handle to the rear, the Slide and Piston Assembly with attached Bolt will remain to the rear. Attach a loaded Magazine to the right side of the Receiver.

To fire: Pull the Trigger, the Slide will be released carrying the Bolt forward to chamber and fire a round. If the Trigger is held to the rear the weapon will continue to fire until the Magazine is empty.

NOTE: This is a dangerous weapon to unload. Even with the Magazine removed, a round remains in the Feedway and must be pushed out manually before the Bolt can be closed.

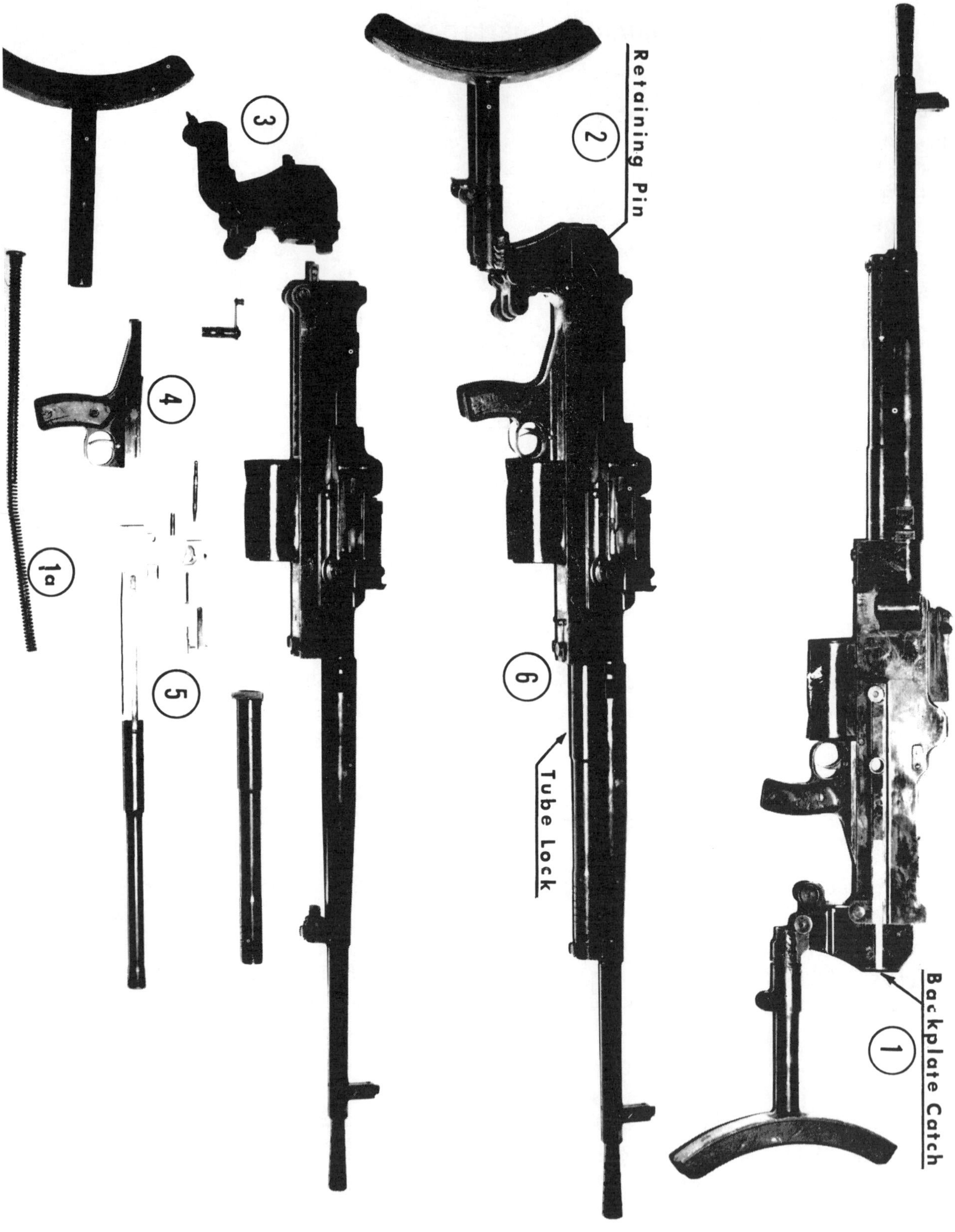
Retaining Pin
Tube Lock
Backplate Catch
1
1a
2
3
4
5
6

7.5-mm M1931A

FRANCE 8-MM, MODEL 1914

MACHINEGUN   FRANCE

8-mm M1914 (HOTCHKISS)

The French M1914 Hotchkiss Machinegun is a gas-operated, strip-clip fed, heavy machinegun which saw extensive use in both WWI and WWII. Limited numbers were recovered in Korea during the Korean Conflict. This weapon was the first truly successful Hotchkiss designed machinegun though the original design appeared in 1895. Many variations of this Hotchkiss system have appeared throughout the world, most notably the Japanese copies of the system. The weapon was unusually heavy for the caliber and is characterized by the heavy finned barrel, designed for sustained fire, and the metal strip-clip feeding system.

FUNCTIONING

This is a gas-operated weapon in which the feeding of the strip-clip containing the ammunition is accomplished by camming studs on the upper surface of the gas piston transmitting the reciprocating motion of the piston into a tranverse motion of the belt feed components. With a loaded strip of ammunition inserted into the feedway from the left, the bolt handle is drawn to the rear where the sear engages a sear bent on the slide holding the slide and bolt to the rear. When the trigger is pulled the sear releases slide and the slide carrying the bolt moves forward under impulse of the recoil spring, the bolt strips a round from the clip and chambers it. At the same time the camming stud on the upper rear portion of the slide which is engaged with a link attached to the rear of the bolt, forces this link down so that it locks in front of a shoulder in the receiver. A forward stud on the slide contacts the firing pin and forces it into the primer. Gas is tapped from the barrel to impinge against the piston forcing the piston rearward. The inston, being a forward extension of the slide, forces the slide rearward causing the cam on the slide to raise the locking pin on the link up and out of its engagement in the locking recesses in the receiver, and the unlocked bolt is carried to the rear by the slide. Feeding cams on the upper surface of the piston rotate a feed pawl to draw the strip-clip into the feedway and position the next round for feeding. This weapon fires full-automatic only and the recoiling parts will move forward immediately and the firing cycle will be repeated until the trigger is released or the strip-clip is empty. Loaded clips can be attached to the strip being fed into the weapon during firing to deliver sustained fire beyond the 30-round clip capacity.

CHARACTERISTIC DATA

Caliber	8-mm
Operation	Gas
Type of Fire	Full-auto only
Rate of Fire	550 rpm (Practical 200)
Type of Feed	Strip - 30 rd cap
Weight, w/mount	106.5 lbs
Overall length	54.1 in
Effective range	2,150 meters

FIELD STRIP PROCEDURE

STEP   ACTION

1. Push in on Recoil Spring Guide protruding from Back Plate inside of Spade Grip.
2. Drive Back Plate Pin out to the left.
3. Pull Back Plate with Recoil Spring and Guide from Receiver.
4. Draw the Bolt Handle to the rear to bring the Bolt, Slide and Piston Assembly rearward and remove these components from the Receiver. Lift the Bolt from the rear of the Slide.
5. Drive the Feed Block Key, located along the lower edge of the Feed Block on the right side of the Receiver, to the rear and remove.
6. Lift the Feed Block Assembly from the Receiver.
7. Slide the Trigger Group to the rear and remove from the Receiver. Disengage the Trigger from the Trigger Group.

ASSEMBLY PROCEDURE

Assemble in the reverse order. Assemble the Trigger to the Trigger Group and slide the assembled group onto the Receiver. Place the Feed Block Assembly into position and drive the Feed Block Key into place. Assemble the Bolt to the camming post on the upper rear of the Slide and slide the Slide, Bolt and Piston into the Receiver. Place the Recoil Spring into the rear of the Slide and push the Back Plate with Recoil Spring and Guide into the Receiver and replace the Back Plate pin. The Recoil Spring Guide protruding from the Back Plate must be pushed in in order to push the Back Plate Pin through the Receiver.

LOADING AND FIRING

To load: Draw the Bolt Handle to the rear and push the Safety Lever to "SAFE." Insert a 30-round strip of ammunition into the Feed Block from the left side, push in until first round in strip is engaged by Feed Pawl. Make sure cartridges are lined up in strip.

To fire: Push Safety Lever to "FIRE." Pull the Trigger. The weapon will fire. This piece fires full-automatic only and will continue to fire until the Trigger is released or the strip is empty. Loaded strips of ammunition can be continuously hooked onto the strip being fed into the weapon so that long sustained fire may be delivered.

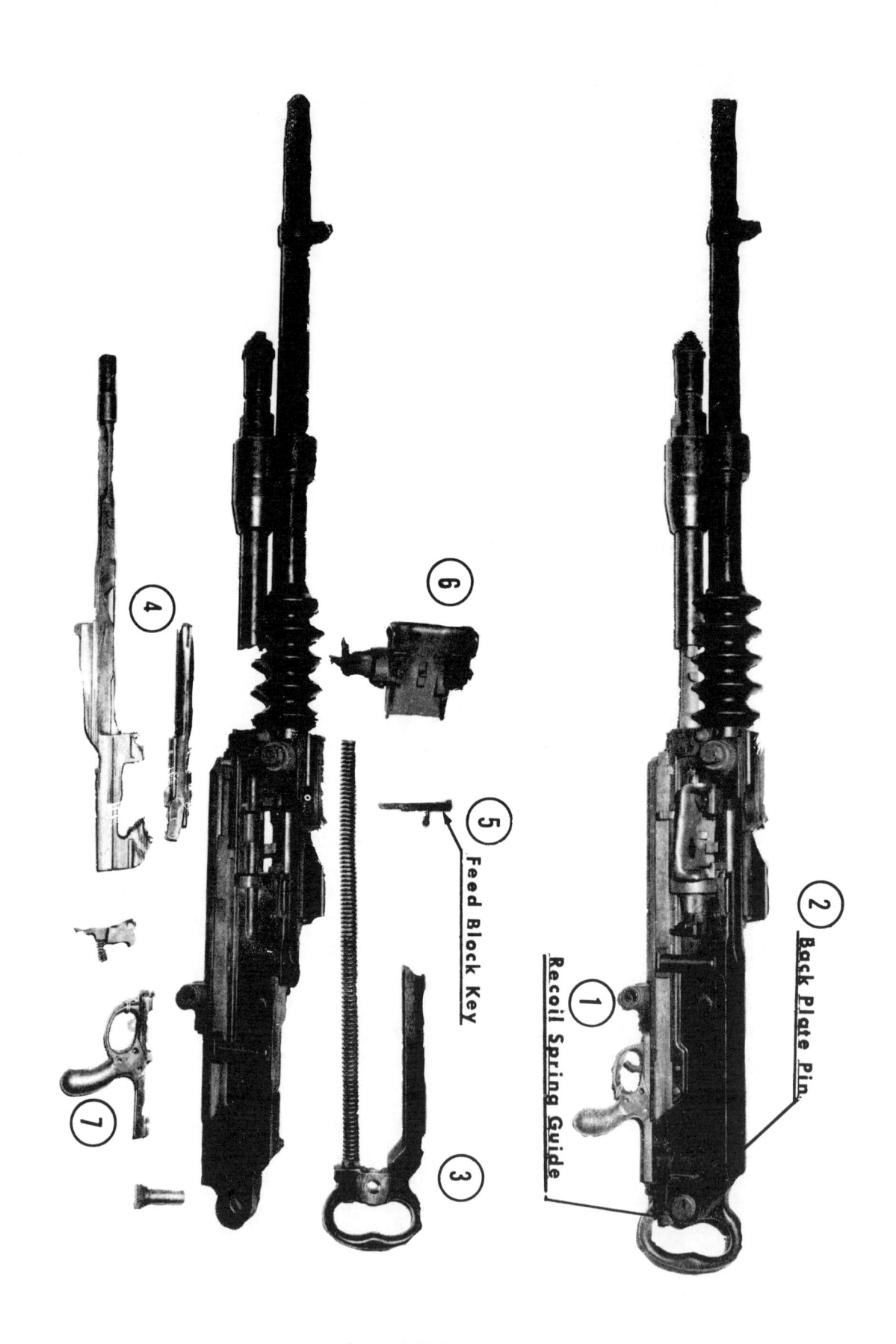

1. Recoil Spring Guide
2. Back Plate Pin
5. Feed Block Key

8-mm M1914

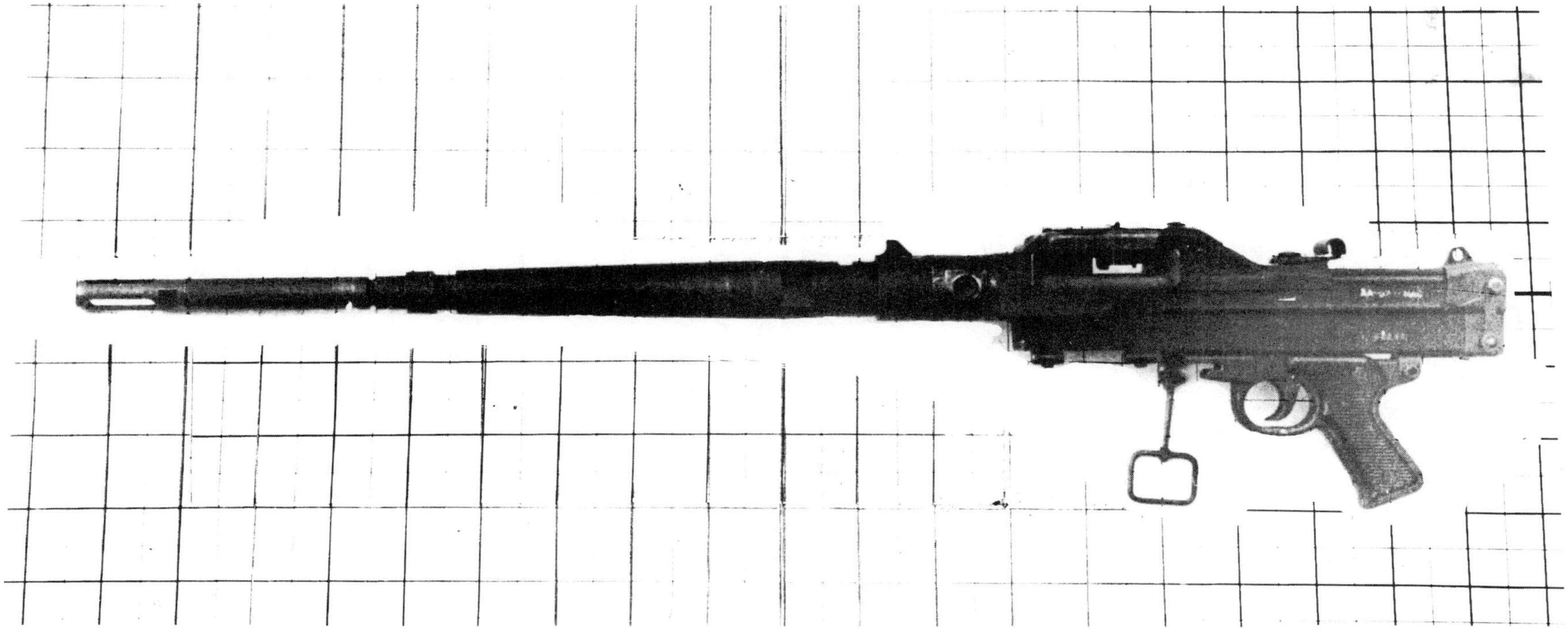

FRANCE   7.5-MM M29, MODEL 1952

MACHINEGUN FRANCE

7.5-mm AAT MLE—52

The French Model 52 Light Machinegun is a retarded blowback weapon which fires full-automatic from an open bolt only. It is bipod or tripod mounted and utilizes a quick-change barrel, a retractable shoulder stock and a belt feed system similar to the German MG-42 Machinegun. This weapon is classed as a General Purpose Machinegun and is replacing the French M24/29 Light Machinegun. A tank version is also mounted in the French AMS—13 Light Tank (illustrated). This weapon is an example of the French design technique of utilizing the best features of a number of weapons to produce a versatile, efficient weapon. The bolt locking system is similar to the German G-3 Assault Rifle except that a retarding lever is utilized to slow the opening movement of the bolt instead of rollers as in the case of the G-3.

FUNCTIONING

With the bolt handle drawn to the rear to open the action, a loaded belt is positioned in the feedway. When the trigger is pulled the sear releases the bolt which moves forward under impulse of the compressed recoil spring, strips a round from the belt and chambers it. The bolt is constructed of two pieces, a heavy rear portion and a light forward head portion. Between the head and the body of the bolt is a locking lever which engages a shoulder in the receiver at one end and the heavy body section at the other end. When the firing pin strikes the primer, pressure in the chamber forces the empty cartridge rearward against the bolt head, the bolt head bearing against the locking lever must overcome the resistance presented by the locking lever bearing against the shoulder in the receiver and the heavy bolt body. By the time this resistance has been overcome the bullet has left the muzzle and the action starts moving rearward. A feed stud on top of the bolt engages the feed lever in the cover to move the belt feed pawl from right to left to position the next round for feeding. This weapon fires full-automatic only and will continue to fire until the trigger is released or the belt is empty.

CHARACTERISTIC DATA

Caliber . . . . .7.5-mm (M29 ctdge)
. . . . .7.62-mm (NATO)
Operation . . . . Retarded blowback
Type of Fire . . . . Full-auto only
Rate of Fire . . . . 650 rpm (Practical 225)
Type of Feed . . . . .Belt - 50 rd cap
Weight, w/mount . . . . 34.2 lbs
Overall length, stock retracted . . . . 38.7 in
Effective range . . . . 2,150 meters

FIELD STRIP PROCEDURE

STEP　　　　　　　　　　　　ACTION

1. Rotate Receiver Pin and remove Back Plate.
2. Raise the Cover, pull the Bolt Handle to the rear, remove Recoil Spring, Guide and Bolt assembly out the rear of the Receiver, remove head of Bolt.
3. Remove the Triggerguard Pin and remove the Trigger Group Assembly.
4. Raise the Feed Block Assembly.
5. Pull Barrel Lock to the rear; swing Carrying Handle clockwise and pull Barrel forward from the Receiver.

ASSEMBLY PROCEDURE

Assemble in the reverse order. Slide Barrel into front of Receiver, turn Barrel clockwise and engage Barrel Lock. Assemble Trigger Group to the Receiver and replace Triggerguard Pin. Assemble Bolt Head to Bolt Body, slide Recoil Spring and Guide into Bolt and slide assembly into Receiver. Slide Back Plate onto Receiver and replace Receiver Pin. Close Feed Block assembly and Cover.

LOADING AND FIRING

To load: Draw the Bolt Handle to the rear and push the Safety Lever to "SAFE." Open the Cover and lay the first round of the loaded belt into the Feed Block Assembly, positioning the first round against the Cartridge Stop. The weapon can also be loaded with the Cover down by inserting the belt tab into the feedway and pulling through until the first cartridge stops against the Cartridge Stop in the Feed Block Assembly.

To fire: Push the Safety Lever to "FIRE" position. Pull the Trigger. The weapon will fire. This weapon fires full-automatic from an open Bolt only and will continue to fire until the Trigger is released or the belt is empty.

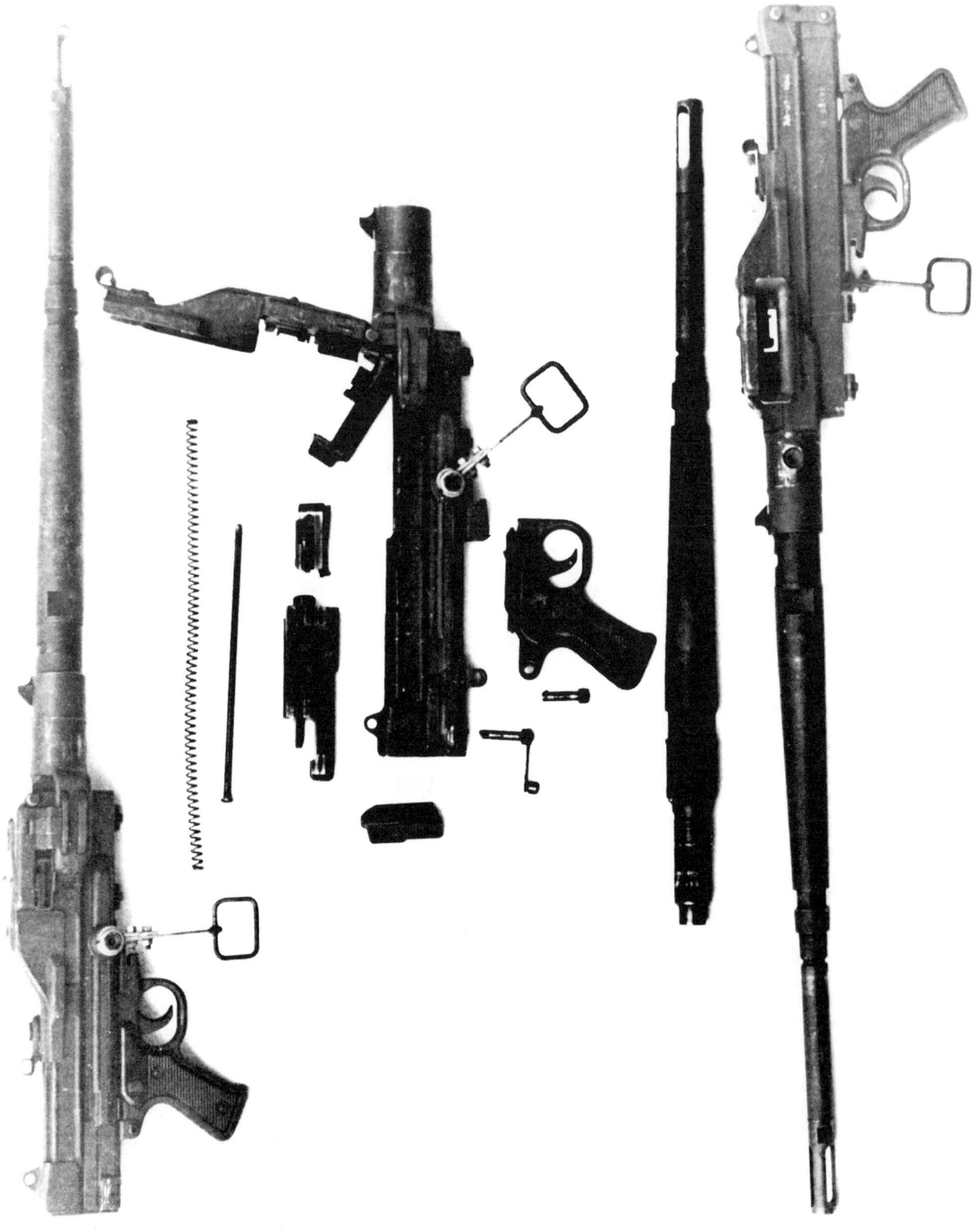

GERMANY   7.92-MM., MG-42

MACHINEGUN   GERMANY

7.92-mm MASCHINENGEWEHR 42 (MG-42)

The 7.92-mm MG-42 machinegun is a recoil operated, air cooled, belt fed machinegun. Recoil is assisted by a muzzle recoil booster. It is fed from the left side, may be fired from a bipod or tripod, and has an extremely high rate of fire. It has a quick change barrel, removable from the right side of the barrel jacket. In WWII the Model 42 replaced the Model 34 as the standard general purpose machinegun of the German Army. The Model 42 was cheaper and simpler to manufacture than the Model 34 and incorporated a modified bolt system. The Model 34 was well-made, utilizing machined parts and components and a complex rotating bolt-head system for locking. The Model 42 made use of many stampings, particularly in the receiver, barrel jacket and bipod construction. The bolt system was changed to a straight reciprocating bolt which accomplished the locking function by the use of locking rollers on each side of the bolt, which are cammed into locking recesses in the barrel extension. After the West German Army was officially founded in the early 1950's. considerable testing of various machineguns took place to determine the weapon the West Germans would be armed with. No weapon tested was deemed superior to the MG-42, and production of a slightly modified model of the MG-42 was started in West Germany in 1957. Slight changes were made in the feed ramp to improve feeding, and a floating accelerator was added to the internal rear portion of the bolt to assure positive locking action during firing. This model, the MG-1 is chambered for the NATO cartridge.

FUNCTIONING

The MG-42 is fed from a non-disintegrating metal belt which may be contained in a steel drum (50- rounds only) or linked together in increments of 50-round belts contained in a metal ammunition box. This weapon fires from an open bolt. With the bolt to the rear, an ammunition belt positioned in the feed-way and the cover closed, the trigger is pressed, the sear disengages from its bent in the bolt and the bolt travels forward under the impulse of the compressed recoil spring. The face of the bolt strips a round from the belt and chambers it. As the face of the bolt comes flush with the rear of the barrel extension (attached to the rear of the barrel) two locking rollers, located on each side of the forward portion of the bolt, are cammed into engagement with recesses in the barrel extension. The extractor slips over the head of the cartridge and the firing pin carried in the bolt strikes the primer, firing the cartridge. During recoil, the barrel extension and bolt are locked firmly together by the engaged locking rollers and recesses in the barrel extension for a fraction of the initial recoil movement. When the barrel extension is stopped in its rearward travel, the rollers are cammed out of engagement and the bolt continues to the rear alone, compressing the recoil spring and stopping its travel against the buffer group contained in the stock. A stud located at the top rear of the bolt engages a belt feed arm in the cover, and imparts a reciprocating action to the belt feed pawl, which pulls the belt from left to right to position the next round in the feedway.

CHARACTERISTIC DATA

Caliber . . . . 7.92-mm and 7.62-mm NATO
Operation . . . . Recoil
Type of Fire . . . . Full-auto only
Rate of Fire . . . . 1,200 rpm (Practical-450)
Type of Feed . . . . Belt - 50 rd cap
Weight, empty . . . . 26.1 lbs
Overall length . . . . 48.31 in
Effective range . . . . 1,890 meters bipod
. . . . 2,300 meters tripod

FIELD STRIP PROCEDURE

STEP   ACTION

1. Open the Bolt by pulling the Operating Handle to the rear.
2. Push the Barrel Release Lever out to the right.
3. Remove the Barrel to the rear.
4. Push forward on the Cover Latch and raise the Cover.
5. Remove the Cover Hinge Pin.
6. Remove the Cover.
6a. Lift off the Feed Block.
7. Pull the Trigger and allow the Bolt to go forward. Disengage the Butt Stock Catch.
8. Twist the Butt a quarter turn and remove to the rear.
9. Remove the Bolt Assembly and Recoil Spring from the Receiver.

ASSEMBLY PROCEDURE

Proceed in the reverse order. Slide the Bolt Assembly and Recoil Spring into the Receiver. Attach the Butt Stock and latch into place. Place the Feed Block into position, assemble the Cover to the Feed Block and put the Cover Hinge Pin in place. Close the Cover, pull the Operating Handle to the rear. Place the Barrel into position in the Barrel Release assembly and swing the Barrel Release Lever in against the Barrel Jacket.

LOADING AND FIRING

To load: Open the Cover, place the first cartridge in the belt against the Cartridge Stop in the Feed Block. Close the Cover. Push the Safety on, from right to left. Pull the Operating Handle to the Rear to open the Bolt. Push the Operating Handle forward again until it locks.

To fire: Push the Safety off, from left to right. Press the Trigger. The Bolt will move forward, chamber and fire a round. The weapon will fire as long as the Trigger is held back.

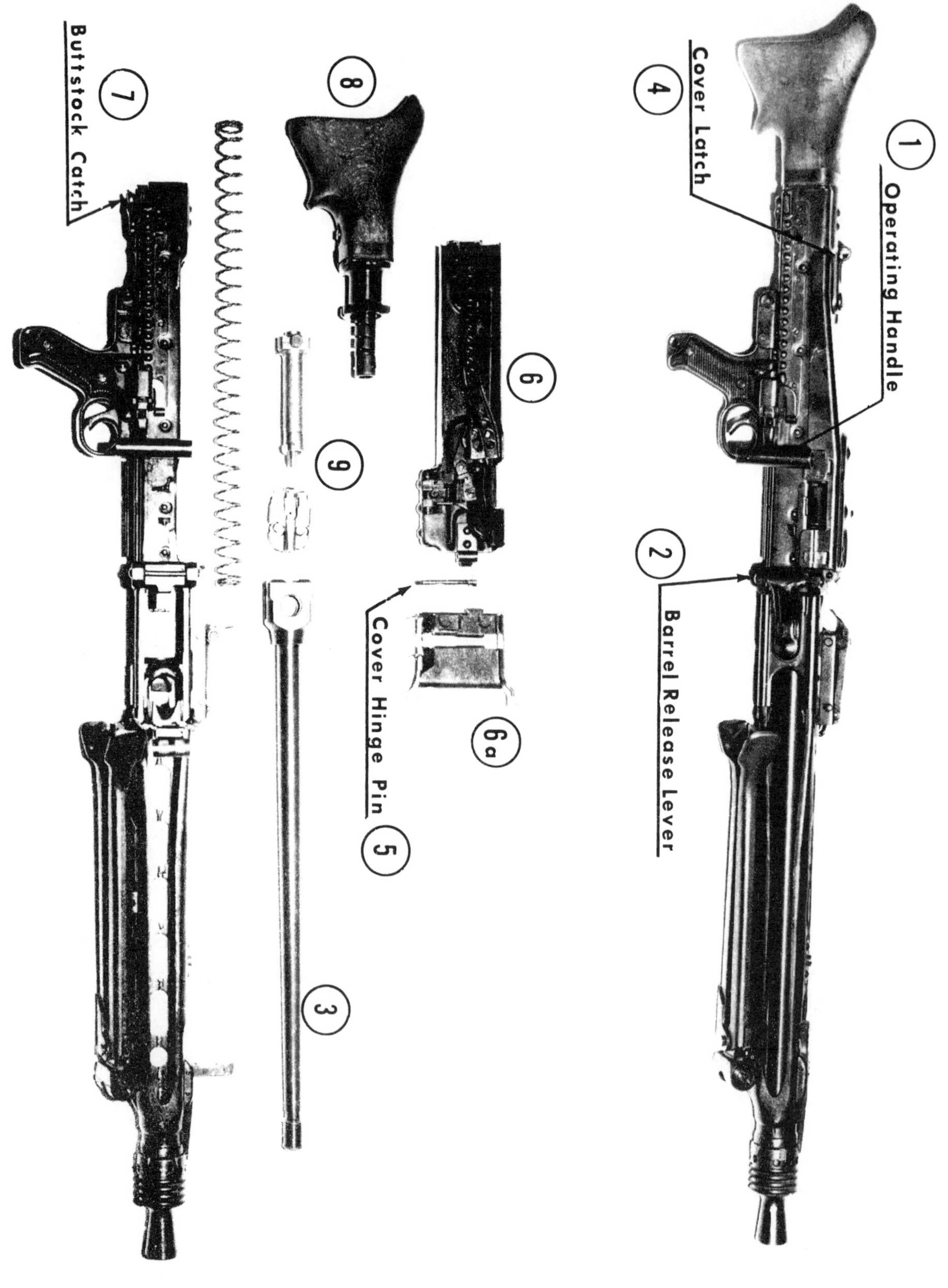
1
Operating Handle
2
Barrel Release Lever
4
Cover Latch
3
5
Cover Hinge Pin
6
6a
7
Buttstock Catch
8
9

7.92-mm MG-42

GERMANY 7.92-MM, MG-34

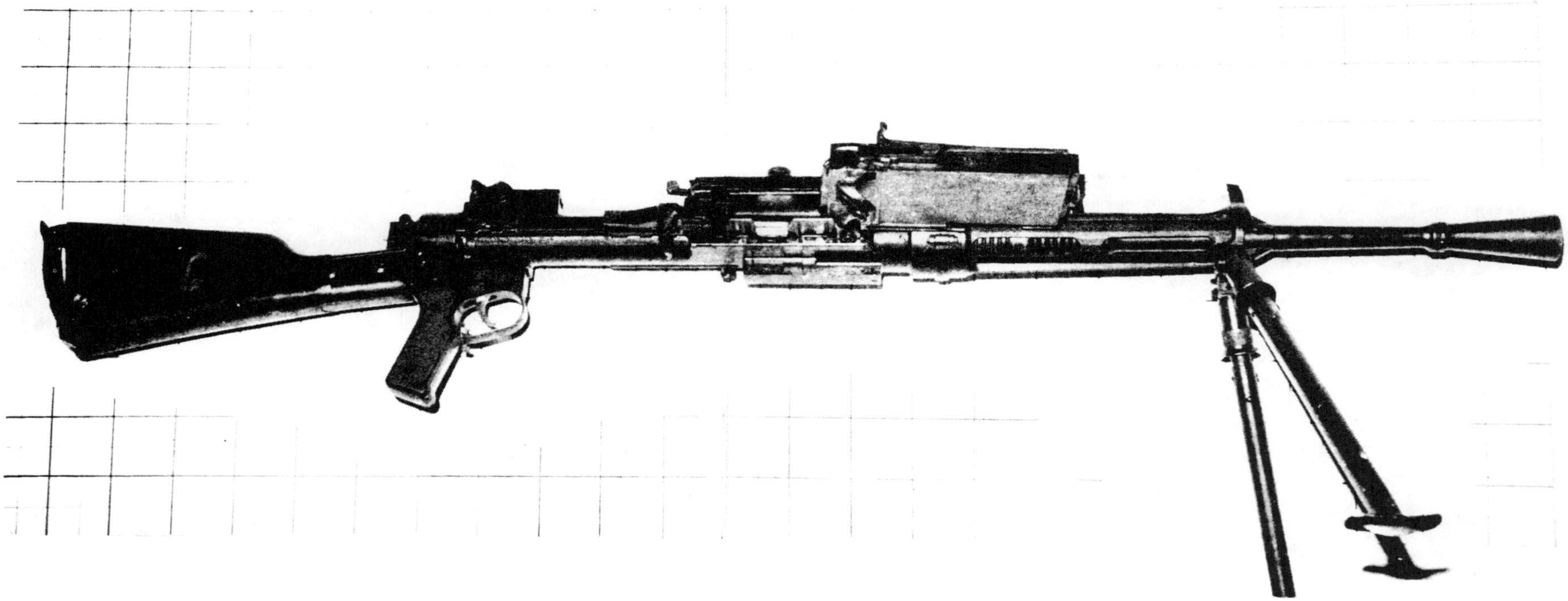

ITALY 6.5-MM, MODEL 30

MACHINEGUN   ITALY

6.5-mm MODEL 1930 (BREDA)

The 6.5-mm Model 1930 Breda Machinegun is a recoil-operated, magazine fed weapon which incorporates a quick-change barrel and a non-removable magazine into its design. The forerunner of this piece is the Model 1924 Machinegun produced by the Breda Plant, Brescia, Italy. The original Model 1924 was finally placed on the marked as the Model 1926 and with minor changes was later designated the Model 1928. All of these models utilized the unusual magazine system whereby the Magazine is pivoted away from the receiver, loaded from a container and then pivoted back into position for firing. In 1930 the Breda Plant merged with the Fiat concern and the Breda-Fiat Plant was opened at Piacenza. The first product of this new plant was the 1930 Model Breda; chambered originally for 6.5-mm, it was later produced for export in 7-mm and 7.92-mm caliber.

FUNCTIONING

This is a recoil-operated, full-automatic fire only weapon, which fires from a closed bolt. It should be noted that during firing, when firing ceases, the bolt should be locked open to prevent "cookoffs." The magazine is loaded by unlatching the magazine housing catch and pivoting the magazine forward on its hinge. A container, or clip, of 20-rounds is inserted into the magazine and the magazine is pivoted back into firing position. The ejection port cover should now be opened. The bolt handle is drawn to the rear and released, the sear engages the sear bent on the firing pin holding the firing pin to the rear and the bolt moves forward to strip a round from the magazine and chambers it. A locking lug on top of the bolt rotates the locking ring on the forward end of the bolt to engage the locking recesses around the end of the barrel. During this chambering action, oil from a cartridge lubricating device has squirted oil on the cartridge as it was stripped from the magazine. This lubricating of the cartridge is necessary due to the violent removal of the empty case from the chamber. A portion of the unlocking cycle is caused by the fired cartridge thrusting rearward against the face of the bolt. When the trigger is pulled, the sear, projecting from the sear housing to engage the firing pin, releases the firing pin allowing the firing pin to move forward under impulse of the firing pin spring and strike the primer. The bolt and barrel locked together by the locking ring moves rearward in recoil, the lug engaging the bolt lock disengages the bolt locking ring and the bolt moves to the rear independant of the barrel, compressing the recoil spring, striking the buffer system and moving forward to chamber the next round. The firing pin is held to the rear until the bolt is fully forward and locked at which time the sear releases the firing pin.This weapon fires full-automatic only and will continue to fire until the trigger is released or the magazine is empty.

CHARACTERISTIC DATA

Caliber	6.5-mm
Operation	Recoil
Type of Fire	Full-auto only
Rate of Fire	450 rpm (Practical-150)
Type of Feed	Box - 20 rd cap
Weight, empty	23.7 lbs
Overall length	48.7 in
Effective range	1,280 meters

FIELD STRIP PROCEDURE

STEP   ACTION

1. Pull Barrel Lock out and down to unlock Barrel.
2. Turn Barrel counterclockwise, slide Barrel forward to disengage the Barrel from the Receiver.
2a. Move Barrel to the rear and remove from Barrel Jacket.
3. Rotate Stock Latch forward, grasp Stock Assembly and twist it counterclockwise, remove from Receiver. Remove Recoil Spring, Guide and Buffer Spring.
4. Draw Bolt Handle to the rear and remove Bolt and Firing Pin with Spring from rear of Receiver.
5. Remove Bolt Handle from Receiver.
6. Release Cover Latch, raise Cover, remove Cover Hinge Pin and remove Cover from Receiver.
7. Slide Magazine forward off its Hinge Plate.

ASSEMBLY PROCEDURE

Assemble in the reverse order. Slide Magazine onto Magazine Hinge Plate. Assemble Cover and Cover Hinge Pin to top of Receiver. Assemble Bolt Handle into Bolt Handle Slot in Receiver. Assemble Firing Pin and Spring into rear of Bolt and slide Bolt into Receiver. Engage Stock Assembly to rear of Receiver and twist down to lock. Makre sure that Stock Latch engages. Slide Barrel forward into Barrel Jacket, then rearward to engage Barrel with Receiver. Pivot Barrel Lock up to lock Barrel.

LOADING AND FIRING

To load: Draw Bolt Handle to the rear and engage Safety Catch to hold Bolt to the rear. Swing Magazine forward to expose Magazine Follower. Insert 20-round charger or container into Magazine and push in until all cartridges are engaged. Open the Ejection Port Cover.

To fire: Draw Bolt Handle to the rear slightly to disengage Bolt from Safety Catch, Bolt will move forward and chamber a round and the Firing Pin will be held to the rear by the Sear. Pull the Trigger. The weapon will fire. This weapon fires full-automatic only and will continue to fire until the Trigger is released or the Magazine is empty.

257

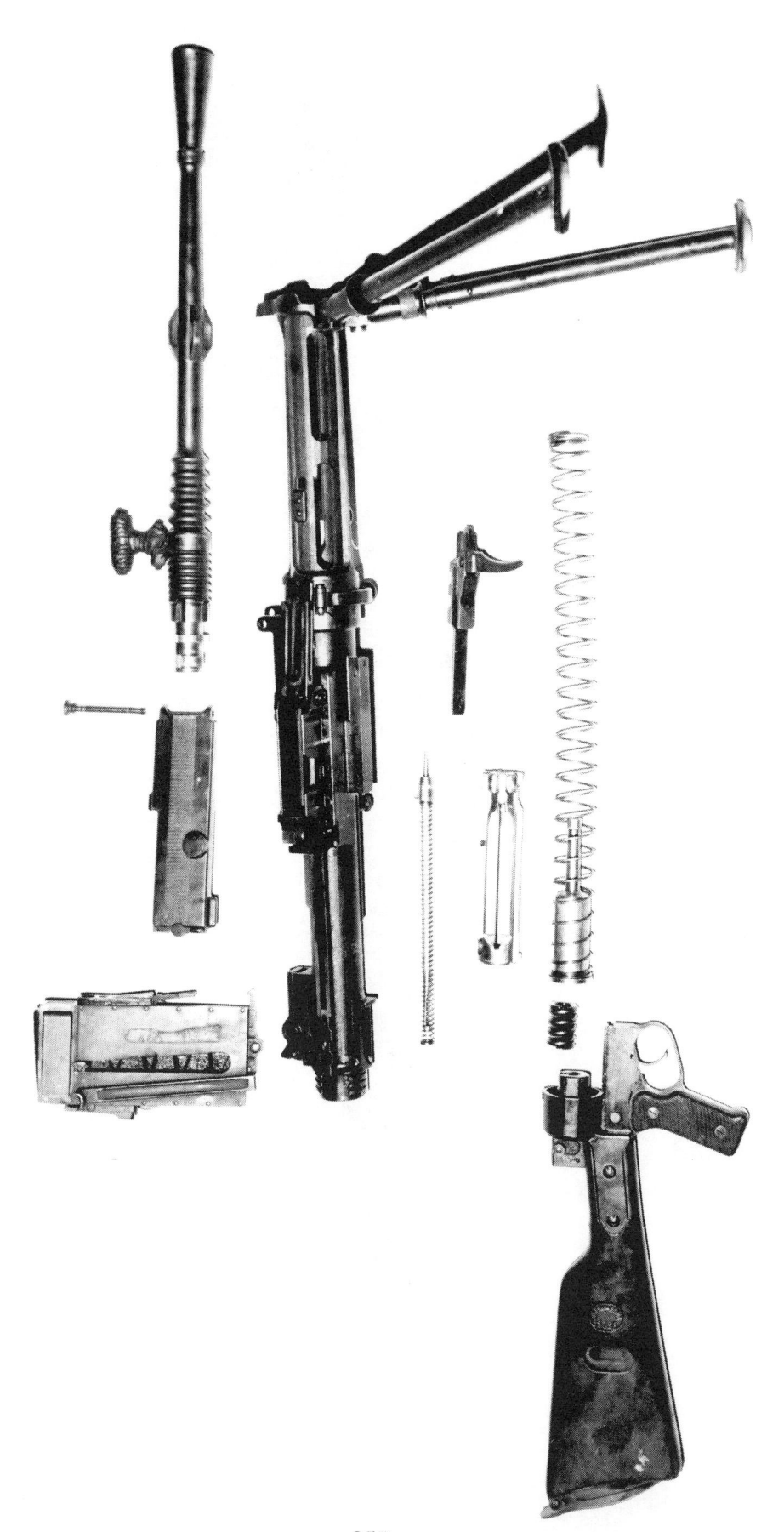

JAPAN 6.5-MM, TYPE 11

MACHINEGUN   JAPAN

6.5-mm TYPE 11 (NAMBU)

The Japanese Type 11 Light Machinegun is a gas-operated hopper-fed, light machinegun copied from the French Hotchkiss design. Developed by General Kijiro Nambu in 1922 it saw extensive use during WWII. The heavy, radial finned barrel, odd-shaped stock and hopper feed mechanism give it a rather unconventional look. Though the locking system, (the rear of the bolt being cammed down by the slide to lock), was conventional enough, the complex hopper feed system was unusual and left much to be desired. This weapon, plus the later models (Type 96, Type 97, Type 99 and Type 92), are obsolete and are not currently in Japanese service.

FUNCTIONING

This is a gas-operated light machinegun which employs an unusual feeding system based on a hopper principle. The feed hopper, a box-shaped device located on the left side of the receiver, is loaded with 6, 5-round strip-clips. These clips are conventional rifle loading clips. When the hopper is loaded a spring-loaded cover is lowered onto the top clip. Pressure from this cover, as well as gravity, keeps the ammunition moving down in the hopper to be fed into the receiver. A complex switching system positions the lowermost, righthand round in front of the bolt for chambering. As each strip-clip is emptied, the ammunition being stripped and positioned for loading, the empty clip is ejected, the next loaded clip dropping into place for feeding. With the hopper loaded and the cover down, the bolt handle is drawn to the rear bringing the piston, slide and attached bolt to the rear where a sear bent on the bottom of the slide is engaged by the sear. When the trigger is pulled the slide is released and moves forward under impulse of the compressed recoil spring. The bolt is carried on the upper rear portion of the slide, a beveled surface on the rear of the bolt being mated to a beveled post on top of the slide. A round is stripped from the hopper and chambered by the bolt, the bolt comes to a stop against the rear face of the barrel, and the slide continues to move forward for a short distance. During this movement the beveled post on the top of the slide operating against the angled surfaces on the bolt forces the rear of the bolt downward so the locking lugs on both sides of the bolt drop in front of locking recesses in the receiver walls. This final movement of the slide also forces the firing pin against the primer. Gas is tapped from the barrel to impinge against the gas piston which is a forward extension of the slide, the slide and piston move to the rear a short distance. Camming surfaces on the slide now force the rear of the bolt upward to disengage the locking lugs on the bolt from the locking recesses in the receiver and the slide, piston and unlocked bolt continue to the rear to stop against the buffer in the backplate. This is a full-automatic weapon and will continue to fire until the trigger is released or the hopper is empty.

CHARACTERISTIC DATA

Caliber 6.5-mm
Operation ....Gas
Type of Fire .... Full-auto only
Rate of Fire .... 500 rpm (Practical 120)
Type of Feed .... Hopper - 30 rd cap
Weight, empty .... 22.7 lbs
Overall length .... 44.1 in
Effective range .... 1,280 meters

FIELD STRIP PROCEDURE

STEP   ACTION

1. Rotate Back Plate Pin down and withdraw from Receiver.
2. Remove Back Plate with assembled Buffer and Recoil Spring and Guide from Receiver.
3. Draw Bolt Handle to the rear and remove from Receiver.
4. Remove Gas Piston and Slide with attached Bolt from rear of Receiver, lift Bolt from top of Slide.

ASSEMBLY PROCEDURE

Assemble in the reverse order. Assemble the Bolt to the Slide and slide Gas Piston and Slide with attached Bolt into rear of Receiver. Assemble Bolt Handle to Bolt Handle slot in Receiver. Assemble Back Plate, Buffer and Recoil Spring and Guide into rear of Receiver, push Back Plate Pin through to left and pivot down to lock.

LOADING AND FIRING

To load: Push Safety Button to "SAFE." Raise the Feed Hopper Cover by lifting up on the Hopper Cover Handle. Holding Feed Hopper Cover open, place 6, 5-round strip clips into Hopper, bullets pointing forward, lower the Hopper Cover until Cover rests on top of the ammunition.

To fire: Draw Bolt Handle to the rear. Slide will be engaged by the Sear and the action will remain open. Pull the Trigger. The weapon will fire full-automatic only and will continue to fire until the Trigger is released or the Feed Hopper is empty.

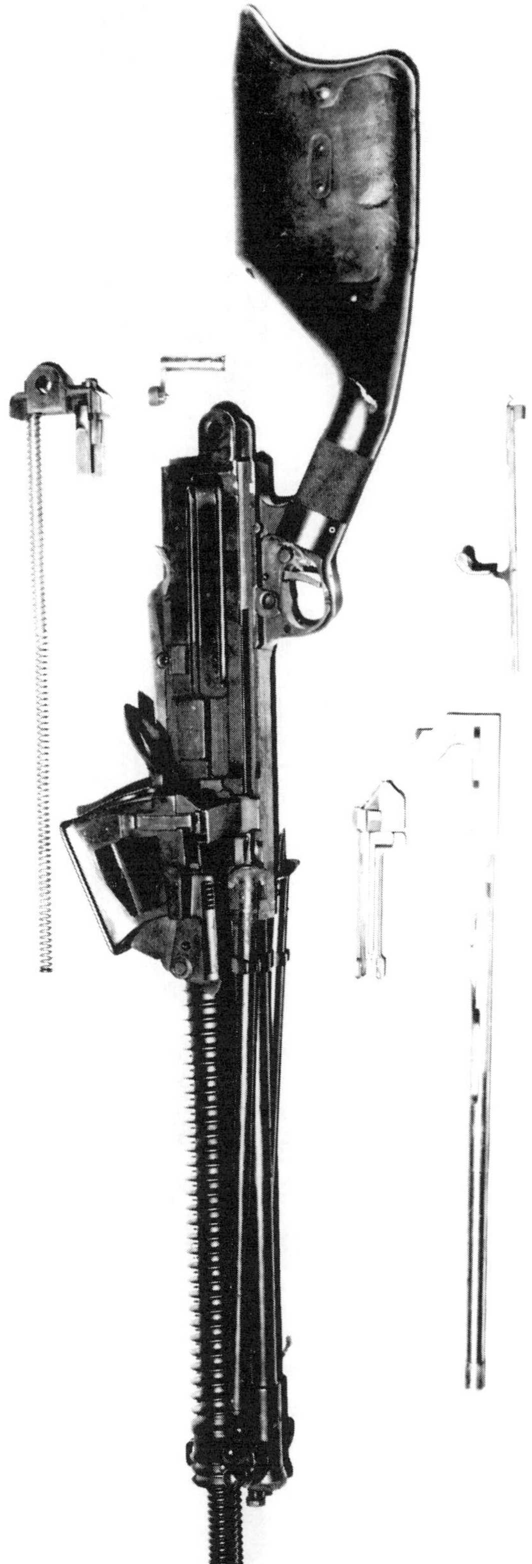

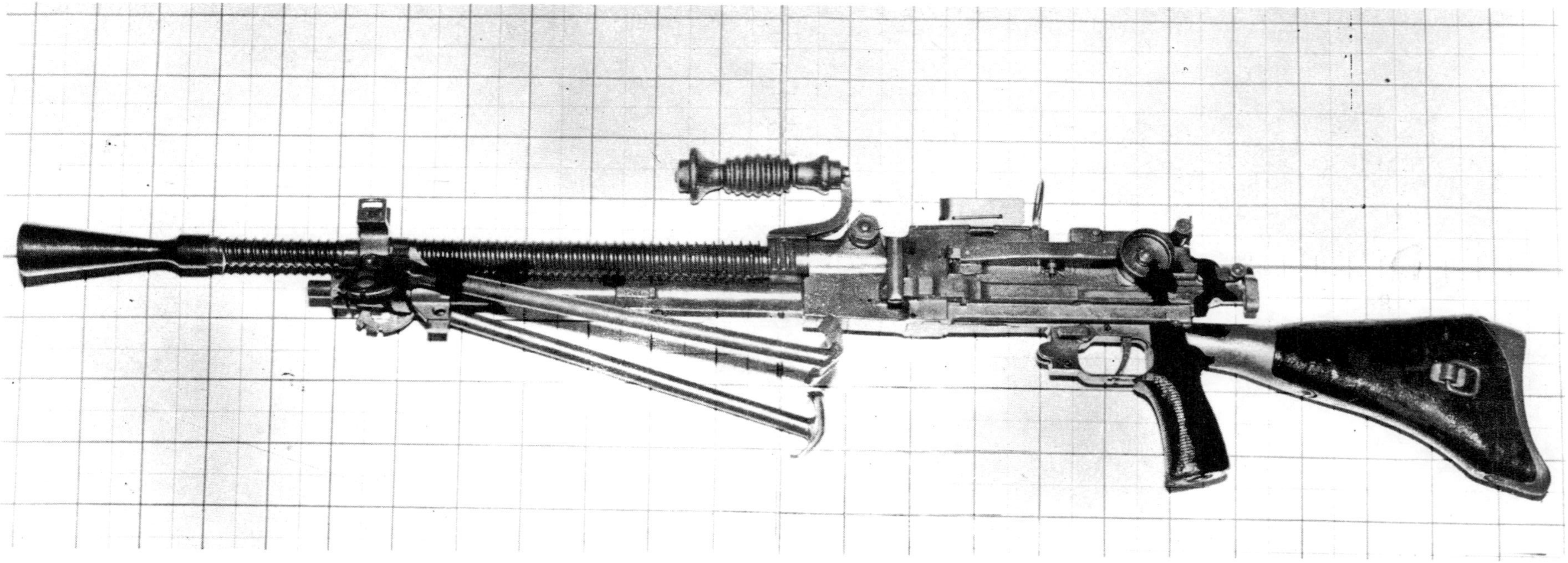

JAPAN 7.7-MM, TYPE 99

MACHINEGUN   JAPAN

7.7-mm TYPE 99

The Japanese 7.7-mm Type 99 Light Machinegun was the last of a series of light machineguns designed by Nambu. The Nambu organization, founded by Kijiro Nambu in 1927, had merged with that of the Chuo Kogyo Kaisha Company in Tokyo in 1937, and the Type 99 Light Machinegun was introduced in 1939 as a result of this merger. The Type 99 utilized the radical bolt lock design and top feed of the 6.5-mm Type 96 Light Machinegun though the barrel lock was changed to incorporate a headspacing device. This is an excellent light machinegun though it is no longer used by the Japanese Armed Forces. This weapon is chambered for the 7.7-mm rimless ammunition and will not chamber the 7.7-mm semi-rim ammunition for which the Japanese Type 92 Heavy Machinegun is chambered.

FUNCTIONING

This is a gas-operated, magazine fed light machinegun which fires from an open bolt, full automatic only. It utilizes a quick change barrel and the barrel is slid straight into the front of the receiver and a cross bolt engages a notch cut in the top of the barrel to hold it in place. The barrel does not turn to lock. With a loaded magazine inserted into the magazine opening in the top of the receiver, the bolt handle, located on the left side of the receiver is drawn to the rear and then pushed forward. The handle does not move with the bolt during firing. The sear engages the slide on which the bolt is carried holding the action to the rear. The bolt lock is a hollow square block of steel carried in the lower forward portion of the receiver. The slide moves back and forth through this lock during its reciprocating movement. When the trigger is pulled, the slide, moves forward under impulse of the compressed recoil spring. The bolt strips a round from the magazine and chambers it. When the bolt comes to a stop against the rear face of the barrel, the slide continues to move forward. As the forward, or camming portion of the lower surface of the slide passes through the lock, the lock is cammed upward so that the upper surface of the lock mates into a cut-out in the bottom of the bolt and the stud on the slide strikes the firing pin driving it into the primer. Gas is tapped from the barrel where it impinges against the face of the gas piston which is a forward extension of the slide. The slide starts rearward and a hump on the bottom of the slide cams the lock down out of its locking cut-out in the bottom of the bolt. With the lock down, the bolt is carried to the rear by the slide. The slide strikes a buffer in the backplate and then moves forward again and the firing cycle is repeated. This weapon fires full-automatic only and will continue to fire until the trigger is released or the magazine is empty.

CHARACTERISTIC DATA

Caliber .... 7.7-mm (Rimless)
Operation .... Gas
Type of Fire .... Full-auto only
Rate of Fire .... 850 rpm (Practical 225)
Type of Feed .... Box - 30 rd cap
Weight, empty .... 22.2 lbs
Overall length .... 42.3 in
Effective range .... 1,620 meters

FIELD STRIP PROCEDURE

STEP   ACTION

1. Unscrew the Barrel Nut (Headspace Adjustment Nut) and pull Barrel Locking Bolt out to the left. Slide Barrel out of Receiver.
2. Pivot up and pull out on the Buffer Lock Pin.
3. Remove Buffer Assembly with Recoil Spring and Guide from rear of Receiver.
4. Remove Slide, Gas Piston and Bolt from Receiver, lift Bolt off of Slide. (Plate covering Bolt Lock, located on bottom front of Receiver, may be swung down to expose Bolt Lock for removal if necessary.)

ASSEMBLY PROCEDURE

Assemble in the reverse order. If Bolt Lock has been removed, replace it and close plate covering opening. Assemble bolt to Slide and slide Slide, Gas Piston and Bolt into Receiver. Assemble Buffer Assembly with Recoil Spring and Guide into rear of Receiver. Push Buffer Lock Pin through Receiver and pivot down to lock. Slide Barrel into front of Receiver. Push Barrel Locking Bolt through Receiver and tighten Barrel Nut. This Barrel is not turned to lock into place. NOTE: If this weapon is assembled without the Bolt Lock the Sear will not release the Slide.

LOADING AND FIRING

To load: Draw the Bolt Handle to the rear and push forward, the Slide and Bolt will remain to the rear. Push the Safety Lever located on the left side of the Trigger Guard ahead of the Trigger to "SAFE." Insert a loaded Magazine into the Magazine port on top of the Receiver.

To fire: Push the Safety Lever to "FIRE." Pull the Trigger. The weapon will fire. This weapon fires full-automatic only, and will continue to fire until the Trigger is released or the Magazine is empty.

1a
4
3
Barrel Nut
1
Buffer Lock Pin
2

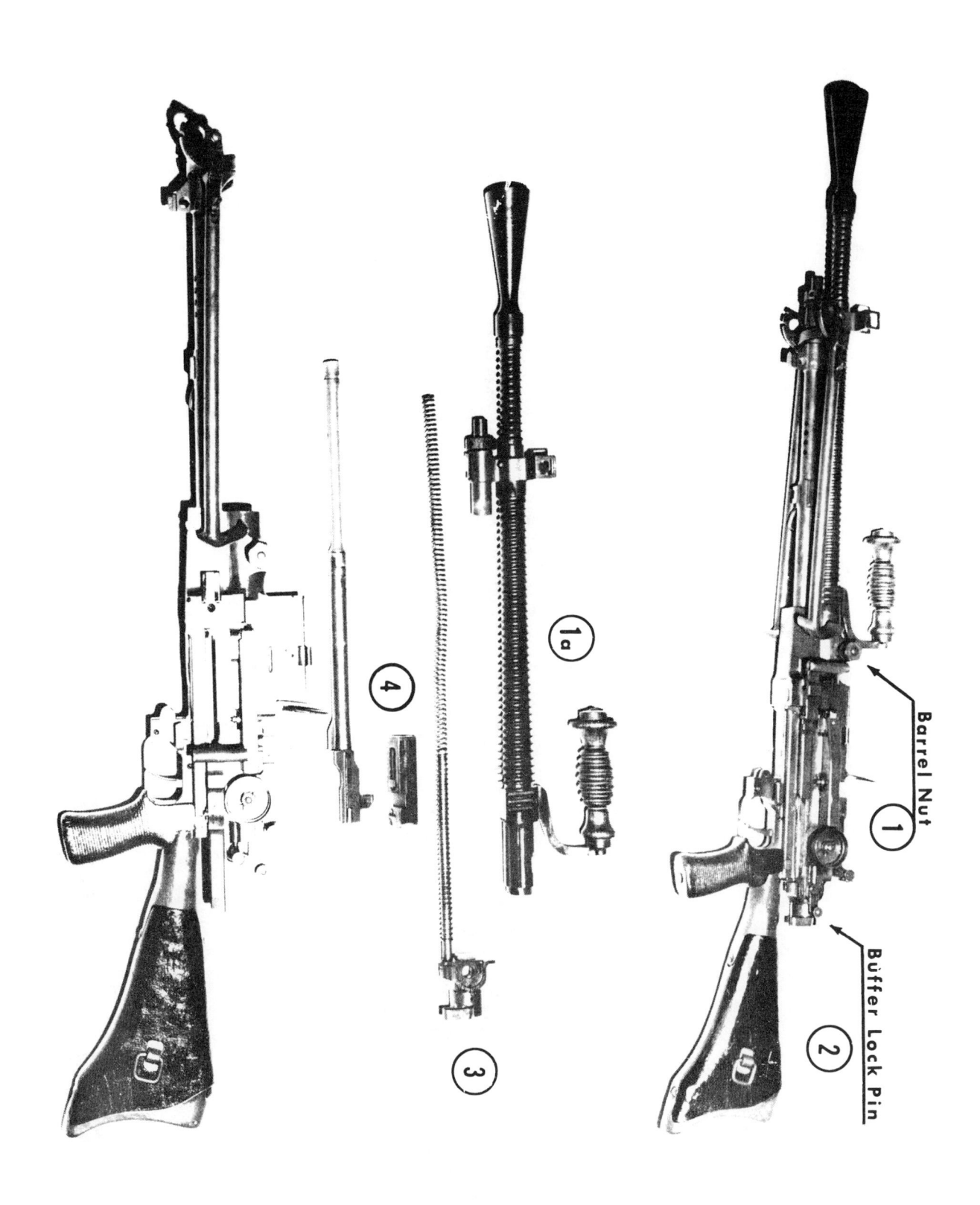

7.7-mm Type 99

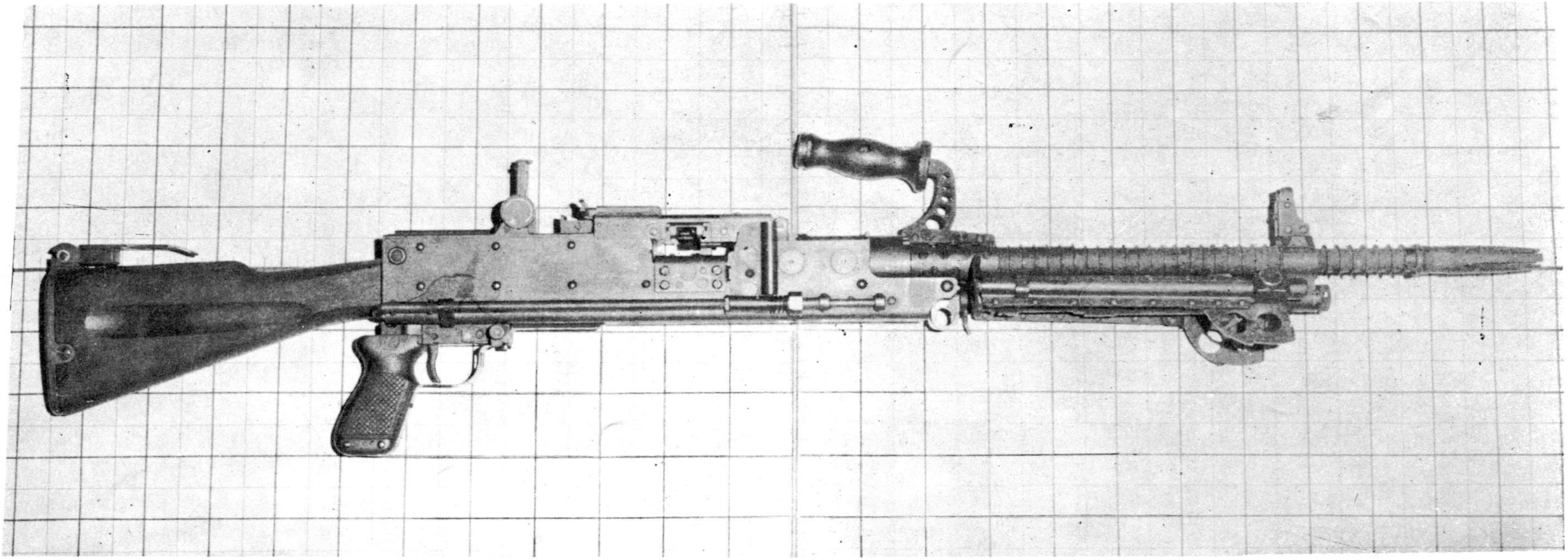

JAPAN 7.62-MM NATO, MODEL 1962

MACHINEGUN   JAPAN

7.62-mm MODEL 62

The Japanese Model 62 Machinegun is the newest machinegun produced by the Japanese defense industry and is currently being manufactured for the Japanese Ground Defense Forces. It is a gas-operated, felt fed machinegun which may be fired from either a bipod or tripod. Most Japanese weapons have been of a uniform inferior design though they have been closely pagterned after such weapons as the Hotchkiss and Bren machineguns or have been faithful copies of the Lewis and Orlikon weapons. The Model 62 machinegun appears to have a number of excellent design features including an independent gas piston with return spring, quick-removable barrel and an excellent flash supressor. The very heavy slide carrying the bolt and an efficient buffer system in the stock allow a relatively "soft" firing action which accounts for a better than usual accuracy in this weapon.

FUNCTIONING

This weapon fires full-automatic from an open bolt only and utilizes an independant gas piston system which is returned to its forward position by its own return spring. With a belt positioned in the feedway and the bolt held to the rear by the sear engaging the sear bent in the bottom of the slide, the trigger is pulled and the sear releases the slide. The slide carries the bolt on its upper surface, the firing pin attached to the slide being positioned in a tunnel in the bolt. The bolt strips a round from the belt and chambers it. As the round is chambered a camming ramp on the rear of the slide forces the rear of the bolt to seat in front of a shoulder in the receiver at the same time that the firing pin strikes the primer. The impulse of the forward moving parts is in effect still felt when the cartridge is fired. Gas is tapped from the barrel to impinge against the face of the gas piston, the gas piston moves rearward to contact the face of the slide. The slide is forced rearward and in so doing the rear of the bolt is cammed down out of its locking recess in the receiver. The bolt and slide continue rearward and the gas piston is drawn forward by the piston return spring. The slide strikes a buffer system in the back plate and starts forward again. The firing cycle is repeated until the trigger is released or the belt is empty.

CHARACTERISTIC DATA

Caliber	7.62-mm (NATO)
Operation	Gas
Type of Fire	Full-auto only
Rate of Fire	650 rpm (Practical 275)
Type of Feed	Belt - 250 rd cap
Weight, empty	23.5 lbs
Overall length	47.6 in
Effective range	1,850 meters

FIELD STRIP PROCEDURE

STEP   ACTION

1. Push Stock Retaining Pin out of Receiver to left.
2. Remove Stock Assembly with Recoil Spring, Guide and Buffer Assembly from rear of Receiver.
3. Raise Cover. (This releases Barrel Locking Plunger.)
4. Draw Bolt Handle fully to the rear and remove.
5. Draw Slide Assembly with attached Firing Pin and Bolt from rear of Receiver.
6. Align Carrying Handle dismounting stud with dismounting notch in Barrel Locking Ring, push Barrel Locking Plunger rearward, turn Carrying Handle until dismounting guide lines are aligned then pull Barrel forward out of Receiver. (Cover must be open.)
7. Remove Gas Piston and Gas Piston Return Spring from Receiver.

ASSEMBLY PROCEDURE

Assemble in the reverse order. Assemble Gas Piston Return Spring to Piston and slide Piston into front of Receiver. Slide Barrel into Barrel Locking Ring with dismounting guide lines aligned, turn Carrying Handle up to lock Barrel into place. Assemble Bolt to top of Slide and slide Bolt and Slide Assembly into rear of Receiver. Assemble Bolt Handle to Receiver. Close Cover. Attach Stock Assembly with Recoil Spring and Guide to rear of Receiver and push Stock Retaining Pin through Receiver.

LOADING AND FIRING

To load: Draw Bolt Handle to the rear and push forward. Bolt and Slide will be held to the rear by the Sear. Push Safety Button to "SAFE." Raise Cover and lay first round in belt against Cartridge Stop in feedway. Close and latch Cover. Weapon may also be loaded by leaving Bolt forward and pulling tab end of belt through feedway and then drawing Bolt to the rear to position first round for feeding.

To fire: Push Safety Button to "FIRE" position. Pull the Trigger. The weapon will fire. This piece fires full-automatic only and will continue to fire until the Trigger is released or the belt is empty.

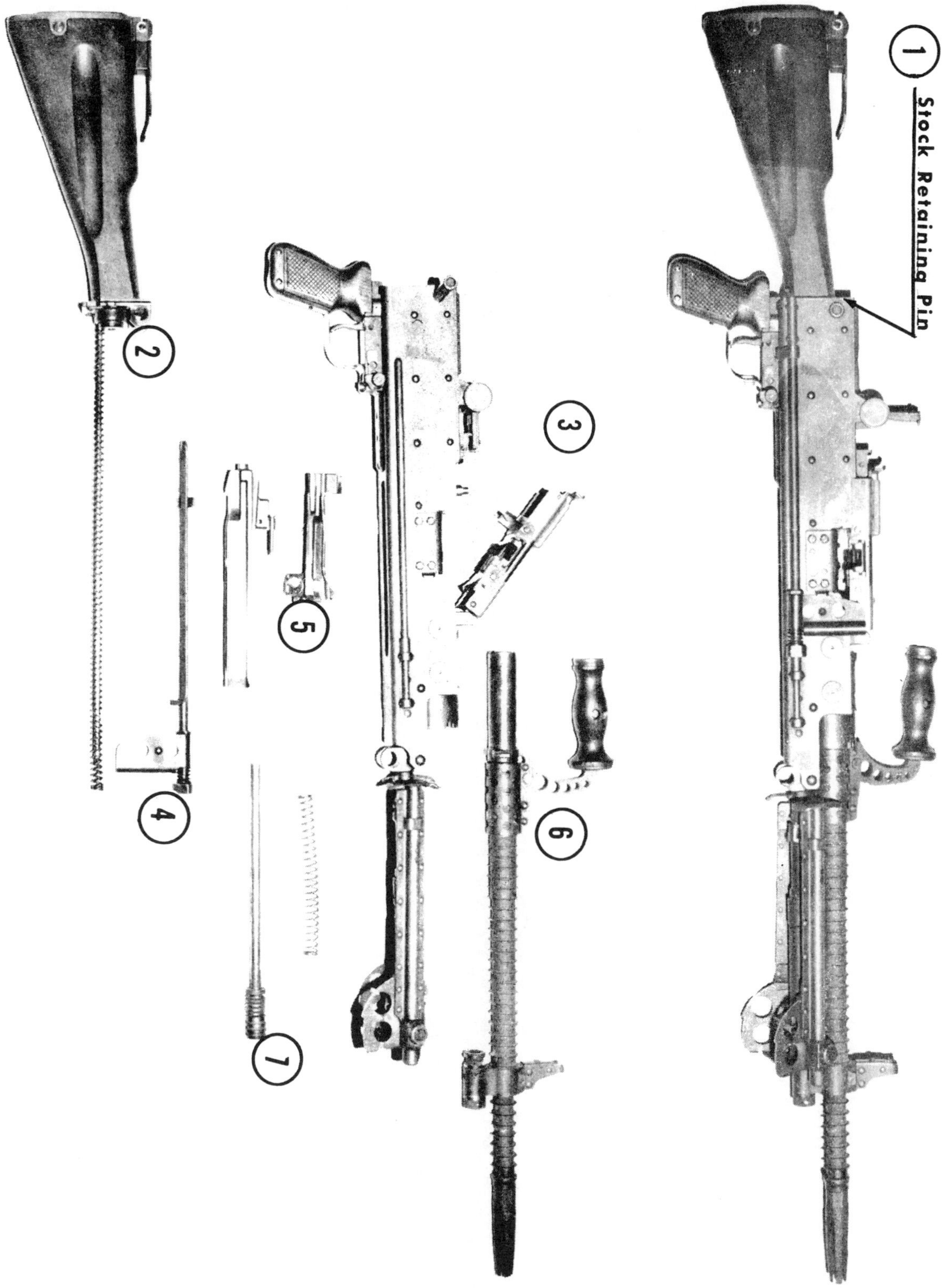
1
Stock Retaining Pin
2
3
4
5
6
7

7.62-mm M1962

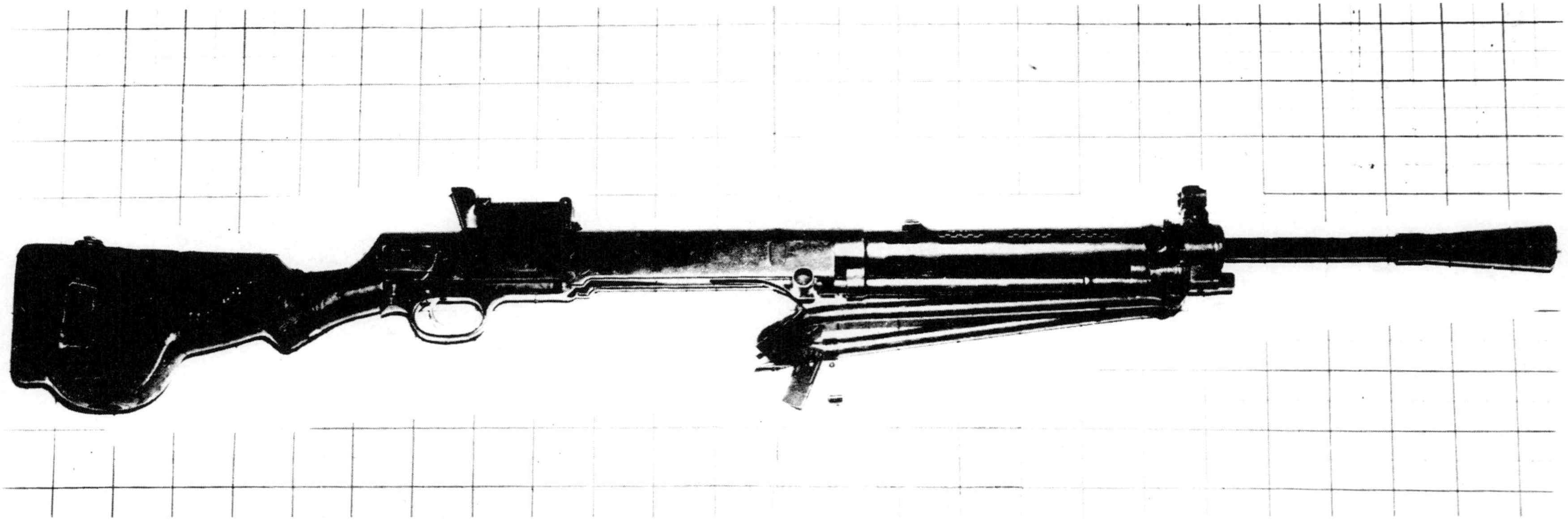

RUSSIA   7.62-MM, DP

MACHINEGUN   U.S.S.R.

7.62-mm DEGTYAREV (DP)

The 7.62-mm DP Machinegun is a gas-operated, pan fed light machinegun designed in 1926-27 by Vasiliy Alellyevich Degtyarev. This weapon became standard in the Russian Army in 1928 and saw extensive service in the Spanish Civil War. It was manufactured and used in large quantities in WWII by the Soviet Forces but has been replaced in recent years by the Russian RPD and RPK light machineguns. The Degtyarev locking system, incorporating pivoting wings on each side of the bolt, is utilized in all Soviet light machineguns. The weapon is fed from a 47-round capacity pan-type drum which is mounted on the top of the receiver. A tank version (DT) of this machinegun, mounting a 60-round capacity drum appeared in 1929. Both the ground machinegun and the tank machinegun were modified in 1944 by repositioning the recoil spring, originally positioned around the gas piston beneath the barrel, to project from the rear of the receiver in a recoil spring tube. These modified models are known respectively as the DPM (ground) and the DTM (tank) machinegun. Although the DP series is now obsolete in the Soviet Army it will be encountered in all the Satellite Armies and is used by many countries outside the Soviet Bloc.

FUNCTIONING

The DP light machinegun is an extremely simple gas-operated weapon. There are only five moving parts which accomplish chambering, locking, firing and unlocking. The 47-round pan magazine consists of a fixed exterior pan shaped housing and a rotating inner center piece which exerts spring loaded pressure against the ammunition. With a loaded magazine in place, the bolt handle is drawn to the rear and a notch on the bottom rear of the bolt engages the sear. The recoil spring positioned around the gas piston, or in the modified models positioned in a recoil spring housing projecting from the rear of the receiver, is compressed. The bolt which is carried on the top of the bolt carrier at the rear of the gas piston, has a pivoted wing mounted on each side of it. These locking wings are cammed in flush with the sides of the bolt by their attachment to the firing pin. When the trigger is pulled, the sear disengages from the bolt and the bolt moves forward stripping a round from the magazine. As the round is chambered, the firing pin which is firmly engaged by a slot at the upper rear of the bolt carrier is pulled forward, moving freely with respect to the bolt which has now stopped its forward travel. This final forward movement of the firing pin forces the locking wings on the bolt outward into recesses in the receiver. As the round is fired, gas is tapped from the barrel to impinge against a cup at the forward end of the gas piston. During the initial rearward movement, the firing pin moves rearward due to its attachment to the bolt carrier. In so doing, it allows the locking wings on the bolt to disengage from the receiver recesses. The assembly continues to the rear until the bolt is engaged by the sear. If the trigger is held to the rear the cycle is repeated.

CHARACTERISTIC DATA

```
Caliber ..................................................... 7.62-mm
Operation ....................................................... Gas
Type of Fire ........................................... Full-auto only
Rate of Fire ............................... 550 rpm (Practical-350)
Type of Feed ....................................... Pan - 47 rd cap
Weight, empty ............................................. 19.8 lbs
Overall length ................................................ 50 in
Effective range ......................................... 1760 meters
```

FIELD STRIP PROCEDURE

STEP   ACTION

1. Draw the Bolt Handle to the rear to lock the Bolt open.
2. Press the Barrel Locking Stud, located on the left side of the front of the Receiver, turn the Barrel up a quarter-turn, slide the Barrel forward and remove.
3. Press the Trigger and allow the Bolt to go forward. Unscrew the Receiver Locking Bolt at the right rear of the Receiver.
4. Pivot the Butt Stock Group down and remove from the Receiver.
5. Unlock and push down the Gas Piston Lock located at the rear of the Gas Piston.
6. Slide the Gas Piston and Bolt Carrier with attached Bolt out of the rear of the Receiver.
7. Lift the Bolt and attached Bolt Locks from the Bolt Carriers.
8. Disengage the Bolt Locks from the Bolt and remove the Firing Pin.

ASSEMBLY PROCEDURE

Assemble the weapon in reverse order. Slide the Firing Pin into the Bolt, place a Bolt Lock on each side of the Bolt and attach the assembly to the Bolt Carrier. Slide the Carrier and Gas Piston Assembly with attached Bolt into the Receiver. Engage the Gas Piston Lock. Engage the forward end of the Butt Stock Group and pivot upward. Screw the Receiver Locking Bolt into the Receiver. Pull the Bolt Handle to the rear to lock the Bolt open. Slide the Barrel into the Receiver and turn it down to locked position.

LOADING AND FIRING

To load: Draw the Bolt Handle to the rear to lock the Bolt open. Place the pan magazine on top of the Receiver with the feed opening of the pan forward and down. Engage the tongues on the forward edge of the pan with the mating stud on the Barrel Jacket and push down firmly so that the Magazine Latch at the front of the rear sight mount engages the rear of the pan.

To fire: This weapon fires from the open bolt. The Grip Safety at the rear of the Pistol Grip must be depressed. Pull the Trigger and the weapon will fire. It will continue to fire as long as the Trigger is held to the rear.

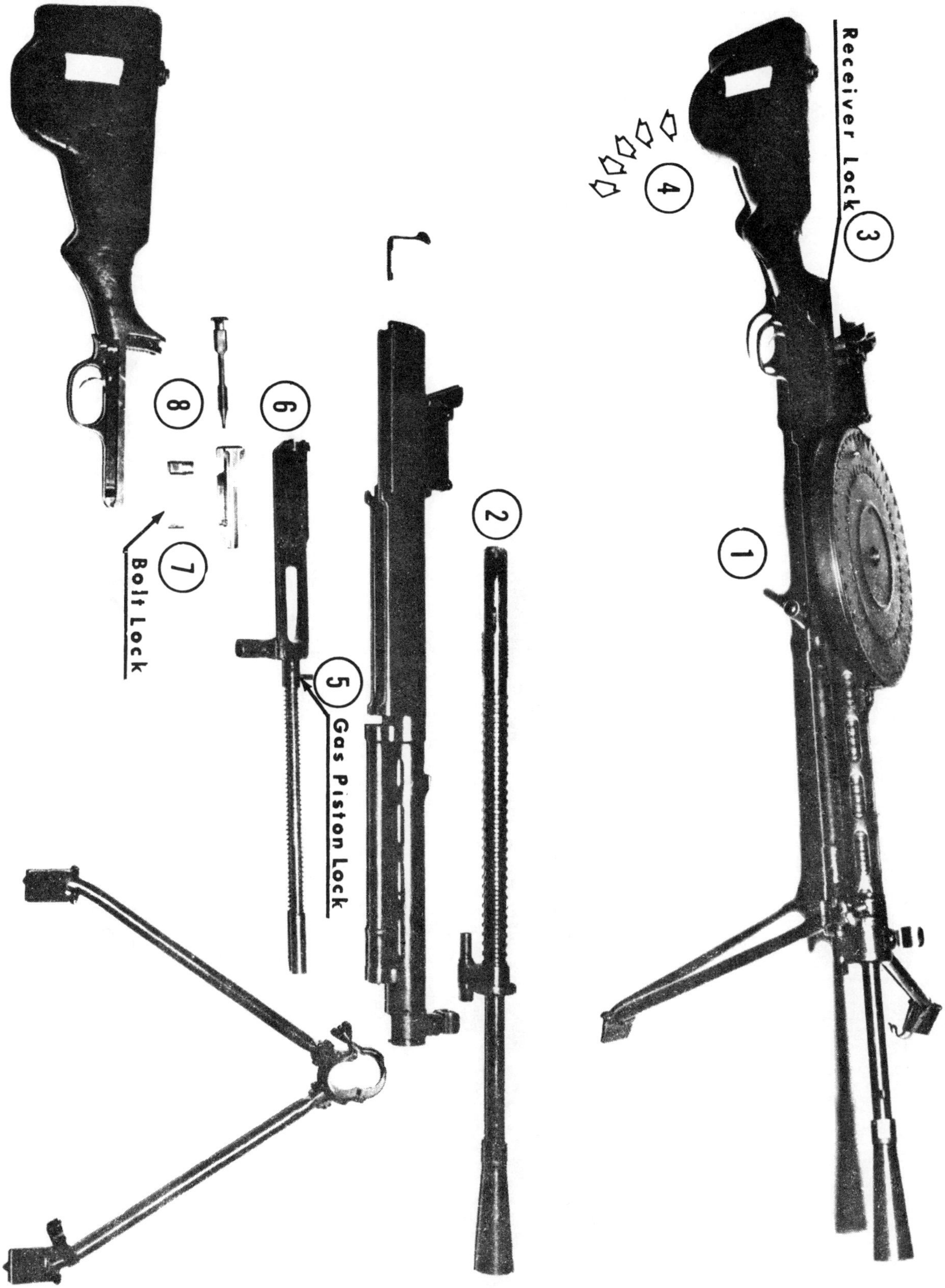
Receiver Lock
3
4
1
2
6
8
7
Bolt Lock
5
Gas Piston Lock

7.62-mm DP

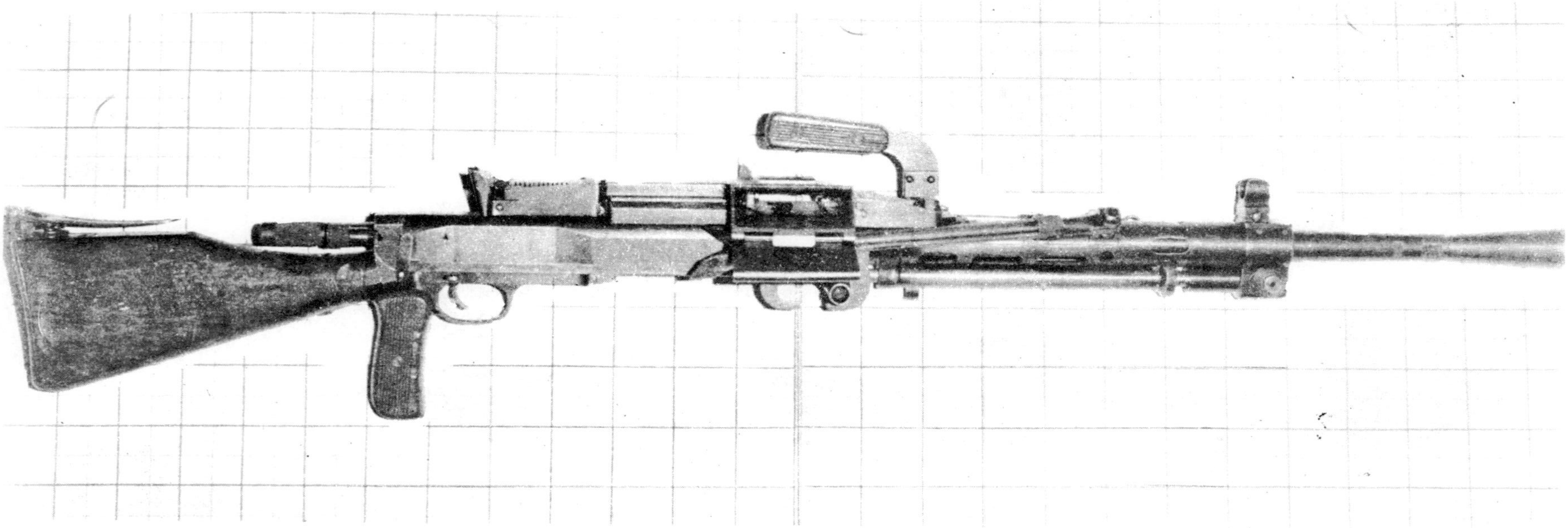

RUSSIA 7.62-MM, RP-46

MACHINEGUN   U.S.S.R.

7.62-mm RP-46 (M1946)

The Soviet 7.62-mm RP-46 Machinegun is designated the Company Light Machinegun M1946 and is the tactical equivalent to the U.S. M60 Machinegun. This weapon is a further modification of the DP series of light machineguns which included the DP (ground), DT (tank) and the DPM and DTM (modified ground and tank). The major modification of the RP-46 was the inclusion of a belt feed mechanism which gave the weapon a belt as well as a pan feed capability. This makes it an extremely versatile weapon, utilized as either a squad automatic weapon, or offensive light machinegun when pan fed or a offensive/defensive light machinegun employed at Company level when belt fed. The belt feed mechanism utilizes a vertically positioned arm which contacts the reciprocating bolt handle and transmits this horizontal movement into a lateral, side-to-side movement of the feed arm components. This weapon is produced by the Chinese Communist and is designated the Type 58.

FUNCTIONING

The RP-46 is a gas-operated, belt or pan fed light machinegun which fires full-automatic from an open bolt only. The bolt is locked by pivoting wings carried on each side of the bolt which are cammed into locking recesses in the sides of the receiver by the camming action of the firing pin. The bolt is carried on the upper rear portion of the slide, a stud on the slide to which the firing pin is attached projects up into the bolt from the bottom. With a round positioned in the feedway, the bolt handle is drawn to the rear. The trigger is pulled, the sear disengages from the sear bent on the bottom of the slide and the bolt, slide and piston move forward under impulse of the compressed recoil spring which is housed in a tube projecting from the rear of the receiver. The bolt strips a round from the belt, chambers it and comes to a stop against the rear face of the barrel. The slide and piston continue to move a short distance and the firing pin, carried by the slide, cams the locking wings on each side of the bolt out into the recesses in the receiver and continues forward to strike the primer. Gas is tapped from the barrel to impinge against the gas piston which is a forward extension of the slide. The slide is driven rearward, drawing the striker rearward to allow the locking sings to be cammed in flush with the sides of the bolt. The bolt being unlocked is also carried to the rear by the slide. This weapon fires full-automatic only and the firing cycle will be repeated until the trigger is released or the magazine is empty.

CHARACTERISTIC DATA

Caliber . . . . .7.62-mm (M1930 ctdge)
Operation . . . . .Gas
Type of Fire . . . . Full-auto only
Rate of Fire . . . . 650 rpm (Practical 350)
Type of Feed . . . . .Belt - 250 rd cap
. . . . Pan - 47 rd cap
Weight, empty . . . . 28.7 lbs
Overall length . . . . 49.7 in
Effective range . . . . 1,760 meters

FIELD STRIP PROCEDURE

STEP   ACTION

1. Push in on Tube Lock and turn clockwise.
2. Remove Tube Lock and Recoil Spring Housing Assembly with Recoil Spring from Receiver.
3. Unscrew Receiver Lock and remove.
4. Pivot Stock and Trigger Group Assembly down and remove from Receiver.
5. Disengage Gas Piston Lock by pushing to the rear and down.
6. Draw Feed Mechanism Latch to the rear, (see step 7) raise Feed Mechanism to disengage Feed Arm from Bolt Handle, draw Bolt Handle to the rear slightly, lower Feed Mechanism. Draw Bolt Handle fully to the rear and remove Bolt, Slide and Piston Assembly from the Receiver.
7. Draw Feed Mechanism Latch to the rear, raise Feed Mechanism up and draw to the rear to disengage from Receiver and remove.

LOADING AND FIRING

To load: Draw Bolt Handle to the rear. Pivot Safety Lever forward to "SAFE." Raise Cover, lay loaded belt into feedway, close and latch Cover. The weapon may also be loaded by leaving the Bolt forward, inserting the belt tab into the feedway with the Cover down, pulling the tab through until it stops. Drawing the Bolt to the rear will now operate the Belt Feed Mechanism and a round will be positioned in the feedway ready for chambering. The Safety Lever should be placed on "SAFE" at this point. To load the 47-round pan Magazine the Feed Mechanism must be removed and the pan is positioned in the same manner as it is in loading the DP or DPM machineguns.

To fire: Pivot the Safety Lever to the rear. Pull the Trigger. The weapon will fire. This piece fires full-automatic only and will continue to fire until the Trigger is released or the ammunition belt or pan is empty.

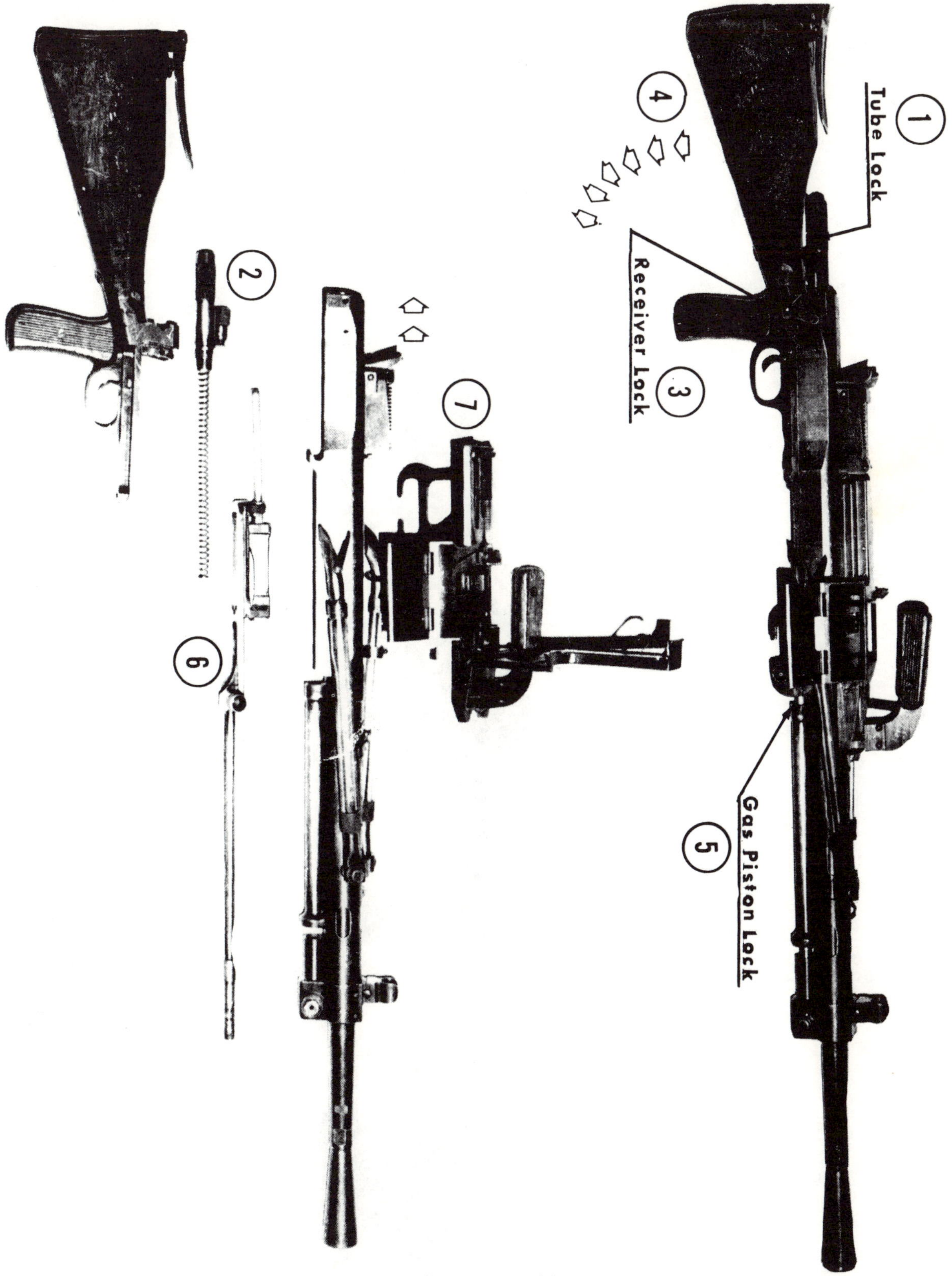
1
Tube Lock
2
3
Receiver Lock
4
5
Gas Piston Lock
6
7

7.62-mm RP-46

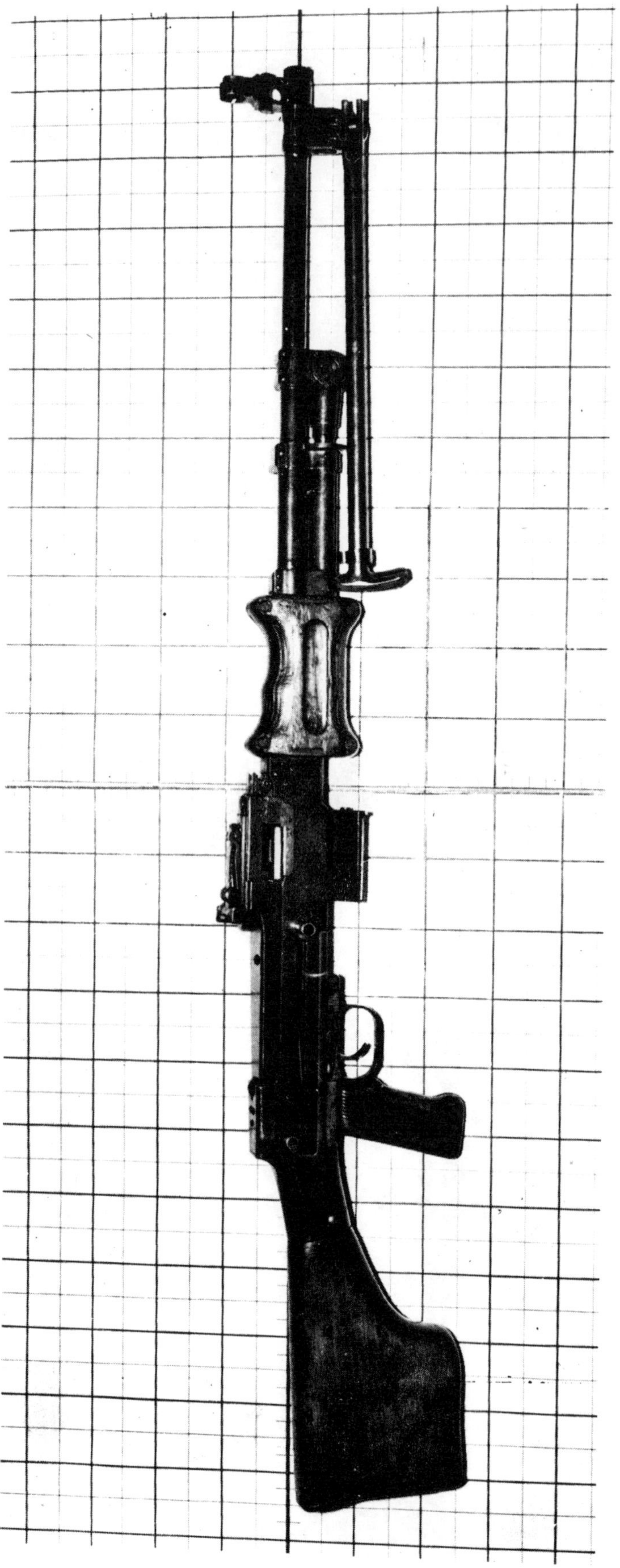

RUSSIA 7.62-MM M43, RPD

LIGHT MACHINEGUN U.S.S.R.

7.62-mm MACHINEGUN (RPD)

The 7.62-mm Ruchnoi Pulemet Degtyarev (RPD) was adopted in 1948 as the standard squad automatic weapon of the Soviet Army. It is chambered for the Model 43 intermediate-size cartridge as are the Assault Rifle (AK) and Carbine (SKS). The RPD is not employed for sustained fire missions. The barrel is chrome-plated and is not of the quick-change type. It is fed from a metallic belt which is contained in a drum attached to the underside of the receiver. The RPD is the lightest belt fed machinegun in use today. The amount of gas taken from the barrel to function the action can be varied by a 3-position gas regulator located at the front end of the gas cylinder in a manner similar to the British Bren gun. Since its adoption in 1948, the RPD has been modified three times. The first modification (1953) included: (1) relocation of the rear sight windage knob from the right side to the left, (2) addition of a rear sight guard, and (3) changing the design of the piston head from female to male with respect to the gas block. A second series of modifications occurring between 1955 and 1958 included: (1) addition of feed and ejection port covers, and (2) changing the bolt handle from a reciprocating, non-folding type to a nonreciprocating, folding type. A third modification enlarged the gas cylinder to cover the end of the piston when cocked and added a bearing to the right rear of the bolt. The RPD is being replaced by the RPK.

FUNCTIONING

This is a gas-operated, full-automatic light machinegun. It fires from an open bolt position. With the bolt to the rear, and the first round in the belt positioned against the cartridge stop in the feedway, the trigger is pulled. The sear is disengaged from the sear notch on the underside of the slide assembly. The gas piston, the slide assembly, and the attached bolt move forward under the impulse of the compressed recoil spring. A stud on the top rear of the slide engages the track of the belt feed lever located in the cover which moves the belt feed slide to index the first round in front of the moving bolt. The bolt strips the round from the belt and chambers it. Continued forward movement of the piston and slide assembly cams the locking wings mounted in each side of the bolt out to engage mating recesses in the receiver. The final forward movement of the slide assembly causes the firing pin to strike the cartridge primer. Gas enters the gas cylinder from the barrel, impinges against the gas piston and drives the piston to the rear. After a fractional movement of the piston and slide assembly, the slide camming against the inner surfaces of the locking wings carried in the bolt, unlock the bolt and carry it to the rear. The recoil spring is compressed by this action and the slide is engaged by the sear if the trigger has been released. If the trigger is still pressed the cycle is repeated.

CHARACTERISTIC DATA

Caliber .... 7.62-mm M-43 (short)
Operation .... Gas
Type of Fire .... Full-auto only
Rate of Fire .... 650 rpm (Practical-375)
Type of Feed .... Belt - 100 rd cap
Weight, empty .... 15.4 lbs
Overall length .... 40.8 in
Effective range .... 1,210 meters

FIELD STRIP PROCEDURE

STEP | ACTION

1. Turn the Butt Trap Cover at right angles to the stock.
2. Place a screwdriver in the top hole in the Butt. Engage the cross-slot in the Recoil Spring Plug and turn one-quarter turn. Remove the Recoil Spring Plug, Recoil Spring and Recoil Spring Guide from the rear of the Stock.
3. Push out the Butt Retaining Pin.
4. Pull the Butt and Trigger Group to the rear and disengage from the Receiver.
5. Raise the Cover Assembly by pushing forward on the Cover Latch.
6. Pull the Bolt Handle to the rear. The Piston and Slide Assembly and Bolt can now be removed from the rear of the Receiver. The Bolt and assembled Bolt Locks can then be lifted from the Slide.

ASSEMBLY PROCEDURE

Proceed in the reverse order. Assemble the Bolt and Bolt Locks to the Slide. Slide the Piston and Slide Assembly with the attached Bolt into the Receiver. Close the Cover. Slide the Butt and Trigger Group onto the bottom of the Receiver. Replace the Butt Retaining Pin. Place the assembled Recoil Spring and Guide and Recoil Spring Plug in the hole in the Butt. Engage the cross-slot in the Recoil Spring Plug with a screwdriver. Push in and turn one-quarter turn to lock in place. Turn the Butt Trap Cover to a vertical position.

LOADING AND FIRING

To load: This weapon is fed from a 100 round link belt which is carried in a drum attached to the bottom of the Receiver. When the drum is loaded the belt loading tab should be left protruding from the trap door of the drum. Assemble the drum to the Receiver and lock into place. Pull the Bolt Handle to the rear. Push the Safety Lever, located above the Trigger on the right side of the Trigger Group, forward to "SAFE." Push forward on the Cover Latch and raise the Cover. Lay the Belt on the feedway so that the first round is against the Cartridge Stop. Lay the Belt on the feedway so that the first round is against the Cartridge Stop. Close the Cover.

To fire: Push the Safety Lever to the rear. Pull the Trigger. The weapon will fire until the Trigger is released or the belt is empty.

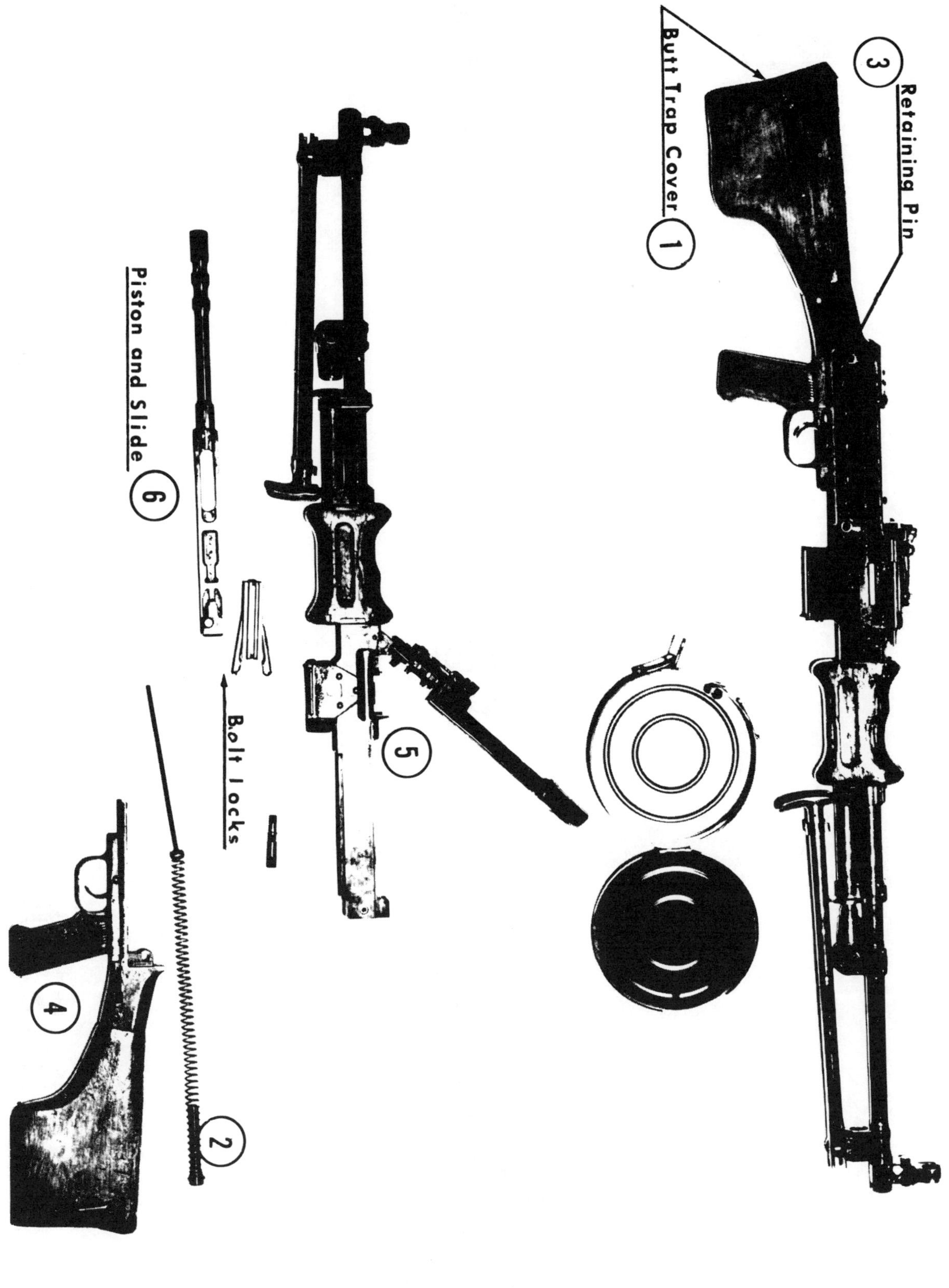

Butt Trap Cover
1
3
Retaining Pin
Piston and Slide
6
Bolt locks
5
4
2

7.62-mm RPD

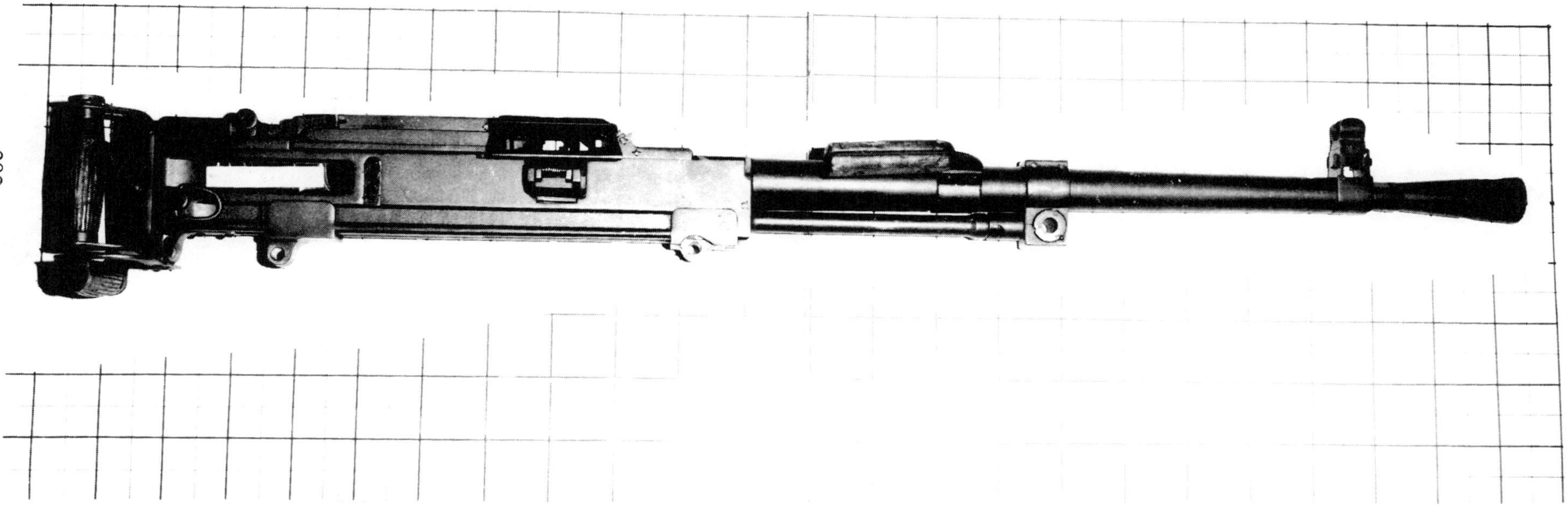

RUSSIA 7.62-MM, SG-43

MACHINEGUN   U.S.S.R.

7.62-mm SG-43 (GORYUNOV)

The Soviet 7.62-mm SG-43 Machinegun is a gas-operated, beltfed machinegun which fires full-automatic from an open bolt only. This is an extremely well made weapon which utilizes a quick-removable barrel and an unusual locking system in which the bolt is cammed to the side to lock. This weapon saw extensive service in WWII and the Korean Conflict. It is standard in many Soviet Satellite countries. The SG-43 replaced the Soviet M1910 Maxim (SPM) in the Soviet Army, and has, since the end of WWII been modified slightly. These modifications include a longitudinally fluted barrel, provision for headspace adjustment and a change in backplate design. Two new mounts also appeared with this modified weapon. The modified weapon is designated the SGM (Heavy Modernized Goryunov).

FUNCTIONING

This is an air-cooled, gas-operated weapon with a quick-change barrel. The bolt rides on a camming stud on the upper rear portion of the slide. With a loaded belt positioned in the feedway, the first round gripped by the spring-loaded claws of the feed carrier, the operating handle is drawn to the rear drawing the slide, piston and bolt to the rear where they are held by the sear, the belt feed slide moves from right to left drawing the next round into position. When the trigger is pulled the slide carrying the bolt moves forward, the bolt pushes the first round out of the feed carrier into the feed tray and into the chamber. The belt feed slide riding in transverse grooves in the top of the slide moves to the right to engage the next round in the belt. When the bolt comes to a stop against the rear face of the barrel, the slide continues for 3/8 inch during which time the camming stud on top of the slide forces the rear of the bolt to swing to the right where it engages a recess in the right receiver wall. The slide strikes the firing pin at this time forcing it against the primer. Gas is tapped from the barrel where it impinges against the face of the gas piston forcing it rearward. The gas piston, which is a forward extension of the slide, forces the slide rearward, the slide cams the bolt out of the locking recess in the receiver wall and carries it to the rear where the sear will engage and hold the action open if the trigger has been released. The belt feed slide, being operated by the moving slide, has moved to the left drawing the next round into the feedway. If the trigger has been pushed in the sear will not engage and the firing cycle will be repeated until the trigger is released or the belt is empty. The barrel can be changed without removing the ammunition belt from the feedway. The change can be accomplished in approximately 20 seconds in the following manner: raising both covers; draw bolt to the rear; push the barrel lock to the left; pull the barrel forward by the barrel handle; slide a new barrel into place; push the lock to the right, drop the two covers into place to latch, release the bolt to move forward to engage the first round; and draw the operating handle to the rear; pulling the trigger will fire the weapon.

Caliber	7.62-mm (M1930 ctdge)
Operation	Gas
Type of Fire	Full-auto only
Rate of Fire	700 rpm (Practical 300)
Type of Feed	250 rd metal belt (non-dis)
Weight, w/mount	62.6 lbs
Overall length, gun only	44.2 in
Effective range	2,300 meters

FIELD STRIP PROCEDURE

STEP   ACTION

1. Push in on Cover Latch and raise Cover and Feed Cover.
2. Remove Feed Carrier from Feed Cover.
3. Pull Back Plate Pin out of Receiver to the right. Hold Back Plate tightly and slide out of rear of Receiver with Recoil Spring.
4. Draw Operating Handle to the rear sharply to bring Bolt and Slide to the rear of the Receiver.
5. Draw Bolt, Slide and Gas Piston out the rear of the Receiver. Lift Bolt off of Slide.
6. Draw Belt Feed Slide out of Receiver to the right.
7. Push Barrel Lock, a rectangular plate located above the Belt Feed Slide opening, to the left as far as it will go, grasp the Barrel Handle and pull the Barrel forward out of the Receiver.
8. Remove the Operating Handle from the rear of the Receiver.

ASSEMBLY PROCEDURE

Assemble in the reverse order. Barrel may be assembled last. Position Operating Handle into the bottom of the Receiver. Slide Barrel into front of the Receiver. NOTE: In assembling Barrel make sure Gas Cylinder on Barrel aligns with the Gas Tube projecting from front of the Receiver. Slide Belt Feed Slide into Belt Feed Slide opening. Assemble Bolt to Slide and assemble Slide, Gas Piston and Bolt into Receiver. Push Operating Handle forward. Assemble Back Plate and Recoil Spring into Receiver and push Back Plate Pin through the Receiver from the right. Assemble Feed Carrier to Feed Cover. Close both the Covers firmly, make sure Cover Latch engages.

LOADING AND FIRING

To load: Raise the Cover and lay the loaded belt on the feedway. Place the rim of the first cartridge into the spring-loaded jaws of the Feed Carrier. Close the Cover. Draw the Operating Handle to the rear and push forward. The Bolt and Slide assembly will be held to the rear by the sear.

To fire: The Safety Lever automatically blocks the Trigger when the weapon is not being fired. Push the Safety Lever up with the left thumb and push in on the Trigger with the right thumb. The weapon will fire. This weapon fires full-automatic only and will continue to fire until the Trigger is released or the ammunition belt is empty.

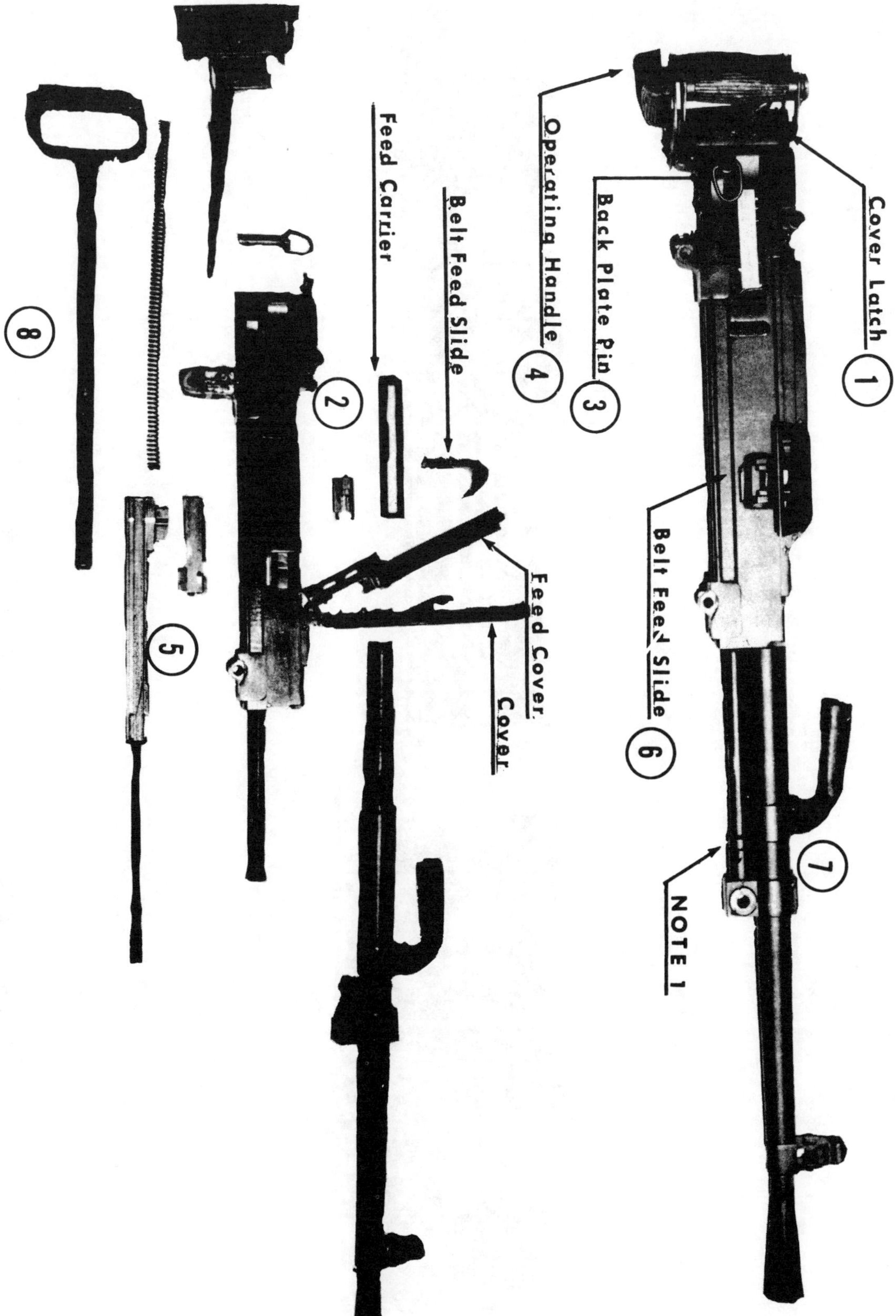

Cover Latch
Back Plate Pin
Operating Handle
Feed Carrier
Belt Feed Slide
Belt Feed Slide
Feed Cover
Cover
NOTE 1
1
2
3
4
5
6
7
8

7.62-mm SG-43

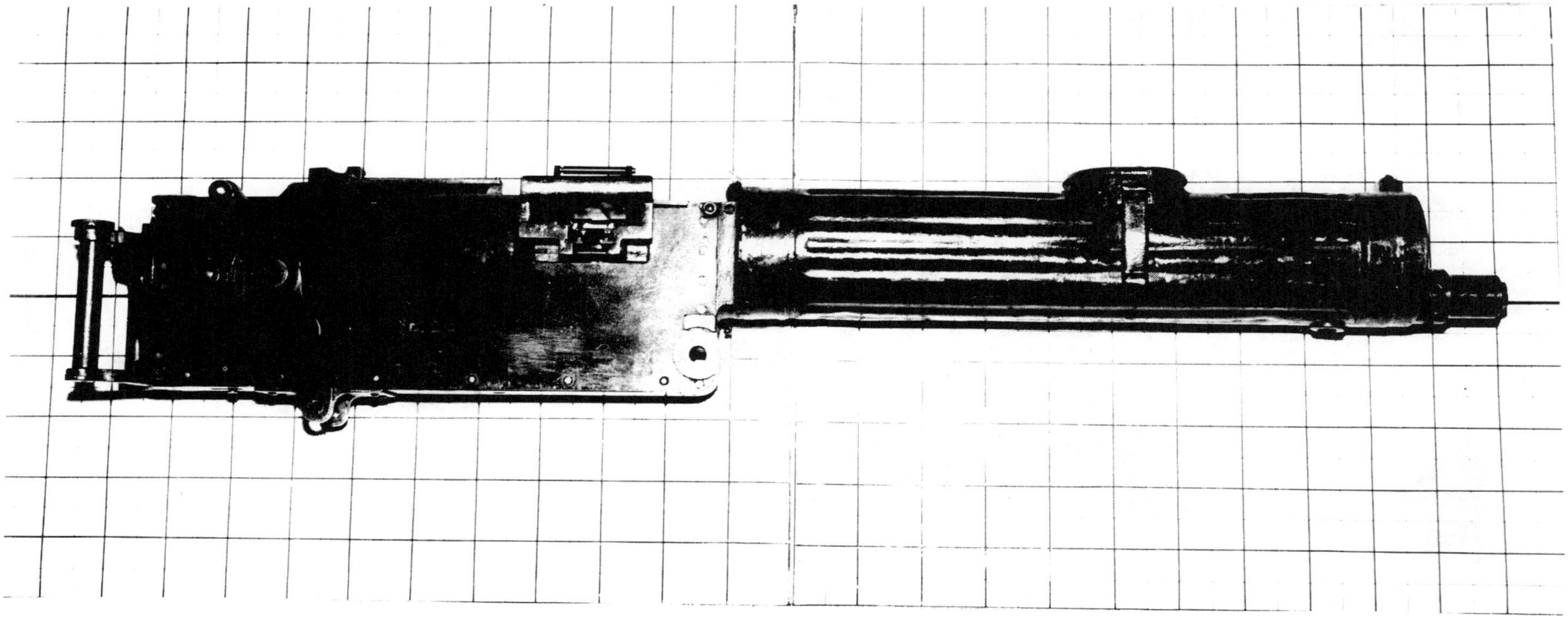

RUSSIA 7.62-MM, SPM

MACHINEGUN   U.S.S.R.

7.62-mm MACHINEGUN M1910 (PM)

The 7.62-mm Maxim M1910 Machinegun is a recoil operated, belt fed water cooled machinegun, employing the toggle joint locking principle invented by Hiram Maxim in 1884. The Maxim design was utilized in the German MG-08 and variations. The Vickers Sons & Maxim (PM) as used by the Soviet Army was first purchased from the Vickors & Maxim plant. Two Soviet designed mounts are available for this weapon, one a heavy two-wheeled mount (Sokolov), and the other a somewhat lighter two-wheeled, dual purpose mount which can be used for ground or AA fire. The Maxim principle is the first successful, mass-produced automatic loading system to see extensive use. The United States did not consider the Maxim machinegun an effective system until 1904. From July 1917 to September 1918, 12,125 Model 1915 Vickers were made by Colt in .30 caliber. More than 7,000 of these accompanied American troops overseas. The Soviet version of the M1910 may be encountered with or without the large cap on the top of the water jacket.

FUNCTIONING

This is a recoil operated machinegun utilizing the toggle joint locking principle in which a two-piece unit joined in the middle by a toggle joint offers resistance to movement of the bolt carried on the forward piece when the two pieces are in line. When the joint is "broken", the forward piece is able to move rearward against a continuously lessening resistance.

To load: The crank handle (operating handle) is pushed forward to draw the lock (bolt) to the rear. The belt is pulled through the feedway until it stops and the handle is released. The vertical reciprocating cartridge carrier on the forward face of the lock will move up to engage the rim of the first cartridge in the belt. Operating the handle again pulls the round from the belt, the cartridge carrier moves down as the lock moves rearward. As the handle is released and the lock moves forward the carrier chambers the round and moves up to grip the next round. The toggle joint which is connected to the crank handle by a pivot point is now down slightly below a straight line and the lock is held firmly against the breech. When the trigger is pulled the sear is released by the trigger bar. The lock carried on the barrel extension which is attached to the barrel remains flush against the breech in a locked position and the assembly moves to the rear under the force of recoil. The curved rear surface of the external crank handle is forced against a camming surface mounted on the outside of the right side plate and in so doing is forced upward. Being connected to the toggle joint the movement of the crank handle breaks the straight line configuration of the front and rear pieces upon which the lock is mounted, the barrel extension reaches its rearmost point of travel and stops and the lock continues rearward. The carrier extracts the fired case and a new round from the belt during this movement. The recoil spring connected by a link to the opposite end of the crank pivot point is expanded and in contracting forces the parts forward into firing position. If the trigger is held the weapon will continue to fire.

CHARACTERISTIC DATA

Caliber 7.62-mm M1908
Operation . . . . .Recoil
Type of Fire . . . . Full-auto only
Rate of Fire . . . . 550 to 600 rpm (Practical-450)
Type of feed . . . . .Belt - 250 rd cap
Weight w/mount . . . . 159.7 lbs
Overall length, gun only . . . . 43.6 in
Effective range . . . . 2,150 meters

FIELD STRIP PROCEDURE

STEP ACTION

1. Press in on the Cover Latch and raise the Cover.
2. Lift the Feed Block off of the Receiver.
3. Push the Crank Handle forward and hold in this position.
4. Grasp the Lock, raise it straight up, twist ¼ turn and disengage it from the stem on the connecting rod.
5. Push the Recoil Spring Housing forward and remove it. Disconnect the Recoil Spring from the Crank link.
6. Push the Backplate Retaining Pin through the Receiver and slide the Backplate up off the Receiver.
7. Remove the Left Sideplate.
7a. Remove the Right Sideplate.
8. Slide the Barrel Extension and Barrel out of the Receiver. Disassemble the Barrel from the Barrel Extension.

ASSEMBLY PROCEDURE

Proceed in the reverse order. Attach the Barrel to the Barrel Extension and slide into the Receiver. Assemble the Left and Right Sideplates to the Receiver. Slide the Backplate down on the rear of the Receiver. Hook the Recoil Spring to the Crank link and attach the Recoil Spring Housing to the Receiver. Lift the Lock connecting stem up and assemble the Lock to it. Drop the lock back down onto the guide rails of the Barrel Extension and operate the Crank Handle to properly position the Lock. Place the Feed Block into position insuring the Feed Lever arm engages the cut-out in the left Barrel Extension side plate. Close the cover and operate the Crank Handle to assure the parts are assembled properly.

LOADING AND FIRING

To load: See explanation of loading in operating instructions.
To fire: Push the Safety Lever located beneath the butterfly trigger to one side with the thumb, and push the trigger in with the other thumb. The weapon will fire and continue to fire until the trigger is released, or the belt is empty. When the trigger is released, the safety blocks the Trigger and must be released to fire again.

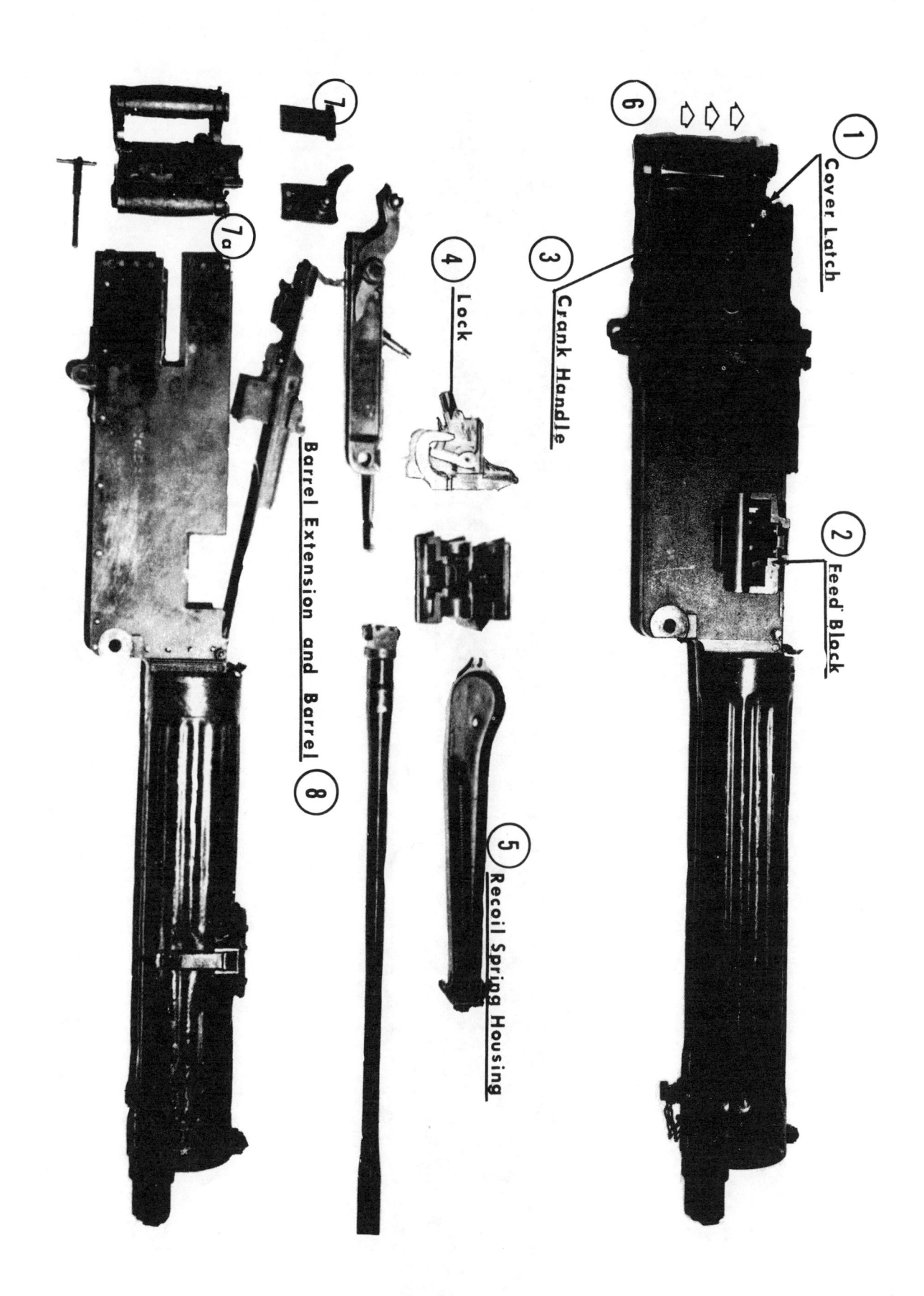

1. Cover Latch
2. Feed Block
3. Crank Handle
4. Lock
5. Recoil Spring Housing
7a. Barrel Extension and Barrel
8.

7.62-mm SPM

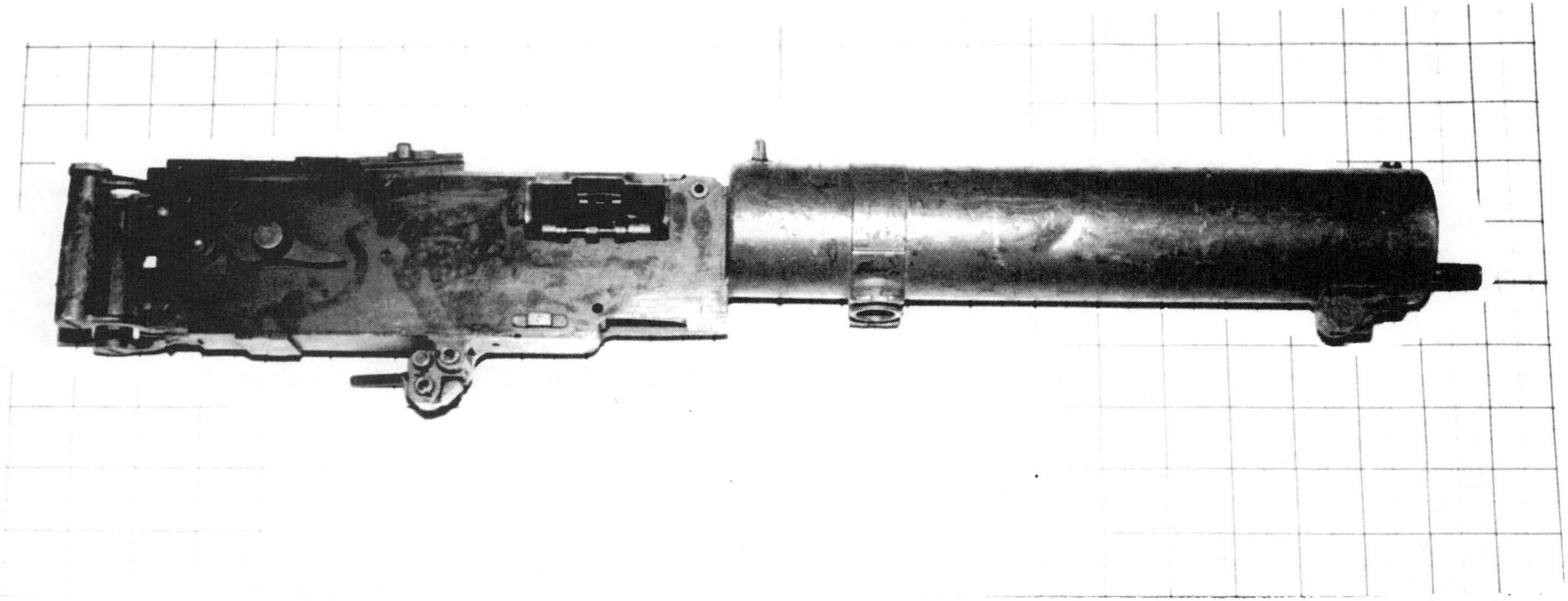

COMMUNIST CHINA 7.92-MM, TYPE 24

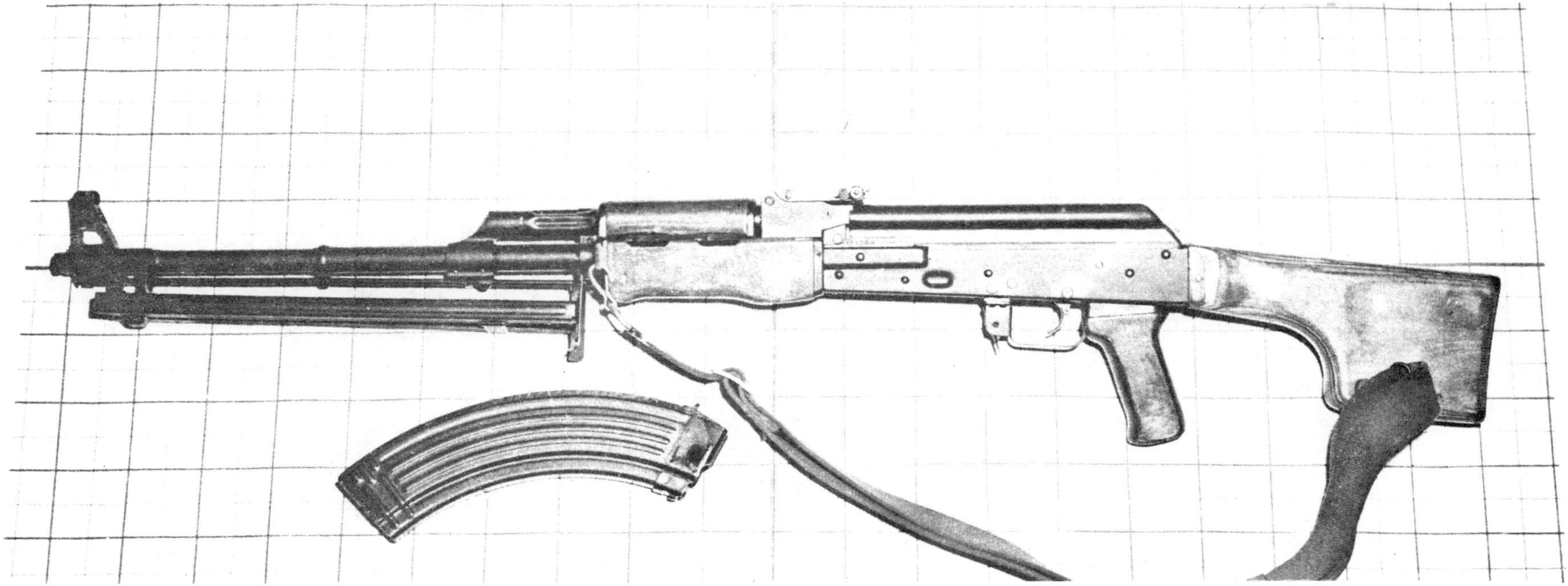

RUSSIA 7.62-MM M43, RPK

LIGHT MACHINEGUN   U.S.S.R.

7.62-mm MACHINEGUN (RPK)

The Soviet 7.62-mm Ruchnoi Pulemet Kalashnikov (RPK) is the standard Soviet Squad Light Machinegun. It has replaced the RPD Light Machinegun. The RPK is identical to the AKM Assault Rifle as far as operation and major component parts are concerned. It is essentially an AK with a longer barrel, modified stock and an attached bipod. It is an extremely well made weapon. Feeding is from a curved 40 round capacity box magazine or a 75 round capacity drum magazine. The barrel is chrome-plated as are those of the standard AK series of weapons. It is chambered for the Soviet M1943 intermediate cartridge as are the other two standard Soviet Squad weapons, the SKS Carbine and the AK Assault Rifle. The Soviet Infantry Squad, due to the elimination of the RPD, now has only one automatic weapon system to learn and maintain, the AKM and the RPK.

FUNCTIONING

The AK Assault Rifle is a magazine fed weapon, which fires from a closed bolt position utilizing a rotating bolt locking system. The safety/select lever is located on the right side of the Receiver above the trigger guard. With this lever in its uppermost position the weapon is on "SAFE;" with the lever halfway down the weapon is set for full-automatic fire; with the lever fully down the weapon set for semi-automatic fire. With a loaded magazine in place, the bolt handle is drawn to the rear drawing the bolt carrier and piston with the attached bolt to the rear, overriding and cocking the hammer and compressing the recoil spring. When the bolt handle is released the bolt carrier and bolt move forward, the face of the bolt strips a round from the magazine and chambers it. The face of the bolt strikes the rear face of the barrel and its forward movement is stopped, the bolt carrier continues forward and cam surfaces in the bolt carrier acting on lugs on the bolt, rotate the bolt to the right, locking lugs on the head of the bolt engage locking recesses in the receiver and the hammer is ready to be released. If the select lever is set for semi-automatic fire when the trigger is pulled, the semi-automatic sear and disconnector pivot, the hammer is released striking the firing pin which in turn strikes the primer. Gas is tapped from the barrel into the gas cylinder to impinge against the piston. The piston and bolt carrier move to the rear, the cams in the carrier rotate the bolt to unlocked position and the carrier and bolt continue to the rear pivoting the hammer rearward where it is engaged by the disconnector and held to the rear. The trigger must be pulled for each shot. If set for full-automatic, a full-automatic disconnector on the bolt carrier strikes the full-automatic sear, rotating it to release the hammer and the hammer pivots forward to strike the firing pin. The firing cycle is no bolt hold-open device on this weapon, when the magazine is empty the bolt will be in the closed position.

CHARACTERISTIC DATA

Caliber . . . . .7.62-mm (M43 ctdge)
Operation . . . . .Gas
Type of Fire . . . . Full and semi-auto
Rate of Fire . . . . 600 rpm (Practical 325)
Type of Feed . . . . .Box - 40 rd cap
. . . . Drum - 70 rd cap
Weight, empty . . . . 14.2 lbs
Overall length . . . . 40.9 in
Effective range . . . . 1210 meters

FIELD STRIP PROCEDURE

STEP   ACTION

1. Push in on the Recoil Spring Guide which protrudes from the rear of the Receiver.
1a. At the same time the Recoil Spring Guide is pushed in raise up on the Receiver Cover and remove it from the Receiver. Push the Recoil Spring Guide in as far as it will go and lift it up and out of the Receiver with the Recoil Spring.
2. Push the Recoil Spring Guide in as far as it will go and lift it up and out of the receiver with the Recoil Spring.
3. Slide the Bolt Carrier, Bolt and Piston rearward until they can be lifted up and out of the Receiver.
4. Turn the Bolt head until the lugs on the Bolt aline with the cam grooves in the Carrier, slide the Bolt rearward until it disengages and then slide it forward and out of the Bolt Carrier.
5. Pivot the Handguard Lock up.
6. Disengage the Handguard from the Receiver and lift it up and off of the Barrel.

ASSEMBLY PROCEDURE

Assemble in the reverse order. Slide Handguard into position and pivot the Handguard Lock down to engage. Assemble the Bolt to the Bolt Carrier and slide the assembled Bolt and Carrier into the Receiver. Slide the Recoil Spring and Recoil Spring Guide into the rear of the Bolt Carrier, push forward until the rear of the Guide clears the rear of the Receiver, and push down to engage the rear of the Receiver. Slide the Receiver Cover into place, push in on the Recoil Spring Guide and push the Receiver Cover down to lock.

LOADING AND FIRING

To load: Insert a loaded Magazine. Push Safety Lever on right side of Receiver up to "SAFE." Draw the Bolt Handle to the rear and release it. The Bolt will move forward and chamber a round.

To fire: Push Safety Lever to type of fire desired. Pull the Trigger. The weapon will fire. If the Select Lever is set all the way down the weapon will fire semi-automatic and the Trigger must be pulled for each shot. If the Select Lever is set in the mid-position the weapon will fire full-automatic fire and will continue to fire until the Trigger is released or the Magazine is empty.

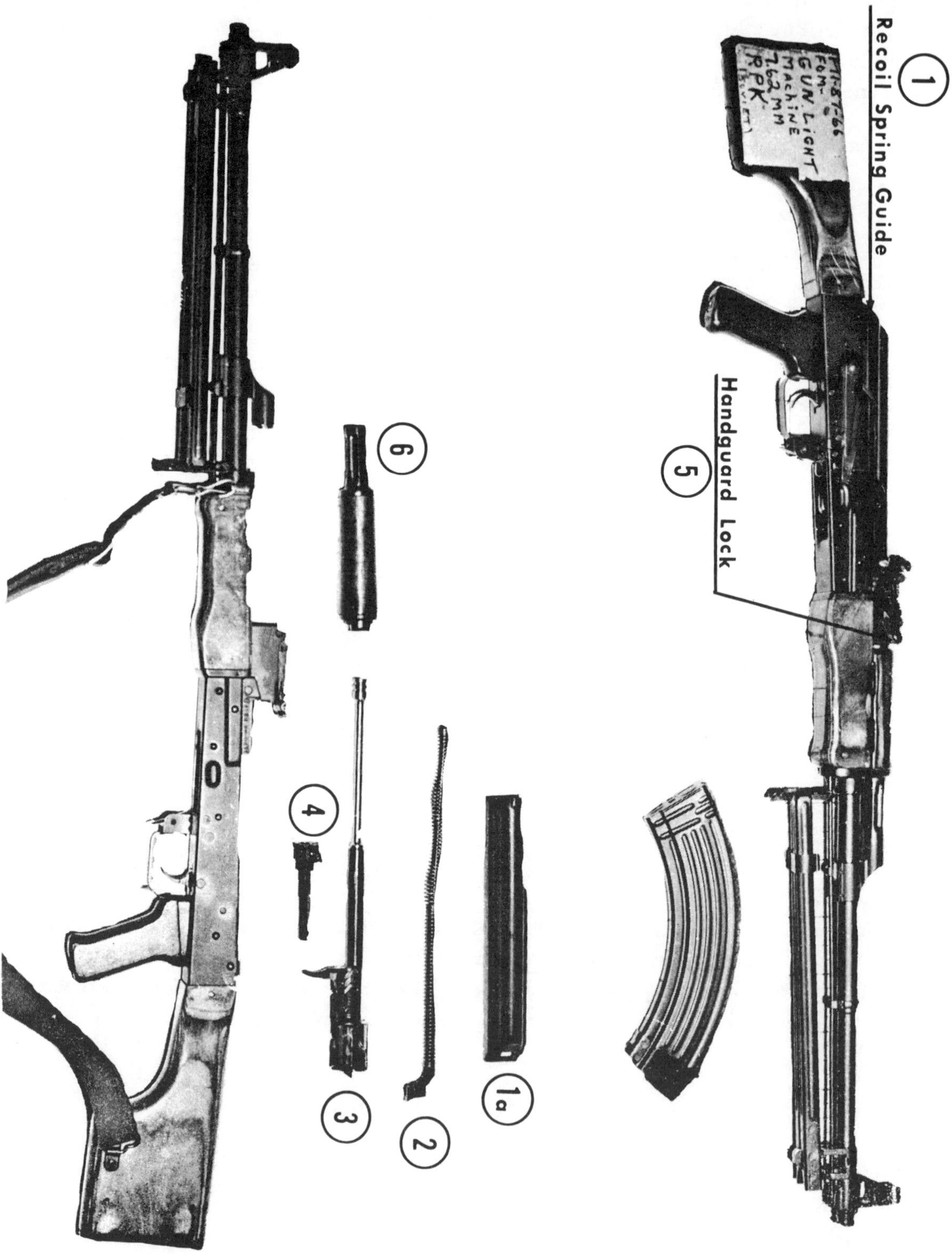
1 Recoil Spring Guide
5 Handguard Lock
6
4
1a
3
2

7.62-mm RPK

SECTION V

GLOSSARY OF SMALL ARMS TERMS

ACCELERATOR.

A component which operates during the rearward movement of the recoiling parts to increase the speed at which certain parts move. In general, the rate of movement of the bolt or breechblock is increased, which increases the rate of fire of the weapon.

ACTION.

The assemble of moving parts in a weapon which (1) feed the cartridge into the chamber (in a revolver, move a loaded chamber into position for firing), (2) seal or lock the chamber, (3) fire the cartridge, (4) unseal or unlock the chamber and extract the fired cartridge case, and (5) eject the empty case.

1. Single Action: A weapon in which the hammer must be cocked before pressure on the trigger will fire the gun.

2. Double Action: In a revolver, a mechanism in which a continuous pull on the trigger will revolve the cylinder to place a loaded cartridge in position, draw the hammer to the rear and release the hammer to fire the gun. In autoloading pistols, a mechanism in which a continuous pull on the trigger will draw the hammer to cock position and release it to fire the round in the chamber. In some cases, the firing pin assembly is drawn to the rear and released to fire the round in the chamber.

3. Bolt Action: A weapon (usually a rifle or shotgun) in which the opening and closing of the breech is accomplished by manually moving the bolt backward and forward in the receiver. This reciprocating action extracts and ejects during rearward movement and loads and locks during the forward movement. In most cases a handle for manually operating the bolt is permanently affixed to the bolt.

ACTUATOR.

A component operated either manually or mechanically which transmits certain action or energy to other components. These components are dependent upon movement of the actuator in order to function.

ASSEMBLY.

A grouping or collection of parts which form a single unit. The unit usually cannot accomplish its designed function unless all the parts are in the assembly; i.e., bolt assembly, backplate assembly, cover assembly, magazine assembly.

AUTOLOADING.

A weapon in which the first round is manually loaded into the chamber and after the first shot is fired, will extract the empty cartridge case, eject it from the mechanism, load the next cartridge into the chamber and leave the hammer or firing pin cocked for firing the next round. The trigger must be released after each shot is fired and pressure must be reapplied to fire the next round.

AUTOMATIC.

A weapon in which the first round is positioned for loading into the chamber, manipulation of certain components then chambers the round. After the first round is fired, the empty case is ejected and a new round is chambered and fired. This action continues until pressure of the trigger is released or the ammunition supply is exhausted. The extraction, ejection, loading and firing operations are performed by utilizing the forces of gas pressure or recoil, coupled with mechanical spring action.

BACKPLATE.

An assembly of parts which make up the rearmost portion of the receiver and is removable from the receiver as a complete assembly. Often contains buffer systems, trigger components and safety mechanisms when part of a machinegun. Not to be confused with Receiver Cap.

BALLISTICS.

The science which deals in the study of the motion and impact of projectiles.

1. Interior Ballistics: The study of the motion of a projectile in a gun barrel or tube. Concerned not only with the projectile itself but with cartridge primer; ignition and burning of the propellant; internal pressures and strains, stresses and torques to which the barrel or tube is subject as the projectile moves toward the muzzle.

2. Exterior Ballistics: The study of the motion of a projectile in flight from the time it leaves the muzzle until impact.

BARREL.

That portion of a weapon through which a projectile is propelled by action of the gases generated by the burning propellant charge.

BARREL EXTENSION.

A component to the rear of the barrel which carries or contains the bolt, breechblock or similar components. In some cases an integral part of the barrel forging, in other cases the barrel may be screwed, sweated, pinned or swedged into the forward end of the extension.

BARREL JACKET.

A metal sleeve or tube surrounding the barrel. In the case of weapons where the barrel is cooled by air, this jacket is perforated to allow air to circulate around the barrel. In cases where the barrel is cooled by water, this jacket is considerably larger in diameter than the exterior diameter of the barrel and is filled with water to accomplish barrel cooling. The front end of the barrel jacket generally supports the muzzle end of the barrel to give added strength and rigidity to the barrel.

BIPOD.

A device used to support a weapon during firing which consists of two separate "legs". Mounted near the muzzle end of the weapon the bipod assembly is usually designed to be folded up against the lower-most side of the barrel or barrel jacket when not in use.

BOLT.

A major component of a firearm whose main function is to support the base of the cartridge and seal the chamber when the cartridge is fired. The bolt contains certain subassemblies such as firing pin and extractor, and may contain other small components such as sear, locking lugs (usually a portion of the bolt) and various springs, pins and small parts. The bolt generally moves forward and backward in the receiver in a motion longitudinal to the axis of the bore. During the forward movement of the bolt the cartridge is chambered and the chamber is sealed by the face of the bolt. During the rearward movement of the bolt, the cartridge (or empty case) is withdrawn from the chamber and ejected from the receiver. The bolt may also be referred to as the breechblock, firing mechanism assembly or lock (Maxim system).

BOLT CARRIER.

A component of the firing mechanism which carries the bolt and which usually contains grooves, cams, lugs etc., which assist in locking the bolt in the forward position during firing. Manual unlocking of the bolt is often accomplished by moving the bolt carrier through an attached handle.

BOLT HANDLE.

A handle (Projection) attached to the bolt which can be grasped in order to manually open or close the action.

BREECH.

The outside rear face of the barrel which meets the face of the bolt or breechblock.

BREECHBLOCK.

A major component of a firearm which supports the base of the cartridge and seals the breech. The use of this term is generally reserved for breech closures which move up and down or to the side rather than in a reciprocating plane. The inside rear portion of the slide in a pistol is often referred to as the breechblock.

BUFFER.

A part intended to absorb the shock of moving parts or check the motion of major components during recoil and/or counter-recoil.

BULLET.

A projectile fired from a gun. Ballistically a bullet is a projectile only after it has left the gun muzzle.

BUSHING.

A detachable metal lining, commonly used around another part to provide a better fit than can be accomplished by direct machining. May also be used to compensate for wear.

BUTT.

In a shoulder arm, the rearmost face of the stock. In a handgun, the bottom of the grip.

BUTT PLATE.

A protective plate attached to the butt. Often designed with an opening to accommodate a cleaning material kit.

CALIBER.

The distance across the bore of a weapon, measured from land-to-land. Also used to express comparative dimensions in ballistics; i.e., a bullet with a length of "three calibers" has a length that is three times its diameter. In connection with weapons other than small arms it may also be used to denote barrel (tube) length; i.e., a 3" - 50 caliber gun has a barrel that has a bore diameter of 3 inches and is 50 times this dimension long, or 150 inches long. (Expressed as 3"50, 75-mm/150, 75-mm/50, or 75/50.)

CANNELURE.

An indented ring or groove around a bullet into which the cartridge case is roll-crimped to keep the bullet firmly attached to the case.

CARRYING HANDLE.

A handle attached to a weapon, usually a rifle or light machinegun, by which the weapon can be easily carried. Normally attached to the weapon at the center of balance. In most cases this handle can be swung or folded out of the way during firing. Often used to perform some function during disassembly such as unlocking certain components.

CARTRIDGE.

In small arms terminology, a cartridge is a complete round of fixed ammunition which is composed of a cartridge case, primer, propellant and bullet.

1. *Ball Cartridge:* Any cartridge loaded with a single projectile.

2. *Blank Cartridge:* Any cartridge which contains no projectile.

3. *Guard Cartridge:* Any cartridge loaded with buckshot or with a standard ball projectile and carrying a reduced powder charge.

4. *Multi-plex Cartridge:* Any cartridge containing two projectiles, one positioned behind the other.

5. *Rim-fire Cartridge:* A cartridge in which the primer mixture is loaded inside the rim of the head of the case. The firing pin can strike this rim at any point in its circumference to ignite the propelling charge in the case.

6. *Center-fire Cartridge:* A cartridge in which a primer, contained in a cup, is positioned in the center of the head of the case.

7. *Rimmed Cartridge:* A cartridge which has a head larger in diameter than the body, forming a rim or flange.

8. *Semi-rimmed Cartridge:* A cartridge which has a head only slightly larger in diameter than the body, with a shallow groove machined around the circumference of the body forward of the head to provide an extractor gripping surface.

9. *Rimless Cartridge:* A cartridge which has a head the same diameter as the body, with a groove machined around the circumference of the body forward of the head to provide and extractor gripping surface.

10. *Belted Cartridge:* A cartridge of the rimless type which has a thick band, or "belt" around the body just forward of the extractor groove to provide greater strength in that portion of the case.

11. *Shot Cartridge:* A cartridge loaded with small shot, usually used for killing small game.

12. Signal Cartridge: A cartridge containing pryotechnic projectiles, either in single color or a combination of colors, used for signalling.

CARTRIDGE CLIP.

A device designed to hold cartridges, which when properly positioned in a weapon allow the cartridges to be fed into the chamber for firing.

1. Bloc Clip: A clip formed of metal in the shape of a square-based "U", designed to be top-loaded into the magazine well of a weapon. The clip holds a number of rounds of ammunition, held firmly by ribbing, guides, or spring tension of the sides of the clip. The cartridges are fed into the chamber from the clip by action of the bolt and the clip is ejected from the weapon when the last round is fired.

2. Charger Clip: A clip formed of metal so designed as to grip the rims of a number of cartridges (usually five). The cartridges are contained in the clip, one above the other, and are held in place by a leaf spring exerting pressure against the heads of the cartridges. A loaded clip is placed in charger guides at the top of the magazine well, and the cartridges are pushed down into the well. The empty clip is then removed from the charger guides, in some cases manually, in other cases by the forward movement of the bolt.

3. Strip Clip: A clip formed of metal or plastic, onto which cartridges are placed and held in position by flexible prongs, formed from the body of the clip, which grip the body of the case. The cartridges lay side-by-side in a horizontal plane, the length of the clip. The clip may be of such a length as to hold 30 or more cartridges. The end of the clip (with bullets pointing forward) is inserted into the feedway of the weapon until the first round is engaged by components of the feeding mechanism. During firing the clip is continuously fed into the weapon by action of feeding components to position each succeeding round for chambering. The empty clip is ejected from the opposite side of the weapon from which it entered. Clips may be hooked together during firing to provide a continuous supply of ammunition.

CASE.

The main body of the cartridge. That part of the cartridge in which the other components are held. Often referred to as the "shell."

1. Bottleneck Case: A case in which the mouth of the case is smaller in diameter than the body, e.g., the body of the case is larger in diameter than the bore of the barrel. Shaped like a bottle.

2. Straight Case: A case which is the same diameter its entire length.

3. Tapered Case: A Case which is tapered slightly from the base to the mouth.

CHAMBER.

An unrifled portion of the bore at the rear of the barrel, which receives and supports the cartridge when the breech is closed. The chamber alines the bullet with the bore and the primer with the firing pin.

CHANGE LEVER.

A component on the exterior surface of the weapon which is connected to components within the weapon. When activated it changes the type of fire from automatic fire to semi-automatic fire and vice versa. Referred to as the Select Lever. May operate as a pivoting lever, a sliding button or a "push through" button (Moving transversely from left to right and right to left).

CHARGER GUIDES.

Slots machined into the receiver opposite the magazine well to rceive the cartridge clip (charger clip). The cartridge clip is held firmly by the guides while the cartridges are stripped manually into the magazine well. Commonly referred to as Clip Guides.

CHARGING.

The action of operating the bolt to ready the weapon for firing.

COCK.

The action of positioning the hammer, or firing pin, so that the spring which imparts motion to these parts is compressed. The hammer or firing pin is held in this position by engagement of a component, usually a sear, which is acted upon by the trigger. When the trigger is moved to release the sear the hammer or firing pin, under impulse of the compressed spring, moves to strike the primer in the cartridge.

LCOCKING HANDLE.

A component protruding from the side of the receiver or barrel jacket which engages certain recoiling components inside the receiver. When drawn to the rear, these recoiling components are also drawn rearward. This action "cocks" the weapon in preparation for firing. (In most belt-fed machineguns this rearward movement of the cocking handle must be accomplished more than once in order to position the first cartridge for chambering.) Most Cocking Handles are automatically disengaged from the recoiling components while the weapon is firing. Not to be confused with Bolt Handle which is a handle directly attached to the bolt.

COCKING PIECE.

A component of the firing mechanism attached to the rear of the striker or firing pin which allows this piece to be drawn to the rear manually to cock the firing mechanism.

COMPENSATOR.

A device attached to the muzzle of a weapon, which due to its design allows the gases following the bullet out of the muzzle to be deflected upward through slots in the top surface of the compensator. The lower portion of the compensator is solid, so that while some gas escapes through the top, gas is also pressing against the bottom. This pressure against the bottom of the compensator, literally pushing the compensator down, pushes the muzzle down. This action tends to retard the muzzle climb which is an instability factor in a full-automatic firing weapon.

COOLING FLANGES.

Rings, ribs, ridges, or flanges, machined into the exterior surface of the barrel circumference. This exposes more of the barrel metal to the air and in effect causes the barrel to cool more rapidly than if the surface were smooth.

CRANK.

A curved arm attached to an axle which is in turn attached to a recoiling component inside the receiver. Actuating the crank manually draws the recoiling parts to the rear (cocking). The opposite end of the crank serves as a lever to transmit recoiling energy to a recoil spring. The compressed energy of the spring is then transmitted back through the crank to force the recoiling parts forward.

DETENT.

A pawl, stud, ball-check or similar movable projection under spring tension which holds a movable or removable part in place until moved. Moving the detent allows the part, against which it is maintaining tension, to be moved or removed.

DISCONNECTOR.

A device incorporated into the action of a weapon which prevents the firing of more than one shot for one pull of the trigger or which prevents the weapon from being fired until the action is fully closed.

EJECTOR.

A cam or projection inside the receiver against which the cartridge case strikes and is thrown clear of the mechanism after it has been drawn from the chamber by the extractor.

1. On hinge-frame weapons, springs working in conjunction with the extractor, force the extractor to the rear after the barrels have reached a position where the cartridge can be thrown clear of the mechanism. This system combines extraction with ejection.

2. In certain weapons the ejector is a spring loaded plunger located in the face of the bolt which exerts constant pressure against the head of the case. When the action opens enough for the case or cartridge to clear the ejection port, this pressure against the head of the case forces the case or cartridge out of the mechanism.

3. In some weapons, the nose of the firing pin protrudes through the firing pin hole in the face of the bolt when the bolt nears its most rearward point of recoil and forces the case from the mechanism.

4. In certain machineguns, the ejector is a portion of the extractor mechanism, extraction of the case and ejection from the receiver being accomplished by the same component.

EXTRACTOR.

A component engaging the rim or extractor groove of the cartridge case while the case is in the chamber, which withdraws the case from the chamber when the action opens. In a revolver, a segment at the rear face of the cylinder which engages the rims of the cases.

FEEDING.

The mechanical action of forcing cartridges from a magazine, bloc clip, strip clip or belt, successively into the chamber.

FEED GUIDES.

Guides surfaces machined into the top of the magazine well, or lips formed at the mouth of a magazine, which guide the cartridges into the chamber.

FEED RAMP.

A ramp machined in the receiver, breech end of the barrel, or other component in this region of the action, which guides the bullet so that the cartridge is properly directed into the chamber.

FEED PAWL

A hinged component designed for limited movement in one direction which is a part of the feed mechanism. This pawl acting through a lever engages succeeding cartridges in the feeding system and draws the cartridge into position for chambering.

FEED LEVER.

A major component of the feeding mechanism which transmits the recoiling and counter-recoiling motion of the bolt into a transverse motion of the feed pawl.

FIRING MECHANISM.

The subassemblies and components in a weapon which operate to function the primer in the cartridge. Consists generally of the trigger, sear, hammer, firing pin or striker and the necessary pins, springs, screws, etc.

FIRING PIN.

That part of the firing mechanism which strikes or contacts the primer of the cartridge to cause ignition of the primer.

1. Inertial: A firing pin shorter than its length of travel, surrounded by a coil spring. When struck by a hammer and driven forward the spring is compressed. The tip of the firing pin functions the primer and the spring immediately withdraws the tip back into the bolt or breechblock. Used in pistols.

2. Free-floating: A firing pin which is confined in the bolt by a retaining pin but is free to move a short distance when struck by the hammer. Used in light rifles.

3. Fixed type: A protrusion machined into the face of the bolt which functions the primer when the bolt has fully chambered the cartridge. Found in most blowback submachineguns.

4. Percussion: A firing pin which is engaged by a sear or other device which holds the firing pin to the rear as the bolt moves forward. This action compresses a firing pin spring which forces the firing pin forward when the firing pin is released. Used in high power rifles and machineguns.

FLASH HIDER.

An attachment attached to the muzzle of a weapon which shields the muzzle flash, or a circular disk attached to the barrel just to the rear of the muzzle to shield the flash from the firer.

FLASH SUPPRESSOR.

A two, three or four prong device attached to the muzzle of a weapon which tends to cool the hot gases as they leave the muzzle behind the bullet. Cooling the gases reduces the flash.

FOLLOWER.

A metal platform on which the last round in the magazine rests. The follower transmits the thrust of the magazine spring to the ammunition in the magazine so that the top round is properly positioned for feeding into the chamber.

FUNCTIONING.

The action of related groups or components in a weapon, working in conjunction with each other, which causes the weapon to accomplish its design mission.

GAS CYLINDER.

In gas operated weapons, an expansion chamber in which the gas piston rides. Generally, gas enters the gas cylinder from the gas port in the barrel where it impinges against the face of the gas piston to drive the piston rearward. After a short rearward movement of the piston, the gas is allowed to escape from the gas chamber.

GAS PISTON.

A piston or rod carried on the forward end of a major recoiling component in a gas operated weapon. The front end of this piston is enclosed by the gas cylinder. Gas entering the cylinder from the barrel strikes the face of the piston driving it rearward. This movement operates certain components which unlock the action, extract the case and performs other functions.

GAS PORT.

In gas operated weapons, a hole drilled in the barrel wall through which gas travels into the gas cylinder.

GRIP.

That portion of a weapon which is gripped by the hand that fires the weapon. On handguns, the handle; improperly called the butt.

GROOVES.

That portion of the rifling in a barrel which in conjunction with the lands, impart the spinning motion to a bullet.

GROOVE DIAMETER.

The inside diameter of the bore of a gun barrel measured from the bottom of one groove to the bottom of the opposite groove. This diameter is larger than the actual diameter of the bullet the weapon is chambered for.

HAMMER.

A component of the firing mechanism which imparts a sharp blow to the firing pin or striker causing the firing pin to initiate the primer in the cartridge case.

HANGFIRE.

Delayed ignition of the powder charge. Unpredictable and dangerous. Not to be confused with Misfire.

HEAD SPACE.

The distance between the face of the bolt when fully closed and the cartridge seating shoulder of the chamber which the rim of the cartridge seating shoulder of the chamber which the rim of the cartridge contacts. In bottle-necked cartridges, that distance between the face of the bolt when fully closed and the tapered diameter in the seating cone of the chamber.

HOLDING PAWL.

A hindged component designed for limited movement in one direction which is part of the feed mechanism. This pawl acting under spring tension engages succeeding cartridges in the feeding system to keep the cartridge from sliding back out of the feedway once they have been positioned by the feed pawl.

HOLD OPEN DEVICE.

A component in a firearm which holds the bolt to the rear when the ammunition supply has been exhausted.

JUMP.

The distance which the axis of the bore rises while the bullet is traveling down the barrel.

KICK.

A generic term used by shooters to describe the rearward thrust a firearm exerts against a shooter. Kick varies depending on such factors as ballistic recoil, shape of stock, muzzle blast and method of holding the arm.

LANDS.

Raised portion between the grooves in the bore of the gun which impart a spinning motion to the bullet.

LAND DIAMETER.

The inside diameter of the bore of a gun barrel measured from the top of one land to the top of the opposite land. This diameter is smaller than the actual diameter of the bullet for which the weapon is chambered.

LOCKING LUGS.

Carefully machined proturberances on the bolt which engage suitable recesses in a non-moving component in the receiver to assist in securely sealing the breech during the initial moment of firing.

MACHINEGUN.

A weapon capable of automatically loading and firing a round of ammunition, extracting the fired case from the barrel and ejecting it from the mechanism, positioning a new cartridge for loading and loading and firing this round. This action is repeated until action by the firer, or lack of ammunition, causes it to cease.

MAGAZINE.

The operating assembly in which ammunition is stored and which feeds this ammunition one round at a time into position so that closing of the action causes the top round to be fed into the chamber.

1. Box Magazine: A box shaped magazine, open at the top, which contains a compound flat spring with a magazine follower positioned at the top. Tension of this spring against the follower forces the follower upward which in turn forces the ammunition carried on top of the follower into position in the open top of the magazine for feeding into the chamber. Various box magazines are identified by their feeding systems as follows.

    a. Single-position-feed, staggered-column. Ammunition is contained in a double column within the magazine but the opening at the top of the magazine is centered so that the rounds are forced from the magazine in a straight line with the chamber.

    b. Two-position feed, staggered-column. Ammunition is contained in a double column within the magazine but the feed lips at the top of the magazine are so designed that the rounds are fed alternately from the left and right side of the opening. In this case a feed ramp assists in guiding the round into the chamber.

    c. Single-position-feed, staggered-column, double-compartment. This magazine contains a vertically positioned wall down the center of it. Ammunition is contained in a double column on both sides of this wall. The opening at the top of the magazine is centered so that rounds are forced from the magazine in a straight line with the chamber.

2. Drum Magazine: A magazine shaped like a drum, with a single opening at one point in its outer circumference. Ammunition contained within the drum is forced, one round at a time (through a combination of springs and followers) into position in the opening where it can be fed into the chamber.

3. Pan Magazine: A flat, circular magazine shaped like a pan, with a single opening on one side which is located on a plane which bisects the outer edge and the center of the pan. The ammunition, which lies flat in the pan with the bullet points facing the center of the pan, is forced, one round at a time (through a spring and follower system) into position in the opening where it can be fed into the chamber.

4. Rotary-box Magazine: A magazine shaped like a small drum, designed to hold 6 to 10 rounds of rifle caliber ammunition. A rotor system actuated by a coil spring within the magazine, positions succeeding rounds of ammunition in line with an opening located at a single point in the outer circumference of the magazine. Movement of the action forces ammunition into the chamber and the rotor positions the next round for feeding.

5. *Tubular Magazine:* A magazine shaped like a tube open at one end, located in such a position on the weapon that ammunition being forced out of this opening is positioned properly for feeding into the chamber.

6. *Hopper-feed Magazine:* A square, box-shaped magazine, into which ammunition in charger clips is placed. An opening near the bottom edge of one wall allows the rounds to be stripped from the bottom-most charger and chambered. Pressure exerted by a spring-loaded cover forces the succeeding charger clips of ammunition down into position for stripping and chambering of the rounds.

7. *Integral Magazine:* A magazine which is not removable from the weapon. This magazine contains all the components necessary to position the ammunition for feeding into the chamber. Ammunition is placed in the magazine manually by the firer.

MAGAZINE HOUSING.

An opening formed in the receiver into which the magazine is inserted. Shaped in such a manner that the lips or feed guides, at the top of the magazine are protected once the magazine has been inserted. The housing usually projects a short distance from the receiver wall.

MAGAZINE WELL.

An opening formed in the receiver into which the magazine is inserted. Unlike the Magazine Housing, the well does not project beyond the receiver wall.

MAGAZINE CATCH/RELEASE.

A component designed to engage the magazine, after the magazine has been inserted into the weapon, to prevent the magazine from falling out of the weapon. Usually spring-loaded, the Catch/Release must be pressed manually in order to disengage from the magazine when the magazine is being removed.

MAGAZINE SAFETY.

A mechanical device built into the action which prevents the weapon from being fired when the magazine is removed.

MAINSPRING.

The spring which supplies the energy for actuating the major components of the firing mechanism such as the hammer, striker, etc. In some weapons the Mainspring is also the Recoil Spring or Operating Spring.

MECHANICAL SAFETY.

An arrangement of components within the action which prevents the weapon from being fired until the action is fully closed and locked.

MISFIRE.

Failure of the primer to function after it has been struck by the firing pin. Not to be confused with Hangfire.

MOUTH

The open end of the cartridge case into which the bullet is inserted.

MONOPOD.

A device attached to a weapon to assist in supporting the weapon during firing; consisting of only one "leg" it may be located near the muzzle or near the butt. In some weapons it may be folded out of the way when not in use.

MUZZLE.

The end of the barrel from which the bullet emerges.

MUZZLE BLAST.

A generic term denoting the atmospheric disturbance of air at the muzzle of the barrel which is caused by the expansion of the powder gases in the air after the bullet has left the barrel.

MUZZLE BRAKE.

A device at the muzzle of the weapon which deflects the emerging powder gases. The energy imparted by this act of deflection pulls the weapon forward to offset some of the rearward motion of recoil.

MUZZLE FLASH.

The incandescent flash in the air at the muzzle of the weapon which occurs when the bullet leaves the barrel. This flash is caused by the expansion of the emerging powder gases, ignition of oxygen in the air and expulsion of burning powder grains.

MUZZLE VELOCITY.

The computed velocity in feet-per-second (fps), at which the bullet leaves the barrel. This velocity is computed by a formula which contains factors regarding propellant weight, propellant composition, bulletweight and configuration, etc.

NECK.

The forward portion of a bottleneck cartridge case which is smaller in diameter than the body of the case.

NOTCH.

A notch or cut-out in a component which is engaged by another component to keep the first component from moving; i.e., the notch in the hammer which keeps the hammer immovable until the sear is withdrawn from the notch; the notch on the undersurface of a bolt-carrying slide which is engaged by a sear to hold the slide immovable until the sear is disengaged.

OGIVE.

The radius of the curve of the nose of a bullet.

OPERATING HANDLE.

A handle (projection) attached to the operating rod, slide or bolt which can be grasped to manually open or close the action.

OPERATING ROD.

In gas operated weapons, the rod which connects the gas piston to other components. When the rod is moved by the force of the gas against the face of the piston it causes the action to unlock and open.

OPERATION.

The procedure by which a person uses a firearm for its intended purpose. Not to be confused with Functioning. See Functioning.

PARABELLUM.

Meaning "For War". The European name for the Luger Pistol. Also applied to the 9-mm German Service cartridge to distinuish it from other 9-mm cartridges.

PIECE.

Refers to the arm under discussion.

PISTOL.

A firearm designed to be held and fired with one hand only, having the chamber integral with or permanently aligned with the bore.

PITCH.

The angle at which the rifling is cut in relation to the axis of the bore. Expressed as the length of the bore required for one complete turn or spiral, e.g., one turn in 16 inches. As pertains to pistol and revolver grips, the angle at which the grip slants in relation to the axis of the bore. In rifle and shotgun stocks, the angle at which the butt plate slopes in relation to the axis of the bore.

PRESSURE.

The thrust of the powder gases expanding in the barrel. Recorded in pounds per square inch (psi) in the United States.

1. *Chamber Pressure:* The pressure generated in the chamber.

2. *Residual Pressure:* The pressure remaining in the chamber after the bullet has left the muzzle.

PRIMER.

The small charge which is detonated by the firing pin which in turn ignites the powder charge or propelling charge in the case or chamber.

PROPELLANT.

The powder charge contained in the case, which when ignited by the primer, propels the projectile from the barrel.

PROJECTILE.

A bullet. Ballistically a bullet does not become a projectile until it is in flight.

RANGE.

1. *Firing Range:* A place where target shooting is practiced.

2. *Accurate Range:* The maximum range at which a particular weapon and cartridge will consistently hit the target.

3. *Effective Range:* The maximum distance at which a particular weapon and cartridge are reasonably expected to kill a particular type of game.

4. *Maximum Range:* The maximum distance that a particular bullet will travel.

5. *Point-blank Range:* The distance at which a particular weapon will consistently hit the target with no sight adjustments being made.

RATE OF FIRE.

The number of rounds a given weapon can fire in one minute, normally given as rounds per minute (rpm).

1. *Cyclic Rate of Fire:* The maximum number of rounds an automatic weapon can fire in one minute.

2. *Accurate Rate of Fire:* The maximum number of rounds an automatic or semi-automatic weapon can fire and consistently hit the target.

RECEIVER.

That portion of a weapon which houses the bolt, or breech-block, certain recoiling components, portions of the firing mechanism, etc., and to which the barrel, barrel jacket, stock, trigger-group, feed mechanism, etc., are attached. In revolvers and hinge-frame shotguns it is called the "frame". In certain pistols the terms "receiver" and "frame" are used synonymously.

RECEIVER CAP.

A circular, cap-shaped component which closes the rear of the receiver, usually found on simple submchineguns.

RECEIVER RING.

That forward portion of the receiver into which the barrel or barrel jacket is threaded.

RECOIL.

The rearward movement of a weapon caused by the expansion of the powder gases which act to thrust the projectile forward in the barrel and react to thrust the weapon rearward.

RECOIL BOOSTER.

A component of a machinegun, usually located at the muzzle, which traps some of the escaping gas in such a manner as to insure positive recoil action when the weapon is fired at angles less than horizontal. May also be designed to increase the rate of fire of a weapon.

RECOIL MECHANISM.

Mechanism designed to absorb the energy of recoil gradually, to avoid violent movement of the weapon during firing, and in some respects protects rapidly moving parts from becoming damaged.

RECOIL SPRING.

A spring which is compressed by the action of certain recoiling parts, and upon expansion forces these parts forward to close and lock the action. Often called the "Operating Spring."

RECOIL SPRING GUIDE.

A rod which is surrounded by the recoil spring, anchored at one end (the rear end usually), which keeps the recoil spring from buckling and twisting while the spring is being compressed by the movement of the recoiling parts. In some cases this guide is a hollow tube, with the recoil spring riding inside. In this case it may be called a "Recoil Spring Housing" or "RecoilSpring Guide Tube".

REVOLVER.

A firearm in which the cartridges are carried in the cylinder, mounted coaxially with the barrel. A mechanism revolves the cylinder so that the cartridges are successively aligned with the barrel.

RIFLE.

A shoulder fired, air-cooled firearm, which fires a spin stabilized projectile. Rotation is imparted to the projectile by spiral grooves engraved in the inner walls of the barrel.

RIFLING.

A series of spiral grooves in the bore of a barrel which imparts a spinning motion to the bullet as it travels the length of the barrel from breech to muzzle.

SAFETY.

Any mechanism incorporated into the action of a weapon which by mechanical or manual manipulation prevents the weapon from being fired. See Mechanical Safety. A Safety is "ON" or "applied" when it is positioned to prevent the weapon from firing.

1. Automatic Safety: A safety which is automatically applied by the movement of certain components of the weapon and must be manually released or set to "FIRE". Examples: Grip Safety, which must be pressed before the weapon can fire; Ejection Port Cover, which must be opened before the weapon can be fired; Magazine Safety, when magazine is removed, safety is automatically applied and weapon cannot be fired until magazine is inserted; Hammer Safety, which automatically blocks the hammer when the weapon is initially loaded and must be placed in the "FIRE" position before the weapon can be fired; Bolt Lock Safety, which is automatically applied if the bolt is not fully closed and locked.

2.. Manual Safety: Operate in conjunction with most of the Automatic Safeties. The Manual Safety takes the form of a swinging lever, a sliding button, a push-through button, etc. The Manual Safety must **bedeliberately** set or applied to "ON" or "SAFE" and deliberately released to "OFF" or "FIRE". Very often Manual Safeties are combined with Fire Selection systems, where the safety must be set to the "FIRE" position before the type of fire desired can be selected.

STRIPPING.

1. As pertains to weapons, means to disassemble. (a) Field Stripping is disassembling as far as necessary for normal maintenance. (b) Detail Stripping is disassembling all parts and pieces that can be removed.

2. As pertains to ammunition, means the failure of the bullet jacket to properly grip the rifling so that bits of the bullet jacket are stripped from the bullet and left in the bore.

3. As pertains to loading a magazine, the act of pressing the cartridges from the strip clip into the magazine.

4. As pertains to loading rounds into the chamber, the movement of the bolt which forces the top round in the magazine into the chamber in preparation for firing.

SUBMACHINEGUN.

A shoulder fired, air-cooled, magazine-fed weapon, chambered for pistol caliber ammunition and capable of full-automatic fire.

SYSTEM.

The type of mechanical operations which cause the weapon to function.

1. *Bolt Operated:* A generic term, refers to a weapon, (rifle or shotgun) in which the bolt is opened and closed manually by the firer.

2. *Recoil Operated:* A locked breech weapon in which the barrel and breech recoil a certain distance locked together and the force of the recoil is utilized to unlock and open the action. Two types: Long recoil and Short recoil.

3. *Blowback Operated:* An unlocked breech weapon in which the force of gas in the chamber thrusts the empty cartridge case in the chamber against the face of the bolt to open the action.

4. *Retarded or Hesitation Blowback:* An unlocked breech weapon in which a series of levers, springs, etc., are utilized to slow down or retard the initial opening motion of the bolt. The bolt is not locked closed at any time, gas in the chamber is utilized to open the action.

5. *Gas Operated:* A locked breech weapon in which gas is tapped from the barrel to strike a piston. The movement of the piston unlocks and assists in opening the action.

THROAT.

The forward portion of the chamber which is tapered to meet the bore diameter.

SEAR.

A component operated by the trigger which fires the weapon.

SEMI-AUTOMATIC.

A weapon in which the trigger must be pulled for each shot fired. All the functions of loading, locking, cocking, extraction and ejection are carried out automatically by the weapon.

SILENCER.

A device attached to the muzzle of a weapon, which absorbs the gases following the bullet from the muzzle in such a manner that the usual explosive sound of the gas is muffled. Silencers to be effective can only be used when the muzzle velocity of the bullet is less than the speed of sound.

SLIDE.

A component which makes up part of the recoiling components and functions to carry the bolt or the hammer or the firing pin or operates the feeding system,etc.

STOCK.

The part or parts attached to the receiver of a weapon which makes it possible for the firer to hold aim, and fire the arm.

1. Fixed Stock: A stock which is rigidly attached to the receiver in such a manner that it cannot be moved or repositioned without deliberately removing some other parts.

2. Folding Stock: A stock which is designed in such a manner that it can be pivoted or folded forward to lay above, below, or alongside of the receiver, thus shortening the overall length of the weapon. In some submachineguns, the weapon may be fired with the stock folded.

3. Telescoping Stock: A stock which is designed in such a manner that it can be pushed forward to shorten the overall length of the weapon. It does not pivot, hinge or swing. In some submachineguns, the weapon may be fired with the stock telescoped.

STRIKER.

A cylindrical shaped firing pin which is carried inside the bolt which receives its forward impetus from its own spiral spring when released by action of the trigger. It is not struck by a hammer. The actual firing pin portion which strikes the primer may be an integral part of the striker or it may be a separate piece attached to forward end of the striker. This term is sometimes improperly used to indicate any firing pin.

TRAJECTORY.

The part of a bullet in flight which describes a downward curve from the muzzle to the impact point.

TRIGGER.

A finger actuated lever used to activate the firing mechanism and so fire the weapon.

TRIGGER BAR.

A connecting bar operating between the trigger and the sear.

TRIGGER GUARD.

A metal loop which partially protects the trigger from damage and from being pressed accidentally.

VELOCITY.

As pertains to projectiles, the speed of the projectile. Instrumental velocity - the velocity of a projectile in flight measured by scientific instruments at a specified point in its trajectory. Usually measured in feet per second (fps). Instrumental velocities always indicate the range at which the readings were made.

TRIPOD.

A stand or mount on which a machinegun rests during firing. Consists of three legs which are adjustable in angle in relation to the long axis of the weapons (and may be adjustable in length) in order to raise or lower the whole weapon. The tripod usually contains mechanisms to elevate and traverse the weapon to a limited degree without moving the tripod as a whole.

TRUNNION.

A component of a machinegun which makes up the foremost portion of the receiver and which usually receives the barrel jacket or the barrel. The trunnion is usually designed to constitute the foremost mounting point for the weapon.

WATER JACKET.

A cylindrical metal jacket which surrounds the barrel on machineguns. It is rigidly attached at its rear to the Trunnion, with a hole in the front end from which the barrel protrudes. This jacket is considerably larger than the barrel in diameter, and is so designed with sealing rings, intake or filler holes, outlet holes, etc., so that it will hold water. The water keeps the barrel cool during sustained firing.

REFERENCE DATA
SECTION VI

COMPARATIVE DATA TABLE -- PISTOLS

WEAPON	CALIBER	OPERATION	TYPE OF LOCK	LENGTH INCHES	WEIGHT OZS	FEED	TYPE FIRE	RATE FIRE	RANGE METERS
M12 Steyr Austria	9-mm Steyr	Recoil	Turning barrel	8.5	34	Box-8 rd	Semi-auto		75
M35 Browning Belgium	9-mm Luger	Recoil	Ribs on bbl mate w/grooves in slide	7.8	32	Box-13 rd	Semi-auto		70
Mk 1 Webley Britain	.455 Webley	Recoil	Step on bbl mates w/recess in slide	8.5	38	Box-7 rd	Semi-auto		70
M1935A MAS France	7.65-mm Long	Recoil	Ribs on bbl mate w/grooves in slide	7.8	25.3	Box-8 rd	Semi-auto		65
M1896 Mauser Germany	7.63-mm Mauser	Recoil	Pivoting block locks bolt & ext	12.2	45	Box-10 rd	Semi-auto		80
P-38 Walther Germany	9-mm Luger	Recoil	Pivoting block locks bbl & slide	8.6	34	Box-8 rd	Semi-auto		70
P-08 Luger Germany	9-mm Luger	Recoil	Toggle joint keeps breech block closed	8.7	30	Box-8 rd	Semi-auto		70
M1910 Glisenti Italy	9-mm Glisenti	Recoil	Pivoting arm locks bolt & ext	8.3	34	Box-7 rd	Semi-auto		60
M1951 Beretta Italy	9-mm Luger	Recoil	Locking wedge locks bbl & slide	8	25.2	Box-8 rd	Semi-auto		70
Type 14 Japan	8-mm Nambu	Recoil	Pivoting block locks bolt & ext	9.2	29.2	Box-8 rd	Semi-auto		60
Type 94 Japan	8-mm Nambu	Recoil	Sliding block locks bbl & slide	7.1	27	Box-6 rd	Semi-auto		50
TT33 Tokarev Russia	7.63-mm Mauser	Recoil	Ribs on bbl mate w/grooves in slide	7.7	32	Box-8 rd	Semi-auto		50
PM Makarov Russia	9-mm Soviet	Blowback	Inertia	6.3	25	Box-8 rd	Semi-auto		50
M1940 Lahti Sweden	9-mm Luger	Recoil	Sliding block locks bolt & slide	10.7	37.5	Box-8 rd	Semi-auto		

COMPARATIVE DATA TABLE -- RIFLES

WEAPON	CALIBER	OPERATION	TYPE OF LOCK	LENGTH INCHES	WEIGHT POUNDS	FEED	TYPE FIRE	RATE FIRE	RANGE METERS
FAL Belgium	7.62-mm NATO	Gas	Rear of bolt cammed down	39.1	8.4	Box-20 rd	Full & Semi	150rpm	540
Type D Belgium	7.92-mm	Gas	Link cammed up by slide	45.2	21.2	Box-20 rd	Full-auto	250rpm	1480
Model 52 Czech	7.62-mm M52	Gas	Front of bolt cammed down	39.4	8.7	Box-10 rd	Semi-auto	30rpm	470
Model 58 Czech	7.62-mm M57	Gas	Rotating bolt head	33.2	7.9	Box-30 rd	Full & Semi	225rpm	540
Madsen Denmark	7.62-mm NATO	Gas	Rotating bolt head	43	10.2	Box-20 rd	Full & Semi	150rpm	540
Model 2 Dom Republic	.30 U.S. Carbine	Retarded blowback	Resisting lever	37.2	7.8	Box-25/30	Full & Semi	100rpm	315
MAS 49 France	7.5-mm M29	Gas	Rear of bolt cammed down	43.2	10.4	Box-10 rd	Semi-auto	40rpm	540
GEW-43 Germany	7.92-mm	Gas	Rear of bolt cammed down	44.2	9.7	Box-10 rd	Semi-auto	35rpm	680
GEW-G3 Germany	7.62-mm NATO	Retarded blowback	Bolthead rollers	40.3	9.5	Box-20 rd	Full & Semi	150rpm	540
FG-42 Germany	7.92-mm	Gas	Rotating bolt	39.5	10.7	Box-20/30	Full & Semi	225rpm	540
Model 40 Russia	7.62-mm	Gas	Rear of bolt cammed down	48.1	8.2	Box-10 rd	Semi-auto	30rpm	540
SKS Russia	7.62-mm M43	Gas	Rear of bolt cammed down	40.1	8.2	Box-10 rd	Semi-auto	30rpm	470
AK Russia	7.62-mm M43	Gas	Rotating bolt	34.2	10.6	Box-30 rd	Full & Semi	225rpm	470
AG42B Sweden	6.5-mm	Gas	Rear of bolt cammed down	48.2	10.3	Box-10 rd	Semi-auto	30rpm	580

COMPARATIVE DATA TABLE -- SUBMACHINEGUNS

WEAPON	CALIBER	OPERATION	TYPE OF LOCK	LENGTH INCHES	WEIGHT POUNDS	FEED	TYPE FIRE	RATE FIRE	RANGE METERS
Mark 1/42 OWEN Australia	9-mm Luger	Blowback	Inertia	32.1	9.7	Box- 32 rd	Full & Semi	125rpm	270
Mark V STEN Britain	9-mm Luger	Blowback	Inertia	30.2	8.7	Box- 32 rd	Full & Semi	125rpm	150
Model 24 Czech	7.62-mm	Blowback	Inertia	26.9	7.2	Box- 32 rd	Full & Semi	175rpm	225
Model 1950 Denmark	9-mm Luger	Blowback	Inertia	30.7	7.1	Box- 32 rd	Full & Semi	125rpm	225
Model 1931 Finland	9-mm Luger	Blowback	Inertia	34.2	11.5	Box & Drum	Full & Semi	250rpm	300
MAS-38 France	7.65-mm	Blowback	Inertia	24.9	7.1	Box- 32 rd	Full- auto	125rpm	125
MAT-49 France	9-mm Luger	Blowback	Inertia	18.3	8.5	Box- 32 rd	Full- auto	125rpm	225
"Universal" France	9-mm Luger	Blowback	Inertia	17.2	7.7	Box- 32 rd	Full & Semi	175rpm	175
Model 1948, C4 France	9-mm Luger	Retarded blowback	Lever overcoming wgt of extension	25.4	6.5	Box- 32 rd	Full & Semi	175rpm	225
MP-40 Germany	9-mm Luger	Blowback	Inertia	24.9	8.2	Box- 32 rd	Full- auto	150rpm	270
MPK Germany	9-mm Luger	Blowback	Inertia - heavy bolt extension	14.8	6.2	Box- 32 rd	Full & Semi	150rpm	175
MP-43 Germany	7.92-mm short	Gas	Bolt cammed down to lock	36.7	8.2	Box- 30 rd	Full & Semi	250rpm	480
M/42 Germany	9-mm Steyr	Blowback	Inertia	33.2	9.5	Box- 30 rd	Full & Semi	175rpm	300

COMPARATIVE DATA TABLE -- SUBMACHINEGUNS continued

WEAPON	CALIBER	OPERATION	TYPE OF LOCK	LENGTH INCHES	WEIGHT POUNDS	FEED	TYPE FIRE	RATE FIRE	RANGE METERS
No 2 Mk A Israel	9-mm Luger	Blowback	Inertia - bolt surrounds barrel	17.3	8.2	Box- 25/40	Full & Semi	125rpm	225
Model 38/42 Italy	9-mm Luger	Blowback	Inertia	31.6	9.7	Box- 20/40	Full & Semi	200rpm	250
LF-57 Italy	9-mm Luger	Blowback	Inertia - heavy bolt extension	16.6	7.1	Box- 20/40	Full- auto	175rpm	200
PPSh-41 Soviet	7.62-mm	Blowback	Inertia	33.2	8.7	Box & Drum	Full Semi	175rpm	200
PPS-43 Soviet	7.62-mm	Blowback	Inertia	24.2	7.2	Box- 35 rd	Full- auto	150rpm	175
M45B Sweden	9-mm Luger	Blowback	Inertia	21.7	6.1	Box- 36/50	Full- auto	100rpm	270
F.V. Mk 4 Swiss	9-mm Luger	Blowback	Inertia	27.2	8.3	Box- 32 rd	Full & Semi	150rpm	135

321

COMPARATIVE DATA -- MACHINEGUNS

WEAPON	CALIBER	OPERATION	TYPE OF LOCK	LENGTH INCHES	WEIGHT POUNDS	FEED	TYPE FIRE	RATE FIRE	RANGE METERS
Model 07/12 Austria	8-mm	Retarded blowback	Heavy breech block and toggle joint	49.3	102.0	Belt-100 rd	Full-auto	225rpm	2180
Lewis Britain	.303	Gas	Rotating bolt	50.6	28.6	Pan-47 rd	Full-auto	450rpm	1870
Type 41 Nat China	.30	Gas	Rear of bolt cammed up	45.7	23.8	Box-30 rd	Full & Semi	120rpm	1620
ZB30 Czech	7.92-mm	Gas	Rear of bolt cammed up	47.9	22.2	Box-20 rd	Full & Semi	120rpm	1620
M1952 Czech	7.62-mm M52	Gas	Rear of bolt cammed up	41.1	18.3	Box & Belt	Full & Semi	350rpm	1620
Madsen/Saetter Denmark	7.62-mm NATO	Gas	Locking wedges	38.2	25.2	Belt-50 rd	Full-auto	450rpm	1890
Madsen, Light Denmark	8-mm	Long-recoil	Pivoting breech block	44.7	24.7	Box-25/30	Full & Semi	125rpm	1270
M1924/29 France	7.5-mm M29	Gas	Rear of bolt cammed up	42.5	20.5	Box-25 rd	Full & Semi	175rpm	1620
M1931A France	7.5-mm M29	Gas	Rear of bolt cammed up	40.6	30.1	Box & Drum	Full-auto	350rpm	1850
M1914 France	8-mm	Gas	Bolt link cammed down	54.1	106.5	Strip-30 rd	Full-auto	200rpm	2150
AAT MLE 52 France	7.5-mm M29	Retarded blowback	Lever overcoming weight of bolt	38.7	34.2	Belt-50 rd	Full-auto	225rpm	2150
MG-42 Germany	7.92-mm	Recoil	Locking rollers in bolthead	48.3	26.1	Belt-50 rd	Full-auto	450rpm	2300
Model 30 Italy	6.5-mm	Recoil	Rotating bolthead	48.7	23.7	Box-20 rd	Full-auto	150rpm	1280
Type 11 Japan	6.5-mm	Gas	Rear of bolt cammed down	44.1	22.7	Hopper 30 rd	Full-auto	120rpm	1280

COMPARATIVE DATA TABLE -- MACHINEGUNS Continued

WEAPON	CALIBER	OPERATION	TYPE OF LOCK	LENGTH INCHES	WEIGHT POUNDS	FEED	TYPE FIRE	RATE FIRE	RANGE METERS
Type 99 Japan	7.7-mm	Gas	Cammed block	42.3	22.2	Box 30 rd	Full-auto	225rpm	1620
M1962 Japan	7.62-mm NATO	Gas	Rear of bolt cammed up	47.6	23.5	Belt-50 rd	Full-auto	275rpm	1650
DP Russia	7.62-mm	Gas	Locking wings	50.0	19.8	Pan-47 rd	Full-auto	350rpm	1760
RP-46 Russia	7.62-mm	Gas	Locking wings	49.7	28.7	Belt-250 rd	Full-auto	350rpm	1760
RPD Russia	7.62-mm M43	Gas	Locking wings	40.8	15.4	Belt-100 rd	Full-auto	375rpm	1210
SG-43 Russia	7.62-mm	Gas	Rear of bolt cammed sideways	44.2	62.6	Belt-250 rd	Full-auto	300rpm	2300
M1910 Russia	7.62-mm	Recoil	Toggle joint	43.6	159.7	Belt-250 rd	Full-auto	450rpm	2150
RPK Russia	7.62-mm M43	Gas	Rotating bolt	40.9	14.2	Box & Drum	Full Semi	325rpm	1210

```
METERS TO FEET
1  m =     3.281'      100  m =   328'
5  m =    16.405'      200  m =   656'
10 m =    32.81'       300  m =   984'
20 m =    65.62'       400  m =  1312'
30 m =    98.43'       500  m =  1640'
40 m =   131.24'      1000  m =  3281'
50 m =   164.05'      2000  m =  6562'
```

```
INCHES TO MILLIMETERS
.10" =  2.54-mm     .70" = 17.78-mm
.20" =  5.08-mm     .75" = 19.05-mm
.22" =  5.58-mm     .80" = 20.32-mm
.25" =  6.35-mm     .90" = 22.86-mm
.30" =  7.62-mm    1.00" = 25.40-mm
.32" =  8.12-mm   10.00" =   254-mm
.35" =  8.89-mm   15.00" =   381-mm
.38" =  9.65-mm   20.00" =   508-mm
.40" = 10.16-mm   30.00" =   762-mm
.45" = 11.43-mm   40.00" =  1016-mm
.50" = 12.70-mm   50.00" =  1270-mm
.60" = 15.24-mm   60.00" =  1524-mm
```

```
POUNDS TO KILOGRAMS
 .10 lb = .0454 kg    10.00 lb =  4.54 kg
 .20 lb = .0908 kg    15.00 lb =  6.81 kg
 .50 lb = .2270 kg    20.00 lb =  9.08 kg
1.00 lb = .454  kg    30.00 lb = 13.62 kg
2.00 lb = .908  kg    40.00 lb = 18.16 kg
3.00 lb = 1.362 kg    50.00 lb = 22.70 kg
4.00 lb = 1.816 kg   100.00 lb = 45.40 kg
5.00 lb = 2.270 kg   200.00 lb = 90.80 kg
```

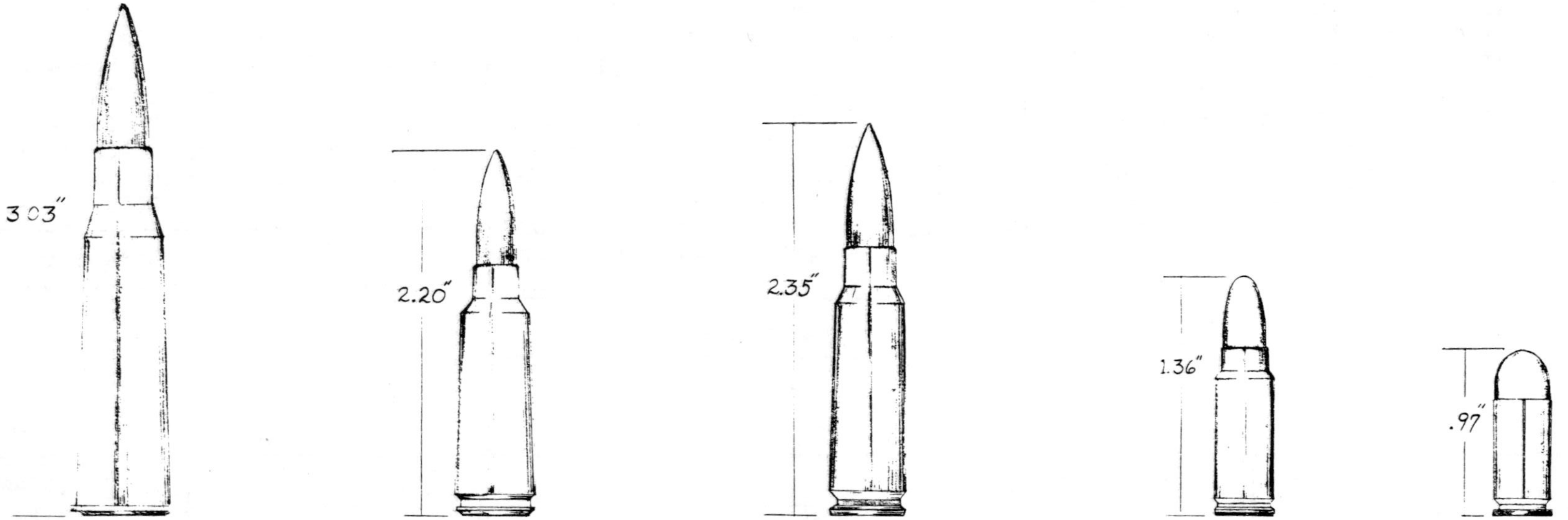

Soviet 7.62-mm M1908	Soviet 7.62-mm M1943	Czech 7.62-mm M52	Soviet 7.62-mm Type P	Soviet 9-mm Makarov
3.03"	2.20"	2.35"	1.36"	.97"

M1940 Tokarev Rifle
M1938 Carbine
M1944 Carbine
  (CHICOM Type 53)
DP & DPM LMG's
  (CHICOM Type 53)
SG-43 & SGM HMG's
  (CHICOM Type 53 & 57)
SPM M1910 Maxim HMG
RP-46 LMG
  (CHICOM Type 58)
	SKS Carbine
	  (CHICOM Type 53)
	AK-47 Rifle
	  (CHICOM Type 56)
	AKM Rifle
	RPK Rifle
	RPD LMG
	  (CHICOM Type 56)
	Czech M52/57 Rifle
	Czech M58 Rifle
		Czech M52 Rifle
		Czech M52 LMG
			TT-33 Pistol
			  (CHICOM Type 51)
			Czech M52 Pistol
			PPSh-41 & PPS-43 SMG's
			  (CHICOM Type 50 & 43)
				PM Makarov Pistol
				APS Stechkin Pistol

SOVIET BLOC AND CHICOM SA AMMUNITION

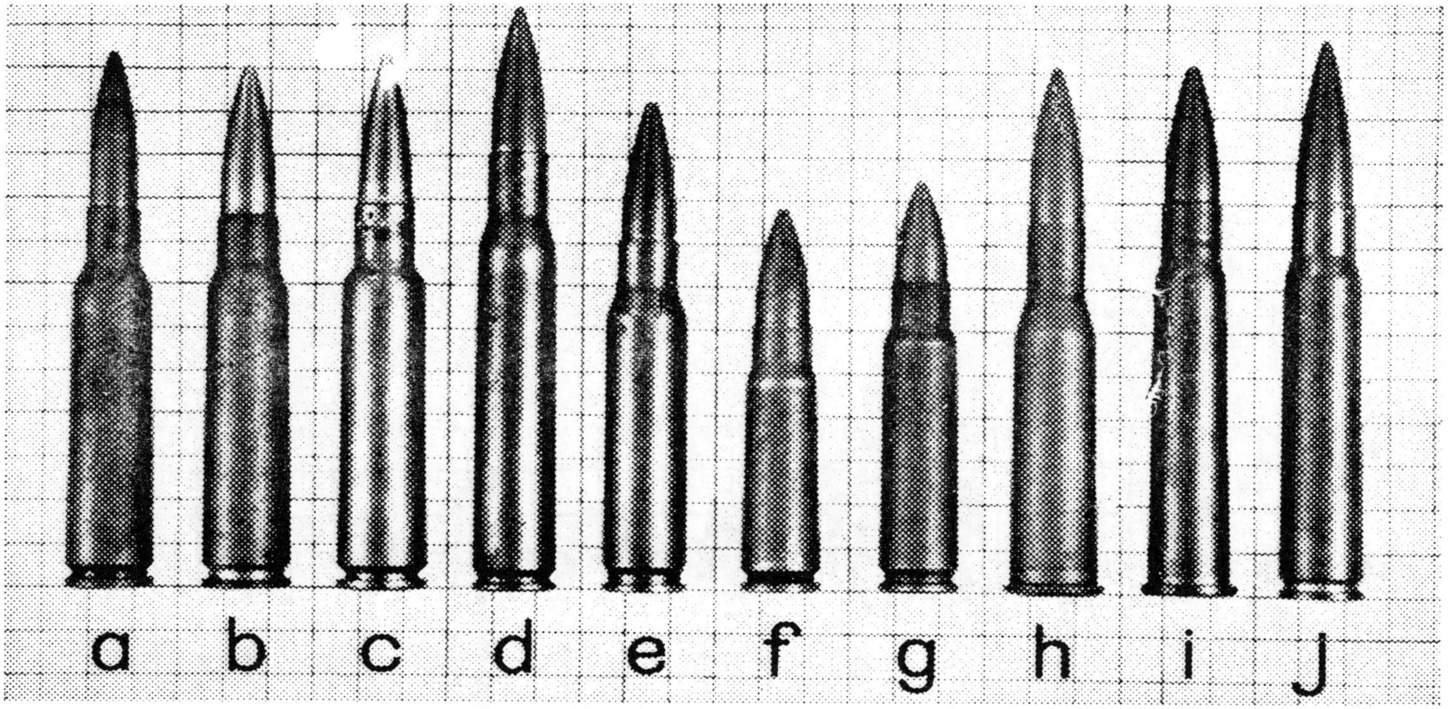

PRINCIPAL MILITARY RIFLE, CARBINE, AND MACHINE GUN CARTRIDGES IN CURRENT USE (ON ¼" GRID):

a. 6.5x55-mm, Swedish
b. 7.5-mm, French
c. 7.5-mm, Swiss
d. .30-06, U.S.
e. 7.62-mm, NATO
f. 7.62-mm M43, Soviet
g. 7.62-mm M52, Czech
h. 7.62-mm M1908, Soviet
i. .303, British
j. 7.92-mm, German

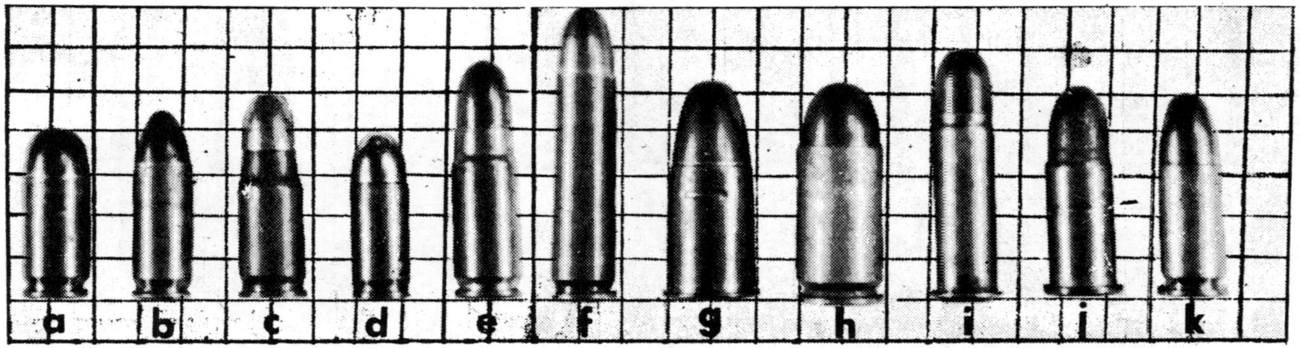

PRINCIPLE PISTOL, SUBMACHINEGUN AND CARBINE CARTRIDGES IN CURRENT USE (ON ¼" GRID):

a. 9-mm Browning Short (.380ACP)
b. 7.65-mm French Long
c. 7.65-mm Luger (.30 Luger)
d. 7.5-mm Browning (.32 ACP)
e. 7.2-mm Soviet Type P (Czech M48)
f. ? U.S. Carbine
g. .455 Webley Auto
h. .45 ACP
i. 8-mm French M1892
j. .38 S&W Revolver (.38 Webley Scott)
k. 9-mm Luger (9-mm Parabellum)